S0-BVE-720

The Minds
of Mass Killers

The Minds of Mass Killers

Understanding and Interrupting the Pathway to Violence

P. SHAVAUN SCOTT

Exposit

Jefferson, North Carolina

ISBN (print) 978-1-4766-8447-5
ISBN (ebook) 978-1-4766-4572-8

LIBRARY OF CONGRESS AND BRITISH LIBRARY
CATALOGUING DATA ARE AVAILABLE

Library of Congress Control Number 2021051169

© 2021 P. Shavaun Scott. All rights reserved

*No part of this book may be reproduced or transmitted in any form
or by any means, electronic or mechanical, including photocopying
or recording, or by any information storage and retrieval system,
without permission in writing from the publisher.*

Front cover image © 2021 vchal/ Barock/Shutterstock

Printed in the United States of America

Exposit is an imprint of McFarland & Company, Inc., Publishers

Exposit
Box 611, Jefferson, North Carolina 28640
www.expositbooks.com

To those whose lives have been lost before their time:
you will never be forgotten.

To their loved ones:
we stand with you and hold hope for healing.

To those who do their utmost to nourish change:
we will not give up the vision for a better future.

Table of Contents

Preface   1

1. At War with Ourselves   7

2. Trends and Typologies   29

3. The Pathway to Violence Stage 1: Grievance   45

4. The Pathway to Violence Stage 2: Ideation
   and Foreshadowing   59

5. The Pathway to Violence Stages 3 & 4: Research
   and Planning   79

6. The Pathway to Violence Stages 5 & 6: Breach
   and Attack   96

7. Into the Mind   110

8. Personality and Bullying   134

9. Complicating Factors: Autism Spectrum Disorder,
   Traumatic Brain Injury, and Trauma   158

10. Racial, Ethnic, and Politically Motivated Violence   178

11. Gender-Based Violence   202

12. The Conspiracy Mindset   219

13. Our Electronic Culture   233

14. Guns, Guns, and More Guns   254

15. What We Can Do   278

Afterword   307

Chapter Notes   311

Bibliography   343

Index   365

Preface

"Complicated problems have many moving parts,
but the relationships between them are knowable."
—*Noemie Bouhana*

"The aim of an argument or discussion should not be
victory, but progress."—*Joseph Jouber*

"We have reports of an active shooter," the newscaster says. We freeze and stop what we're doing to listen. We're riveted by cable TV or a radio broadcast, and our heart rates speed up with a rush of adrenaline. Family members look at each other as somebody says, "Where now—a school? Church? Grocery store?"

It could be any of those places; experience has shown it could even be a shopping mall, a nightclub, or the local Walmart.

As disturbing as each incident is, what may be more alarming is that these events now seem commonplace in the United States. Though statistically the odds of any one of us being a victim of a mass shooting are exceedingly small, these attacks are increasing. This has a direct influence on our perception of safety as we go about our daily lives. The world begins to *feel* dangerous, and we may change our behavior in response.

One-third of Americans now report that they avoid certain places due to fear of mass killings. Schools across America engage in lockdown drills, which can be psychologically traumatizing to students and teachers. Some parents advocate homeschooling due to fears for their children's safety, and many teachers have left the profession due to stress-induced anxiety.

Anxiety has skyrocketed in recent years across the population, creating a steady hum of intrapsychic noise. Hypervigilance has become

1

the new normal. A car backfires on a public street, and bystanders duck or run.

Some foreign governments now issue travel warnings for their citizens seeking to visit the United States, warning them about the gun violence that seems ubiquitous here.

Some politicians have advocated for weapons training for teachers and arming all school personnel. Others suggest requiring that elementary school children wear bulletproof backpacks. In many places, schools are being redesigned into fortresses with bulletproof glass and barred windows.

Are we safe anywhere? Why is this happening? When will it stop?

These questions consume social media for a day or two after each violent event as politicians offer "thoughts and prayers" and battles over gun control are fought on Facebook and Twitter. Eventually, everybody throws up their hands.

Is this the way we have to live now? Is there anything we can do?

This book will answer many of these questions. While we don't understand everything about why individuals commit mass murder, we do know a lot. Research is ongoing, and what we currently know has been synthesized in this book.

As a mental health therapist, I've performed dozens of risk assessments and worked in a forensic capacity with killers. I've studied the criminal mind and the impact of violence on victims for close to 30 years.

I'm also a mom, and there's nothing more important to me than children's safety. Since I believe our society can do a much better job of violence prevention, I'm passionate about this subject.

However, we can't do anything without the facts and an in-depth understanding of the problem.

Though I'm a clinician, this evidence-based book is written for the layperson as well as professionals: parents, educators, religious leaders, and anyone who wants a deeper understanding of the phenomenon of mass violence. Mental health and school counselors who do not have specialized training in forensics will also find it helpful.

Chapter 1 explores the current state of our search for accurate data on mass killers and identifies common terminology and definitions. The history of mass killings in the United States is reviewed from the country's inception to the present time.

Chapter 2 gives the foundational concept of pattern analysis and basic categorizations of mass killers that researchers have developed. We look at five factors that influence violent behavior and see that things commonly believed about these killers are not valid. Two distinct modes of violence are explained.

Chapter 3 takes us to the first stage of the pathway to violence and the concept of the injustice collector. We contrast two cases of mass killers who had different grievances but very similar psychological processes.

Chapter 4 moves to the second stage of the pathway to violence and explores the thinking patterns common to most mass killers, including distorted thoughts and violent fantasies.

Chapter 5 explores the third and fourth stages of the pathway to violence and describes how mass killers engage in research and planning, often long before their planned attack.

Chapter 6 discusses the final stages of the pathway to violence, defining empathy and how it impacts behavior. We learn what is different about mass killers that can cause them to lack compassion for others.

Chapter 7 provides an overview of the complexities in assessing mental illness and defines major mental illness and its relevancy to mass killings. Various factors that influence the way our minds develop are detailed.

Chapter 8 defines personality as well the way personality develops and evolves over the lifespan. Personality features often found among public mass killers are identified and defined.

Chapter 9 explores how other vulnerabilities and differences found in some individuals can contribute to the phenomena of mass killings. The impact of trauma, traumatic brain injury, and autism spectrum disorder are explored.

Chapter 10 looks at the increasing role of extremist ideology in mass violence and domestic terrorism, particularly the dangers of the rising militant far-right and the culture of white supremacy. We see that specific personal characteristics can propel an individual with vulnerabilities toward violent, extremist behavior.

Chapter 11 focuses on subcultures centered on the hatred of women (misogyny), particularly the unusual subculture of involuntary celibates, and its relationship to mass killings.

Chapter 12 examines the role of the conspiracy mindset in violent extremism and breaks down the thinking errors that feed hate-based and politically motivated violence. The role of political leaders in influencing conspiracism is clarified.

Chapter 13 explores the relationship of cable television news, the internet, and video games in both copycat behavior and social contagion. The controversial issue of content moderation and the effects of deplatforming are examined as well as ways families can develop guidelines for healthy media use.

Chapter 14 discusses the relationship of guns to public mass killings and the hot topic of gun safety legislation. Reasonable ways to increase gun safety are explored as well as the history of gun legislation in the United States.

Chapter 15 identifies a comprehensive vision for bringing change. The ways we can work to help children develop into healthy adults who will turn away from violence are delineated as well as multiple ways to intervene when there are problems or red flags. Resources for finding mental health and crisis services are identified along with lists of red flags indicated that quick action should be taken. Activities to create positive social change are explored, including content moderation in social media platforms. Included is an in-depth look at prevention strategies as well as ways to intervene in the pathway to violence long before a potential mass killer picks up a weapon.

The Afterword presents a case study from my practice where specific interventions contributed to a good outcome for an adolescent at risk. There are reasons to hold hope.

Case studies have been woven into each chapter to provide examples of the concepts covered. Repetitive themes will be noticed throughout because mass killers share certain similarities, even when they appear to have little in common at a superficial glance. You will recognize the multiple steps on the pathway to violence apparent in each case presented.

Data has been gathered and reviewed from the FBI, the CDC, the U.S. Secret Service, forensic researchers, and epidemiologists worldwide.

I've studied all information about mass killers available in the public domain, including their journals, social media posts, stories written for school, and manifestos posted online. I've pored over the details of their histories and the factors that led to their deadly decisions.

We all like a linear narrative with clear cause and effect, but that approach fails us when it comes to mass killers. Mass shootings result from multiple factors with many variables that coalesce to create violent behavior. That is what makes this topic complicated. Nonetheless, much can be understood, and we are not powerless.

For every complicated problem, the solution is equally complex. I like to think we are up to the task if we understand all aspects of the problem and create a vision to work together for a safer, more peaceful world. When we see that mass killings follow patterns, they are to some degree preventable. Anything that can be predicted can be prevented— if we know what to do.

I hope that we can use this information to do a much better job of prevention; collectively, we can make a difference, at least some of the time. As epidemiologists tell us, anyone who has died from a firearm has died from a preventable injury. This is a public health crisis.

We deserve to live in a world that is safe from mass killings. This is the future I want for my children and all of us.

Author's note: *The personal case studies presented from my practice represent composites of multiple actual clients. Names and other identifying details have been changed and modified in the interest of privacy.*

1

At War with Ourselves

"Parents had to gather away from the elementary school while squads of police with military-style weapons searched the campus. Helicopters were flying overhead. Parents were not told what was going on. We could only text our children and instruct them on barricading themselves in the classrooms and hiding. The children had to use buckets to go to the bathroom in front of other students. These buckets are now in each classroom because active shooter lockdowns are so common. Parents pray each day when we drop off our kids at school that our babies are safe and we don't get texts like I did this afternoon that my son's school was in lockdown because of a possible active shooter."—Dorian Beach, January 18, 2020, Santa Monica, California

This mother's experience is every parent's nightmare. Lockdown drills are now a routine part of the school experience in America, with most public schools scheduling multiple drills per year.

Schools no longer feel like safe places, and all of us ask ourselves why. We flash on the 2017 Route 91 Harvest Music Festival in Las Vegas, where one 64-year-old man left 61 people dead and 867 injured, and all the other mass shooting attacks that have happened since then. We ask ourselves if we're safe anywhere, why so much about our society has changed, and if there is anything we can do to ensure the safety of our loved ones.

Our collective imagery about life in America has darkened. We sense it.

The active shooter has become the modern boogeyman, a terrifying monster in military gear who could appear out of the ether at any time or place to murder our children in their classrooms, at a concert, or a shopping mall.

We want to do something, but for the most part, we're baffled.

Though no shooter was found in that Santa Monica elementary school on that chilly January day, the psychological effects of the school lockdown live on for Dorian Beach and her child. School lockdowns come with emotional consequences. They teach us to expect the worst and change our view of the world.

Most of us will never forget the blank-eyed faces of the adolescent killers who have stared from television screens. Echoes of Columbine, Sandy Hook, Parkland, and dozens of other schools where children have been victimized continue to reverberate. The list of the infamous murderers grows longer every year. We can easily visualize the memorials to the dead that we've seen on the news, the white crosses and flowers, the candlelight vigils, the photographs of smiling faces of happy children who are no longer with us.

After each event, we collectively say, "Never again!" which inevitably is followed by "It happened again."

How many times have we said, "This is madness!" and "It makes no sense"?

There have been more school shootings in the past 20 years than most of us can track. A database on school shootings, going back to 1970, shows there were more school gun incidents and more deaths in 2018 than any other year on record.[1] The year 2019 brought a total of 417 mass shootings across a wide variety of locations in the United States.[2] Four of the deadliest mass killings in history occurred between 2016 and 2020. And in just one month in spring 2021, there were 45 mass shootings of various sorts across the country.

School shootings are just one subset of public mass killings. The phenomenon is spreading beyond schools and into other public locations. In early March 2021, a 20-year-old Florida man with a semiautomatic weapon murdered eight people in a killing spree in three spas owned by Asian-Americans. Six days later, a 21-year-old man in Colorado killed 10 strangers in a supermarket.[3] There is a contagion effect with each mass killing, something that will be clear throughout the text of this book. You will notice patterns.

Indirect Victims

As a therapist, I work with distressed adults and children, both victims and perpetrators of violence. Part of my role is to assess the potential for any one of my high-risk clients to become violent and help those victimized by violence recover from the trauma. Both are imperfect and complicated processes.

This is particularly apparent with children who live in fear of violence. They are indirect victims, no matter how removed they are from witnessing violence first-hand. Kids see horror stories on the news and then practice drills at school where they hide in closets or rehearse throwing P.E. equipment in hopes of stopping an armed attacker.

Kids are more fragile than adults and don't have coping skills to help them manage stress from their environment. They're sensitive to changes in routine and the emotional states and behavior of the adults around them. Violence changes their perceptions of the world and their sense of safety in it.

Since children don't have well-developed coping skills, they're quick to react to stress with changes in behavior that are often not understood by adults. When they're unable to put their feelings into words, they may become moody, argumentative, or apt to have health complaints. Kids are affected by the environment they live in far more than we realize.

The brain is rapidly maturing during childhood, constantly incorporating information from its surroundings permanently into its structure. The environment in which we grow up is a significant factor in the kind of adults we eventually become and partly determines how we relate to others and engage with the world.[4] Kids who perceive the world to be a dangerous place become anxious and often grow into anxious adults. Living under the threat of violence changes the way we're wired.

Anxiety disorders in childhood are rising dramatically, and many believe that lockdown drills are one factor.[5] On this topic, psychologist and violence researcher Jillian Peterson says,

> In schools, we're running our kids through lockdown drills, we're spending billions of dollars on homeroom security, we're putting police officers in the corridors, and we're even arming our teachers. It's safe to say it's not

working because you can't get to true prevention until you understand who those motivated offenders are and why they're motivated.

As a parent of three kids, I'm concerned with research showing that these drills are traumatic, and my own research showing they increase anxiety. This generation is known as the "school shooting generation," and they have more mental health problems than generations before them.[6]

Mental health clinicians who work with children agree with her.

Trauma Stories

Play therapy is the preferred modality when I work with young children. Since pre-adolescent kids are not cognitively mature enough to describe complex emotions with words, it's through play therapy that they can act out what they are feeling with the stories they create in play. In the safety of the therapy office, surrounded by toys, their inner experiences are expressed organically as repetitive themes.[7]

I recently began working with seven-year-old Olivia, who is experiencing anxiety symptoms. It's become a common scenario.

Olivia has a long brunette braid hanging between her shoulders. She wears a pink and white striped t-shirt, blue jeans, and pink sneakers. Though Olivia avoids eye contact, she eagerly plays with the toys which dominate one section of my office. We sit on the floor together as she manipulates small figurines in the play therapy dollhouse.

"The kids and their mom are in bed," she says, leaning forward and placing three dolls in the bedroom. Her voice is soft. "They don't know the bad guy is coming, so they can't wake up and hide. If they don't hide, he is going to shoot them."

She chooses a brawny military action figure and puts a rifle in his hand to represent the bad guy as she positions him to peek in the windows of the dollhouse. She then repositions the tiny family figurines inside the house, hiding them behind furniture. Her voice becomes loud and pressured as she pretends to speak for the mother, telling the kids, "Hurry! Hide!"

Olivia's mother reports that she complains of stomach pain and cries when it's time to get ready for school in the morning. She begs to sleep with her mom at night and often wakes with nightmares. Her mother associates her symptoms with lockdown drills in her school along with things her peers have told her about school shooters. Based upon the themes in Olivia's play, I believe she is correct.

It's my job to help Olivia find ways to manage her fears. I want to help her learn to soothe herself, accept comfort from her mom, and learn techniques to calm her nervous system. The story she tells explains at least one source of her anxiety. It's challenging to help her find coping skills, particularly when the stress is ongoing.

Though Olivia is struggling, I question if it's appropriate to diagnose her with a mental health disorder when there are rational reasons for her fears.

There is now a $3 billion school security industry built on the concept that lockdown drills are necessary; the business has taken on a life of its own. Ninety-five percent of American schools now schedule regular lockdown drills in hopes of preventing deaths from school shootings.[8]

It's questionable if lockdown drills enhance safety for a variety of reasons. It's clear they are scaring many of the children they are designed to protect.[9]

What will the long-term consequences be for children who grow up under threat of being murdered in their schoolroom or playground? The most prominent unions of educators in the country, the American Federation of Teachers and the National Education Association, call for schools to eliminate them for precisely this reason.

"Those terrifying and traumatizing drills—they have no basis in fact, and they harm more than they help," said Randi Weingarten, the president of the American Federation of Teachers, in a 2019 interview with National Public Radio.[10]

In my therapy practice, I treat elementary and secondary school children displaying various stress-induced somatic symptoms—including headaches, stomach aches, and insomnia—following school lockdown drills. Instead of places where students feel welcomed, some kids experience school as something closer to a war zone.[11]

Such stress is hard on the developing nervous system.[12] None of us can focus on learning when we're upset. Under emotional stress, the brain's capacity to think is reduced; upset kids can't effectively process new information, disrupting their learning ability.[13]

It's hard on the parents and teachers too. Dedicated teachers are increasingly leaving the profession due to stress,[14] and many parents advocate for homeschooling due to fears of random violence.

Elementary school children are not the only ones at risk of school shootings. College students have also been targeted: Virginia Tech in Blacksburg, Virginia; Umpqua Community College in Roseburg, Oregon; Oikos University in Oakland, California. The list goes on as geographic targets keep expanding outside of academic settings.

It takes nothing more to become the target of a public mass killer than being in the wrong place at the wrong time, and though the risk to any one of us is small, that knowledge festers just beneath the surface of our collective psyches.

In the past five years, random public mass killings motivated by racism, religious hatred, politics, and misogyny have increased dramatically.[15] Synagogues, mosques, African American churches, and women at both a yoga studio and a fitness club have been hit. So have Latino families shopping at Walmart, Asian women at spas, and fans at a country music festival.

In Aurora, Colorado, patrons at a movie theater were attacked by a gunman; 12 were killed and 70 injured.[16] In April 2020, during the heightened stress of the Coronavirus pandemic, FBI agents in Missouri were forced to kill a white supremacist planning to bomb a hospital in a predominantly Black community where Covid-19 patients were recovering.[17]

Let that sink in. Patients in the *hospital* were targeted.

We want *someone* to take decisive action to stop it, but there's little agreement on what to do. If we desire to facilitate change, we must start with an in-depth understanding of what's going on and why it's happening. At present, popular culture is ridden with inaccurate information and myths.

The Search for Decisive Data

Interpreting data about public mass killings is challenging since we immediately enter a definitional quagmire. Differences in how mass killings are defined create difficulty in arriving at a consensus about the number of victims or the kinds of incidents that are most common. Decisions about what constitutes a mass killing have been made arbitrarily by those from many different disciplines (journalists, researchers, law enforcement) and are often subject to debate.[18] Media outlets, law enforcement agencies, and academic researchers often use entirely different definitions and terminology.[19]

Though much research has been done, the methodology has differed from study to study; some sample sizes have been very small, with conflicting definitions of what constitutes a mass killing. For example, some researchers consider a minimum of three deaths to be a mass killing; others count four. In one study by the U.S. Secret Service, the threshold was one—if other criteria were met. Some conflate domestic homicides with mass killings, while most do not. Some include workplace rampages, robberies, and gang-related crimes; others don't. Many only focused on shootings within schools. Many studies only included murders that were committed with firearms, excluding those where explosives, knives, or other deadly weapons were used.

Without a clear consensus on precisely what we're studying, we can find ourselves befuddled.

Interpreting the Data

How many have to die in a gun incident for it to count as a mass killing?

There are problems with compiling data strictly according to the number of fatalities in any single event. One killer may kill two victims but wound 20, thereby not meeting the specified fatality threshold for inclusion in a mass killing database. Another perpetrator may drive a motor vehicle into a crowd with the intent of killing many; if only one dies and 15 are injured, this attack is also not counted among most statistics.

The fact that a knife or motor vehicle is used instead of a gun excludes an entire category of murderers from a database that only counts gun deaths. Another killer may plan to murder hundreds with an interrupted bombing plot, thus resulting in zero deaths. These cases are not counted in most studies, though all are relevant to the topic of who mass killers are, their motivations, and the social trends that influence them. As targeted public mass killings increasingly move out of school settings, we need to understand if there are perpetrator similarities, regardless of the location of the crime.

In studying characteristics of perpetrators, the total number of the dead isn't necessarily relevant since actual death tolls will vary based upon the following factors:

- the marksmanship of a shooter;
- the skill level of a bomb-maker;
- the ready availability of emergency medical care for those injured; and
- the proximity of law enforcement at the time of the event

It's not the body count that's most relevant when examining the psychology and motivations of the perpetrator. Yet, body counts and methods of attack have determined what and how data is reported.

In developing prevention efforts, the killer's motivations, intentions, and observable behavior are more relevant than the type of weapon used or the ultimate number of fatalities. We need to understand the risk factors and warning signs that can lead someone to a pathway to violence in order to know how to interrupt them.

The ideal goal is to intervene long before a would-be mass killer picks up any type of weapon.

Following are four non-government organizations and two federal law enforcement agencies that compile data on mass killings, each with different criteria: the Gun Violence Archive, the FBI, *Mother Jones Magazine*, Guns and America, and the Violence Project. Numerous other sources have also published their statistics on public mass killings, including the *Washington Post, The New York Times,* and *Vox.*

- The Gun Violence Archive is a nonprofit organization that has been tracking gun-related violence in the United States since 2013. They define a mass shooting as "any incident of **four or more fatal or nonfatal injuries**, not including the shooter including domestic homicides and gang violence."[20]
- *Mother Jones Magazine* keeps an extensive database of mass

shootings which is often cited in media reports. They define mass shootings as **"three or more fatalities** in a single incident, in a public place, excluding the shooter." *Mother Jones* excludes the "crimes of armed robbery, gang violence, or domestic violence in a home."[21]

- Guns and America are organizations of journalists around the country coordinated by WAMU, the NPR station based in Washington, D.C., and affiliated with American University. Guns and America has created a public media fellowship program they describe as doing "in-depth research on complex issues" in 10 locations around the country. Guns and America define mass shootings as "the **shooting of two or more** people in a single incident in a public place, excluding crimes of robbery, gang violence, and domestic violence, focusing on cases[22] in which the motive appears to be indiscriminate mass murder."[23]

- The Violence Project, a nonpartisan think tank implemented by researchers Jillian K. Peterson and James A. Densley, documented 167 mass shootings between 1966 and 2019 in their *Violence Project Database of Mass Shootings in the United States*, which was published in 2019 and updated in 2020. This project was funded by a grant from the National Institute of Justice.

  The Violence Project research is unique in that each perpetrator was coded on 200 life history variables and thus is broader in scope and more detailed than any data previously compiled.[24] The Violence Project follows the Congressional Research Service definition of "a multiple homicide incident in which **four or more victims are murdered with firearms**—not including the offender—within one event, and at least some of the murders occurred in a public location or locations in close geographical proximity (e.g., a workplace, school, restaurant, or other public settings), and the murders are not attributable to any other underlying criminal activity of commonplace circumstance (armed robber, criminal competition, insurance fraud, argument, or romantic triangle)."

- The FBI refers to mass shootings as "active shooter incidents." They exclude gang or drug-related violence and state "an active shooter is an individual actively engaged in killing or attempting to kill people in a populated area." The FBI counts each incident even if there are no casualties.[25]

- The U.S. Secret Service National Threat Assessment Center (NTAC) has been analyzing data on targeted violence in schools since 1999 and has released recent research reports on what we know about perpetrators, including interrupted attacks. The NTAC does not limit its data to weapons used with firearms or the number of victims.[26]

There are no definitive statistics on how many potential mass killings are interrupted before violence occurs since these situations are not always reported. It's impossible to know every time a school counselor, mental health therapist, or family friend has made some kind of intervention with a person on a pathway to violence that interrupted what could have been a future attack.

For this book, I will examine what we know about the trends in public mass killings and the characteristics and traits found among perpetrators, regardless of the ultimate number of fatalities. Public mass killers, active shooters, and those increasingly designated as domestic terrorists essentially represent a single offender type; they are people who commit rampage attacks in public places and attempt to harm multiple victims beyond a single target. For this examination of the motivation of these individuals, there is no minimum threshold of victims established. Attempted and planned attacks count, even when plots have been thwarted before anyone was hurt.[27]

Mass killings due to gang violence or violence committed in a crime like a robbery are excluded since offenders perpetrate these crimes with different motivations from the public mass killer. Intra-familial violence and domestic homicide are only included if others outside the home are killed during the same episode.

Unless otherwise noted, I will primarily reference longitudinal data provided by the NTAC, the FBI, and the Violence Project; I will also include case studies of public mass killings and thwarted mass killings that did not involve a firearm as well as those that do not meet criteria for a specified number of fatalities.

This book focuses on violence committed in the United States unless specifically indicated otherwise. Case studies of mass killing events in other nations will be presented when similar behaviors and motivational patterns have been observed. Recent public mass killings have occurred in the United Kingdom, Canada, New Zealand, Thailand, and Norway, following patterns seen in the United States.

Categories of Mass Killers

Attempts to categorize types of mass murder have also been arbitrary,[28] and this is a process that continues to evolve.[29]

Based on common historical law enforcement typologies, I use the following four distinct groups for clarity and to define this book's scope: serial killers, spree killers, workplace killers, and public mass killers. School shooters are a subset of the last category and are further broken into subsets of K–12 killers and college/university killers.

Long a source of fascination in Hollywood films and true crime documentaries, the serial killer stalks single specific victims in different locations over time, often with an extended cooling-off period between crimes.[30] This type of killer may travel to distant places over months or even years and live a seemingly everyday life between episodes. Serial killers, while infamous, are quite rare.[31] Since their motivations and methods are unique from other killers, they are *not* this book's subject.

The psychological information in this book applies to the following categories since research has determined that the differences between them are mainly superficial, and they share similar psychological processes[32]:

- **Spree killers** are defined as those who kill multiple victims in different locations in a very short period, often on the same day but no more than seven days apart. Spree killers have no cooling-off period and do not resume their everyday lives between murders. The D.C. snipers, who killed 17 people and wounded 10 in random shooting attacks in Washington, D.C., in 2002 over 23 days, are an example of spree killers. Like the others identified here, spree killers are generally motivated by anger.[33]
- **Public mass killers** attack multiple victims at one time, in one

location. Such killers are often motivated at least in part by extremist beliefs, particularly racist, misogynistic, or right-wing ideologies.[34] Fame is an additional motivating factor for this type of murderer.[35] Victims are usually not specifically targeted; instead, individuals are attacked randomly based upon the location where they happen to be and the symbolic representation they hold to the shooter. Public mass killers are not confined to schools. Restaurants, nightclubs, concerts, retail stores, and community events have also been targeted.

- The term "domestic terrorist" is sometimes used for mass killers. The word "terrorist" implies to many that there is a specific political motivation attached to the attack. Since such motives can be difficult to determine, I use the term **violent extremist** to describe killers with various extremist ideological motivations, whether or not the criminal justice system has formally identified them as terrorists.

- In the mid–80s, a spate of workplace rampages in post offices[36] resulted in the now common euphemism for workplace violence: "going postal."[37] The **workplace rampage killer** is typically an employee or ex-employee of a company with a grudge against his employer and has been subject to layoff, firing, or disciplinary action. This type of killer returns to a workplace to target specific victims, usually supervisors or other employees. He has stated grievances and rationale for his actions. Unlike other public mass killers, this perpetrator knows his victims personally. The workplace rampage killer shares many characteristics with other mass killers.

Characteristics

There is no single profile of a public mass killer, though characteristic patterns in behavior and thought can be observed—despite differences in weapons, ideology, personal history, age, and race.

The general term "shooter," though popularly used, can be viewed as something of a misnomer. Many mass killers have planned to use a combination of explosives as well other weapons during their attacks.

The Columbine killers in Littleton, Colorado, are commonly referred to as school shooters, but their primary plan to destroy their high school involved several massive bombs, which they placed in various locations around the school. When the bombs failed to detonate as planned, they used their guns as Plan B.[38] If their bombs had successfully detonated, the death toll would have been in the hundreds rather than just over a dozen.

Since it's harder to build a bomb than to pick up a gun, guns are the most common weapon used by mass killers. Those armed with military-grade semiautomatic firearms have had the greatest number of victims.[39]

Recent Trends

The summer of 2019 was particularly bloody. Between Memorial Day and Labor Day, there were 26 mass shootings in the United States, leaving 126 people dead. The end of the summer was shocking, as near back-to-back mass killings happened in Gilroy, California; El Paso, Texas; and Dayton, Ohio. Those who followed the daily news were understandably rattled.

Each of the three perpetrators used a military-grade semiautomatic weapon (often termed "assault weapon"). Each perpetrator expressed common motivations among contemporary mass killers: racism, power, misogyny, and the desire for fame.[40]

Following is a summary of these three end-of-summer events in 2019. They represent the most recent trends in public mass killings, particularly regarding the type of weapons used and the motivations of the perpetrators.

Gilroy, California

"Because I'm really angry."—Gilroy mass killer

Gilroy is a quiet Northern California community of 60,000 people with a strong agricultural history. It is best known for growing garlic. On a beautiful day in late summer 2019, Gilroy was celebrating its 41st annual Garlic Festival, which Latino families heavily attend. As usual, it was a happy and crowded event, filled with parents and children.

Shortly before 6:00 p.m. on the final day of the festival, a 19-year-old white man used bolt cutters on a chain-link fence to enter the site and evade security. He was dressed in military fatigues with a bullet-proof vest and carried a semiautomatic rifle. He brought multiple high-capacity magazines.

It took less than one minute for him to kill three and wound 17 others as he fired wildly into the crowd filled with families with young children. Within 60 seconds of opening fire, he was wounded by police present to guard the festival; he then shot himself in the head, dying instantly.[41]

The Gilroy perpetrator made a racist post on Instagram attacking Latino immigrants just minutes before the attack.

Killed were a six-year-old Latino boy, a 13-year-old Latina girl, and one 25-year-old white male, all strangers to him.

When a bystander asked him why he was shooting, he responded, "Because I'm really angry."[42]

The Gilroy killer, a white male from a middle-class family, had no known history of violence or mental illness. For months, he had made racist posts on social media and explored various violent ideologies online. He'd also created a list of potential targets, subsequently discovered in his bedroom by investigators. In addition to the Garlic Festival, his target list included religious organizations, courthouses, federal buildings, and political institutions. Law enforcement officers found a wide variety of extremist political literature in his bedroom.

Neighbors in the local middle-class neighborhood where the shooter lived with his parents reported that he had seemed like a quiet, everyday teenager who stayed out of trouble.[43]

El Paso, Texas

"This attack is in response to the Hispanic Invasion of Texas."—El Paso mass killer

On August 3, 2019, just six days after the Gilroy shootings, a 21-year-old white male with right-wing, white supremacist views drove 650 miles from his home in Allen, Texas, to the city of El Paso. He chose El Paso because it has a high population of Mexican immigrants.[44]

Carrying a semiautomatic rifle, he began shooting in the El Paso

Walmart parking lot and then moved inside the store, where he targeted shoppers. Minutes before the attack, this perpetrator published a 2,300-word manifesto in the online forum 8chan, stating that he was hoping to kill as many Mexicans as he could.

The attack lasted less than six minutes. He killed 22 and wounded two dozen more before being captured by police. Witnesses said he appeared to target Latinos while allowing blacks and whites to run from the store. In his manifesto, the El Paso shooter stated that he was targeting Mexicans, whom he blamed for taking American jobs and resources.

In his manifesto, he cited "an invasion of immigrants" and included a plan to separate America by race; he stated that he was inspired by the mass shooting at the Christchurch, New Zealand, mosque where a white supremacist killed 51 Muslims just weeks previously.

The El Paso shooter lived with his grandparents in Allen, Texas, as he attended community college. He had no prior history of involvement with law enforcement. A former high school peer described him as sometimes irritable and short-tempered, but he had no other observable mental health problems. He was from a middle-class family, his mother a nurse and his father a mental health counselor.

His family stated after his arrest, "His actions were apparently influenced and informed by people we do not know, and from ideas and beliefs we do not accept or condone. He was raised in a family that taught love, kindness, respect, and tolerance—rejecting all forms of racism, prejudice, hatred, and violence."[45]

This was the deadliest attack on Latinos in modern American history and the seventh deadliest mass shooting since 1949.[46]

Dayton, Ohio

"All shall be annihilated."—Dayton mass killer

On August 4, just 13 hours after the El Paso shooting, it took only half a minute for a 24-year-old white male in Dayton, Ohio, to kill nine people and wound 17 more with a semiautomatic weapon.[47] He was shot dead by police just 32 seconds after he fired his first shot.

The Dayton shooter had gone to a bar with his sister and a male friend in the city's downtown historic district, a pleasant area filled with restaurants and pubs, typically crowded in the evening. Wearing body armor, a mask, and hearing protection, he began shooting indiscriminately into the crowd outside the bar. Most of the victims were in their 20s or 30s; six were black, and three were white. His 22-year-old sister was one of those killed.

This perpetrator did not leave a written manifesto, but those around him had long noticed his unusually violent interests and proclivities. Many were quick to report to the news media shortly after his death.

The Dayton shooter lived with his middle-class parents, who appeared to be both loving and traditional in their social media postings. He grew up in an intact family, with an older sister he seemed to care for—the one he was to murder. He had been active in musical theater in high school and enjoyed performing in front of an audience. With a superficial glance, one could say he seemed to be a typical young adult.

But peers from the high school described him as a joker who could often be charming, though episodically odd and menacing. Girls were told to stay away from him. There were disturbing things about him that can be noted in his musical expression.

The Dayton shooter was a vocalist for a "pornogrind" band, an extreme form of metal music focused on the murder of women, sexual violence, rape, and gore. The bands he performed with were called Menstrual Munchies and Putrid, and the songs had names like "Six Ways of Female Butchery" and "Preteen Daughter Pu$$y Slaughter."[48]

In 2012 this perpetrator was suspended from high school when he was found to have created a hit list and a rape list; both lists contained the names of his schoolmates. A girlfriend broke up with him in May 2019 because she found his interest in mass shootings and other violent behavior disturbing.[49]

In high school, he often spoke of killing others and was obsessed with guns. In the past, sketches he'd posted on social media had captions like "All Shall Be Annihilated," "Bloodlust," and "Bloody Massacre."[50] It's unknown if any adults were aware of his social media activity.

It took less than one minute to kill three and wound 17 in Gilroy. It took only 32 seconds to kill nine and wound 17 in Dayton. In El Paso, 22 were killed and 24 wounded in less than six minutes. The damage that a mass killer can do in a short time with a military-grade semiautomatic weapon is terrifying.

Pattern Recognition

The sciences of psychology and epidemiology intersect. Both are based upon pattern recognition. By carefully observing details of violent events and then moving backward with a timeline, it's possible to analyze a host of variables that precede violence. With this process, we find recognizable patterns. Though the behavior makes no sense to a casual observer, once we enter the mind of a killer in the context of his life, we can usually see how it makes sense to him.

Forensic psychology is the branch of the study of human behavior that intersects with the law and criminality.[51] Since 1983 the U.S. Centers for Disease Control (CDC) has designated violence as a preventable public health issue and formed an epidemiology branch to study patterns in violence. Both forensic psychology and epidemiology base research on sophisticated analysis of patterns.

By recognizing and analyzing patterns of human behavior that regularly repeat, we can identify common factors that can then be named, analyzed, and categorized. Pattern recognition allows us to determine why behaviors happen and discover how best to keep harmful behaviors from reoccurring.

Tracking public mass killings in the United States can give a person whiplash because they often happen in bursts. One seems to lead to another, which leads to another, creating a behavioral chain with each new mass killing making another link. This is known as the contagion effect, which is explored further in Chapter 12. There are reasons that these murders are connected, with recognizable cultural templates and scripts that have evolved in the past two decades.[52]

Though the reasons are multifactorial and complex, that doesn't mean they cannot be understood. Mass killings are horrifying but not incomprehensible. By dissecting these events and breaking down the components, we can gain a sense of control over an anxiety-provoking subject; it helps us understand. This is where we need to begin with the task of reducing violence.

There is no question that mass killers emulate those who have gone before them.[53] Violence spreads like a virus, mainly through the internet.

Attempting to clarify behavioral patterns seen in mass killings is complicated since our access to information varies from one perpetrator to another. Sometimes there is a great deal of information on a specific perpetrator available in the public record; there's very little at other times. Many perpetrators leave a florid social media trail complete with manifestos and videos on social media, but some do not. Some killers have simply attracted more attention, gotten more widespread media coverage, or had family members who have been willing to grant extensive media interviews. We know a great deal about many perpetrators, but much less about others.

We do know that at least half of them plan to die during their attacks, either by suicide or at the hands of law enforcement officers. This leaves us without the ability to question them directly after the attack. With a dead perpetrator, we're left to gather evidence as best we can from other sources.

When we think of random mass public killings, most of us think of gun violence. Because guns are ubiquitous in the United States, firearms are often the weapon of choice for mass killers. However, some have planned to use explosives, often in addition to firearms. Some have tried to kill numbers of people using other weapons like knives, melee weapons, and even motor vehicles.

While the chosen weapons may differ, there are multiple similarities among mass killers, aside from their preferred murder weapons. Those similarities, as well as differences, will be explored.

Since nearly 98 percent of random mass public killers have been male,[54] I use the pronoun *he* in this book, except when otherwise indicated.

Since fame is a major motivating factor for a large percentage of mass killers, I will avoid mentioning these perpetrators by name.[55] Instead, I will reference them by the cities or locations where they attacked, along with many relevant details about their crimes and their known or publicly available histories. While we need to learn from their actions, we can do our best to avoid turning them into perverse celebrities by focusing excessively on the gruesomeness of their actions.

We need to understand that every time most of us see a news story that masks us gasp with horror, others are watching the same event who respond with "Cool!"

Our Violent Heritage, from Past to Present

School shooters and public mass killings may seem to be a modern phenomenon, but the forces driving the problem are rooted in United States history.

Violence has always been an integral part of American culture, despite our expressed desire to live peacefully.

From the genocide of our native indigenous people, the Revolutionary War, two hundred years of slavery and racist lynching, the Civil War, the Ku Klux Klan, and cross burnings, World War I and World War II, multiple political assassinations, and near-constant involvement in ongoing foreign conflicts, there has never been a sustained period where Americans can say they have been free from entanglements with violence.

Racially motivated hate crimes have always been a concern for minority groups,[56] though this has generally flown beneath the radar of the majority in recent decades. Black people were lynched into the early part of the 20th century, something often forgotten by contemporary white people.[57] More recently, the Black Lives Matter movement has highlighted the disparities in treatment between whites and Blacks by police and in the criminal justice system, which has typically gone unrecognized by whites. During the Covid-19 pandemic, hate crimes directed at Asian-Americans soared.[58]

Hate crimes directed at racial minorities have been considered aberrations by most white people since the days of slavery and Jim Crow. This misconception is only recently being challenged and examined in the mainstream, as racial hate crimes increasingly garner media attention.[59] White supremacists openly call for a whites-only ethno state in the Pacific Northwest, as they advocate for a bloody race war. Reports of white supremacist propaganda more than doubled in 2019,[60] and hate crimes have continued to climb. Racially based hatred has become an increasing factor in mass killings and is discussed extensively in Chapter 10.

Despite its violent history and overall poor treatment of racial minorities, most United States citizens have been able to go through their daily lives with a reasonable expectation of personal safety. Violence episodes tended to be discrete, and public mass violence was rare.

Generations of children went to school each day without fear of being murdered in their classrooms.

Though rare until recent years, mass killers are not an entirely new phenomenon. In reviewing history, we can see that the motivational patterns of the killers have been consistent from past to present.

- **Winfield, Kansas, 1903**

    The first recorded random public mass killing occurred on August 13, 1903, in Winfield, Kansas, when a 34-year-old white army veteran opened fire at a crowded outdoor music festival, killing nine and injuring 25 in a crowd of over 1,000 people.[61] Others heard him muttering about plots against him, and he left behind a rambling, paranoid note that vengeful annihilation was imminent to all those who plotted against him. He killed strangers.

- **Bath, Michigan, 1927**

    The next incident of mass public violence by a lone perpetrator occurred in 1927 in Bath, Michigan, when a 55-year-old white farmer and former member of the school board bombed the local school, killing 47 and injuring 58, most of them children.[62] He'd lost re-election to the school board the year before and had been embroiled in a dispute over property tax increases to benefit the school. The Bath, Michigan, perpetrator had rigged explosives throughout the school in the months before the attack. On the day of the bombing, he murdered his wife, firebombed his farm, then detonated his truck with dynamite, killing himself and rescuers. He left a written manifesto blaming others for his anger and an in-depth accounting of all his grievances against the community.

- **Camden, New Jersey, 1949**

    Twenty-two years later, on September 6, 1949, a 24-year-old white ex-soldier in Camden, New Jersey, killed 13 people in 20 minutes with a handgun he had purchased at a sporting goods store.[63] The New Jersey killer, who had served in World War II as a tank gunner, was reportedly engaged in petty disputes with neighbors and had nursed grudges against many others. He proceeded to fire randomly around his neighborhood, killing several children as well as adults. At the time of the shootings, he was captured by police and eventually diagnosed with paranoia and dementia praecox (an early term for schizophrenia). He died in prison in 2009 at age 88.

- **Austin, Texas, 1966**

The case most often cited as the first modern school shooting occurred in Austin, Texas, on August 1, 1966, at the University of Texas in Austin.[64] In that incident, a white 25-year-old former Marine who had training as a military sniper climbed to the observation deck of the 33-foot-high clock tower and picked off fellow students below. He killed 14 and wounded 31 in a two-hour rampage.

The clock tower shooter had murdered his wife and his mother earlier in the day. There is no single motive for his actions, and like most of these incidents, there seem to be multiple contributing factors. He had grown up using firearms, and as a child, his father was very proud of his marksmanship. Most of his victims were shot in or near their hearts. A pregnant woman was shot in the abdomen, killing both her and her unborn child.

The clock tower shooter, an architectural engineering student, had recently complained of rage episodes, confusion, and thoughts of violence. He left a suicide note asking that his brain be examined after his death. At autopsy, a brain tumor was discovered; while it has been speculated that the brain tumor may have contributed to his behavior, there is no way to verify this. While brain tumors in rare cases can cause personality changes, there is no evidence that they provoke people to murder others.[65]

The Texas clock tower shooting was the first mass killing event to be covered live by television news as it was unfolding. TV news stations placed camera crews at the scene while helicopters hovered overhead as both police and civilian snipers tried to hit the shooter. The horrifying drama dominated the airwaves as it was happening in real-time until a sniper killed the perpetrator four hours after the shooting began.

Media coverage is highly relevant to the phenomenon. Extensive media coverage has since become the goal for most modern mass killers.[66] After the Texas clock tower shooting, which received comprehensive media coverage, incidents of mass violence began increasing in frequency.[67]

None of these early random mass public killers had the advantage of semiautomatic weapons or 24/7 coverage on cable news. That is no longer the case.

Something We Must Accept?

Most people are alarmed about school shootings and other public killings but don't know what to do. Many assume we must accept that mass killings are something we have to live with or that arming teachers, pastors, grocery clerks, and yoga teachers is the only way to fight back. If this were to happen, America could quickly become the land of perpetual gunfights.

I think we can do better than this. The United States is awash in guns, and more guns have not been proven to make society safer. Since many shooters use a family member's gun,[68] it's highly questionable if a more heavily armed society would solve the problem of public mass killings.

This leaves us asking, "What *can* we do?"

We start by understanding what's happening and why. If we can predict behavior, there are ways to prevent it. Mass shootings are both predictable *and* preventable.

Personal safety as we go about our daily lives should be the most basic of human rights. Every time there is another mass shooting, it affects us all—even if we're in another part of the country.

2

Trends and Typologies

We now have substantial data about mass killers; we know more about them and their motivations than ever before. Though researchers have organized data into various conceptual categories, specific facts and trends have become apparent, even when researchers have developed somewhat different typologies and terminology to describe the perpetrators.

In this chapter, we review current research about trends and basic typologies as well as brief but relevant case studies. We also learn about the two different types of violence and how these types of violence manifest differently in the brain.

There is no single profile of a mass killer, no one neat category. Nonetheless, there are patterns that help us understand what is happening, considering multiple variables. Public mass killers share similarities in key ways, even when they appear to be superficially different.[1]

This is what we know: public mass killings are not going away. They are increasing in frequency, expanding to more locations, and becoming more lethal when they occur. In the past decade, more mass killers have been motivated by hate-filled, extremist political and racist ideology, and the number of mass murderers who used military-grade semi-automatic weapons has increased from 25 percent to 39 percent.[2]

Racial hatred, misogyny, and military-grade firearms are part of a deadly perfect storm—and the internet is providing fuel toward radicalization.[3]

The public mass killers of today are most apt to be angry young men. Usually, but not always, they are white, with a grievance against society. They have come to believe that murder is a justifiable solution to their perceived problems or to further an ideology for which they are willing to die. They are apt to target racial and ethnic minorities or women. While most use firearms, many use explosives or other weapons as well.[4]

While the bulk of research has been limited to mass killers who used firearms, there is a conceptual link to those who use other weapons. The perpetrators' psychological processes are the same, no matter the specific ideology or choice of weapon.[5]

The actual case studies presented throughout this book will share many commonalities. You will notice repetitive themes and patterns.

Cultural Touchstone

"Everyone is going to die."[6]—Columbine killer

Though it was not the first school shooting, the cultural touchstone for contemporary mass killers happened on April 20, 1999, in Littleton, Colorado. It was not a coincidence that this was Adolf Hitler's birthday and one day after the anniversary of the Oklahoma City bombing in 1995. Murder anniversaries tend to be significant to mass killers.

On that spring day, two Colorado high school seniors, now known as the Columbine killers, committed the deadliest school shooting up to that time. It has since inspired multiple copycat attacks, attempted attacks, and a cult of fetishists known as "Columbiners,"[7] discussed in Chapter 12.

The Columbine killers murdered 12 students and one teacher in a rampage that captured the country's attention for months. In addition to the 13 killed, 21 others were injured.

Political activist Michael Moore made a film about the event in 2002 titled *Bowling for Columbine*. While Moore intended to highlight the need for gun control, subsequent mass killers have instead used it for inspiration. There is a complicated interplay between the media and the mind of a killer, further explored in Chapter 12.

These two high schoolers had hoped to kill hundreds; their goal was to be the most famous mass killers in the country's history. They wanted to top the number killed in the 1995 Oklahoma City bombing of the Murrah Federal Building, where 168 died, and 680 were injured.[8]

Mass killers now rank those who have gone before them according to "kill scores." Each hopes to earn the number one spot on the list. It sounds a lot like a video game competition.

While the Columbine killers are often referred to as "school shooters," a more apt description would be "shooters/attempted bombers."

As documented by many journalists, including Dave Cullen, who spent a decade on his book *Columbine*, the adolescents did extensive research for their plot for a year before the attack, planning every detail down to the minute. They built four large bombs out of propane tanks; they placed two in the school cafeteria, timed to detonate when the area would be most crowded with students. They rigged explosives in their cars, which were strategically placed in the campus parking lot.

The plan was to detonate the car bombs as first responders arrived, thus dramatically expanding the number of victims outside the school building. They placed two additional bombs strategically at a nearby park to create a diversion for law enforcement.[9]

If the Columbine killers had been better bomb makers, they would have killed hundreds, but bomb-making was not their particular talent. When all the large bombs failed to detonate, they used their semiautomatic firearms and smaller pipe bombs as their backup plan.

They became celebrities to other angry young men who have since tried to emulate them.[10] Most significantly, they offered the world a template that others continue to follow to this day.

Patterns in Data

By analyzing multiple mass killing attacks, we can clearly understand the social forces and psychological processes at play. We can study the events, the weapons used, and the personality characteristics of the perpetrators.

When looking at modern mass killings patterns, most researchers in the United States begin counting forward from the Texas clock tower shooting in 1966. The researchers from The Violence Project identify 167 mass shootings from 1966 to 2019.[11]

More than half of the total occurred since 2000.

It is striking that 20 percent of the total number of mass killings in the past 50 years occurred in the five years between 2014 and 2019.[12]

The death count per mass shootings has also increased alarmingly; eight of the deadliest mass shootings in the United States have occurred in the past five years. In each case, the gunman used one or more semi-automatic, military-grade firearms.

- San Bernardino in 2015 (14 dead)
- Orlando in 2016 (49 dead)
- Las Vegas in 2017 (58 dead)
- Sutherland Springs in 2017 (25 dead)
- Parkland in 2018 (17 dead)
- Thousand Oaks in 2018 (12 dead)
- Virginia Beach in 2019 (12 dead)
- El Paso in 2019 (12 dead)

Mass shootings are also happening with increasing frequency internationally, as the template from the United States spreads to other countries:

- Finland in 2008 (9 dead)
- Norway in 2011 (69 dead)
- Christchurch, New Zealand in 2019 (51 dead)
- Thailand in 2020 (29 dead)

Surviving Multiple Events

Statistically, the odds that any one of us will die in a public mass killing are extremely low; nonetheless, there are now people who count themselves as the unfortunate survivors of more than one such incident.

What are the odds of surviving one mass public killing in Nevada, only to die in another in California the following year? As mass shootings increase in frequency and lethality, we see a new and unsettling trend.

Consider Las Vegas, Thousand Oaks, and Gilroy.

"I hope people call me insane."—Borderline Bar shooter, Thousand Oaks[13]

Twenty-seven-year-old Telemachus "Tel" Orphanos, a Navy veteran, survived the Las Vegas music festival shooting on October 1, 2017, only to be murdered 11 months later in November 2018, at a massacre in Thousand Oaks, California. It happened at the Borderline Grill, a country-western bar frequented by college students; it was jammed with patrons that night.

Tel, a part-time security guard at the Borderline, was there to socialize and dance with his friends when a 28-year-old former Marine entered, throwing smoke bombs and shooting into the crowd. The killer carried a legally purchased Glock .45-caliber handgun, modified with an extended magazine to hold additional ammunition rounds.

Tel attempted to help other customers flee when he was stabbed and shot by the perpetrator. He died at the scene.

The killer paused to make an Instagram post during the attack in which he wrote: "I hope people call me insane ... [laughing emojis] ... wouldn't that be just a ball of irony? Yeah.... I'm insane, but the only thing you people do after these shootings is 'hopes and prayers' ... or 'keep you in thoughts' ... every time ... and wonder why these keep happening."[14]

Unfortunately, he was correct.

Mass killers are increasingly foreshadowing, or "leaking," their intentions on social media before attacks; some even live stream during the murders.

Ironically, 45 others who survived the Thousand Oaks attack had also survived the Las Vegas attack.

Tel Orphanos was not one of the lucky ones.

Survivors of the Las Vegas Harvest Music Festival murders were also present at the Gilroy Garlic Festival mass shooting. One of them, Alicia Olive, told CNN, "I don't know how it'll be when I go out now. I know I feel a lot of the same things as I did when Vegas happened." She stated she intends to dedicate herself to supporting survivors of gun violence and advocating for stricter gun laws because "there's a reason why I'm still here today."[15]

Researchers and Typologies

Since completed public mass shootings are relatively rare events, the sample size for research on the perpetrators is understandably small. Nonetheless, researchers have found consistent patterns. We understand many factors involved in mass killings, but this knowledge is not always easily accessible to the public.

The U.S. Secret Service's National Threat Assessment Center (NTAC) has published multiple reports summarizing research on targeted mass violence events in schools going back to the 70s. The NTAC first published the *Safe Schools Initiative* in 2002, based on an analysis of school shootings from the early 1970s to 2000.

In 2018, the NTAC developed *Enhancing School Safety Using a Threat Assessment Model: An Operational Guide for Preventing Targeted School Violence*; in 2019, they published the most comprehensive review of school attacks ever published by the federal government: *Protecting America's Schools: A U.S. Secret Service Analysis of Targeted School Violence*.

In 2021, the NTAC released a study titled *U.S. Secret Service Analysis of Plots Against Schools,* which examined 67 serious, planned attacks in K–12 schools, which were thwarted between 2006 and 2018. In 43 of the cases, there was adequate open-source information to review details and backgrounds of the perpetrators; the findings of this report are consistent with the results of other researchers. The conclusions of the report are consistent with the findings of other researchers. The essential motivations consistently found among school perpetrators are identified as

- grievances;
- a desire to kill;
- suicidality; and
- a desire for fame, emulate previous attackers, exceed the number of victims of previous attackers.

Also focusing on school shootings, psychologist Peter Langman has performed detailed case studies of 64 perpetrators of multi-victim school shootings in the United States between 1966 and 2015. His research has focused primarily on mass killings in which the killer used a firearm in a school setting. *The Journal of Campus Behavioral Intervention* published his *Multi-Victim School Shootings in the United States—A Fifty-Year Review* in 2016. Langman has also published two books on the topic, *Why Kids Kill* (2010) and *School Shooters: Understanding High School, College, and Adult Perpetrators* (2015). His extensive online repository of information on school shooters is available at www.schoolshooters.info.

Langman organizes school shooters into subsets by the type of school targeted. He identifies three categories: Secondary School Shooter, College School Shooter, or Aberrant Adult School Shooter. He then used the following three psychological typologies within those categories to describe the perpetrators.[16]

Following is a summary of Langman's typologies.

- **Psychopathic Shooters**

  Those who evidence traits of the personality disorder known as the psychopath, also described as antisocial personality disorder in the *Diagnostic and Statistical Manual of Mental Disorders (DSM-5)*. Psychopathic personality traits are often associated with callused, cold, and methodical perpetrators; they are usually free of major mental illness symptoms, such as psychotic disorders, which cause delusions and hallucinations.

  The word "psychopath" is often confused with Langman's second category, "psychotic," but they are entirely different.

- **Psychotic Shooters**

  Psychotic individuals experience severe mental illness symptoms, which include false beliefs (delusions) and seeing or hearing things that are not real (hallucinations). These symptoms are most commonly seen among individuals on the schizophrenic spectrum. While most severely mentally ill people are never violent, a small subset can engage in violence under certain circumstances. Only 10 percent of public mass killers have been identified as motivated solely by psychosis.

- **Traumatized Shooters**

  These perpetrators have a significant history of abuse, bullying, or trauma, which may have influenced their behavior.

It is important to note that these categories can overlap, with one perpetrator meeting criterion in more than one subset.

Langman's model, though limited in scope to school shootings, is extremely valuable. His detailed case studies are exhaustive and tremendously helpful in gaining insight into public mass killers' minds.

The Violence Project researchers, Peterson and Densley, have broadened their research set to include mass shootings outside of school settings; it is clear that the targets are now expanding into other locations beyond classrooms.

The deadliest mass shooting in U.S. history (as of 2019) occurred in 2017 at the Harvest country music festival in Las Vegas, where 58 died. The second-deadliest event was at the Pulse Nightclub in Orlando, Florida, in 2016.

The Violence Project researchers have also broken their data into typologies of mass shooters based primarily upon the shootings' locations.[17]

These are the Violence Project subsets with a summary of the categories.

- **K–12 School Shooters**

  Based upon the Violence Project analysis of 13 mass shootings in K–12 locations and 154 attempted mass shootings, the K–12 school shooter is usually a white male (85 percent) and usually a student or former student of the targeted school. Most of them have reported a history of trauma.

  They are nearly always suicidal and are most likely to live in a suburban or rural setting. Eighty-seven percent reveal (foreshadow or "leak") at least some aspects of their plans prior to the attack; 80 percent evidence a high degree of advance planning.

  Most K–12 shooters use guns legally owned by family members and have a previous interest in firearms.

- **College/University Shooters**

  This category is based on nine mass shooting incidents that have occurred in college settings. Five of these men were white, three were Asian, and one was biracial. Most were students at the schools; one was a school custodian. Three had a documented history of schizophrenia, and most of the others had reported histories of mental health problems.

All nine of these shooters were suicidal, and all but one used legally obtained firearms—most of these perpetrators left behind videos or manifestos. All nine took their own lives at the scene.[18]

- **House of Worship Shooters**

The Violence Project identified 11 incidents in the United States as house of worship shootings between 1980 and 2019. Several of these attacks were committed by male white supremacists targeting racial or ethnic minority groups (a Sikh temple, Jewish synagogues, and an African American church were targeted). These racist perpetrators did not have a history of major mental illness.

Men involved in domestic and familial disputes, which spilled over into the church setting, committed three others. The others appeared to be individuals who were psychotic and carried grudges against the church group for various reasons. At least two were former members of the U.S. military; most used semiautomatic weapons.

- **Restaurant/Bar/Nightclub Shooters**

Twenty-four shooters in restaurants, bars, or nightclubs are identified in the Violence Project database. Most were white males with no connection to the target. One-third showed evidence of a thought disorder, which can be indicative of a mental health problem. Sixty-seven percent had a history of violence. Twenty-two percent were military veterans.[19]

- **Retail Shooters**

Twenty-two mass killings at retail establishments are identified in the Violence Project data. Some of the murders occurred outside of retail establishments, ranging from a Walmart, a car wash, a supermarket, a hair salon, and multiple shopping malls.[20]

- **Workplace Shooters**

There are more mass killings in the workplace than in any other location. The Violence Project counts a total of 47.

Workplace mass killers are typically employees or former employees at the workplace, usually a blue-collar company. Most were male and in their 40s.

Eighty-three percent of the workplace perpetrators recently been fired from their jobs or had faced a recent disciplinary action. Thirty-one percent had a military background, and most used their own legally obtained handguns. Seventy-eight percent were suicidal.

There is no dominant racial group in the workplace shooter category.[21]

- **Government/Civic Importance**

  Five incidents were committed at governmental agencies or involved matters relating to the government. White men committed two, a black man committed one, one perpetrator was a Native American woman, and one perpetrator was an Arab male who was a naturalized U.S. citizen.[22]

- **Other**

  Of the 167 shootings in The Violence Project database, 39 shootings were not within their four specified subsets; these are referenced as "other."[23]

Both Langman and the Violence Project researchers have focused solely on mass killings committed with guns. Though they have organized their data differently, the typologies they have developed are complementary and overlapping. All will be broken down precisely in the following chapters.

Relevant Factors Common to All

Though there is no single profile that captures the complexity of those who commit mass killings, all share variables from five specific factors that influence their behavior.[24]

- **Personal-level factors** include psychological issues, family background and relationships, demographic backgrounds, and personal history.

- **Community-level factors** include social environment issues such as work and school environments.
- **Group factors** include affiliation with specific groups, including online contacts and communities.
- **Sociopolitical-level factors** include collective grievances, external events, politics, and the media.
- **Ideological-level factors** include influences by charismatic leaders and movements that justify narratives that tie together all the other factors.

Specific Commonalities

- Ninety-eight percent of mass killers are male, which is not surprising since males commit 90 percent of all violent crimes. The race of perpetrators varies, but overall, the majority have been white. Workplace shooters and college/university shooters are the exceptions to this.
- The perpetrator typically attempts to kill as many people as possible.
- Mass killers motivated by extremist ideologies (racism, misogyny) generally do not know their victims personally. Workplace killers and most K–12 school shooters are "insiders" who may know some or all of their victims, though K–12 school shooters do not typically target specific victims.
- Most mass killers are also suicidal; they plan to kill themselves or die when shot by law enforcement during their attacks (known as "suicide by cop").
- Many mass killers have had a long-standing interest in firearms and other weapons; many have had family members in the military.
- Eighty-seven percent of the K–12 school shooters at least partially revealed ("leaked") their plans in advance.
- Many mass killers adopt a warrior persona and wear military commando-style attire during their attacks, including flak jackets or bulletproof vests.

- Many bring multiple weapons and military paraphernalia, including grenades.
- Public mass killers commit planned predatory violence.

This final fact is foundational.

Predatory vs. Affective Violence

"Cold-blooded killer" is a common trope in fiction, but hot-blooded killers are far more common. We have more experience with the latter since we are far more likely to witness hot-blooded violence in a parking lot after a fender-bender than find ourselves face-to-face with a cold-blooded hitman.

If you have ever driven past a raging person on the highway or ducked out of the way during a bar fight, you recognize the kind of violence that is emotionally hot, volatile, and spontaneous. It is reactive and usually based on some perceived threat or slight. We have all experienced reactive hot impulses to some degree, but hopefully not often. It can lead to outcomes such as arrest and incarceration.

Psychologists refer to hot-blooded violence as "affective" violence.

Contrast this with the behavior of a trained assassin or military sniper. The sniper is logical, practiced, and detached. He has prepared in advance and is methodical rather than quick and reactive. The sniper follows a plan. A sniper's heart rate does not even elevate when he points his gun and pulls the trigger at the person he has designated as his target.

Psychologists refer to cold-blooded violence as "predatory" violence.

Predatory violence unnerves us. Most of us will never engage in it or witness it.

Neuroscientists recognize that these two modes of violence are qualitatively different and involve activation of separate brain regions; we describe them as neurobiologically distinct.[25]

Predatory violence is difficult for most of us to comprehend since it is far outside of typical human experience; most of us will never go through a daily routine of plotting murder.[26]

Public mass killers engage in predatory violence. They are cold and methodical. Their behavior is targeted and premeditated. They plan their attacks for hours, days, months, or even years in advance. In this way, we can think of mass killers as hunters.[27]

A mass killing is never a spontaneous response to one particular event. It is more likely to result from long-held grievances than a fender-bender in a parking lot.

Affective violence is more common. If someone threatens our child at the playground or our dog at the dog park, most of us are quick to see red and take offensive action.

There are physiological processes that motivate these two different types of violence.

The Brain and Aggression

It's helpful to understand some basics about the brain and nervous system to differentiate types of violence. Most simply, we can use a model called the triune brain developed in the 1960s by neuroscientist Paul Maclean. This model of brain structure and function is based on three specific regions of the human brain that are responsible for specific, distinct, mental activities.

- The **brain stem**, also called the "reptilian brain," controls automatic bodily functions like respiration, heart rate, and breathing.
- The **limbic system** is the center of emotion, somatosensory awareness, and implicit memory. The amygdala, an almond-shaped structure known as the center of fear and aggression, is located within the limbic system.
- **The frontal lobe**, the front of the brain, just behind the forehead, contains the prefrontal cortex, often called the "thinking brain," and is the center of cognition, conscious thought, self-awareness, planning, executive functioning, explicit memory, and verbal language. The prefrontal cortex is the part of the brain that sets goals and plans complex tasks and inhibits impulsive behavior.

Current thinking is that actual brain functions are not separated so distinctly; however, this basic model provides a sense of how the aggression types are neurobiologically different. Affective violence is driven by the amygdala, the center of fear and aggression. Predatory violence is driven by the prefrontal cortex, the thinking and planning part of the brain.

When we perceive an environmental threat, the amygdala automatically activates the fight-or-flight response by sending out signals to the nervous system that release a cascade of the stress hormones cortisol and adrenaline. These stress hormones prepare our body to run from danger or to fight by increasing blood sugar for more energy. Our heart rate increases. Our airways open up to take in more oxygen. Our pupils dilate to enhance our vision. Blood flow increases to our arms and legs to increase our strength and speed. While this is happening, blood flow is directed away from temporarily non-essential functions like digestion.[28]

This amygdala response happens *before* our prefrontal cortex—the thinking part of our brain—is even consciously aware of what is happening.

This is a crisis response, designed by evolution to save our lives in an emergency. Our neurobiological systems react instantaneously to help us either run from a mountain lion or fight to save our lives.[29]

To make it more complicated, the threat may be purely psychological, yet neurobiology works the same way. Finding one's spouse with a lover has provoked more than a few hot-blooded murders. Though there is no physical threat, the psychological threat may feel the same, and the body responds accordingly.

In hot-blooded violence, the prefrontal cortex, the thinking part of the brain, is essentially booted offline, which is why this emotional violence can get a person in trouble. Though our reflexes are heightened, our judgment gets worse.[30]

Researchers initially explored the difference in these two modes of violence by studying cats' behavior and brains.[31]

Imagine a cat confronted by an aggressively barking dog. The cat instantaneously responds with an immediate burst of speed, automatically leaping onto a fence or climbing a tree to escape the danger. If an escape route is not available, the cat's claws extend, and its back arches;

it hisses, yowls, and bares its teeth. If cornered, it will fight, swiping aggressively at the dog's snout. This all happens instantaneously, with no pre-planning.[32]

The cat is in fight or flight mode with activation of its autonomic nervous systems. The amygdala sends out the distress signal to the rest of the body, resulting in a surge of adrenaline. The heart rate speeds up as sight, hearing, and other senses become sharper. The cat is prepared to fight to survive.

This is affective violence. The intense energy expended in this emergency response lasts only for a brief period. The goal at that moment is to escape or reduce an immediate threat by fighting back.

Now imagine the same cat is in the back yard and spies a bird that has landed on the patio. The cat becomes stealthy, quiet, with claws contracted. It creeps forward cautiously, careful to make no sound as it stalks the bird with precision. The cat is laser-focused but calm and moves toward the prey with intention. The goal is clear; it wants to kill that bird.

This is predatory violence. Unlike the amygdala-driven fight/flight mode, the cat can sustain this predatory behavior for an indefinite period. Stalking takes time, and the cat is in no hurry.[33]

A different region of the brain activates predatory violence, the prefrontal cortex.[34]

Predatory mass killings are typically motivated by revenge, extremist beliefs, or some distorted sense of injustice, and are often not based on objective fact. The prefrontal cortex operates with no time limitations, and the individual can remain cool, calm, and goal oriented.[35] He experiences heightened clarity of thought.

Predatory violence can be considered the most dangerous manifestation of violence because it's goal-directed and planned in advance. As someone said in the 1800s in France, "Revenge is a dish best served cold."

Predators plan, fantasize about a goal, acquire resources, and rehearse in advance. They choose symbolic targets and select dates for attacks that have personal meaning for them.

Predators experience minimal emotion at the time of their actions; instead of flooding stress hormones, the predator's heightened clarity of thought allows for methodical, precise behavior. This planned, purposeful violence is not limited to a brief period. They ponder, they study, they prepare. They take their time.

Predators who commit public mass killings focus on injustices and revenge. These cold, methodical killers are commonly referred to as "injustice collectors."

3

The Pathway
to Violence Stage 1
Grievance

In this chapter, we learn that there is a clear pathway to violence common to nearly all mass killings and review two cases to illustrate the process. Emphasis is on the first step of the pathway: the accumulation of grievances, which may be part—or all—imaginary.

In this context, a grievance is a slight, often minor, that an individual perceives to be an injustice. Such grievances are often based on misperceptions and become amplified in the mind of a killer.

Injustice Collectors

Mary Ann O'Toole is a retired senior FBI special agent and criminal profiler who spent decades studying mass killers. She was the first to coin the term "injustice collector" as a descriptor for school shooters and similar killers. The term has since become commonly used by criminologists and other violence researchers to describe those who transform private feelings of anger, fear, and shame into a distorted sense of power and a desire for vengeance by creating scapegoats upon whom they act out.

In O'Toole's words, "An Injustice Collector is someone who sees injustices in many, if not most, things that happen to them in life. Injustice Collectors can misperceive the smallest slights and turn them into major events. Keeping a scorecard in their heads, they can accumulate injustices for years. Their response to these injustices—real or perceived—can be extremely disproportionate to the original grievance."[1]

It's important to note that the injustices are *perceived*, not necessarily objectively real. In everyday human experiences, injustice collectors may misattribute minor events as personal slights and persistently believe they have been mistreated. They focus on these slights, keep lists of grievances, and ruminate. They stew with thoughts of revenge. This behavior often starts during adolescence, sometimes earlier. Injustice collectors look at life through a filter of paranoia. Someone is always doing something to them or failing to recognize their intrinsic value and worth.

While most injustice collectors do not act out violently, some are prone to extreme overreactions that are dramatically disproportionate to what the original slight may have been. This thinking style eventually becomes apparent in their interactions with others.[2] This thinking style is the first step toward violence, which leads us to the first myth about mass public killers.

Myth: "He just snapped"

Most of us can't imagine why anyone would rationally plan to murder a group of innocent people. We make the most common assumption that something unusually traumatic must have happened to cause the mass killer so much emotional distress that he had a mysterious breakdown, grabbed a gun, and started randomly shooting.

But that's not how it happens.

A public mass killing is an endpoint on a defined pathway with a sequential series of planned, methodical actions.[3] When we look at all public mass killings, an observable template emerges, though there are unique aspects in how the pathway to violence manifests and progresses with each killer. The grievances differ. The duration of stages varies. Their motives and justifications are not all the same. They don't all use the same weapons. But the progression follows a pattern that may involve weeks, months, or even years in the process that initially begins with grievances.

And there are personality similarities among injustice collectors.

Though they may differ in multiple ways, their grievances are exacerbated by an inflated sense of entitlement and privilege and a narcissistic style of thinking that results in a heightened sensitivity to being insulted or unrecognized by others.[4]

Step One: Grievance

Though mass killers tend to have a long list of grievances that are used to justify their behavior, most of these grievances are grounded in distorted perceptions and thinking errors. These are abundantly clear in the two cases that occurred in Isla Vista, California, and Utoya, Norway.

The Isla Vista Killer

Santa Barbara is an idyllic place, one of the gems of California overlooking the Pacific Coast. Its Mediterranean climate, beautiful downtown area, and stately Spanish-style architecture have made it a haven for the wealthy and privileged. The sun shines nearly every day of the year, and the white-washed walls of the adobe buildings and their red tile roofs contrast with the crisp blue of the sky and the ocean.

It's the home of the University of California, Santa Barbara, adjacent to the small, densely packed community of Isla Vista, where thousands of college students reside.

On the evening of May 23, 2014, a late model black BMW cruised slowly through the streets of Isla Vista. The 22-year-old, dark-haired man behind the wheel had a good-looking haircut and wore stylish clothes.

He had three semiautomatic guns, 400 bullets, and an assortment of knives with him.[5]

The driver of the BMW was hunting, making his way to a sorority house. Earlier that afternoon, he had stabbed to death three young men in his apartment; all UCSB students, two were his roommates, and one was an acquaintance. All were Asian males.[6] The perpetrator's father was white, his mother Asian.

The killer attacked them by surprise, one by one as they entered the shared apartment; now, he was heading to a sorority residence where he hoped to kill dozens of young female students before hunting down anyone else he could find on the street.[7]

He'd planned to kill the pretty college girls for two years. He had already uploaded the video in which he detailed his plans and motives to YouTube just before he left his apartment that evening. The Isla Vista killer had made several videos revealing the content of his thoughts, which were, in essence, a list of grievances alongside striking self-aggrandizing narcissism. The final video in the series was titled "Retribution."[8]

In "Retribution," he preens and smirks at the camera as he describes his plan to murder. His speech is clear and articulate; he has a broad vocabulary. He's playing the role as if he's a movie star, but he comes off like a sinister cartoon character. Acting came easily to him since he grew up on the fringe of the Hollywood elite.

Sitting in his BMW, he stares into the camera, clearly comfortable. He is parked at the beach, and the light that shines across his face is romantic and golden. Tall palm trees of idyllic Santa Barbara are visible in the background.

Despite chronic social problems, the Isla Vista killer is quite physically attractive, stylish, and well-groomed. He's well-spoken. But his verbiage is over-the-top theatrical, and he inserts a maniacal chuckle repeatedly (subsequently referred to by others as "a creepy laugh") as if he fancies himself an evil genius in a blockbuster film. His tone is arrogant and pretentious. Several times he points an index finger dramatically at the camera.

He's enjoying himself.

Following is the transcript from the "Retribution" video:

Well, this is my last video; it has all had to come to this. Tomorrow is the day of retribution, the day in which I will have my revenge against humanity, against all of you. For the last eight years of my life, ever since I hit puberty, I've been forced to endure an existence of loneliness, rejection, and unfulfilled desires all because girls have never been attracted to me. Girls gave their affection and sex and love to other men but never to me.

I'm 22 years old and I'm still a virgin. I've never even kissed a girl. I've been through college for two and a half years, more than that, actually, and I'm still a virgin. It has been very torturous. College is the time when everyone experiences those things such as sex and fun and pleasure. Within those years I've had to rot in loneliness. It's not fair.

You girls have never been attracted to me. I don't know why you girls aren't attracted to me, but I will punish you all for it. It's an injustice, a crime, because…. I don't know what you don't see in me. I'm the perfect guy and yet you throw yourselves at these obnoxious men instead of me, the supreme gentleman.

I will punish all of you for it [laughs] on this day of retribution. I'm going to enter the hottest sorority house of UCSB. And I will slaughter every spoiled, stuck-up, blond slut I see inside there. All those girls I've desired so much, they would have all rejected me and looked down upon me as an inferior man if I ever made a sexual advance towards them [scoffs] while they throw themselves at these obnoxious brutes. I'll take great pleasure in slaughtering all of you.

You will finally see that I am in truth the superior one. The true alpha male [laughs]. Yes, after I've annihilated every single girl in the sorority house, I will take to the streets of Isla Vista and slay every single person I see there. All those popular kids who live such lives of hedonistic pleasures while I've had to rot in loneliness for all these years. They've all looked down upon me every time I tried to go out and join them, they've all treated me like a mouse.

Well, now I will be a god compared to you. You will all be animals. You are animals and I will slaughter you like animals. And I will be a god. Exacting my retribution on all those who deserve it. You do deserve it. Just for the crime of living a better life than me. All you popular kids, you've never accepted me, and now you will all pay for it. And girls, all I ever wanted was to love you, and to be loved by you. I've wanted a girlfriend. I've wanted sex. I've wanted love, affection, adoration. You think I'm unworthy of it. That's a crime that can never be forgiven.

If I can't have you girls, I will destroy you [laughs]. You denied me a happy life, and in turn, I will deny all of you life [laughs]. It's only fair.

I hate all of you. Humanity is a disgusting, wretched, depraved species. If I had it in my power, I would stop at nothing [points finger at camera] to reduce every single one of you to mountains of skulls and rivers of blood. And rightfully so. You deserve to be annihilated and I'll give that to you. You never showed me any mercy and so I will show you none [laughs].

You've forced me to suffer all my life and now I'll force you all to suffer. I've waited a long time for this. I'll give you exactly what you deserve. All of you. All you girls who rejected me and looked down upon me and you know, treated me like scum while you gave yourselves to other men. And all of you men, for living a better life than me, all of you sexually active men, I hate you. I hate all of you. I can't wait to give you exactly what you deserve. Utter annihilation [laughs].

Grievances and Misogyny

The Isla Vista killer also wrote a dense, 137-page autobiographical manifesto that begins at his birth and proceeds chronologically through the years of his life to the day of his death. The document focuses on hundreds of grievances and elaborate plans to take revenge—for injustices that, for the most part, occurred only in his mind. He convinced himself that the difficulties he had in his life had nothing to do with him; they were all external, entirely the fault of others.[9]

He focused mainly on women. Since puberty, he'd thought of little else, perseverating on sex. And rather than reflecting on what he might be doing wrong in his social relationships, he externalized the blame to women—beautiful young women and the young men with whom he imagined they had sex.

He made it clear that he wanted to kill the pretty girls, the "hot" ones that he blamed for rejecting him—although he had no specific girls in mind. The sorority girls were symbolic to him—symbols of the kind of girls with whom he'd constantly desired to have sex. Blondes, with cascading hair—popular girls who dated other boys, but never him.

The Isla Vista killer had been angry about this for years. Over and over in his videos and his written manifesto, he raged the same complaint: "It's not fair."[10]

As with all injustice collectors, his belief system became the organizing principle of his life.[11]

His complete list of grievances went back to early childhood, and in his manifesto, he mentioned by name everyone he perceived to have ever wronged him. The slights were often minor, but he explicitly stated them anyway. This killer wanted the world to get his message: the murder spree was not his fault.

Investigative Summary

The official Investigative Summary from the Santa Barbara County Sheriff's Office gives the following chronology of events on May 23, 2014[12]:

1. The suspect murdered his two roommates and one of their friends in his apartment by stabbing them to death. The three victims were murdered separately as they entered the apartment at different times on May 23, 2014.
2. Several hours after the initial murders, but minutes prior

to the subsequent events, the suspect uploaded a self-made video onto the internet titled "Retribution" and emailed a 137-page autobiographical manifesto to family members and acquaintances expressing anxiety, severe unhappiness, and anger. The online posting and email that afternoon and evening foreshadowed the events that were soon to occur. Minutes later, the suspect drove to a sorority house where he pounded on the front door trying to gain entry. Unsuccessful in this attempt, he returned to his vehicle and then shot three female students on the public sidewalk, killing two and severely wounding the third.

    3. He then drove to the area of 6560 Pardall Road, where he fired a round into a closed and occupied building in an apparent attempt to shoot occupants. Continuing eastbound, he then shot and killed a male victim standing in front of a market.

    4. The suspect used his vehicle to intentionally strike a male victim, causing injury.

    5. As he continued to drive, he shot two victims, a male and a female, wounding them both.

    6. He shot and wounded the next victim, a female, near the intersection of El Embarcadero and Sabado Tarde.

The report continues with the account of the suspect driving slowly around Isla Vista, alternately shooting pedestrians and bicyclists while intentionally swerving and attempting to run into numerous individuals with his vehicle. A total of 14 were wounded, and nine were killed.[13]

Several of the wounded mentioned that the gunman pulled up close to them in his car, lowered his window, and smiled as he shot them. Some mentioned "a creepy laugh."[14]

A young woman walking down the street reported that the driver of the black BMW pulled up near her and said simply, "Hey, what's up?" He was calm and relaxed.

She described him as "a totally normal guy with brown hair and sunglasses." She turned her head to reply, "What's up?" just before he shot at her with his black Sig Sauer semiautomatic pistol. She felt the bullet whiz by her face.[15]

"It was like looking into the face of the devil—it was terrifying," she said in a news clip. She turned to run and was able to escape.[16]

Within approximately eight minutes from the time the shooter fired his first shots, police engaged the suspect with gunfire, wounding him. He then shot himself in the head behind the wheel of his car, dying instantly.[17]

History

By all objective measures, the Isla Vista killer had been born into privilege. Born in London, he moved to Los Angeles with his parents and a younger sister at age five. His father, a film director who had worked on *The Hunger Games*, provided a decidedly upper-class lifestyle; despite working a great deal, he appeared to give his son everything he wanted. His mother was intensely devoted to him; even after his parents' divorce when he was seven, he describes a childhood filled with playdates, private schools, international travel, and parental kindness. He attended red-carpet premieres of Hollywood films with his family, rubbing elbows with film stars.[18]

He was always painfully shy and had difficulty making friends. He was of short stature and slightly built and perseverated on this as a child.[19] He also didn't like that he was half Asian.

While some might say he was indulged, it's clear his parents had tried desperately to help him. As his father would say later in a televised interview with Barbara Walters, "I had no idea of the darkness he was hiding." His parents were unaware that he had been purchasing weapons and ammunition and had no idea he was planning violence.[20]

Both his manifesto and videos reveal that he was decidedly class conscious, even as a young child. He felt entitled and unique. Maintaining an air of wealth and prestige was very important to him, possibly because he was raised on the fringe of the Hollywood elite and focused on comparing himself with the rich and famous. He was obsessed with social hierarchy. He wanted the best of everything and boasted that his designer sunglasses had cost $300 in one video.[21] His late-model BMW was a gift from his mother.[22]

In his writings, he also revealed a plan to murder his stepmother, a former actress, as well as his nine-year-old brother. His stated rationale was jealousy over his younger brother, who had just gotten a modeling contract, and anger over his stepmother's attempts to limit his obsessive video gameplay.[23]

Jealousy and rage consumed him.

The Isla Vista killer had a complicated mental health history and had been in treatment with several therapists over the years. However, his actions were clear, precise, and goal directed. He planned carefully and knew exactly what he was doing.[24]

Though he had been bullied in high school, he did not target anyone who had ever bullied him. Some stated that they had tried to befriend him in college but were rebuffed.

Most of us find ways to cope with the social hierarchies that confront us in life as well as our inevitable human deficits. Rather than finding productive ways to cope with his problems, the Isla Vista killer became an injustice collector. He rationalized, "I didn't start this war. But I will finish it. Finally, at long last, I can show the world my true worth."[25]

The war was his creation. It existed only in his mind. It started when he was a youngster who took his fear, anger, and shame and began to keep score of injustices that transformed his pain and anger into sadistic fantasies.

The grievance phase on the pathway to violence is unique to each individual. It may last for weeks, months, or years. The perpetrator perseverates on how he has been slighted and develops paranoid fears about the damage being inflicted upon him by others. Simmering with anger, he eventually focuses on retribution. Cognitive distortions, or thinking errors, become cemented over time as the killer becomes convinced his point of view is correct and that violent action is a justifiable solution to his grievances.

The sense of being aggrieved may become so distorted that it can be described as paranoid and delusional. His thinking may not be grounded in objective reality; some or all of the perceived slights may be imaginary.

Oslo/Utoya, Norway

The majestic mountains, waterfalls, and fjords of Norway are breathtaking. With a remarkably low population density, highly educated populace, and low crime rate, Norway's citizens rate themselves among the happiest people in the world.[26] However, in recent years there have been rumblings of civil unrest and a rise of right-wing hate groups.

Racism is at the heart of it.

Traditionally Norway has been a racially and culturally homogenous white, Christian country. In the early 90s, this began to change as the government welcomed non-western immigrants. These immigrants, predominantly Muslim, have continued to increase in number through the years, much to the dismay of a small percentage of white, right-wing Norwegians. Multiple cultural conflicts have been reported.[27]

Far-right white nationalist groups have since become active to limit immigration and maintain Norway as a predominantly white country. Some would like to expel all Muslims. A small number of individuals have resorted to violence.

One became a mass killer.

A Knight Templar

On July 22, 2011, a 32-year-old Norwegian man and self-described "Knight Templar" emailed a 1,500-page, single-spaced manifesto of grievances to one thousand people. He claimed to have spent the previous nine years writing it. The title of what he referred to as his "book" was *2083—A European Declaration of Independence*.[28]

After emailing his manifesto to 1,000 people, the Norwegian killer donned a police uniform before parking a cargo van on a busy street in the city center of Oslo. He left the van directly outside the Ministry of Justice and the Prime Minister's office, the seat of Norway's government. He lit a fuse that would detonate a 950-kilo bomb inside the van that he'd rigged to explode six minutes later, while he escaped in another vehicle parked nearby.[29]

The Norwegian killer had hoped to make the government center collapse, killing hundreds as well as the prime minister.

The windows of the government center blew in, immediately killing eight with a wave of pressure that shook the ground for blocks. Smoke gushed out of the building as several stories burned. Hundreds of citizens flooded the streets, running.

But he wasn't finished. This was only stage-one of his three-stage plan to save the world.[30]

"Attack that which they hold dear"

The Norway killer then drove 45 kilometers directly to Utoya Island, an isolated, pine-covered campground where hundreds of children were on summer holiday for a youth leadership camp sponsored by the political party that he hated. Riding to the island on a ferry, he impersonated a policeman and stated he was there to secure the island and protect the children.

After crossing on the ferry, he first shot and killed the one volunteer security guard on the island and then another adult leader.

Calmly, he began to stalk the children in different locations on the island. Dozens fled and desperately tried to hide or escape by swimming to the mainland. They were screaming, crying, and begging for their lives.

Children spread out across the island, hiding. They hid behind buildings, rocks, outhouses, and lying in tall grass. Some hid behind rocks at the shoreline. Many tried to staunch their friends' bleeding as they hid.

If they cried for help, he shot them. He held his gun just millimeters from their heads and fired. Some children jumped in front of others in an attempt to save them. He shot every child he saw.[31]

The bodies of dead children littered the island. The rocks on much of the island were stained red.[32]

The Norwegian killer murdered 69 of them and injured over 200 before surrendering to the authorities. Yet, his mission wasn't finished; surrendering after the rampage was part of his grand plan.

The Ultimate Goal

The murder of the children on Utoya was only the second stage. The essential part would follow at his trial.

His goal was to drive the Muslims out of Norway, though he didn't kill Muslim children. He killed children of the political party that he blamed for allowing Muslim refugees into the country, a party that embraced multiculturalism.

He envisioned the dissemination of his 1,500-page manifesto as the most crucial part of his plan. The murders were to call attention to it.

The title of what he called his "book" was *2083*, which signified the year when he believed a "pure Europe" would finally be restored—if modern Knights Templar crusaders followed his plan.

The book is an elaborate and exhaustive collection of imagined injustices. He described world history from the perspective of far-right extremism and particularly focused on the interactions between European Christians and Islamic countries and cultures. Much of this was lifted from online right-wing and anti–Muslim sources. He attempted to create a guide for a multiphase war, something of a combination philosophical tutorial, a treatise on "cultural conservatism," and a field guide for other right-wing extremists to advance his anti–Muslim agenda.[33]

It's strikingly narcissistic. He included his personal history, a chronology of his life from birth up to the date of his attack. He responds to his questions with details about his favorite hobbies, beverages, music, cologne, sexual habits, and computer games—he even included his curriculum vitae, written in the faux-interview style.[34]

The Norwegian killer offered guidance in waging a multiphase war with advice on weapons, body armor, tactical training, and potential use of chemical, biological, and nuclear weapons. He shared his views on the evils of "cultural Marxism," which includes feminism, and the necessity to return to traditional gender roles of the 1950s. He railed against homosexuality and sexual promiscuity, even discussing his mother and sister's history of sexually transmitted disease. He railed against those who would "pollute" racial purity by intermarriage, naming several celebrities as examples of this. He called for white Europeans to rise against governments seen as secretly controlled by Jews whose aim is to dilute white racial purity by enabling immigration.[35]

As is typical of right-wing views, he expounded on the need to return to the social order of the 1950s, a time when men and women knew their place in their respective gender roles. Women were to be homemakers, dress in a traditionally feminine manner, and rear children. Their access to birth control was to be limited, with abortion only allowed in cases of rape. Men were to be powerful, masculine, and the breadwinners for their families.[36]

He included a highly detailed organizational structure of a modern "Knights Templar" organization that existed only in his imagination.[37] His view of himself was bizarrely grand.

His grand intention was for his trial to draw attention to his book containing his map to change the world. The entire treatise was evidence of his strangely inflated view of himself.

The Norwegian killer had been involved in extremist far-right youth groups since age 16. He began formulating his plan at age 22 and spent nine years writing this manifesto. He never claimed to be an unhappy or traumatized person, instead describing himself as happy and close to his family and friends, though he shared that he kept most of his beliefs and plans secret.

At his trial, his attorney fought to have him declared insane to avoid prison. The would-be crusader maintained that he was not mentally ill and knew exactly what he was doing. He was clearly not psychotic.[38]

He made a white power salute on the first day of his trial and smiled smugly during most of it. His arrogance was palpable.

The court ultimately accepted the psychological evaluation that indicated a diagnosis of Narcissistic Personality Disorder and Antisocial Personality Disorder, neither of which can be legally used to mitigate responsibility for murdering others.[39]

The Similarities

The Isla Vista killer and the Norwegian killer were superficially different from one another. Their beliefs and causes were different. Yet, on the psychological level, there were many similarities.

Both left extensive, detailed manifestos which provide us with in-depth examples that illustrate their cognitive style. Though the content of their thoughts differed, their thinking styles were similar. They focused on grievances and compiled them for years. They both perceived themselves to be victims.

They came to believe that mass murder was justified, even virtuous, through their distorted perceptions.

They built their identities upon their grievances, and revenge became their reason for living.

Most public killers start as injustice collectors. They are typically narcissistic and believe they are unique; when disappointed or frustrated by life, they externalize their distress and blame others. Rather than seeking productive coping skills, they organize their thinking to create targets for retribution. They *become* their mission. This is the first step on the pathway to violence. Public mass killers do not "just snap." They have reasons for their violence—dozens and dozens of reasons.

4

The Pathway
to Violence Stage 2

Ideation and Foreshadowing

"Serial killers are lame. Everyone knows that mass murderers are the cool kids."—Newtown killer, November 4, 2011, 4:44 a.m., Shocked Beyond Belief Forum[1]

In this chapter, we explore the second phase of the pathway to violence, ideation and foreshadowing. The case study presented illustrates the entire pathway to violence but highlights how abundant evidence of ideation and foreshadowing is often ignored. Opportunities for intervention along the path can be repeatedly missed, with tragic results.

Distorted Thoughts and Fantasies

After the initial grievance phase, the mass killer continues to externalize blame for his real or imagined problems and comes to believe that violence is the appropriate method to address his grievances. He begins to focus on a target for retribution and starts fantasizing about plans. Often those targeted in the fantasies are symbolic representations with whom he has no personal history.

This is the ideation phase, which often includes foreshadowing.[2] Foreshadowing, also called leakage, is when the killer's interests in violence or mass murder leak out in observable behavior or discussion with others. It's the time when his peculiar thoughts and interests in murder may become known by those closest to him. This is not necessarily parents (though it can be), but may include peers, teachers, or those he interacts with online.[3]

During the ideation phase, violent fantasies become increasingly detailed. Killers begin to research, study, and ultimately fixate on other murderers who have gone before them. Adolf Hitler, Charles Manson, and the Columbine killers are popular with public mass killers, though the list of perverse role models expands with each new incident.

They study each other. The killer begins to identify himself with the group. Mass murderers from the past offer a template for future violent actions that start to manifest in the would-be killer's imagination.

As the potential mass murderer becomes increasingly focused on violence, the fantasies correspondingly become increasingly elaborate and sadistic.

They fall in love with the sense of messianic, God-like power; they will ultimately decide who dies.

The Isla Vista killer not only fantasized about murdering women; in his manifesto, he wrote of his fantasies of putting them in concentration camps and torturing them or dipping them in boiling water. He wanted to eliminate women from society, other than a few who would be kept alive for breeding.[4]

The Norway killer fantasized about his violent crusade to change history as a modern Knight Templar. He believed others would be so impressed with his manifesto that they would follow his plan.[5]

Not every person who fantasizes about violence eventually moves to act on the thoughts, but those who act have spent time fantasizing about it, often for a long time.

The internet has made this process easy. Not only can would-be murderers research other killers and their methods, but they can also connect with like-minded souls through websites and online message boards. It's easy for them to become psychologically consumed and filter out peers with more normal interests over time.

In their internal world, they come to identify themselves as righteous killers long before they act.

It is now possible to trace where killers have gone online and determine the content of their computer hard drives through forensic computer analysis. Often, shocking hidden inner worlds are discovered.

This second phase on the pathway to violence, ideation and

foreshadowing, offers an opportunity for intervention that could prevent forward movement on the pathway—if those around the killer notice, take decisive action, and seek help.[6] Once again, we see patterns.

Myth: Mass Killings Are Senseless and Unpredictable

Just because mass killings don't make sense to us, that doesn't mean they don't make sense in the mind of the killer. There are, in fact, layers of inter-related reasons that include the killer's biology, psychology, family, and surrounding social system.

Newtown

There had not been a single murder in Newtown, Connecticut, for 30 years. Nonetheless, on December 14, 2012, the quiet, upper-middle-class community became the scene of one of the most horrifying mass murders in history. The location was Sandy Hook Elementary School. The victims were first-grade children and their teachers.

While this incident stands out as one of the most horrifying due to the young ages of the victims, it's also one of the well-documented cases where abundant foreshadowing was ignored.

The 20-year-old perpetrator had three guns and was dressed head to toe in black. He wore sunglasses and a military hat and was so gaunt and pale he looked like a specter.[7]

December 14 was the anniversary of another school shooting, back in 1991. Since the Newtown killer was an expert in mass murder, the date chosen was likely no coincidence.[8]

Mass killers pay attention to anniversaries.

Sandy Hook Elementary—The Breach

Sandy Hook Elementary School was home to 456 students at the time of the shooting and had a sophisticated security protocol. The doors to the school were locked after the children arrived in the morning. During school hours, visitors could only be individually admitted through a locked door after identification via a live video monitor.[9]

It sounds secure, a far more sophisticated procedure to enter than found at most elementary schools. But even this level of security was not enough to avert tragedy. The gunman had once been a student at Sandy Hook; he knew the layout, and he had a plan.

Shortly after 9:35 on a weekday morning, the gunman pulled his mother's Honda Civic into the emergency zone in front of the school entrance, leaving the car there. He then entered the school by shooting his way through a glass panel next to the locked front doors of the school. He was armed with his mother's Bushmaster XM15-E2S rifle and 10 magazines with 30 rounds each. He also carried a Glock and a Sig Sauer handgun. There was a shotgun in the trunk of his car.[10]

The school intercom system was turned on for morning announcements, and those initial shots were broadcast into every classroom.[11]

The school principal ran toward the sound of the gunshots, followed by the school psychologist and a lead teacher. In the seconds it took to realize that there was a gunman in the school, all three women began shouting, "Shooter! Stay put!"[12]

Several of their colleagues nearby heard the warnings and were able to hide in closets and under desks, which saved their lives.

Though the principal was only 5'2", she charged at the gunman in an attempt to grab the rifle. He shot her multiple times; she died instantly. The psychologist was shot immediately after and also died. The teacher was hit twice, and the shooter moved on, assuming she was dead. She was subsequently able to crawl into a classroom and hide.[13]

The school janitor yelled, "Put the gun down!" as he ran through the halls, warning others.[14]

Walking through the school office, the killer failed to see the staff that were hiding. The rooms appeared empty, and he moved on to the first-grade classrooms.

Multiple 911 calls were made from cell phones just after the first shots. The school custodian made at least three and remained on the line with police dispatch for 10 minutes as gunfire went off in the background.

The killer had entered the school just after 9:35, and the murders began immediately. At 9:36, the first Newtown police dispatch went out that there was a shooting at Sandy Hook Elementary. At 9:37, Connecticut State Police were also dispatched to the school.[15]

Carnage

The Sandy Hook teachers were at a disadvantage. Classroom doors could only be locked with a key from the outside of the rooms. Teachers could not lock the doors from the inside and opening the door could put them face to face with the gunman. The teachers in the classrooms nearest the front of the school did not have time to get their doors locked before the gunman entered.[16]

After the initial murders near the office, the killer turned to the first-grade classroom where he had once been a student. The teacher, a substitute, had herded her five- and six-year-olds to the back of the room and was attempting to hide them in the bathroom in the rear of the class.

The shooter started shooting immediately, frequently stopping to reload as he hit each victim multiple times. In less than 40 seconds, he left 16 dead. The first-grade teacher, her aide, and 15 students were killed. Fourteen were killed at the scene; one was later transported to the hospital, where she was pronounced dead.

The sounds of screaming, crying, and gunfire were carried over the school public address system, which was still on. The *pop-pop-pop* of shots echoed around the school.

Smoke and the smell of sulfur enveloped the school as he made his way to a second nearby classroom, where children huddled together as that teacher also attempted to move others into the bathroom. A handful of children hid under their desks.

When the killer entered the second classroom, he initially shot the children under the desks. A first-grade boy shouted at his classmates to run for safety before he was shot and killed. Several were able to run out, but others were shot as they ran.

The teacher put herself between the gunman and the remaining students who were huddled on the floor. He killed her. A special education teacher would later be found dead, cradling the body of a six-year-old.

The gunman's weapon jammed as sirens were heard approaching the school. Several more children were able to run from the room.

Around the school, teachers hid children in bathrooms and storage closets. The gunman pounded on the door of a 4th-grade classroom, shouting, "Let me in!" That teacher had been able to get the door locked. The children stayed silent. The perpetrator moved on.

In other classrooms, children cried as their teachers told them to hide. Holding hands and hugging, some whimpered and asked for their mothers while others looked shocked. Many teachers whispered to the children, "I love you." Some prayed.

Several survivors reported that they heard the gunman cursing and shouting, "Look at me!" and "Come over here!" and "Look at them!"

At 9:39, just four and a half minutes after the first 911 call, Newtown police arrived at the scene. A final shot from the gunman was heard at 9:40. He sat down in a back corner of one of the classrooms and shot himself in the head with his Glock, dying instantly.[17]

Aftermath

Newtown police entered the school at 9:45. At 9:46, Connecticut State Police arrived. No shots were ever fired by police, and they began evacuating the survivors room-by-room as they swept the school for bombs or other perpetrators.[18]

The rapidity of the police response no doubt saved dozens of lives. The Newtown killer had murdered 26 children and staff in less than five minutes.[19]

Police who arrived at Sandy Hook were not prepared for what they found. The scenes in the two first-grade classrooms were horrific. There were dead children everywhere.

Three officers who were early arrivers collapsed to the ground outside of the first classroom. Other officers embraced one another as tears rolled down their cheeks. *How could someone do this to children?*

As one officer carried a child out who was barely breathing, he whispered to her, "You're safe now—your parents love you."[20]

It took several hours to identify the gunman accurately; he carried his older brother's driver's license in his wallet.

In the Colonial home on the quiet street that the gunman shared with his mother, police found her in bed, clad in pajamas. Before he left for Sandy Hook, her son had shot her four times in the head while she slept.

When law enforcement searched the home, they found the windows in his bedroom and basement wholly covered with black trash bags, taped shut to seal out all light.

A stockpile of various guns, ammo, and knives was found, unsecured, all around the home. At least 1,600 rounds of ammunition were in multiple locations in shoeboxes and peanut cans.[21]

Spreadsheet of Murder

In the killer's bedroom, officers discovered a massive spreadsheet seven feet long and four feet wide. The Newtown killer had ranked hundreds of mass killers from around the world in order from most kills to least, along with the precise make and model of the weapons used. The data was typed out in tiny nine-point font.

This carefully researched document had been years in the making. Studying and ranking mass murderers had been an organizing focus of the emaciated young man who stayed isolated in his dark room, illuminated only by the glow from his computer monitor.[22]

Investigators determined that the Newtown killer had spent years planning. There had been foreshadowing in his behavior for at least a decade. Those who could have noticed and intervened did not. There were countless missed opportunities for intervention throughout his life.

Law enforcement officers also found his NRA certificate in his bedroom, along with his first-grade report card from Sandy Hook Elementary School. There were military fatigues in his closet as well as three Samurai swords.

A holiday card in his room was from his mother; the enclosed Bank of America check had a notation that specified the money was to be used to buy a new handgun.[23]

At a news conference about the murders at Sandy Hook Elementary School later that evening, President Barack Obama broke down in tears. Calls for gun control went out around the country; gun-control opponents called for all teachers to be armed.

Questions

This nightmarish incident at an elementary school seemed particularly senseless. How could someone kill small children?

This case became the object of intense focus in law enforcement agencies, the news media, and various other government agencies. Multiple detailed reports were written on the incident, the subsequent investigation, and the perpetrator.

One exceptionally detailed report was created by the Office of the Child Advocate of the State of Connecticut. The Child Advocate's office monitors and evaluates public and private agencies that exist to protect and advocate for children. One of the primary areas of focus by the Child Advocate was to assess factors that may have led to the incident.

The information on the perpetrator of the Sandy Hook Elementary School murders reveals copious details about his life; however, it concludes that no specific cause could be determined for his actions.[24]

I believe that's only partially correct. There was certainly no single cause for the carnage; however, if we put ourselves inside the killer's mind, we can get a sense of his reasoning and understand that multiple factors over many years contributed to the tragedy.

Determining causality is always challenging; there is never a simple cause-effect relationship with one event that leads to mass murder. There is never a single cause. Multiple interrelated factors are woven together from the killer's neurobiology, history, family, and social setting. When we can look at all the factors, we can begin to understand.

Mass killings always make sense in the killer's mind,[25] even if they make no sense to the rest of us.

Since there is copious, detailed information in the public domain about the Newtown killer, we can follow the process.

History

The Newtown killer was unusual in nearly every way, starting with being born into a family with a peculiar focus on firearms.

He shot his first gun at age four when his mother took him out for target practice. Firearms would continue to be a central organizing factor in the family as he grew up,[26] despite his family's appearance on the surface to be otherwise typical.

He was born into an upper-middle-class family in 1992 in New Hampshire. His father was a corporate accountant; his mother became a stay-at-home parent after his birth. He had one sibling, a brother, four years older. The family moved to idyllic Newtown, Connecticut, when the boy was six years old, purchasing a large Colonial home on over two acres, with an in-ground swimming pool. His parents built a swing set with a wooden slide for him in the backyard.[27]

But the perpetrator was odd, even as a small child. Though he appeared healthy at birth, he had an episode of sleep apnea during which he stopped breathing at eight days old and was admitted to the hospital. This event may have been a factor in subsequent developmental delays.[28]

Medical records indicate that he did not speak until he was three. He had extreme temper tantrums and repetitive, stereotypical behaviors. As he got older, his eating behavior became idiosyncratic; he had multiple rituals about food. There was a limited range of foods he would eat, and the food had to be arranged a certain way on the plate. Only certain dishware could be used.[29] This child demanded a great deal of work and accommodation from early on.

Hypersensitive to touch, he required that all tags be removed from his clothing. He didn't allow others to touch him. He smelled things that weren't there and washed his hands obsessively—a behavior that would leave his hands red and raw throughout his life.[30]

He would eventually come to refuse to touch doorknobs and became upset if his mother touched them.[31]

The Newtown killer always had an aversion to playing with other children and maintained physical separation from groups of kids.[32]

He was evaluated at age three at a child development intervention program, where he was diagnosed with "sensory-integration disorder." This is not a stand-alone condition; rather, sensory-processing problems are typically found among those on the autism spectrum. It's unknown how much about this condition was explained to the parents at that time, and this center's services only went through age three, which made him ineligible for ongoing services at the agency.[33]

People with sensory processing problems are typically oversensitive to things in their environment. Common sounds, lights, and colors can be painful or overwhelming. They may be uncoordinated, bump into things, or be poor at sensing where their limbs are in space. They typically have an awkward, stiff gait. Nearly always, they have problems engaging in activities with peers.

The Newton killer had all those symptoms and more. He would not receive an adequate mental health assessment for another 10 years.[34]

Yet, he always had an affinity for firearms. He enjoyed shooting guns and developed a fascination with them as a young boy. His mother, who grew up in a hunting culture, encouraged this hobby; it became the only activity they could engage in together. The Newtown killer became a perfect shot as a child.

"A normal, weird little kid"

In an interview with journalist Andrew Solomon that was published in *The New Yorker*, his father stated he came to view him as "a normal weird little kid."[35] His mother made a point of describing him to others as "borderline autistic" but "high functioning." In those conversations, she also stressed that he was "gifted."

Her need to put a positive spin on the situation with her extremely troubled child says a great deal about her finesse with denial. She was not viewing him or his difficulties realistically, which became a significant part of the problem as the years went on.

More Than "Autistic"

In truth, he was at the very least on the autistic spectrum with multiple co-occurring diagnoses. He displayed severe obsessive-compulsive disorder and personality pathology; he was *not* "high functioning," though he was of average intelligence. It has been speculated that he may have been developing a psychotic disorder, perhaps schizophrenia, on top of everything else. In childhood, the symptoms of autism and schizophrenia can appear similar and can be difficult to differentiate.[36]

His parents were too close to the situation to realize how much was wrong with their son. Since he was never in sustained treatment, the source and progression of his developmental and psychiatric problems continue to be a topic of speculation among professionals.

Treatment and Missed Opportunities

Mental health diagnoses are best made longitudinally over time, particularly with children. In an initial assessment, a clinician only sees an individual for one visit, a tiny, discrete slice of their lives. It's like viewing a single frame in a movie. It's a snapshot, not a whole photo album. Over time, strengths and weaknesses become more apparent, and diagnoses are typically adjusted as more information is gathered— if the individual remains in appropriate treatment. The Newtown killer did not.[37]

The boy received speech therapy and occupational therapy from kindergarten through 4th grade, in sessions that lasted only 30 minutes. His psychiatric problems, as evidenced by his extreme social withdrawal and obsessive behavior, were never addressed. Considering the extent of his disabilities, this was entirely inadequate and largely the result of a school district with minimal resources for disabled children.[38]

A more aggressive regimen of intervention at this point would have been the first way to interrupt the pathway to violence. This kind of intensive treatment was not available through the Newtown public school system.[39]

Observers noted his mother to be extreme and overbearing; she reacted with dramatic intensity to any sign of her son's distress. She hovered protectively. She seemed to become emotionally enmeshed with him in a way that prevented her from having a realistic perspective; she increasingly sank into denial.[40]

This blind spot contributed to the lack of seeking out appropriate treatment for him.

Despite his social problems, teachers and peers attempted to be supportive. In extensive interviews with teachers and other students, no one recalled him ever being bullied.[41] In *The New Yorker* interview, his father suggested he may have been teased about his awkward physical gait in middle school, but any teasing that might have occurred was mild.[42]

Foreshadowing

Foreshadowing began in 5th grade when the Newtown killer worked with another boy to create a book called *The Big Book of Granny*. It was filled with gruesome violence, far beyond the kind of fantasy violence common to children.[43]

Granny was an old woman with a cane who uses it to murder others. Granny wants to taxidermy a boy for her mantle. Another character in the book, Dora the Berserker, says, "I like hurting people—especially children."

The Big Book of Granny was professionally spiral bound with a purple cover. An adult had been involved in its final production, but no adult raised the alarm.[44]

The Newtown killer subsequently got in trouble for trying to sell copies of the book at school. The original copy of *The Big Book of Granny* was found among his possessions in his bedroom after his death. While young children may play war games with violent themes, this sadistic preoccupation was not usual. Neither is it typical behavior for those on the autism spectrum.

There was also a story in *The Big Book of Granny* about a boy who shot his mother in the head with a shotgun.

Once again, an opportunity for professional intervention was missed.

His mother and father separated during his fifth-grade year, though his father spent time with him on weekends for several years. The father took a backseat in all significant parenting decisions, and the boy's mother had primary control. They would later divorce.[45]

Evaluations and More Missed Opportunities

Teachers noted violent themes and disturbing drawings throughout his public school years. Parents were sometimes notified, but there was never any professional intervention.

A psychiatrist did not evaluate the Newtown killer until he was 13, at which point his father said, "It was crystal clear something was wrong."[46] The odd little boy was turning into a genuinely bizarre young man and was unable to make a successful transition to middle school.

At that time, the diagnosis assigned by a psychiatrist was Asperger's Syndrome (which has now been subsumed into the broader category of autism spectrum disorder), with co-occurring obsessive-compulsive disorder and anxiety. The youngster was noted to have significant social impairments. His IQ was noted to be average, and he had no learning disabilities.[47]

Violence is *not* a typical characteristic of individuals on the autism spectrum; most autistic children are far more likely to internalize their distress than to externalize their unhappiness with violent fantasies. In this case, it appears that the autism diagnosis served to cover the fact that there was much more going on. He was not a typical child; neither was he a typical autistic child.

The boy refused to accept the diagnosis, maintaining that there was nothing wrong with him. This belief would harden into concrete as he got older.

Both he and his mother refused to consider psychotropic medication, which would have helped with his anxiety and obsessive symptoms. No behavioral treatment plan to address his social problems was initiated.[48]

Thus, we count another missed opportunity for intervention.

His parents had him assessed again one year later at the Yale Child Study Center, and the same diagnosis was confirmed: autism, anxiety, and obsessive-compulsive disorder. The multidisciplinary treatment team at the Yale Child Study Center was decidedly proactive; they were alarmed at the lack of appropriate treatment for a child with such severe problems. The treatment team provided his parents with an action plan that offered some hope of improvement. Psychotropic medication was one part of that plan. Once again, his mother refused to support medication.[49]

After staff urging, she agreed to have him try a brief trial of Lexapro, a common SSRI (selective serotonin reuptake inhibiter, often used to help with anxiety and OCD). She reported to the treatment team that the medication was discontinued after three days due to dramatic "side effects." It's questionable if he ever actually took the drug.[50]

There was never another trial of psychotropic medication, despite continued mental deterioration.[51]

His mother increasingly became a prisoner to his demands; she changed her behavior to accommodate him. At Yale, the evaluating psychiatrist noted, "He is intolerant if mother leans on anything in the house because it is 'improper.' ... He is intolerant of her if mother brushes by his chair and objected to her new high heel boots 'because they are too loud.' ... If mother walks in front of him in the kitchen, he would make her redo it." The report noted that the boy's parents seemed to be creating "a prosthetic environment which spares him having to encounter other students or work to overcome his social difficulties."[52]

If this pattern were not interrupted, he would get worse.

It was also pointed out in the report from the Yale Child Development Center that his parents were primarily worried about his schooling rather than his social problems. Yet, the treatment team deemed the social problems to be the primary concern. A comprehensive plan for treatment, which included medication, therapy, and a special intensive day school to meet his needs, was recommended.[53]

The boy's mother rejected the recommendations and terminated treatment there.

His symptoms at middle school were disabling, yet he was mainstreamed into regular classes. He had severe panic attacks, and his mother came to school to manage him. He very seldom spoke and never made eye contact. He couldn't tolerate colored graphics in his textbooks, so his mother made black and white copies of each page for him. He could not adapt in school, and he began having screaming tantrums and refusing to go.[54]

Though he was mentally preoccupied with violence, he never acted out violently with peers; the violence always leaked out in his writing.[55]

Nonetheless, his mother continued to buy him guns and take him target shooting. Shooting guns and playing video games (up to 14 hours at a time, alone, in his basement) or playing Dance-Dance-Revolution at a nearby movie theater (up to 10 hours straight) were the only activities he enjoyed.[56]

Dangerous Preoccupations

His parents failed to monitor his usage of the internet, where he spent all his time when not gaming. He avoided sunlight, covered his windows with trash bags, and hated coming out of his basement game room. He dressed in military fatigues while he gamed and entertained the belief that he would become an army ranger when he turned 18.[57]

Online he was frequenting sites focused on mass murder and weapons, and he developed an encyclopedic knowledge of both. He particularly admired one murderer and became fascinated with him: the Norwegian killer, who had targeted children.[58]

One of the internet monikers he went by was Kaynbred. Psychologist Peter Lankford has postulated that he may have been identified with Cain, the first murderer among humanity, as identified in the Bible. Cain killed his brother Abel out of jealousy. As Langford points out, Abel was the high-functioning brother.[59]

The Newtown killer shunned personal contact with others and would close his door when his mother tried to speak with him.[60]

Psychiatric problems often worsen with developmental transitions, partly for biological reasons. Hormones influence neurotransmitters which can intensify symptoms, and each developmental transition brings many new challenges that severely mentally ill individuals may not have the capacity to master. When severely mentally ill individuals fail to master regular developmental tasks, they become increasingly isolated and cut off from peers.

His mother briefly enrolled him in a more structured Catholic school, where he was also unable to function. Special education services were not provided. There were multiple points where the educational system could have interrupted the pathway if services had been available.[61]

After that, at his mother's insistence, he was transferred to a home study program ostensibly monitored by the school district. In truth, there was no oversight, and he was tutored at home by his parents for one year. After this period, he briefly attended local college classes to earn high school credit. There he sat in the back of the room, refusing to interact.[62]

His mother had a sustained pattern of appeasing him, doing almost anything to keep him from being distressed.[63] In this case, the mother's protective intuition was not serving her son.

The Newtown killer never accepted that he had mental health problems and continued to refuse treatment. His father described him as arrogant.[64] He disliked birthdays, Christmas, and all other holidays and would not tolerate his mother putting up a Christmas tree.[65]

He mandated that his mother get rid of her cat because he did not want it in the house.[66]

Over time he developed an elaborate philosophy on the premise that culture was to blame for "raping" children by attempting to socialize them. He described longing to live with apes, where he would be free of human society.[67]

Worsening Symptoms

The killer's mother never had guests in her home because her son didn't allow it; though her friends had heard her speak of her son, most had never met him.[68] He changed his clothing several times a day, requiring his mother to do his laundry daily.[69] He never allowed her into his room, and when he left the house, she felt it would violate his privacy to enter.[70] She accommodated him.

If his mother had gone into his room, she might have noticed the gruesome photos of dead bodies he had printed out from the internet or the seven-foot-long spreadsheet of mass murderers.[71]

Multiple opportunities to interrupt the pathway to violence were missed.

Accommodating his increasingly restrictive demands was not the right approach. As predicted by the Yale Child Study Center, instead of improving, he became increasingly ill.

He was also anorexic. At age 20, he stood six feet tall and weighed 112 pounds.[72] Gaunt and strange in appearance, he never made eye contact and refused to speak. He refused to see or communicate with his father during the final two years of his life, despite his father's repeated attempts to contact him by phone and email.[73] He interacted with no one other than those in online message boards focused on weaponry or mass murder.[74]

The Newtown killer was an expert on both topics, even editing Wikipedia pages with facts on firearms and details about mass murder.[75] He was active in the online message system for the Super Columbine Massacre's role-playing game for three years (later renamed Shocked

Beyond Belief). He had developed a reputation as a pedophile due to some postings that justified sex between children and adults. His online writings reveal a broad vocabulary, macabre themes, a droll sense of humor, and a pessimistic outlook.[76]

Among his other writings was found an essay that was an elaborate defense of pedophilia. It was 35 pages long, and he identified it as a college entrance essay, though the stated limit on an essay for college was 500 words.[77] The Newtown killer had a lot to say on the topic.

He had also written the beginning of a screenplay on the topic of "The beauty in a romantic relationship between a ten-year-old boy and a thirty-year-old man."[78] Though he was preoccupied with this theme, there is no evidence he ever acted on sexual urges with anyone.

In the message board, he had cataloged all Columbine-related movies and television shows. He knew each plot in detail.

Perverse Role Models

The Newtown killer also wrote with deep admiration for the mass killer of children from Norway, which occurred two years previously. He studied the Norway killer's voluminous manifesto online and made multiple references to the Norwegian attacks in the forum. The following was about the Norway mass killer:

> The format and organization of everything involved was such an impressive instance of mass murder self-actualization that it seemed fictional. I wouldn't call it encouraging, but it seemed motivational enough in some sense that it was the kind of thing you would find in a particularly macabre self-improvement book. Probably owing to watching too many mass murder movies, reading excerpts like this almost had me at the edge of my seat in anticipation.[79]

Notable is the emotional excitement that had him at the edge of his seat in anticipation as well as the statement "impressive instance of mass murder self-actualization." He then posted a lengthy passage from the Norwegian killer's manifesto.[80]

There were similarities.

The Norwegian killer had a massively high kill score; he had murdered children who had no way to defend themselves. As stated in his manifesto, he didn't target those he hated in the ruling political party; he attacked those they loved, in his words, "something they held dear."[81]

The Newtown killer would similarly target children.

Both the Newtown killer and the Norwegian killer had played the same war simulation video game, Call of Duty: Modern Warfare; this was the game the Norwegian killer had used as part of his practice with weaponry and marksmanship.[82]

In these online forum postings, he referred to the Columbine killers as "ubiquitous morons" even though he knew every obscure detail about them, every movie, book, or media reference.

There was no cultural reference or obscure fact about mass killers that he didn't know, including the lyrics of pop songs about them.

It is clear from the voluminous content of his writing that he thought of little else during the last few years of his life.

Anger at Human Culture

The young man who never fit in often railed against human culture in his writings: "You know what I hate!?! Culture. I've been pissed out of my mind all night thinking about it. I should have been born a chimp. I would even settle for a post-language hunter-gatherer society."[83]

He stated that he spent a great deal of time thinking about primates and identified with Travis the chimp. This case also occurred in Connecticut and received extensive worldwide media coverage in 2009. Travis was a chimpanzee who had been adopted as an infant and raised to behave as if human. He slept in the same bed as his owner, ate steak and lobster, drank wine from stemmed glasses, watched TV, and used a computer. He accompanied his owner to work every day. Travis's life came to an end when he was shot by police after mutilating and nearly killing his owner's friend in an unprovoked attack.[84]

In the Newtown killer's mind, the problem was not Travis; the problem was a society that expected Travis to act civilized. Travis had to murder someone; he couldn't help himself.

"My wet dream is living in the wild with apes."[85]

His anger at culture was a consistent theme in his writing in the final years of his life.

Culture. I've been pissed out of my mind thinking about it all night. I should have been born a chimp.

Enculturing human children is all terrifying enough.

I spent all day ruminating over how much I hate culture.

I hate how I spend 99 percent of my time upset about culture.[86]

Mental Illness

In Peter Langman's words, "He was profoundly anxious around people and never developed the social fluency that most children do. Growing up did not come naturally to him. The conventions that govern social interaction were foreign to him, and he struggled in the presence of other people. No wonder that he felt that socialization is a process of 'submission' and 'indoctrination.'"[87]

His behavior was increasingly bizarre, possibly psychotic. His family didn't seem to know what to do—and thus did nothing.

The original diagnosis of autism likely hid the fact that he had developed other serious mental illnesses. It is common for multiple problems to co-occur in one individual.

The Newtown killer's tendency to become fixated and perseverative on specific topics indicates obsessive-compulsive disorder, as had been previously diagnosed. Behavioral therapy and psychotropic medication can often provide relief from this problem; he received neither.

His parents shielded him from effective interventions. No one was looking closely enough to see a growing danger. The Newtown killer had been fascinated with hurting people for years. He'd started writing about hurting children back in 5th grade.[88]

There had even been foreshadowing about a boy who shoots his mother in the head in *The Big Book of Granny*.

There was plenty of leakage, plenty of forewarning—if anyone had made an effort to look.

The Progression

It began with grievances and collecting injustices. He blamed society for everything that had gone wrong.

For the Newtown killer, a man with severe neurobiological impairments who could not function in society, we see a pathway of progression to violence that began with frustration over his neurobiology. He had failed to achieve success in every significant area of life. He externalized blame, collected injustices, and became angry. Eventually woven in were a hatred of school, a fixation on shooting and weapons that his parents facilitated, pathological obsessions with mass murderers, immersion in a perverse online culture that glorified mass killers, the eventual externalization of the blame for his failures into a global hatred of society, failure to receive adequate treatment (in part due to parental denial and resistance), and enmeshed family dynamics, which all created the perfect storm.

The violent culmination of his life was an enactment of mass murder for revenge, power, and infamy.

He blamed society for all his problems, and he wanted to hit society in the heart. Just like the killer in Norway, he tried to kill those we hold dear—our children. He wanted to experience God-like power, and he wanted to be famous.

Elementary school children are quickly dominated and easy pickings for a man with no connection to humanity, one who is seeking a high kill score.

The Newtown killer wanted to make it to the top of the seven-foot list. He would have God-like power. His life would then have meaning and he would never be forgotten.

When we look at all the factors, there is no mystery here. Mass murders may not make sense from the outside looking in, but if we look outward from the killer's point of view, we can see how he came to do what he did.

Public mass killings are not senseless. They just don't make sense to us.[89]

5

The Pathway
to Violence Stages 3 & 4

Research and Planning

"I'm going to be the next school shooter of 2018."—Parkland killer

This chapter examines the elaborate actions taken by perpetrators in three mass killing events to illustrate that these events do not occur suddenly and randomly. These stages—which may go on for weeks, months, or even years—are when those who know a perpetrator are most apt to become aware of a violent plan.

As fantasy progresses into action, mass killers move from thought to behavior. They set dates and times for an attack, gather information, and scout locations. Many create maps, plan transportation routes, study explosives for research. Some plot ways to prevent their victims from escaping, like barring doors. Once they have a sense of what they want to do, they create specific plans and begin creating timelines and acquiring weapons. Many go target shooting, practice with explosives, and buy specific military-type attire and gear.[1]

This phase is when aspects of their plans are most apt to be leaked on social media or to friends; those witnessing it typically assume they are joking and minimize the threat. If confronted, they often say they aren't serious. And many individuals who make verbal threats aren't. This makes threat assessment exceptionally complicated.

This is a critical phase in the pathway to violence because action taken by others has the potential to interrupt an attack. Though most who make threats never actually commit violent acts, all threats need to be taken seriously and reported.[2]

We have no statistics on how many potential attacks are interrupted as a result of those who make reports.

The following three cases provide extensive documentation of the stages of research and planning. Notice that these three cases share similarities and differences; all reveal multiple steps on the pathway to violence.

Aurora

It was July 12, 2012, in Aurora, Colorado, at the midnight showing of the latest blockbuster Batman film, *The Dark Knight Rises*. The film had been playing to sold-out audiences, and that night the theater was packed with 400 people. Thirty minutes into the movie, at about 12:30, a man near the front of the theater with bright orange hair stood up and threw two tear gas canisters into the audience. The gas created a cloud that obscured the crowd's vision and immediately irritated their throats and eyes. Many in the crowd thought it was a stunt or a special effect related to the movie. The perpetrator planned for it to be disorienting. The delay would give him more time to accomplish his goal.

He was dressed all in black and was wearing a gas mask, ballistic helmet, and bullet-proof military-style vest and leggings as well as throat and groin protection.[3]

Using three different semiautomatic guns in succession, the gunman fired first toward the back of the room and then directly toward people seated at the end of the rows as he strolled up and down the aisles. One bullet passed through the wall and hit three people in the adjacent theater.[4]

Many theater patrons thought someone was lighting firecrackers. As patrons became aware that those around them were being shot, they flooded into the aisles, attempting to flee.[5]

In just seconds, the 24-year-old killed 12; 70 others were shot. Twelve more were injured as the crowd fled.[6] Three men were killed as they protectively shielded their wives or girlfriends with their bodies.[7]

The theater's fire alarm system began sounding almost immediately, and multiple 911 calls were made at 12:39. Police arrived at the scene within 90 seconds.

Minutes later, at 12:45, the shooter was captured in the theater parking lot, sitting in his car.[8] Police described him as "very calm."[9]

Overt Warnings

The Aurora killer was brilliant. He was in a Ph.D. program in neuroscience at the nearby University of Colorado; despite his academic achievements, he had been fantasizing about murder for at least a decade.

It was not a secret. He'd recently sought therapy for repetitive thoughts about killing people and had shared this obsession with at least two mental health clinicians at his campus mental health clinic; both clinicians were extremely concerned that he might act on his fantasies.[10]

These clinicians attempted to intervene with what information he had given them. However, this perpetrator was intelligent, strategic, and cagey enough to provide them with no specifics about his plans. While mental healthcare providers are legally required to report explicit threats of violence, laws are unfortunately vague about navigating these gray areas when no specific plans are revealed.

For multiple reasons, including laws regarding confidentiality and preventing unjustified confinement, no effective intervention was implemented despite the killer's warnings.[11]

Research and Planning

The Aurora killer called the attack his "mission." He had dyed his brown hair bright fluorescent orange in preparation for the event. With his wild-eyed stare, he looked a great deal like the mad Joker from the Batman comics.[12] He had an affinity for Batman.

He chose the midnight screening of the premiere of the film *The Dark Knight Rises* because he hoped fewer children would be present. He preferred to avoid shooting children if he could, though when he shot randomly into the theater crowd, he hit a four-year-old girl four times, killing her; he also shot her pregnant mother.[13]

Prior to the theater shootings, he took the time to rig his apartment with homemade explosives and various incendiary devices, hoping to kill law enforcement officers who would arrive after his main event. The explosives were disarmed the following day without further casualties.[14]

The apartment was decorated with copious Batman paraphernalia.

Like all mass killers, this perpetrator wanted to kill as many as he could. He'd previously visited the theater on a scouting expedition and made detailed notes.[15]

He kept a notebook for six weeks before the attack which detailed specific plans, including a map he'd drawn of the theater, showing the seating arrangement and exits. His maps revealed strategic, military-type planning.

The Aurora killer liked movie theaters and spent time researching which one would best meet his purposes. He chose that specific one because it had doors that he could lock to increase the number of casualties. Also, it was located in an area where he thought the police response would take longer.[16] That did not prove to be true.

He considered other locations for a mass shooting, including an airport, which he ultimately ruled out due to the high level of security present there.

Weaponry

The perpetrator began purchasing weapons in May, about eight weeks before the July attack. It was surprisingly easy to do. His first purchase was a Taser disguised as a cell phone, ordered through Amazon. He also ordered a large combat-style knife. Shortly after, he purchased two grenade-style canisters of tear gas along with a gas mask; all were purchased legally, online.[17]

In the coming days, he bought a Glock handgun at a local sporting goods store and hollow-point bullets, which increased the weapon's killing power. Following was the purchase of a Remington 12-gauge tactical shotgun at another sporting goods store. He ordered a pair of handcuffs and small jagged pieces of metal called road stars, which are thrown onto a street to cause tires to blow out. His final weapon purchase was at another sporting goods store, a semiautomatic military-grade rifle.[18]

In early June, the Aurora perpetrator finished his online orders with a special low-light sight with night-vision capability, designed for combat in the dark. He spent an additional $1,200 on hollow-point ammunition for the firearms and a green-dot laser sighting system that can be mounted under a rifle or handgun barrel.[19]

All weapons and paraphernalia were purchased legally. He signed forms certifying that he had never been convicted of a felony at each store and that he had never been psychiatrically hospitalized. This was true. He also indicated that he had no mental or physical impairment that would preclude safe use of firearms.[20]

Of course, he chose not to reveal he had been in mental health treatment for obsessive thoughts about murder; such records would not show up on a background check.

Store clerks followed the legally mandated procedure for the quick online background check, which took only a few minutes. They found nothing. His record was clean and clear, with no criminal history.[21]

In late June, he applied for membership at a shooting range but was turned down for unknown reasons.

In an eerie twist, the Aurora killer had purchased opaque black cosmetic contact lenses at a costume store, which made his irises appear black. Since they reduced his vision, he didn't wear them during the attack but put them in at home days before to take menacing selfies. He wanted to look scary and intimidating, and he pulled it off.[22]

With bright orange hair and crazed black eyes, he cast himself in the part of an evil supervillain in a highly stylized theatrical production.

The Aurora killer had considered using explosives and chemical or biological agents for the rampage but was worried he might accidentally blow himself up.

Survivors were traumatized, as were much of the American public who were left to wonder if going to a movie theater was safe.

Parkland

The bio on his Instagram account read "annihilator." He was 19.[23]

This dark-haired young man posed like an action movie star in the photos he posted on Instagram. Like others before him, he loved the camera and had a dramatic flair.

In one image, his menacing eyes peer around a black semiautomatic gun that partially obscures the lower part of his face. In another, he wears a bandanna around his mouth and is armed with knives. Both photos could have been used for an action movie poster.

He wanted to look scary. He pulled it off.

On February 14, 2018, he became known as the Parkland shooter. This perpetrator killed 17 people and injured 17 more at Marjory Stoneman Douglas High School in a shooting rampage that lasted six minutes.[24]

It was Valentine's Day. He arrived at the school in an Uber, carrying his semiautomatic rifle in a gun case, along with a backpack. He told the driver that he was carrying a guitar in the case for a music class. The Uber driver said, "He seemed just like a normal person." The ride cost $4.53.[25]

The Parkland shooter entered a school building with multiple classrooms and, 15 seconds later, began firing randomly into several rooms on the first floor, where he killed 11. He then pulled a fire alarm and moved to the second floor, where he again fired into several classrooms. Progressing to the third floor, he killed six persons in the hallway and attempted to shoot out the school windows to target others below who were fleeing down below. Since the glass was hurricane resistant, he could not break the window, and his gun jammed. If he'd succeeded in breaking the window, the number killed would have multiplied several times.

At that point, he dropped the gun on the floor and exited the building, blending in with the crowd of fleeing students. Walking off campus, he went to a nearby Subway sandwich shop and calmly bought a soda.

School staff recognized him from video surveillance footage, and he was arrested nearby about an hour later, wandering through a neighborhood.[26]

The Parkland shooter was a former student at the school who had been expelled the year before due to chronic discipline problems and violence.

Social Media Footprint

This perpetrator left a vivid trail on social media, including many threatening posts on YouTube, Instagram, Facebook, and in private chat groups. His internet network was vast. He had multiple social media accounts on all popular platforms, and his posts provided consistent evidence of his obsession with guns and killing. His threats were flagrant, sometimes specific: "I'm going to be a school shooter."[27]

Though this perpetrator had been a special education student and had challenges with academics, he was prolific and talented online. While he lacked social skills in real life, he created an image of someone important and powerful on the internet.

In the virtual world, the Parkland shooter was an outlaw.

He frequented various extremist websites and was very active in one Instagram chat group, mainly focused on racist extremism. He wrote about killing Mexicans, keeping Black people in chains, and cutting their necks. He said he hated Jews because he believed they wanted to destroy the world.[28]

When another member wrote about hating gay people, the Parkland killer responded, "Shoot them in the back of the head."

In a different chat, he wrote, "I think I'm going to kill people." When challenged by other group members, he responded that he was "only joking."

He also wrote about his obsession with guns. He legally purchased an AR-15 at age 18, approximately one year before the attack. He also passed a background check, despite his history of violence. The AR-15 and other guns were constant topics of conversation in the online groups.[29]

Posturing as a warrior, he posted selfies he'd taken wearing body armor and firing a gun out of a window.

He also wrote about killing small animals and posted an image of a disemboweled frog. Others were disturbed by this and worried that he might be killing other small animals.[30]

The Parkland killer made videos on his cell phone just before the attack. He was energized and confident, with a sparkle in his eyes. He outlined his plans, pausing to giggle periodically. One has the sense he's having fun. The rest of the time, he speaks in a menacing, grim monotone that's reminiscent of Arnold Schwarzenegger in the Terminator movies. He was rehearsing.[31]

"I'm going to be the next school shooter of 2018," he begins with a smile. "My goal is at least 20 people with an AR-15 and a couple tracer rounds. The location is Stone-Douglas, in Parkland, Florida. It's going to be a big event." He draws out the word *biiiiig* for emphasis. "When you see me on the news, you'll all know who I am [giggles]. You're all going to die [pew-pew-pew-pew-*pew*]. Oh yeah. Can't wait. Today's the day. The day it all begins. All the kids in school will run and hide. From the wrath of my power, they will know who I am."[32]

He closed the video with a description of his detailed plan for the day that began with an Uber ride to school.

Foreshadowing, Leakage, and Missed Opportunities

The Parkland killer told family, friends, and acquaintances of his desire to kill. While some didn't take him seriously, a number attempted to report his threats, but no action was taken by authorities.

He had grown up with his widowed adoptive mother and half-brother and displayed severe behavioral problems for many years. A public record request obtained by CNN showed that from 2008 to 2017, at least 45 calls were made to law enforcement about the perpetrator's violence in the family home.[33]

His half-brother would later state that the Parkland killer had pointed a rifle at him and at an earlier time at their mother. Neither called the police. If they had, his weapons would have been confiscated, and he would have had a record with law enforcement that might have precluded him from subsequently purchasing firearms.

There were similar problems in school. He was viewed as dangerous. In November 2016, a school administrator sent an email to staff asking that they notify the administrator immediately if he showed up on campus with a backpack.[34]

In 2016 and 2017, one to two years before the rampage, the FBI received multiple calls about threats involving a school shooting that identified the Parkland shooter by name. Reports were made to the FBI about the same individual who posted a message in September 2017 on YouTube about becoming a school shooter. Still, the agency said they could not identify the person.[35]

This is curious, considering that the YouTube account was in his legal name, which has an unusual spelling.

In January 2018, a call was made to the FBI tip line with a direct complaint that the same person, identified by name, had made a death threat. The information was not forwarded to the local FBI office, and no action was taken.[36]

In 2016 the FBI tip line received approximately 1,300 tips per day, and dozens of calls are made daily to field offices. Only about 100 of those tips are determined to be "actionable."[37] It's easy to understand the impossibility of following up on every tip, considering finite resources.

His history was fraught with problems. The Parkland killer was diagnosed with developmental delays at age three and spent nine years in behavioral health treatment.[38] He would acquire additional diagnoses as he got older. In middle school, he attended a school for students with emotional and behavioral disorders but was mainstreamed to Marjory Stoneman Douglas High School in January 2016. It was a poor fit, and he began making threats to shoot up the school one month later. He was consistently aggressive.[39]

He was finally expelled from the high school for fighting on February 8, 2017. Three days later, he bought his AR-15 rifle.[40] This was one year and six days before the rampage.

At age 18, one year before the shooting, he discontinued all mental health treatment, his legal right as an adult.[41]

Many student survivors of the Parkland shooting took to the airwaves to lead a national fight for gun reform legislation; two others subsequently committed suicide.

Columbine

They've become icons among a strange subculture of mostly young men that are fascinated by violence: two suburban teenagers in long black coats and black combat boots, one tall and lanky with longish hair, the other shorter with a military look.

A generation has grown up watching footage of them on news programs and documentaries since their 1999 rampage. Perhaps more than any others, they are credited with creating a cultural template or script for the killers to follow.

These two best friends also loved being on camera. The Littleton, Colorado, killers filmed themselves posturing with their sawed-off shotguns and semiautomatic weapons, target shooting in the forest with friends, and laughing as they blew gaping holes in trees and bowling pins: "Imagine what that would do to somebody's fucking brain."[42]

The two teens also made videos for their school cable network in which they played hitmen, videos that are filled with macho posturing and bravado. They wore long, black duster coats, hip in the 90s, which gave them an outlaw vibe. There were always guns, presumably props for the school videos, along with commando jargon and lots of laughter.[43]

At the time, this may not have appeared to be more than the type of adolescent fantasy play that is common among young men, but hindsight provides a different perspective.

They appear comfortable in the videos, laughing, never awkward on camera. They enjoyed violence, and they wanted to be famous. In their minds, they were badass outlaw killers.

The two teens spent at least a year and a half planning what they came to call "Judgment Day." The goal was to kill more than ever before in a single event; they wanted to produce a spectacle that would make them famous.

In one of their final videos, they laughed as they speculated which director would make the film of their rampage, settling on either Steven Spielberg or Quentin Tarantino.[44]

Could they top the Oklahoma City kill score? They planned to and chose the anniversary date for their attack.

The young men kept journals in the final year of their lives in which they recorded their thoughts and feelings. They also used the journals to plan their production, creating detailed down-to-the-minute scripts for what they hoped would be the largest mass murder in history.[45]

They also made a series of videos in which they explained their plans and their rationale. Recorded in the basement of one of the killers' homes, these came to be known as the basement tapes. They did their utmost to ensure they would not be forgotten.

Judgment Day was to be grand in scope. Not only did they hope to blow up their school, but they were also going to wipe out all law enforcement and medical first responders who arrived on the scene to help.[46]

Teamwork

I'll refer to them by their self-selected nicknames: Reb (chosen for the high school mascot) and Vodka (because he was known to drink copious amounts of it). They were both seniors. Vodka was 17; Reb had turned 18 just 11 days before the April 20, 1999, attacks.[47]

Reb was the charming one. He was considered good-looking, with dimples and a ready smile; some would say he had a sweet face, which was topped off with a short, military-style haircut. Reb was extroverted, socially adept, and had no trouble talking to girls. He was smart and a straight-A student.[48]

In his journal, Reb bragged about his finesse with lying and his ability to manipulate others.[49] He knew how to suck up to adults and tell them precisely what they wanted to hear.

Vodka was tall and skinny, with gangly limbs and long, straggly hair. He was shy and much less confident, though he was liked by those who knew him well. Others described him as angry and menacing. Prone to depressive rumination in his journals, he often wrote of his yearning for true love and a girlfriend. Vodka was also bright, though he didn't put much energy into schoolwork.[50]

It's been commonly opined that Reb was the dominant friend and a classic manipulative psychopath; Vodka has come to be seen as his depressed companion, a follower who likely would not have acted without his friend's leadership.[51]

Both boys attended football games, dances, and school plays. Vodka had taken a date to the school prom just three days before the rampage and appeared relaxed and smiling in his tuxedo.[52]

Despite inaccurate press reports at the time, which portrayed them as bullied loners, both boys had many friends. They were not significantly bullied; actually, they were more apt to bully others and joked about it in their journals.[53]

Both were employees at a popular pizza restaurant, where Reb essentially functioned as manager. The restaurant owner trusted them, and they often worked shifts together.

Both Vodka and Reb were raised in loving, intact upper-middle-class families; they were free of trauma histories. On the surface, the Columbine killers appeared decidedly normal.[54]

Vodka had been accepted at Arizona State University for the coming fall semester. He had recently visited the campus with his father in preparation, though he had other plans.

Reb had hoped to enter the Marines after high school but had not yet been accepted. It's unclear why.[55]

During an interview with the Marine recruiter on April 2, Reb indicated he was interested in weapons and demolitions training.[56]

A year before the attack, both boys were arrested for burglarizing a van and spent a few months in a court-ordered diversion problem. Each had individual counseling with probation officers in the program; they were determined to be doing well, considered not at risk of further offenses, and discharged from the program early. Reb was particularly praised by his counselor, who described him as "open, pleasant, courteous, and honest." The impression he made on her was glowing—and utterly false.[57]

Research and Planning

Both Reb and Vodka identified with the film *Natural Born Killers*; in their journals, they used the initials *NBK* for what they intended to do on Judgment Day. They had memorized every line from the movie.[58]

Their journals also revealed that Reb was fascinated with Adolf Hitler and the Oklahoma City Bomber. He was prone to drawing swastikas and *SS* symbols in his writing and using phrases written in German, particularly "*Ich bin Got*" (I am God). In bowling class, he frequently made Nazi salutes. He had written an essay his senior year on the Nazis and their philosophy of extermination. Reb also made repeated mention of his thoughts on natural selection as well as racist and anti-gay rants. He also detailed violent rape fantasies.[59]

Following is a quote from Reb's journal:

People that only know stupid facts that aren't important should be shot, what fucking use are they. NATURAL SELECTION. Kill all retards, people with brain fuck ups, drug addicts, people who can't figure out how to use a fucking lighter. Geeeawd! People spend millions of dollars on saving the lives of retards, and why. I don't buy that shit like "oh, he's my son, though!" so the fuck what, he ain't normal, kill him. Put him out of his misery. He is only a waste of time and money, then people say "but he is worth the time, he is human too." No he isn't, if he was then he would swallow a bullet cause he would realize what a fucking [illegible] he was.[60]

On the day of the murders, Reb wore a T-shirt with the words "Natural Selection."[61]

Vodka particularly admired Charles Manson. He enjoyed the book *Helter Skelter* about the Manson murders and often referenced it.[62] He wrote a paper about Manson and the Manson family murders for school, which evidenced admiration for his beliefs. In another nod to Manson, Vodka had spray-painted "death to pigs" on the wall of a local pawnshop.

He was also known to admire Hitler and also gave Nazi salutes in bowling. Another student reported that he had once painted a swastika on his face.

From Vodka's journal, referencing a video game:

HELL ON EARTH19 Ahhhh, my favorite book. We, the gods, will have so much fun with NBK!! Killing enemies, blowing up stuff, killing cops!! My wrath for January's incident20 will be godlike. Not to mention our revenge in the commons. GAWWWD sooo many people need to die. & now, a fun look at the past: (science-desk style) ((You know what I hate??? PEOPLE!! YEAA!!))[63]

On the day of the murders, Vodka wore cargo pants and a black T-shirt with the word "Wrath."

Both killers dressed up for the rampage, wearing black combat boots and their long, black duster coats, which helped cover their firearms. The coats were edgy. The film *The Matrix* was released the previous month; Neo wore the cool, long, black coat. They shared a pair of fingerless black leather gloves. Style mattered.

Their journals created detailed drawings of the clothing they would wear on judgment day, which included cargo pants, tactical vests, and suspenders. They'd drawn diagrams of exactly where they would strap knives, guns, ammunition, and explosives on their bodies during the attack.[64]

Reb had studied bomb-making online with *The Anarchist's Cookbook*; he sketched out designs for seven large bombs. He drew diagrams of bomb placement to maximize the kill ratio.[65]

As broken down by journalist Dave Cullen, their attack was carefully scripted into three acts and detailed in writing with military precision.[66] They hoped to double or triple the number of fatalities of the Oklahoma City bombing, which killed 168 people and injured hundreds.

- Act I: They would bomb the high school commons at lunch, while two other bombs went off at a nearby park as a distraction. Each bomb was strung with nails and BBs to create shrapnel.
- Act II: They would exit to their cars in the adjacent parking lot, where they would put on infantry-style jackets. These would allow them to strap on additional ammo and explosives. Each would have a duffle bag and backpack with weapons. Taking rehearsed strategic positions targeting the exits, they would shoot any survivors who attempted to run from the school. They'd even made up hand signals to coordinate during this phase.
- Act III: Their cars had been rigged with explosives. As law enforcement, paramedics, and news crews arrived on the scene, they would detonate their vehicles. They wanted to kill everyone. They also accepted that they would be dead by the end of it.

From Vodka's journal:

Walk in, set bombs at 11:00, for 11:17. Leave, Drive to Clemete Park Gearup. Get back by 11:15. Park cars, set car bombs for 11:18, get out, go to outside hill, wait. When first bombs go off, attack. Have fun![67]

Of course, when none of the giant bombs detonated, they improvised. Walking through the school throwing pipe bombs, they yelled and laughed while stalking and shooting students and teachers. Many were shot at close range, some directly in the face as they begged for their lives.

It's not uncommon for psychopaths to have sadistic streaks. The

Columbine killers enjoyed themselves as they enacted a twisted movie script.

Weaponry

In November 2018, Vodka had convinced an unsuspecting female friend who was 18 to help them purchase firearms at a nearby Denver gun show. Since both boys were 17 at the time, under Colorado law, they needed an adult present to make the purchase. There were no background checks done at the gun show, where they are not required; even if there had been, the girl would have passed. She had no criminal history.[68]

The boys bought two 12-gauge shotguns, a 9mm semiautomatic handgun, and a carbine rifle, along with a supply of ammo. They would later saw off the shotgun barrels, which made them easy to conceal. All were subsequently hidden in their bedrooms at home, along with copious bomb-making supplies.

Their parents had no idea.[69]

Over the coming months, they would repeatedly go target shooting and practice setting off explosives. They weren't alone in the target shooting videos. Friends from school—other boys and at least one girl—were there, posing, shooting, and laughing about entry and exit wounds.[70]

It was widely known among their peers that they were into explosives and guns. They often made remarks about blowing up the school. Reb had made jokes about killing jocks and asked one friend for advice on making napalm.[71]

All friends claimed ignorance of the plans for murder, despite the copious leakage. Few confided to adults about the guns and explosives.

Reb had been in trouble in the past for making pipe bombs and posting threats against a school friend on his website. The parents of this friend had made multiple complaints to police about the threats against their son's life, and though a request for a search warrant had been filled out, no action was taken by the local police. Another opportunity to interrupt the pathway was missed.

Reb's parents knew he had a history of antisocial behavior, but they had cracked down on him and thought he was now on the straight and narrow path.[72]

Vodka's parents had no idea he had a drinking problem; they were clueless that their son was known among his peers by the moniker "Vodka."[73]

Both sets of parents were responsible people who loved their kids, but all were in the dark about the violent plans and accumulated weaponry. Both boys laughed on the basement tapes about their ability to fool people. They could fool anybody, and they were proud of it.[74]

Differences/Similarities

What are the clear differences and similarities in these three cases?

The Aurora killer and the Parkland killer had a history of mental health problems, though their diagnoses were very different. While the Aurora killer was academically gifted and in a Ph.D. program in neuroscience, the Parkland killer had been diagnosed with multiple learning disabilities and been a special education student.

Despite this, they were both capable of creating detailed plans, avoiding detection, and executing complicated, strategic actions.

The Columbine killers had no history of serious mental health problems; both were highly intelligent and good students. They were popular and involved in many school activities.

In all three cases, there was significant leakage in advance of the rampages. The Columbine killers had been involved in the diversion counseling program through the probation program and had graduated early, with praise from the counselors. Manipulation can come very easily to most perpetrators of predatory violence.

Multiple reports to various law enforcement agencies were made long in advance in the case of Parkland. Numerous reports had been made to police about one of the Columbine killers.

Mental health therapists attempted to make reports about the Aurora killer, but laws limited what actions could be taken. Tragically, none of these reports led to effective intervention.

In all three cases, mental health clinicians or probation counselors had contact with the perpetrators before the attack but were unable to take action to prevent the killings that followed.

There are reasons for this, some involving restrictions on how mental health professionals can take action in cases of possible dangerousness and the ability of an adept psychopath to fool others, including professionals.

Obvious similarities in all three cases include the photos and videos posturing with multiple weapons as well as the stated desire to be famous. Each was fixated on his projected image as a macho killer with godlike power.

Each of these perpetrators engaged in cold, methodical, predatory violence that was extensively planned in advance. Their behavior was cruel and sadistic.

They all wanted to achieve a high kill score and dehumanized their victims. None of them targeted anyone in particular. Those who died were simply in the wrong place, at the wrong time.

6

The Pathway
to Violence Stages 5 & 6
Breach and Attack

"Blacks are trying to take over—I've got to stop it."—Charleston killer

They ran down the halls laughing as they killed people. "This is awesome!" one of the killers yelled. "It's what we've always wanted to do!"[1] "What is fun in life without a little death?"—Columbine killers

In this chapter, we explore more about the psychology of killing and the lack of empathy that characterizes cold, methodical killers. We learn that there are two aspects of empathy and the neurobiological basis for both and how empathy is developed. We also explore the related concepts of theory of mind, dehumanization, and "us versus them" thinking.

The case study highlights how a profound absence of empathy is apparent during the breach and attack stages.

Breach and Attack

During the final two stages of the pathway to violence, breach and attack, the mass killer moves into predatory action and initiates the planned attack. He may dress up in combat gear before breaching the target location; he may smuggle in weapons in advance and carefully plan where to enter or exit while making attempts to dodge security. Once inside the target location, he initiates a devastating attack, most often targeting strangers.

We tend to think of the breach into a target location as an aggressive, forced entry. Often it is. The Gilroy killer cut through a fence to enter the Garlic Festival venue, then immediately began shooting into the crowd. The El Paso killer began firing in the parking lot of Walmart before he moved inside. The Newtown killer shot out the glass door panel to enter Sandy Hook Elementary just before firing at the school staff. But not all breaches are done aggressively. Sometimes they are stealthy, up close, and personal.

The Charleston church mass murder is an example of a stealthy breach, and something about it seems particularly unsettling. It was up close; the perpetrator sat next to the victims for 30 minutes in a Bible study. He spent time looking directly into the eyes of the people who had welcomed him warmly before he shot them.

It feels incomprehensible. We realize there is something different about a person who can do this.

What happens in the mind of a perpetrator during this time? Why would anyone crave this experience?

Though they may look like any one of us on the outside, clearly, there are internal qualities that make mass killers different from the rest of us.

To understand the final phases of the pathway to violence, breach and attack, it's helpful to explore the concept of empathy—what it is, how it manifests, and why some people seem to lack it.

While we can objectively review mass shooters' behavior and the preparations that lead up to an attack, imagining the subjective inner experience of the attacker at the time of the rampage is another matter.

It seems incomprehensible, but often, they are experiencing a state of heightened energy and euphoria.

How can seemingly ordinary people be so cold-blooded?

On Killing

Our society sanctions certain kinds of killing, specifically in the contexts of the duties of law enforcement officers and military personnel. But even sanctioned killing is complicated, multi-layered, and fraught with misunderstanding.

In modern societies, we are socialized not to kill. Murder is considered the most egregious criminal offense, which—some would say ironically—is often punished by the death penalty.

David Grossman, a psychologist and retired army ranger who has taught psychology at West Point, explores the psychological aspects of killing in his two books, *On Killing: The Psychological Cost of Learning to Kill in War and Society*[2] and *On Combat.*[3]

Grossman makes the case that most people deeply resist killing another human being, even during military conflict. However, with specialized and intentionally designed conditioning methods, this natural resistance can be overridden.

Grossman presents evidence that only a small percentage of soldiers in battle actually fired their weapons in wars before Vietnam. He cites a 2000 study by S.L.A. Marshall, which found that the ratio of rounds fired versus actual hits to enemy combatants was only 15 percent in World War II.[4] Marshall found that most soldiers were not aiming to hit their targets, despite the imminent danger to their lives. This was attributed to the inherent empathy inside the soldiers who were resistant to killing others.[5]

Because of the individual soldier's reluctance to kill, modern methods of military training were developed to override the natural resistance through the use of specific conditioning methods that include

- using man-shaped targets instead of bullseye targets in marksmanship practice;
- practicing and drilling how soldiers are actually expected to fight;
- dispersing responsibility for the killing throughout the group; and
- displacing responsibility for the killing onto the commanding officer and military hierarchy.

The newer training methods worked. By the time of the Vietnam War, 90 percent of U.S. soldiers fired their weapons directly at enemy combatants. The kill rate went up accordingly.[6]

Grossman stresses that even when sanctioned by superiors, the act of killing is psychologically traumatic for the killer. Taking another human life comes with high psychological costs. It's more disturbing to kill a person than to witness the death of another or live with the constant stress of being in battle.

"Looking another human being in the eye, making an independent decision to kill him, and watching as he dies due to your action combine to form the single most basic, important, primal, and potentially traumatic occurrence of war," Grossman says.

Such is not the case for mass killers. What is different about them? Concerted conditioning methods are required to train law enforcement officers and military personnel to kill, yet mass killers seek out the experience enthusiastically.

How can they seem so at ease with murder?

The mass killer can enact a violent rampage with no psychological distress. In fact, most enjoy it. One factor that makes them different appears to be a reduced capacity for empathy.

Empathy

The development of empathy has everything to do with how we relate to others. We'll begin by carefully defining it and then move to explore how it develops.

Put most simply, empathy is the ability to identify with others and have compassion for them.

A more complex exploration reveals that empathy can be further broken down into two components: *affective* empathy and *cognitive* empathy.

Affective empathy refers to the emotions we experience in response to observing others' feelings; this happens through observing their body language, tone of voice, and the way they are communicating. Affective empathy is when we *feel* what we observe others to be feeling.[7]

Cognitive empathy allows us to *think* about what another is experiencing and intellectually understand the reasons for their feelings.[8]

While associated, these two human experiences are neurobiologically distinct; they each involve different brain regions. Since these different brain regions do not always operate in unison,[9] it's possible to experience one type of empathy but not the other.

Affective empathy allows us to intuitively sense what someone else is feeling through feelings that occur responsively within us. This includes subtle physiological changes in our bodies. We *feel* their pleasure, joy, or excitement internally as well as their stress, anxiety, and anger.[10]

When we see another person smiling, we reflexively smile back. If we are in a room with a person crying, we experience a sense of sadness and have an urge to comfort them or alleviate their distress. If we're with someone who is in pain, our bodies become tense, our blood pressure may go up, and we feel a sense of physical agitation. Our bodies may re-experience sensations from times past when we were in pain. Simply by observing emotional expressions, activation of similar networks in our own brain areas occurs. These automatic responses happen beneath our level of conscious awareness; generally, we don't notice that this is happening and may not be able to describe what we are experiencing in words.[11]

"I feel your pain" is more than just an expression; it's a description of affective empathy. Affective empathy lets us know when another needs acknowledgment, attention, or an offer of help.

Though affective empathy allows us to sense someone else's distress, it doesn't necessarily let us to know how to help effectively.

In fact, too much affective empathy can get in the way of helping. It's possible to have such a strong emotional response to another's pain that we become emotionally overwhelmed and unable to act helpfully. When we are overly sensitive to others' emotional distress, our stress hormone levels elevate, forcing us into a fight or flight state. Becoming emotionally overwhelmed can keep us from thinking clearly, as the strong amygdala response reduces the functioning of our prefrontal cortex.[12]

Imagine witnessing a catastrophic car accident in which someone is severely injured. Affective empathy causes us to feel a compulsion to help, but we can only pull out our phones to call 911 or practice CPR by thinking clearly. If we respond to others' emotions with such intensity that we are completely overwhelmed, we can decompose into a sobbing puddle in the middle of someone else's crisis.

This has particular application for those who work in medical, social work, or other helping professions. If we begin to *live* others' experiences rather than just *observe* them, we are likely to be less helpful and ultimately more likely to experience burnout. We experience their trauma as our trauma. Ideally, we need to observe others with compassion and caring, take appropriate action, and then be able to let go.

Contrast this with cognitive empathy, which is the ability to think about what another person is experiencing, to take another's perspective objectively. Cognitive empathy allows us to describe what another is feeling and to understand the circumstances that explain why they are feeling it. We can put words to the experience.[13]

But intellectual insight alone doesn't necessarily prompt us to behave altruistically. It's possible to have cognitive empathy without a correlating emotionally empathic response. Cognitive empathy allows us to understand another's experience intellectually yet remain detached and devoid of compassion for them.

A predatory salesperson may recognize the vulnerability of an older person who has recently lost a spouse. While the salesman recognizes their grief and pain through cognitive empathy, they see them as an easy mark for exploitation. If the salesperson is deficient in affective empathy, they can engage in self-serving, manipulative behavior with no pangs of conscience.

The development of cognitive empathy without affective empathy can make a person dangerous. Psychopathic people are an example of this. They are good at reading others and recognizing their emotional fragility and vulnerability. But instead of caring about them or being moved to compassion, they see opportunities to take advantage of them.

Theory of Mind

It's when affective empathy and cognitive empathy integrate that humans are most apt to behave pro-socially, altruistically, and with less reactivity.

This integrated empathy is also called "theory of mind." Theory of mind allows us to understand others' thoughts as well as sense their feelings. Theory of mind is what allows us to take the perspective of another. Theory of mind is what people are describing when they speak of "emotional intelligence."

The capacity for theory of mind differs dramatically from one person to another; as with most human traits, it can be viewed on a continuum from minimal to strong.

Those with a strong theory of mind have the greatest capacity to have positive and successful social relationships in their families, workplaces, and communities. They understand others and are able to engage positively with them. Theory of mind is what allows us to show up for others emotionally and build solid relationships. Without this, loved ones often feel neglected and unheard.

Those lacking theory of mind have difficulty keeping close friends or having successful romantic relationships; since they don't understand people on a gut level, they are prone to misperceiving and alienating others. They are also prone to perceptual errors that impair their ability to connect and cause them to incorrectly interpret others' intents.

How Empathy Develops

How does empathy develop? Why do some people have more than others? Like all facets of human personality, it's complicated.

Like other personality features, empathy is the result of multiple, complex, interacting factors that include genetics, environment, and social context. While humans seem to be hardwired to develop empathy, it unfolds gradually throughout childhood, and many variables influence it.[14]

Affective empathy emerges first, during infancy. Babies begin absorbing and reflecting the emotional states and expressions of those around them shortly after birth. They are soothed by soft sounds and their mother's voice. They smile in response to a parent's face. Their brains and bodies respond to the emotional states of those nearby; after just a few weeks, they begin to laugh in response to funny looks made by their caregivers. And since empathy is reciprocal, we feel distressed when we hear young children cry.[15]

Parents and children attune to one another's emotional states and develop an attachment based upon empathy. It can be described as a mutual dance, set off by an innate hardwiring for connection, developed and enhanced by caregivers. Nurturing and attuned caregivers allow babies to associate positive human interactions with feelings of calm and safety.[16]

Children who feel safe and loved are more apt to become sensitive to others' emotional needs. This process of the bonding that develops between babies and their caregivers is also referred to as "attachment." Those with secure, positive attachments in childhood are thought to grow up more apt to have healthy attachments to others.[17]

As little humans mature, they become increasingly aware of the emotional states of others outside of their immediate family. Toddlers as young as 18 months old often show responsiveness to other infants or toddlers in distress.[18]

During preschool years, most children begin to display early cognitive aspects of empathy. If they see another child upset, they think about what to do. They may get their parent to comfort them or give them a toy they believe will help. They understand that corrective action can be taken to make him feel better. Cognitive empathy expands around age six as children develop the ability to attach words to feelings and grow in the ability to take another's perspective.[19]

Empathy develops over time in the context of caring relationships and modeling by others. Most children naturally integrate the way caregivers treat them into the way they interact with others. One cannot "teach" a child to have empathy. It's something that develops internally from the combination of their unique genetics and environment.[20]

In a recent example of this, I was caring for a friend's four-year-old little girl, Emma, and took her along with me on a trip to the grocery store. Seeing a homeless man sitting outside the parking lot, Emma looked at me and said, "Where is the bag for him?"

"What bag do you mean?" I asked.

"The one with the bottle of water, the snacks, and the five dollars," she said. She explained that whenever she and her mom are out, they keep little bags ready with a few essentials to give to any people in need that cross their path. Emma had integrated compassion and empathy from daily observation of her mother's way of relating to others. Children do indeed learn what they live.

As Canadian empathy researcher and child advocate Mary Gordon says, "Empathy is caught, not taught."[21]

Unfortunately, there are times when this aspect of normal

development veers off track. For complex reasons that can be both genetic and environmental, an individual may fail to develop the normal human capacity for emotional attunement and attachment to others.

These individuals misperceive others' intentions, develop distorted ways of viewing the world, and may even dehumanize others and move into various kinds of criminal behavior. They have personality features that can make them difficult for others to relate to.

In mild cases, they may simply not do a very good job of attuning to loved ones' needs as a friend or relationship partner. In more extreme cases, they may have what can be described as "personality disorders." This will be discussed in more depth in Chapter 8.

Other brain differences can impede the process of experiencing empathy. It's commonly been thought that individuals on both the autistic and schizophrenic spectrums have struggles with developing empathy and a correlating theory of mind, but this capacity varies widely among individuals. Many people on these spectrums have noted that while they feel compassion for others, they are not always sure how to express it, resulting in others incorrectly assuming they are devoid of empathy.

There can be distinct differences in neural processing that cause those with schizophrenia or autism to experience relationships with others in atypical ways, which are covered in-depth in subsequent chapters.[22] There can be perceptual differences which sometimes manifest as difficulties understanding sarcasm, misreading others' feelings, or misunderstanding their intentions—though this in no way causes them to act with cruelty and has nothing to do with the way they were parented. We've all got subtle differences in our neurobiological hardwiring.

These differences in hardwiring sometimes involve something called the mirror neuron system.

Mirror Neurons

In recent decades, brain researchers have learned that an important biological factor that occurs in the process of experiencing empathy involves the mirror neuron system, which is located in the prefrontal cortex of our brain.[23]

Mirror neurons were discovered by a team of neuroscientists at the University of Parma in Italy in the early 1990s. These researchers found that certain groups of neurons in the brains of macaque monkeys not only fired when a monkey performed an action—such as grabbing a piece of fruit—but also fired when the monkey simply *watched* another monkey grabbing a piece of fruit. In other words, the brain responded the same way whether the monkey was taking action itself or just watching another taking action.[24]

Human brains work the same way. Studies have demonstrated that while we are simply observing emotional facial expressions, activation of the same brain areas occurs in our own brains.

Just by observing another person, our brain creates an internal virtual simulation of their experience. If I watch you eating ice cream, my brain creates the sensation in my mind; I recall the taste and texture and may start salivating.[25]

Mirror neurons allow us to experience on an internal "gut" level what other people are experiencing. When I see you smiling, my neurons for smiling also fire up. If I see you cry, my own mirror neuron system causes me to experience sensations of sadness.[26]

In one interesting study, female volunteers underwent brain scans while they received a painful electrical shock to their hands. While they received the shock, a defined segment of their brains identified as a "pain matrix" was activated. Afterward, they received a signal that their husbands were also receiving similar shocks. This information activated a similar pain matrix again in their brains. Just knowing that their loved ones were in pain caused them to sense pain as well.[27]

The mirror neuron system is thought to be one crucial aspect of the experience of human empathy and the accompanying development of theory of mind. It helps us understand and connect with others. It has been speculated that differences in the mirror neuron system may be a factor in autism.[28]

Flawed theory of mind can result in a tendency to grossly misinterpret the intentions of others, resulting in perceptual distortions and thinking errors. These distortions can allow one to justify antisocial behavior without any sense of personal distress for harm that may come to others.

It's clear that mass killers operate with impaired empathic abilities.

Without the ability to sense the terror and pain of others, the mass killer feels no corresponding sense of dread, regret, or guilt.

In his mind, he is justified in killing others due to his personal grievances. In fact, he may enjoy the experience.

There appears to be something that has interfered with the normal development of empathy in those who become mass killers. That's a critically important point because empathy is what puts the brakes on the worst of human impulses.

Dehumanization

It's no surprise that so many mass killers have idolized the Nazis. Perhaps the most efficient mass murderers in history, they created massive killing centers to kill millions. There is no better role model for the process of dehumanization.

When we hear an individual or group of individuals describe others as "animals," "vermin," or with racial or ethnic slurs, we're witnessing dehumanization.[29]

Put simply, dehumanization is the process whereby someone identifies others as different from himself and less than human. It's a cognitive distortion that allows humans to commit terrible atrocities by creating false excuses for immoral behavior.[30]

In the process of dehumanization, an individual or group is identified by simplified characteristics, such as "lazy," "dishonest," or "evil." By thinking of others in this way, a perpetrator of violence rationalizes that they deserved their fate.

Dehumanization is at work in war and genocidal atrocities, when one group of people decides that another group of people should be persecuted or killed. In their mind, it allows them the justification to do so and to adopt a self-concept of righteousness in the process.

Mass killers motivated by racial hatred elevate their own race while dehumanizing others. Men motivated by gender hatred dehumanize women.

And some mass killers consider themselves godlike, with the tendency to dehumanize everyone. The Columbine killers referred to the students and teachers they intended to kill as zombies: lesser, non-human life forms that they were used to killing in videogames.[31] The Norwegian killer dehumanized those of other races and political parties. The Isla Vista killer dehumanized all women and racial groups other than white.

Certain personality types, particularly those with narcissistic and psychopathic traits, are low in empathy and are innately prone to dehumanizing others. They view others as nothing more than props in their personal theatrical life drama.

Dehumanization is the default lens through which they look at the world.

"Us" Versus "Them"

Another factor involved in the process of empathy is the way humans are biologically wired to unconsciously sort people into categories of "us" or "them."[32]

This means that we automatically categorize other people according to how much they are alike or different from us.

Research with brain scanning has shown that humans have an immediate amygdala reaction when shown faces of a person of another race. This causes feelings of fear or uncertainty, which may be subtle and under the level of consciousness; this emotional response can result in aggressive thoughts and reactions. This same instantaneous "us versus them" processing also occurs as we categorize others by gender, social, or economic status. The response does not activate when shown faces of "our own kind." This effect is even observed with babies and young children.[33]

We can override this amygdala response with intentional activation of the logical part of our brain, the prefrontal cortex—when the brain is working optimally. The prefrontal cortex, the analytical part of the brain, can calm down the amygdala and thus reduce its innate reactivity.[34]

However, suppose one is part of a social group that encourages the members of the group to maintain fear of those who are different. In that case, the resulting group validation amplifies perceptual distortions and intensifies feelings of anxiety and thoughts of aggression.[35]

This "us versus them" thinking describes the process of racism, which the Charleston church shooter illustrates. This event is a striking example of a person devoid of empathy. A young white man, he chose to murder black members of a church who had welcomed him to Bible study—just because they were black.

Charleston

It was a Wednesday night Bible study in mid–June 2017 at an African Methodist Episcopal Church in downtown Charleston, South Carolina. The church is a beautiful, historic building, painted white, with a tall steeple rising above the rooftops in the neighborhood.

That evening, as they gathered for fellowship and prayer, the black congregation kindly greeted a young white man, who was a visitor. He had seemingly just wandered in the door, and the pastor invited him to take the seat at his side.[36] The 21-year-old was visiting the church for the first time, and he had an unusual bowl-shaped haircut. There were 12 members of the congregation present, ranging in age from 26 to 87.[37]

One of the parishioners happened to be a state senator, who handed the young man a Bible to use for reference during the study. They were friendly, warm, and kind.

He sat with them for about a half-hour, listening as they discussed their faith in God and their love for each other. Midway through the service, when they closed their eyes for prayer, the young man pulled a Glock .45 from his fanny pack and stood up.[38]

He addressed the group by saying, "Blacks are trying to take over." He then began firing indiscriminately and hurling insults and racial slurs. He yelled that he wanted to start a race war between whites and Blacks.

This perpetrator hit parishioners with 60 of the 70 shots he fired. Nine were killed; three were wounded but survived. When he was finished shooting, he told one survivor that he was leaving her alive to explain what had happened. He wanted the world to hear his message.[39]

The Charleston shooter then tried to shoot himself but had run out of ammunition. He ran out of the door and fled the scene in his car.

Alerts with images of the shooter obtained from security footage went out in the media the following day. That morning, a motorist 245 miles away in Shelby, North Carolina, recognized the killer's bowl-shaped haircut as he drove down the highway. She notified the police. When an officer pulled him over, the killer was calm, polite, and acknowledged what he had done.[40]

Digital Footprint/Leakage

The Charleston killer left copious evidence of his extremist, racist views online and was active on various white supremacist websites.[41] He spent months accumulating grievances.

In the way of leakage, he had posted photos on his Facebook page wearing a jacket with white supremacist emblems. There was a Confederate flag sticker on his license plate. In other images, he posed holding his gun in one hand and a Confederate flag in the other.[42]

This perpetrator told multiple friends that he wanted to start a race war and supported racial segregation in the United States. No one reported him to authorities.

Several days before the church rampage, he made statements to friends that he wanted to commit a mass shooting at a college; one friend had briefly hidden his gun. It is speculated that he didn't follow through with the attack at the college due to the security that was present.

In a videotaped interview with investigators, the Charleston killer was polite, soft-spoken, friendly, and calm when he explained he had ultimately chosen a Black church because he thought he would meet with no resistance there. That particular church was chosen for its history of civil rights activism. He'd found it on Google.[43]

He had no remorse, and he had no empathy.

Investigators determined from his computer and phone analysis that the Charleston killer was radicalized online through interactions with racist extremist groups. At his trial, his defense attorney stated, "Every bit of motivation came from things he saw on the internet. That's it ... he is simply regurgitating, in whole paragraphs, slogans, and facts—bits and pieces of facts that he downloaded from the internet directly into his brain."[44]

His gun had been legally purchased from a retail store with money he received for his birthday.[45]

7

Into the Mind

"He had to be crazy. No normal person would do this."
"This is a spiritual problem. I think he was demon-possessed."
—Comments on social media

Since murdering strangers makes no sense to most of us, it's commonly assumed that mass killers must be mentally ill. In this chapter, we explore the definition and manifestations of mental illness, along with the myths and facts relevant to violence and mental illness.

Mental Health/Mental Illness

Are mass killers mentally ill? Or do we blame the devil? The response to that is complicated.

The quick response is that the majority of mass killers are not severely and chronically mentally ill. Major mental illness is evidenced by delusions and hallucinations termed "psychotic symptoms," which cause people to have a break from reality and fail to fully understand what they are doing.

Recent data from The Violence Project indicates that from their sample, only 10 percent of mass killers have been motivated solely by a major mental illness. Another 11 percent had symptoms of psychosis that were a minor influence in the crime, and in 9 percent of the cases, psychosis played a moderate role. Overall, 70 percent of mass killers are free of major mental illness.[1]

This is supported by an FBI study released in June 2018, which indicates that only three killers out of 65 studied had a major mental illness. Only 25 percent of mass shooters in the study had ever been diagnosed with *any* kind of mental health problem, including minor conditions.[2]

"The conclusion that all active shooters are mentally ill is both misleading and unhelpful," the FBI report states.

Even if major mental illness is only a factor 10–20 percent of the time, it's still important that we understand this subset of mass killers to intervene early on the pathway to violence. Several high-profile cases have been perpetrated by individuals with well-documented severe and chronic mental illness.

Since specific interventions can be taken in these situations, it's highly relevant in prevention.

This requires that we explore the topic of mental illness in-depth and work through another labyrinth of concepts and terminology. The term "mental illness" is a catchall phrase used to describe many different conditions; it can be confusing.

In the broadest definition, a mental illness is a health condition that involves changes in emotion, thinking, behavior, or a combination of these, which causes distress. This resulting distress leads to impairment in functioning in one or more areas of life, such as self-care, school or work, and personal relationships. However, defining "distress" and "impairment" leaves us with a wide swath of gray zone.

Most of us use the words "depressed" or "anxious" to describe everyday moments of sadness or worry, which are part of the everyday experience of being human. Most of the time, these feelings are primarily situational and quick to pass. Such brief episodes of unhappy mood states don't impact our daily functioning in significant ways.

But depression and anxiety *can* certainly be types of mental illness when they grow in intensity and duration and keep us from functioning normally in significant areas of our lives. As with any other health condition, a mental illness can be mild, moderate, or severe.

Traditionally, Americans have gone out of their way to avoid being tagged with a diagnosis of mental illness. Terms like "crazy," "nuts," and "psycho" have been used to describe those with psychiatric disorders; such labels inaccurately implied major character flaws, which resulted in the shaming of those afflicted. The resulting social stigmas have been used to persecute the mentally ill, and in many cases, deny them access to employment, housing, and education.

For millennia, mental illness has also been misidentified as a spiritual problem; it's still common among certain religious groups for severely mentally ill people to be labeled as "demon-possessed." These errors have resulted in millions of individuals failing to receive the mental health treatment that could have helped them recover or given them a much-improved quality of life.

The stigmas and social persecution that can accompany mental illness can cause as much harm as the illness itself.[3] That societal baggage is still being unpacked and sorted and will hopefully continue to diminish as our culture grows in awareness of the interrelationship between human biology, environment, and the development of the mind.

In truth, anyone can have a mental illness; there should be no "us versus them" dichotomy. Understanding the basic facts about these conditions will help to reduce the stigma and guide intervention strategies designed to help those who struggle with mental health concerns.

What About "Insanity?"

It's common in popular culture to use the word "insanity" as a synonym for major mental illness. However, this use of the word is dated; "insanity" is no longer used by mental health professionals to describe a person with a mental health condition. In current usage, the word is a legal term used in criminal proceedings when someone fails to have the mental capacity at the time of the crime to understand that what they did was wrong.

If someone commits murder and has such severe mental illness that they could not be aware that their actions were wrong, a court may find them guilty of the crime but "legally insane." In this case, they would be placed in a secure forensic mental health facility rather than a prison.

A related concept is "competency to stand trial." "Competency" means that a person can understand the legal proceedings against them and play a role in their defense. A person will be determined to be incompetent to stand trial when they are so severely mentally ill that they cannot understand the court process or work with their attorney. In those cases, they may also be sent to a secure mental health facility to receive treatment to be "restored to competency," at which point the court proceedings for the crime are continued.[4]

It is difficult for a defendant in a murder trial to meet the criteria for an insanity defense. There is an exceptionally high bar. Evidence from multiple mental health experts must prove that they could not understand what they were doing. Even those with major mental illnesses generally understand that murder is legally wrong, despite their perceived justifications.

Another Organ in the Body

The brain is an organ in the body, and like the heart or pancreas, it can become ill and fail to function correctly.

Our neurobiological system is intertwined with all our other organs and body processes. The mind-body connection is a biological reality, and conditions that affect the brain also affect other bodily functions.[5]

We now recognize that while some mental health problems are related to environmental stress, others develop from genetic factors. In most cases, mental health problems result from both and the way they intermingle.[6]

At least one in five Americans will experience a mental health problem; depression and anxiety are the most common general diagnoses.[7] These problems amplify during times of social stressors such as war, pandemics, or political instability.

At least half of all adults will experience some kind of mental health concern at some point during their lifetime.

The Gray Zone

Is all emotional distress a mental illness? Does that mean that any time I'm upset, there is something wrong with my brain? Definitely not.

Grief is an example of an extremely painful but normal universal human experience. We all become bereft when a loved one dies. It's normal to feel incredibly sad, long for our loved one, cry, remain tearful, lose appetite and weight, and find it difficult to concentrate. When suffering from grief, much of our functioning is temporarily impaired.

Yet some people can continue to function reasonably well while mourning, returning to work after a brief absence and never failing to care for themselves. Others may become so despondent they take to bed for weeks at a time, cease working, and cannot effectively meet their basic needs. Most people fall somewhere between those two extremes. Personality factors are also involved in how we experience grief and how incapacitated we may become when experiencing it.

When it comes to grieving, the boundaries between normal sadness and clinical depression are anything but clear. In a situation where someone seems to be exceptionally functionally impaired, a mental health clinician is often consulted to help sort out what's going on. Therapy and group support can assist in developing a plan to help a person feel better and experience an improvement in the quality of their life.

Some have argued that "mental health condition" is a better descriptor than "mental illness" for these milder, common problems, which can often be directly related to situational factors and environmental stressors. What begins as a mild symptom can progress to a mental health condition and may evolve to a serious mental illness over time.

Mental health practitioners typically assess the pattern and severity of a person's symptoms, the social stresses they are experiencing, and to what degree a person's ability to function is impaired. Only then can they work to determine the most accurate diagnosis and a corresponding treatment plan.

Major Mental Illnesses

Normally, when we describe our experiences, thoughts, and feelings to one another, we assume a shared understanding of what it's like to think and perceive the world. We assume we can discuss what we are thinking without having to describe how our brains process reality. This is not true for someone with a major mental illness.

Major mental illnesses are a small subset of mental health conditions. These severe, often chronic, mental conditions have been identified as having a clear basis in the biology of the brain, though for the most part, this is not entirely understood. The brain is an exceptionally complex organ, and while neuroscience research has made tremendous progress in recent years, there is still much we are in the process of discovering.

Unlike the more common and transitory minor mental health concerns, major mental illnesses like schizophrenia, bipolar disorder, and severe major depression have the potential to impede or disrupt an individual's ability to function in relationships, education, work, and self-care throughout their lives. In some cases, these conditions prevent people from being able to work or live entirely independently.

Each of these conditions is known to cause psychosis, which is when an individual's basic processes of perceiving and thinking are affected by the illness. Though psychosis manifests uniquely for every person, there are characteristic symptoms.[8]

When psychotic, people cannot think normally, cannot perceive the world accurately, and experience disorganized thoughts. They also commonly experience entrenched false beliefs (delusions) and see or hear things that are not objectively real (hallucinations).

Symptoms of psychosis are described below, along with the most common major mental illnesses. However, it's important to note that these symptoms can be caused by other factors, including head trauma, a medication reaction, or in response to the use of an illicit substance. Only a professional can determine the cause in a given situation.

These descriptions are *not* presented for the purpose of diagnosis but for informational purposes relevant to understanding the topic of mental illness. Only a licensed and qualified mental health professional can perform a mental health evaluation and assign a diagnosis.

Since people with untreated major mental illnesses are often unable to maintain employment or consistent relationships with others, they make up at least 40 percent of the homeless population in the United States. When highly symptomatic, some require psychiatric hospitalization to keep them safe.

To complicate matters, people with a condition causing psychosis generally don't realize they are ill. "Anosognosia" is the term for the lack of insight experienced by a mentally ill person who doesn't understand that the voices they are hearing aren't real or that their bizarre beliefs aren't objectively true; instead, delusional thoughts and auditory hallucinations are experienced as their reality. They don't realize that what they are seeing and hearing isn't shared by others. This makes it very difficult to engage them in treatment since the anosognosia renders them unable to realize that their beliefs and perceptions are false and that they need help.

It's common for family and friends of someone experiencing psychotic symptoms to find that they refuse all attempts to get them treatment. Many of those family members fail to find needed resources and eventually give up attempting to help.

Before the 1970s, people with major mental illnesses tended to be housed in massive institutional state mental hospitals. When the government shut down those hospitals in the 1970s, the mentally ill were turned out to the streets. Urban areas are now flooded with a chronic, impoverished, homeless population due to this healthcare failure.

Diagnosis

Unlike other biological illnesses, severe mental disorders can be complicated to diagnose and treat due to the current state of science. While medical science has improved in many areas in the past 100 years, we still have a long way to go when it comes to the brain.[9]

Diabetes is diagnosed by measuring glucose levels in the blood. CT scans can discover tumors in the body. But there are no lab tests or imaging studies that can diagnose mental illness. Instead, clinicians must rely on the things patients verbally relay about their symptoms and by monitoring their observable behavior. This is an imprecise and imperfect practice and is often best accomplished over time.

A century ago, heart disease was poorly understood. Physicians could only observe a patient's physical symptoms and listen as they described their complaints because there were no tests to measure cholesterol, no EKGs to measure electrical impulses, and no CT scans to check for artery blockages. Now, doctors have multiple ways of precisely measuring the state of a person's heart and have accordingly developed corrective treatments that significantly improve health and extend life.

The brain is the most complex organ in the body. We're now in the phase of the treatment of major mental illnesses that we were with heart disease 100 years ago. In the coming decades, researchers hope to make similar headway with mental illnesses as they develop more precise ways to measure and determine exactly what is happening in the brain when things go wrong.

A Few Basics on Brain Biology

The brain makes up only 2 percent of our body weight, but it consumes 20 percent of the oxygen we breathe and 20 percent of the energy we take in. The brain controls virtually everything we experience, including moving, sensing our environment, regulating our involuntary body processes such as breathing as well as generating and controlling our emotions. Hundreds of thousands of chemical reactions occur every second in the brain; those reactions underlie the thoughts, actions, and behaviors with which we respond to environmental stimuli. The brain dictates the internal processes and external behaviors that allow us to survive.[10]

The neuron, or nerve cell, is the basic functional unit in the brain. Neurons communicate with other neurons through a combination of electrical signals and chemical messengers called neurotransmitters.

Most scientists believe that some mental illnesses are caused by problems with the neurotransmission system in the brain. For example, the neurotransmitter serotonin is lower in people with major depression, which has led to the development of medications that increase the amount of serotonin available to neurons (Selective Serotonin Reuptake Inhibitors, or SSRIs). It's believed that other neurochemical disruptions involving dopamine, glutamate, and norepinephrine may be involved in schizophrenia.[11]

Genes also have a role in mental illness. Genetic components have been identified in schizophrenia, bipolar disorder, autism, and ADHD. In studies done with twins, identical twins are much more likely to share these conditions than fraternal twins; these illnesses clearly run in families.[12]

Additional factors that determine how genes are turned on include head injury, exposure to toxins (including lead and tobacco smoke), and poor nutrition.[13]

No single gene determines any one of these conditions; scientists believe that it is the interaction of several genes that trigger these illnesses. Precise genetic testing for all the possible gene variables does not yet exist due to the number and complexity of the genes that are involved.

To complicate things even further, it's the combination of genetics, neurochemicals, environment, and social factors that all come together to determine if and how a mental illness is manifested and how mild or severe it is.[14]

This intertwining process is referred to as the process of epigenetics.

Epigenetics

Epigenetics is the process of how the genes we inherit are turned on (expressed) or turned off (not expressed) based upon environmental influences. We call this the science of gene expression.[15]

For decades people have tried to answer the question about all human behavior, "Is it caused by nature (inherited) or nurture (upbringing and environment)?"

We now understand that there is no "either/or." Both are intertwined.

This is explained by Robert Sapolsky, professor of biology and neurology at Stanford University, in his book *Behave: The Biology of Humans at Our Best and Worst* (2017):

> A behavior has just happened. Why did it happen? Your first category of explanation is going to be a neurobiological one. What went on in that person's brain a second before the behavior happened? Now pull out to a slightly larger field of vision, your next category of explanation, a little earlier in time. What sight, sound, or smell in the previous seconds to minutes triggered the nervous system to produce that behavior? On to the next explanatory category. What hormones acted hours to days earlier to change how responsive that individual was to the sensory stimuli that trigger the nervous system to produce the behavior? And by now you've increased your field of vision to be thinking about neurobiology and the sensory world of our environment and short-term endocrinology in trying to explain what happened.

And you just keep expanding. What features of the environment in the prior weeks to years changed the structure and function of that person's brain and thus changed how it responded to these hormones and environmental stimuli? Then you go further back to the childhood of the individual, their fetal environment, and then their genetic makeup. And then you increase the view to encompass factors larger than that one individual— how has culture shaped the behavior of people living in that individual's group?—what ecological factors helped shape that culture—expanding and expanding until considering events umpteen millennia ago and the evolutions of the behavior.

"To put it simply," Sapolsky says, "we have to think complexly about complex things."

It's not genes *or* environment that makes us who we are; it's genes *plus* environment and the way they intertwine.[16]

The Role of Environmental Stress

Some researchers believe that we can be too quick to diagnose someone experiencing any psychological distress as mentally ill when, in fact, symptoms of anxiety and depression can be very logical and coherent responses to environmental stress.[17]

When we are stressed, our sympathetic nervous system is activated, resulting in a flood of neurochemicals that generate our fight/flight response by activating the amygdala. While this is appropriate if we're running from a tiger, it's harmful if we persist in this high-adrenaline state over days, weeks, or months. This nervous system hyperarousal can cause multiple mental health symptoms in the short term, including insomnia, depression, and anxiety disorders. Chronic flooding of stress hormones in the brain can also cause thinning in the frontal cortex, the cognitive part of the brain, which reduces an individual's ability to control impulses over the long term. Living in an environment of prolonged stress changes our biology in multiple ways; all facets of our health can suffer.[18]

Socioeconomic status is relevant since it affects many factors directly related to health. Poverty directly impacts the quality of nutrition and exposure to toxins like lead paint, both of which have a dramatic negative impact on our neurodevelopment.

In war-torn and conflict-affected countries, the incidence of depression and anxiety symptoms increases dramatically. Many believe these emotional symptoms that occur in life-threatening situations are natural responses to trauma and danger that help us focus energy to engage in protective action in the short term. In that way, some emotional responses serve as part of our natural threat detection system.[19] But if the distress is severe and ongoing, those emotional responses become overwhelming.

Contrast the lives of two parents in their 30s who represent common subtypes of modern Americans.

- A single mother works a minimum wage job with irregular hours; her parents are deceased, and she has no financial or emotional support from any other family members. She has diabetes, or another chronic illness, and limited access to healthcare. She also lives in a low-income area that is high in violent crime, and she relies on public transportation to get to work. This woman is often sad, tearful, and suffers from panic attacks. She also complains of having a poor memory, which affects her work performance. She never knows from one week to the next if she'll be able to afford groceries or pay her rent. Her children need more support and are thus struggling in school.
- Contrast this with another individual, a woman of the same age with a six-figure income, a supportive partner, excellent childcare, and an extensive family support network. She may also have a health condition; however, she has excellent medical insurance and easy access to health care. This mother lives in a quiet neighborhood and takes her car to work, which accords her a flexible work schedule. She has time to relax, enjoy friends and hobbies, and sleeps and eats well. She is generally optimistic and hopeful and free of anxiety symptoms. Environmental stressors are greatly diminished for this person and help to cushion her from developing stress-related symptoms. Her children have after-school tutors and are thriving in school. Their future is optimistic, and they are hopeful. In safe and supportive environments, incidents of anxiety and depression decrease—and the reverse is also true.

The following factors have been shown to increase the risk of mental illness due to the state of prolonged stress that they introduce into life[20]:

- poverty and economic hardship;
- exposure to violence;
- severe family discord;
- abuse, neglect;
- parent's mental illness; and
- death of close family member or friend.

Increasingly, researchers are suggesting that we look at the socio-cultural factors affecting mental health and work to better support safe and healthy environments.[21]

All of us will experience mental health symptoms if we are under enough environmental stress. However, specific symptoms are experienced differently from person to person due to genetic factors and the unique factors found in each environment.

Environmental stress may serve to set it off or make an existing condition worse for someone with a genetic vulnerability to one or more major mental illnesses.

Stress is a normal part of the human experience; overall, our emotions serve the evolutionary purpose of helping us stay alive. However, there are times when the thinking, perceiving, and processing system can go awry, and at those times, our minds can become our worst enemies

The Number of Major Mental Disorders in the General Population

Numerous efforts to define serious mental illness and identify how many experience it have come to similar conclusions and report similar numbers of people who have it. Two respected federal agencies are consistent with other research[22]:

- The Center for Mental Health Services defined severe mental illness when it was created in order to distribute mental health block grants to states proportional to the number of the seriously mentally ill in each state. They defined serious mental illness as a condition that "resulted in functional impairment which substantially interferes with, or limits, one or more major life activities." They identified these as "schizophrenia-spectrum disorders," "severe bipolar disorder," and "severe major depression."

- The National Institute of Mental Health (NIMH) states that serious mental illness is relatively rare, affecting only 5 percent of the population over 18. NIMH identified serious mental illness as schizophrenia; the subset of major depression called "severe, major depression"; the subset of bipolar disorder classified as "severe." NIMH identifies 1 percent of the population as having schizophrenia, 2.2 percent of the population with severe bipolar disorder, and 2.0 percent of the population as having "severe, major depression."

Thus, we can say with reasonable certainty that between 4 and 5 percent of the adult population of the United States suffers from a major, severe mental illness.[23] These individuals typically have psychosis, evidenced by delusions, hallucinations, disorganized thinking, and loss of touch with reality.

Many of those individuals receive no treatment due to the unavailability of resources.

The good news is that with consistent psychiatric treatment, which includes psychotropic medication to minimize the psychotic symptoms, most improve. Unfortunately, accessing treatment can be exceedingly difficult.[24]

Types of Major Mental Illness

Following is a list of major mental illnesses and a description of typical symptoms found with each. Each of these illnesses is evidenced by psychotic symptoms, which means they cause delusions and hallucinations. Not all of these symptoms are found in every person with the condition.

Schizophrenia[25]

Schizophrenia is a complex disorder that can present with a variety of subtypes. Speaking generally, the person with schizophrenia experiences a break with reality in their thoughts, feelings, and sensory experiences. The illness typically emerges in the late teens or 20s. Though children can develop schizophrenia, it is rare before adolescence.

People with schizophrenia typically experience delusions that often involve themes of persecution, conspiracies, mind control, or malevolent supernatural forces. Some individuals may believe that they are a famous person.

Hallucinations are also common. Auditory hallucinations are far more common than visual hallucinations and cause the person to hear voices; the voices often criticize them or tell them that someone will harm them.

When experiencing hallucinations and delusions, a person with schizophrenia may perceive the television to be giving them direct messages; they may think that aliens or evil spiritual forces are transmitting messages inside their head. Such delusions and hallucinations can be frightening and often cause a great deal of anxiety for the afflicted person. Symptomatic individuals may become consumed by these delusions.

Since people with schizophrenia often experience difficulty organizing their thoughts, their speech may sound nonsensical and difficult to understand. They often ramble and may speak aloud as if having a conversation with a person or entity that is not there.

Some persons with schizophrenia become suspicious and distrustful of others' intentions and can thus become hostile and withdrawn. These fears can develop into elaborate paranoid delusions involving law enforcement agencies, people of other races, or extraterrestrial forces.

It is impossible to reason a person out of these symptoms since they experience their perceptions as real. Attempting to try to convince them otherwise generally results in them becoming increasingly agitated and paranoid.

Schizophrenia doesn't come on suddenly. In the early phases of schizophrenia (called the "prodromal phase"), which occurs before active hallucinations and delusions, the individual may experience flat emotions, a lack of facial expression, and limitations to their ability to maintain grooming or practice essential self-care. They often withdraw from family and friends, become irritable, and start to experience unusual beliefs. The prodromal phase may go on for several years and eventually result in a psychotic "break" when they begin to experience hallucinations and delusions.

Though there is no cure for schizophrenia, symptoms can improve dramatically when a person receives appropriate mental health treatment. Psychiatric medications can reduce delusions and hallucinations, and supportive counseling can help suffers gain more insight into managing their illness. Life-skills training and community support can specifically address challenges to help people with schizophrenia function well and effectively manage their lives. It's also essential for the family members of a person with this illness to receive counseling to understand how to help them best.

Major Depressive Disorder, Severe[26]

In major depression, an individual typically experiences an extreme sense of sadness, hopelessness, loss of interest in activities that were previously enjoyed, and some combination of oversleeping or insomnia, weight loss or weight gain, difficulty concentrating, physical slowing, feelings of worthlessness, inappropriate guilt, and recurrent thoughts of death or suicide. Many describe a sensation referred to as "leaden extremities"; it becomes hard to move. Approximately 20 percent of those with major depression develop psychosis, which causes them to become delusional; their thoughts commonly involve an unreasonable sense of self-blame and self-loathing. They may develop persecutory delusions and believe that their loved ones don't care about them. These individuals are at high risk for suicide. Hallucinations are also possible and can be similar to those experienced in schizophrenia.

Major depression is always serious, and requires mental health treatment, though many times, family members seem unaware that a loved one is struggling. When psychotic features are present, immediate help is critical. For major depression with psychotic features, research has shown that antipsychotic medication combined with antidepressant medication provides the best treatment outcome.[27]

Bipolar Disorder, Severe[28]

A person with bipolar disorder alternates between episodes of major depression and mania. During the depression, the symptoms previously listed under major depressive disorder are experienced. During mania, the person experiences an abnormally and persistently elevated mood (feeling euphoric) or extreme irritability. They typically have a decreased need for sleep, experience racing thoughts, and become extremely talkative. Many develop overly inflated self-esteem (grandiosity) and become excessively involved in risky or pleasurable activities such as fast driving or unsafe sex. They lose reasonable judgment and may over-spend; normally law-abiding people can engage in criminal activity when in a manic episode.

How long an individual experiences each mood state varies tremendously. Some people may be primarily depressed with rare episodes of mania, or the reverse can also be true. Bipolar Disorder has two subtypes: type 1 and type 2. In type 1, psychotic symptoms are present, which include delusions and hallucinations. In type 2, the mood extremes are less severe, and generally, psychotic symptoms are not present. Both types of bipolar disorder can become manageable with medication and therapy, and many people function exceptionally well after they receive treatment, which should include psychiatric medication and psychotherapy.

It's important to realize that people with psychotic disorders generally don't perceive themselves as mentally ill. This presents particular difficulties with convincing them to seek treatment. Without family members who can actively facilitate the process, very few will seek treatment on their own.

The Diagnostic and Statistical Manual of Mental Disorders (DSM): *Some Cautions*

It's become common in popular culture to hear popular media references to *The Diagnostic and Statistical Manual of Mental Disorders (DSM)* as "the mental health Bible." This is a highly inaccurate and problematic description.

The *DSM* is published by the American Psychiatric Association and contains general definitions of mental disorders to establish a standard nomenclature for qualified mental health clinicians.[29] It is by no means "the Bible," and it should not be considered a fixed gospel.

The *DSM* is constantly in revision as we learn more about mental health conditions. New versions of the DSM evolve and are published every few years; there are always changes. This reflects the process of evolution in our understanding of mental disorders. Revisions of the *DSM* will continue as we continue to gather research.[30]

Since the *DSM* allows practitioners to use standard terminology, it's beneficial when a patient moves between providers. If someone is assigned a diagnosis of schizophrenia or bipolar type 1, clinicians understand the basic information on what symptoms the client is experiencing. However, this is only foundational. Those *DSM* diagnostic codes do not give all relevant information about a person or what they are experiencing.

The *DSM* is divided into multiple discrete categories with a general checklist for each diagnosis. A specific number of criteria are to be met for a particular diagnosis to be assigned. However, a trained mental health professional does not diagnose by checklist alone; the checklist is only one component of a mental health assessment.

In truth, many mental health disorders have overlapping symptoms. Hallucinations may be the result of schizophrenia, or bipolar disorder, a medication side-effect, or an effect of an illicit drug like methamphetamine. Which diagnosis is the best fit in any given situation can only be determined by an extensive assessment process, ideally including a thorough clinical history.

Symptoms of depression may result from multiple causes, including hypothyroidism, grief, or some forms of dementia.

The *DSM* is only a guide, and it takes an experienced clinician to understand the intricacies that are involved in making a diagnosis. An initial diagnosis is always a hypothesis and is usually specified as provisional. Often, in complicated cases, a valid diagnosis can only be assigned over time as the clinician has observed the symptomatic individual at various times and assess all relevant variables, including information from family members. Lab work is generally done to look for other physical illnesses that could be causing the symptoms.

Because of this, it's not uncommon for mental health providers to assign one diagnostic code when they initially meet a patient and modify that to a different *DSM* diagnosis at a later date when they have more information.

To complicate things further, most people with severe mental health symptoms have a combination of diagnoses. Real people often don't fit the neat, discrete categories presented in the *DSM*, rather they experience overlapping features of several disorders. These nuances cannot be captured by a checklist in the hands of a non-professional. Only a skilled mental health provider can decide which diagnosis is the best fit among several possible. This is also why people may receive different diagnoses from different providers at different points in time.

The diagnostic process is also moving away from the discreet categories of mental disorders as currently listed in the *DSM*, where conditions are identified with checklists. Instead, many mental health conditions can be viewed as existing on a continuum. This classification system is called the dimensional model and views mental disorders as part of a spectrum that includes a range of linked conditions.

Autism, schizophrenia, and bipolar disorder are examples of conditions that are now viewed dimensionally.[31] The varying elements of a spectrum disorder are thought to be caused by the same underlying mechanism, though they differ in severity. Using a dimensional model allows for more inclusive umbrella terms that can more accurately reflect a given person's experience.[32]

Because of this, I exclude the categories with symptom checklists from the *DSM*. A person displaying *any* of the symptoms described above should have a thorough assessment from a licensed mental health clinician.

Finding Treatment

To prevent incidents of violence that mental health conditions have influenced, we must help people access treatment as soon as symptoms manifest and *before* they progress. People with major illnesses generally need help from friends and loved ones to access care.

Those who are unsure how to access mental health treatment can start by consulting with a primary care physician. Primary care doctors have a basic understanding of mental illness and should refer to local specialists. In addition, state or county health departments typically offer mental health services, and most communities have crisis contact phone numbers where referrals can be made for ongoing treatment. In a crisis, treatment can be initiated at a hospital emergency department.

There are several categories of mental health service providers, and often they work as a team. Psychiatrists are medical doctors who specialize in diagnosing and treating mental illness. These physicians are typically the prescribers of psychotropic medication for major mental illnesses. Psychiatric nurse practitioners also specialize in this area and have extensive education and training in mental health assessment and psychotropic medication.

Additional assessment services can be provided by licensed clinical psychologists, who also offer psychological testing for diagnostic clarity. Many mental health professionals provide psychotherapy and counseling, including licensed professional counselors, licensed marriage and family therapists, and licensed clinical social workers.

Additional resources and information on finding mental health treatment services are provided in Chapter 15.

Tucson—A Schizophrenia Case Study

On January 8, 2011, a 22-year-old driver ran a red light in Tucson, Arizona. A state game and fish officer, who happened to be behind him, switched on his emergency lights and quickly pulled him over.[33]

The young man was odd in appearance. He wore a black beanie pulled low over his forehead, and as he pulled it off, the officer noticed that along with a shaved head, he had entirely shaved off his eyebrows. He was wearing a black hoodie, and there was a black backpack in the rear seat.

Inside the backpack were a 9mm Glock and multiple large-capacity magazines. Since the officer had no reason to search the car, he never discovered the bag's contents. Even if he had, the gun and the ammo had been legally purchased. The young man had spent months in planning and preparation.

The driver was polite; he kept his hands on the steering wheel as directed. The officer checked for warrants and found nothing. His record appeared to be clean. When the officer told the driver that he would give him a citation instead of a ticket, the young man began to cry.

"Are you okay?" the officer asked. The driver replied, "I've just had a rough time. I'm okay. I just thought you were going to give me a ticket."

When the officer asked if he was sure he was okay to drive, the young man said, "Can I thank you?" and stuck his hand out to shake hands with the officer. He was incredibly polite.[34]

"Be safe," the officer responded.[35]

The driver drove off to continue on his mission at a Safeway grocery store, where Congresswoman Gabriele Giffords was hosting a meet-and-greet event she called "Congress on the Corner." A lengthy line of constituents had formed to meet with her. It was a beautiful, sunny day, and the mood was festive.[36] The killer was ready to breach and attack.

At approximately 10 o'clock, the young man walked to the front of the line and fired off 31 shots in 30 seconds, shooting Congresswoman Giffords at point-blank range. The bullet entered just above her left eye, fractured her skull, passed through her brain, and fractured the top of both her eye sockets.[37]

Then, shooting into the crowd, he murdered nine others, including a nine-year-old girl and a federal judge. One man shoved his wife to the ground and covered her with his body. He was shot in the back and killed. A mother pinned her daughter against a wall, covering her with her body. She was also shot and killed.[38] Nineteen others were injured.

Gabby Giffords was left gravely wounded. She lost her left eye and would be permanently disabled due to traumatic brain injuries. It was considered miraculous that she survived.

The rampage stopped when the perpetrator emptied his magazine and fumbled while reaching into his pocket for another. A member of the crowd hit him with a folding chair, while another man grabbed his arm and forced him to the pavement.

The Tucson killer was an only child who lived with his parents in a middle-class Arizona suburb.[39] As a child, friends recalled him as ordinary and nerdy. He loved music and was talented at playing saxophone. But he began to change during his junior year in high school.[40]

He grew strange and distant. He was fired from jobs at Quiznos and an animal shelter because he couldn't follow basic instructions.[41] Friends stated that he walked around angry, with his hands balled into fists. He began using lots of illicit drugs and had a run-in with police over the vandalism of a street sign. He was beginning to accumulate grievances.

The killer began to discuss bizarre topics, such as learning to dream while conscious and believing that this would give him the power to fly. Effective treatment at this phase might have made a dramatic difference in what was to come.

He stated that he could invent a new grammar that would reduce all government to a mere word. It was this thought that led him to Representative Giffords. When she visited his high school to meet with students in 2007, he stood up to ask her, "What is government if words have no meaning?" Understandably, Giffords skipped to the next question, which incensed him. He expected her to respond to his delusion, and she passed.[42] He was gravely offended.

Enraged at Giffords, he would fixate on her and obsess about killing her for the next four years.

A Downward Spiral

His behavior became increasingly odd in the coming years, and he continued a downward spiral. Neighbors of the family described them as becoming increasingly isolated and private. No one knew what was going on inside the family home.[43]

By age 20, the Tucson killer made no sense when he spoke, sometimes in random streams of words. He sent strange text messages to former friends that were impossible to understand.[44]

And there were the bizarre videos he posted on YouTube, in which he ranted about creating currency and recited random series of numbers. The government, he said, was trying to control him. Those who had contact with him began to describe him as weird and scary.[45]

The Tucson killer enrolled in community college, where he

alarmed both students and teachers with rambling, odd rants about war, killing people, and strapping bombs to babies. When his concerned English teacher contacted campus police about him, she described him as "creepy" with "a dark personality."[46] Everyone around him observed leakage.

Other teachers also made complaints to campus police. He would laugh hysterically to himself in class while shaking and trembling.[47] A female classmate was so frightened of him that she began sitting near the door to escape if need be.[48]

He made another video which he posted on YouTube in which he called the community college a "genocide" school and stated, "We're examining the torture of students" and "mind control." Other students told teachers they were scared of him.[49]

Due to his disturbing behavior, school officials decided that he would be expelled until he had received a mental health assessment. Campus police were sent to his home where, in front of his parents, they reviewed the reports of his increasingly bizarre behavior in class. They described the content of the "genocide" school video. They advised his parents to get him a mental health evaluation. They also suggested that the parents remove any guns from the house.[50]

Though his father removed a shotgun from his possession after the meeting, this one intervention was not nearly enough.[51]

On the day of the expulsion, the community college police contacted the U.S. Bureau of Alcohol, Tobacco, and Firearms to ask for any records relating to the perpetrator and guns. The ATF responded that they had no information regarding this individual.[52]

His parents were aware that something was wrong. They heard him in his room laughing and talking to himself. Despite all this, he could stroll into a Sportsman's Warehouse in Tucson and legally purchase the Glock he would subsequently use in the murders.[53]

His father would later state that he could not get his son to agree to a mental health assessment or treatment.[54] As an adult, he had the right to refuse treatment. Nothing he had done was against the law.

Approximately two weeks before the killings, the Tucson perpetrator visited two friends who shared an apartment and said, "Guess what? I got a gun." When asked why he had purchased it with such a large quantity of ammunition, he replied, "Home protection."[55]

Even amid his severe mental illness, he knew enough to hide his real intentions.

Incompetent to Stand Trial

Two months after the murders, a hearing was held to determine if the Tucson killer was competent to stand trial. Two psychiatrists testified that he spoke nonsense and was delusional. At that time, he was formally diagnosed with schizophrenia.[56]

Since it was determined he could not have a rational understanding of the proceedings, he was ruled incompetent to stand trial. The court ordered him to be placed in a secure federal facility for a year in hopes that psychotropic medication would restore him to sanity so that he could be tried. An order from the judge was required to force him to take antipsychotic medication while hospitalized.[57]

Months after starting medication, he improved enough to understand the legal proceedings. He was restored to competency and accepted a plea bargain to avoid the death penalty. On November 15, 2012, the Tucson shooter was sentenced to seven consecutive life terms in prison, plus 140 years, without the possibility of parole.[58]

Recovery and Activism

Gabrielle Giffords left Congress following the shooting and resulting brain injury. She has since become known for her remarkable resiliency and her advocacy against gun violence. She and her husband Mark Kelly founded a non-profit organization Giffords Courage to Fight Gun Violence, which advocates increased gun safety laws.[59] Giffords and Kelly also told the story of the shooting, the aftermath, and their fight to enact stricter gun control legislation in their 2017 book titled *Enough: Our Fight to Save America from Gun Violence*.[60] In November 2020, Mark Kelly was elected to the U.S. Senate, representing the state of Arizona.

Perspective

While major mental illness is relevant to the topic of mass killings, it's essential to keep it in perspective. Most mentally ill individuals will never commit a violent crime; they are much more likely to become victims than perpetrators.[61]

The Tucson killer presented with classic signs of severe schizophrenia, with intensely paranoid delusions. He had become progressively more mentally ill over five years. After the murders, his parents stated to the media, "We have no idea why this happened."[62]

Even though the Tucson killer was extremely psychotic with disorganized thinking, delusions, and hallucinations, his symptoms did not prevent him from making complex plans and initiating actions. Once again, multiple opportunities to intervene on the pathway to violence were missed.

As the FBI says, "In light of the very high lifetime prevalence of the symptoms of mental illness among the U.S. population, formally diagnosed mental illness is not a very specific predictor of violence of any type, let alone targeted violence. Careful consideration should be given to social and contextual factors that might interact with any mental health issue before concluding that an active shooting was 'caused' by mental illness."[63]

This begs the question, if 70 percent of mass shooters are *not* mentally ill, what is it that makes them different from the rest of us?

This brings us to the following topic: personality.

8

Personality and Bullying

Since most mass killers do not have a major mental illness, how else do we account for their behavior? We find relevant variables when we examine personality characteristics that often cluster in mass killers. In this chapter, we define and clarify what personality is, how it develops, and the times it's of particular concern. We review specific personality traits that have been associated with mass killers. We also examine the issue of bullying in the context of incidents of mass violence.

It's important to re-emphasize that no single variable results in someone becoming violent or committing *any* crime. Like all human behavior, violent crime results from multiple intertwining factors that occur both within an individual and externally in their environment. However, specific personality characteristics *can* indicate vulnerability areas for potential violence in a small number of people with those traits.

Personality

When we notice people around us, we are aware of how different they are from one another. Some are quiet, some talkative. Some are easy-going, others anxious. Certain people love adventure, and others are cautious. Our personality causes us to interpret and interact with the world in specific and unique ways. None of us are exactly alike, but there are overall patterns found in humans.

Personality can be described as an individual's characteristic patterns of thought, emotions, behavior, social interactions, and coping skills that are regular and consistent over time in various settings. Our personality determines how we think, the way we express emotion, how we control our impulses, and how we relate to other people.

Early personality is apparent at birth; babies are born with clear differences in temperament, primarily due to genetics and the prenatal environment, including the mother's nutrition, exposure to substances, and hormones during pregnancy.[1] Infants may be fussy, demanding, anxious, good-natured, excitable, relaxed, or prone to tantrums.

These initial temperamental tendencies gradually develop into personality characteristics that become apparent during early childhood and continue to evolve as a child gets older. Personality evolves from the complex weaving together of many factors, including biology, neurology, caregiving, and social environment, resulting in each individual's development of a unique personality.[2]

Though it tends to be relatively stable over time, personality develops over the lifespan and is not set in concrete. During childhood, there is particular flexibility in how personality goes on to develop. A shy child can often be helped with coaching to become less fearful. A child who tends to be impulsive can gain skills in applying their internal brakes before acting. A child prone to worrying can learn to self-soothe and calm down.[3]

While parents can support and help shape their child's developing personality, they can't fully mold it. Parents who have raised more than one child can attest how completely different each child is, even when they are raised under near-identical circumstances.[4]

As children mature, personality continues to be shaped by the environment, though it becomes less flexible over time; traits become increasingly hardwired in the nervous system. Thus, the primary aspect of a person's core identity that remains stable in various environments.

Adolescence is an important time in development; while the emotion-driven limbic system is fully operational in the teen years, the prefrontal cortex, the thinking part of the brain, is the last brain region to reach maturity, at about age 25. Teens are notorious for heightened emotionality, poor impulse control, and bad judgment. The prefrontal cortex is the part of the brain that cautions "you'd better not do that" and functions to put the brakes on the emotional limbic system.[5]

Peers and the surrounding culture exert a much more significant influence on personality development during adolescence[6]; this includes people met online and through social media and the type of electronic media consumed. Online culture is powerfully influential, and adolescents now spend hours every day on the internet. It's also the time when parents have decreasing influence and are least likely to know what their offspring are up to.

Males commit most violent behavior, which peaks in late adolescence and early adulthood, including premeditated and impulsive murder.[7] It has often been said, "The greatest crime-fighting tool is a thirtieth birthday."[8]

Moving from adolescence to adulthood, social maturity increases, and most people tend to become more emotionally stable and conscientious.

We bring to adulthood personalities that have already influenced our lives in profound ways. Our personalities have everything to do with our perceptions of the world and our decisions regarding education, careers, and relationships.

Personality also explains why two people in similar circumstances may respond very differently.

Personality Traits

Specific individual characteristics of personality found in each person are described as "personality traits." Various traits in combination are the building blocks that make up one's personality.

We're used to thinking in absolutist terms when it comes to personality. Someone is labeled as an "introvert" or an "extrovert" or "Type A." However, these crude categorical distinctions about supposed personality types fail to capture the complex nuances that make each one of us unique.

Personality traits can be viewed as specific basic dimensions common to all people, with each trait existing on a continuum, or spectrum, from low to medium to high. We are each at a different place on the spectrum for every trait. For example, when we talk about "extroverts" or "introverts," we're not describing entirely different types of people, but more accurately, where a person falls on the continuum of the trait of extraversion.[9]

Everyone has different combinations of personality traits that vary in intensities, with certain ones tending to dominate our personalities in unique patterns. They are not binary, not good or bad. All traits can be considered "healthy" or "unhealthy," depending upon how they impact our lives. When traits cause consistent problems in life, they are referred to as "maladaptive."

While personality traits are relatively stable over the lifespan, some may shift over time. Most adults become more agreeable, conscientious, and emotionally resilient as they age, but these changes tend to unfold across decades rather than weeks. Sudden and dramatic changes in personality are rare.[10]

Ways to Conceptualize Personality

Understanding personality is not an exact science. Different theorists have conceptualized personality in different ways, and our understanding continues to evolve.

In 1936, psychologist Gordon Allport found that one English-language dictionary contained more than 4,000 words describing various personality traits. Allport subsequently developed a system to categorize those traits.[11] In the 1940s, Allport's initial list of over 4,000 traits was condensed down to 171 by psychologist Raymond Cattell, when he eliminated uncommon traits and consolidated others.[12] Cattell rated a large sample of individuals for these 171 distinct traits. Using multivariate analysis, Cattell identified closely related terms to eventually consolidate and reduce his list to 16 fundamental, key components of personality. This method allowed researchers to view individuals holistically, reflecting personality strengths as well as weaknesses.

According to Cattell, these 16 traits are the source of all human personality. He developed one of the most widely used personality assessments known as *The 16 Personality Factor Questionnaire.*[13]

Current theories of personality show a great deal of overlap, despite differences in terminology. Researchers who agree conceptually often use different terms and continue to build off one another's work and refine their predecessors' work, as is common in all areas of science.

The Dimensional Five-Factor Model

The most recent edition of the *Diagnostic and Statistical Manual, DSM-5,* includes a newer model for understanding personality that has gained favor with researchers over the past two decades. This is a dimensional model called Five-Factor Model or the Big Five. Over the past 20 years, research has suggested that personality pathologies can be conceptualized as extreme, maladaptive variants of the personality traits common to us all. This means that an individual with a problematic personality has characteristics we all have, but to a more intense degree.[14]

The Five-Factor Model condenses essential core personality components down to these broad traits, each existing on a spectrum[15]:

- openness (intellectually curious, artistic, and imaginative vs. disinterested in art, beauty, and abstract ideas);
- conscientiousness (orderly, hardworking, and responsible vs. disorganized and distractible);
- extraversion (outgoing, assertive, and energetic vs. quiet and reserved);
- agreeableness (compassionate, respectful, and trusting vs. uncaring and argumentative); and
- neuroticism (prone to worry, sadness, and mood swings vs. calm and emotionally resilient).

The dimensional model frames maladaptive personality traits as *quantitatively* different rather than *qualitatively* different.[16]

These five personality factors cover a group of narrower personality facets and 25 additional maladaptive traits that occur at extreme degrees.[17]

For example, extroversion is often thought to be a positive trait. Extroversion is characterized by social confidence and the ability to connect with others easily. People high in extroversion enjoy meeting others, make friends easily, and can thrive in many social environments.

However, when this trait is *extreme* on the high end, it can result in excessive attention-seeking or dramatic outbursts that can cause problems in job settings or relationships.

Those lower on the extroversion trait are quieter, thoughtful, and tend to be uncomfortable in large groups. However, they often make profound connections with a small group of people and do well in groups of people they know well. On the *extremely* low end, they may be inhibited, socially phobic, and experience social isolation.

Agreeableness is thought to make one cooperative, pleasant, and kind. Agreeable people are friendly and cooperative, trusting of others, and altruistic. Those high in agreeableness work well as members of a team and are considered likable. They are apt to avoid conflict and tend to work as peacemakers. This can be a tremendous asset in a work environment.

However, on the *extreme* high end, agreeableness can manifest as non-assertiveness and people-pleasing acquiescence; too much amiability can cause a person to become a doormat, quickly taken advantage of by others.

People *extremely* low in agreeableness tend to be suspicious and more prone to conflict. They are often perceived as selfish and unlikeable, which negatively impacts their ability to make friends or function well in groups. Others tend to avoid them.

Conscientiousness is considered a positive trait. Those high in conscientiousness have a strong sense of ethics. They are hardworking, responsible, and follow through on their goals and commitments. They are driven to succeed in academic achievements and in meeting their career goals. Conscientious people can be counted on to pay their bills on time.

However, when taken to an *extreme* on the high end, conscientiousness manifests as perfectionism, obsessive tendencies, workaholism, self-punishing behavior, and excessive criticism of oneself and others.

People *extremely* low in conscientiousness show less motivation and follow-through. They may have trouble setting goals, managing their finances, or staying employed. They also tend to be impulsive and not consider how their actions impact other people. They tend to act on whims without consideration for consequences.

Extremes in either direction have the potential to become maladaptive; to make it more complicated, each of our traits intersects in patterns that are unique to each of us.

A thorough mental health assessment is complicated since the five personality factors are further broken down with multiple additional variables.[18]

Personality Disorders in the DSM-5

The topic of "personality disorders" is frequently discussed in popular media, usually to describe someone with extremes of pathological behavior that cause consistent problems for themselves or others. Depending on which disorder, they may be chronically self-sabotaging, deceitful, abuse substances, have difficulties in interpersonal relationships, engage in violent or manipulative behavior, and in various ways cause harm to family members, loved ones, co-workers, or constituents.

The *DSM* defines a personality disorder as "an enduring pattern of inner experience and behavior that deviates markedly from the expectations of the individual's culture, is pervasive and inflexible, and has an onset in adolescence or early adulthood is stable over time and leads to distress or impairment."[19]

Ten separate personality disorders are identified in the original *DSM* structure (which is offered as one of two models in the *DSM-5*). Each is considered a single, discrete diagnosis. These 10 disorders are clustered into three groupings based upon similar qualities (Clusters A, B, and C).[20] Within each cluster, there is much overlap between the disorders. This can make the diagnosis process confusing, as a clinician must choose between very similar conditions to determine which the closest fit is for an individual.

Personality disorders have always been classified in a separate section in the *DSM* because they are often a focus of treatment in psychotherapy. However, they are not considered "mental illnesses" in the same way as schizophrenia, major depression, or bipolar disorder, which are diseases of the brain caused by biochemical disruptions in brain chemistry. Anxiety, mood, or psychotic disorders *happen to* a person, whereas a personality disorder is *who* that person *is*.[21]

Most clinicians are hesitant to diagnose minors with personality disorders since it's understood that adolescence is a tumultuous time full of dramatic change. Many aspects of personality continue to be flexible and apt to evolve with maturity. Therapists are reluctant to assign a diagnosis like a personality disorder unless they are sure it's warranted, though research shows that personality disorders often become apparent in adolescence.[22]

Antisocial Personality Disorder, the *DSM*-equivalent closest to the trait of psychopathy, cannot be diagnosed before age 18; a precursor diagnosis of Conduct Disorder is given to minors who display similar characteristics.

Since personality is how one's perceiving, thinking, and behaving patterns have developed within our identity structure, a personality disorder cannot be corrected with medication or eliminated with psychotherapy. However, in many cases, therapy can help individuals with a personality disorder learn to mitigate the harm resulting from their ways of thinking and ingrained behavior patterns, eventually helping them manage their actions and impulses more effectively.

More Than One Category

But there is another layer of complexity. Most people experiencing severe mental health-related problems have more than a single categorical diagnosis; a biochemical illness like depression, schizophrenia, or bipolar can be layered as a *secondary* diagnosis on top of a *primary* personality disorder. When there is a second diagnosis in addition to the first, each diagnosis is called "comorbid." This means that two or more diagnoses occur together.[23]

It's important to realize that not all people with personality pathology can be easily identified. They often come from "good" families. Many have not been abused. Many people with personality disorders appear superficially normal. Those who have manipulative traits can be masters of impression management and blend in with their peers and colleagues.

Individuals with these pathological personalities can be found among highly successful professionals, politicians, and salespeople as well as incarcerated criminals. The number of successful people with personality pathology is far greater than we imagine because they can be sophisticated at avoiding detection. Often, only those in close relationships with them are the only ones who come to understand that something is wrong.

In the *DSM* section on personality disorders, each of the 10 disorders is primarily diagnosed by a checklist of specified criteria. If enough of the requirements are met for a specific disorder and not better accounted for by another condition, a clinician can assign that personality disorder as a diagnosis.[24] In many cases, because one person shares several traits with more than one disorder, that person ends up with a combo pack of personality disorders when features from several categorical diagnoses overlap.[25]

In other cases, the individual with personality problems doesn't have the entire cluster of traits that meet the criteria for any one of the *DSM*-identified personality disorders. In this case, the symptoms are considered "subclinical." Subclinical symptoms still cause difficulties and are thus worthy of attention in mental health treatment.

Most of us are familiar with the personality disorders commonly described in pop culture. People frequently diagnose politicians and ex-romantic partners as "narcissists" or "borderlines," with wide variations in the accuracy of such assessments. Checklists for personality disorders are abundant on the internet, with limited degrees of validity. Accurately assessing personality is complicated, and that familiar caveat needs to be applied once again: *only a mental health professional can or should assign a diagnosis.*

Advantages of the Dimensional Model

With the dimensional model, which is offered as the alternate model in the *DSM-5*, personality problems are classified according to which specific traits are present and at which level of severity. This means that extreme problematic characteristics are recognized, even if the combination of traits does not align with any one of the 10 *DSM* personality disorders. This allows for a trait-specific personality assessment without attempting to fit an individual into a single discrete disorder.[26]

Thus, a person who has traits of both narcissistic personality *and* borderline personality can be diagnosed accordingly with those traits, whether they meet full *DSM* criteria for either personality disorder.

Since most individuals with personality problems have traits from more than one of the single personality disorder categories in the *DSM*, we can understand a person with greater clarity by looking at the specific maladaptive traits.[27]

Another advantage of the trait-specific diagnostic process is that it also allows for an individualized recognition of positive and adaptive personality traits, which are also relevant to a holistic understanding of a person. We shouldn't restrict our focus to simply what is wrong.

It would be inaccurate to state that all mass killers share a single personality disorder or an identical trait cluster. When there are similar traits, they will be at different degrees of severity on the spectrum and manifest differently. Despite this, the pattern of personality traits displayed by mass killers does show commonalities and certain consistencies.

None of these traits, alone or in combination, should indicate that a person will become violent, but when they are extreme and cluster in a significant pattern, this can indicate *vulnerability* for potential violence.

In cases where killers have left behind videos, social media posts, and written manifestos, many of these extreme traits can be clearly observed. This does not mean that we can retroactively identify a specific individual with a personality disorder according to *DSM* criteria; it's possible to have many of these traits without meeting full criteria for a single specific personality disorder.

The whole purpose of diagnosis is to drive decisions regarding the best way to understand a person in order to provide intervention and treatment. The trait-specific model allows us to do this.

Traits Often Found in Mass Killers

Researchers have identified five pathological personality features that are often found among mass killers[28,29]:

- paranoia;
- narcissism;
- psychopathy;
- Machiavellianism; and
- sadism.

It's important to emphasize that most people who have some or many of these personality features never commit acts of violence. Most never commit any kind of crime. But when present, these traits can indicate areas of amplified concern.

When it comes to mass killers, it's important to emphasize that no single individual will have all of these features. Some may have few, others many. The degree of severity of each feature will always differ from person to person.[30]

These traits are on the spectrum from mild to moderate or severe, and many people possess some of these qualities in mild forms.[31] We are *all* capable of being a little narcissistic or manipulative. You will also notice that facets of several of these traits overlap with others.

Another critical point is that it is possible to have these personality features *in addition to* a major mental illness like schizophrenia, bipolar disorder, or another comorbid condition like autism.

People with these particular personality pathologies typically have no insight that anything is wrong or realize how other people see them. Intensely absorbed in themselves, they have limited—if any—ability to take others' perspectives.

Paranoia, Key Facets[32]

- **Hypersensitivity**: Hypersensitivity to perceived slights or criticism. Over-reacts to benign social circumstances where they believe they are not adequately recognized or respected. Ascribes malevolent motives to others when they do not exist. These perceptions are generally not grounded in reality.
- **Suspiciousness**: A general suspiciousness of others. Socially withdrawn. Assumes (often with no evidence) that others are out to get them or think negatively about them. Misperceive benign remarks as attacks. Since they do not discuss their suspicions with others, there is no opportunity to receive feedback, allowing them to adjust their incorrect assumptions. Consistently scan the environment for evidence to confirm their suspicions, and often find like-minded others on the internet who do the same. Combing their environment for threats, they create enemies where they don't exist.

- **Rumination and revenge fantasies**: Keeps track of every action they count as a slight. Thoughts are focused on these slights, and the individual takes pleasure in plotting elaborate fantasies of revenge. These fantasies can come to consume their thought life and grow increasingly detailed over time. In a circular thinking process, they justify their revenge fantasies by focusing on the perceived slights.
- **Social rank and status**: Obsessed with social position and status, and misperceive that others are critical of them or view them as inferior.
- **Envious, entitled, self-justifying**: On the emotional level, they can become overwhelmed with envy and believe they are entitled to special treatment. Cognitively, they distort reality to justify these feelings. They can give a well-crafted argument to justify their suspicions and refuse to consider alternate positions.

Paranoid individuals do not realize that their perceptions and feelings are inaccurate. They believe their thoughts are normal. Any misfortune in life is attributed to ill-will from others. It is this paranoid perception that creates an injustice collector.

It's important to remember that *feeling* persecuted and *being* persecuted are two different things. The person with the paranoid personality trait does not realize this.

Narcissism, Key Facets[33]

- **Grandiosity**: An exaggerated sense of self-importance. Fantasize about their superiority to other people. Exaggerate their achievements and talents, and expect to be recognized as superior without commensurate achievements.
- **Fantasies**: Preoccupied with fantasies of unlimited success, power, brilliance, attractiveness, or ideal love.
- **Specialness**: Believe that they are "special" and unique and can only be understood by other high-status people.
- **Admiration**: Needs excessive admiration and quick to become angry when they don't receive it.

- **Entitlement**: Expect unreasonable favorable treatment and are quick to become angry when they don't receive it.
- **Interpersonally exploitative**: This trait results in the manipulation of others to achieve their ends.
- **Lack of empathy**: People high in narcissism are unwilling or unable to identify with the feelings of others; they are devoid of compassion.
- **Envious**: Jealous of others' success or believes that others are envious of them.
- **Arrogant**: Displays arrogant, haughty behaviors or attitudes.

Psychopathy, Key Facets[34]

- **Lack of affective empathy**: A key hallmark of the psychopathic feature is a lack of emotional concern and compassion for others. This quality allows a psychopathic individual to harm others to obtain a goal with no guilt or remorse. They tend to be callous and contemptuous of others' feelings, rights, and suffering. They may experience cognitive empathy, which they use to exploit others' vulnerabilities.
- **Disregard for others' rights**: Unconcerned about others' rights and lies, cons, or manipulates others for personal gain or pleasure.
- **Superficial charm**: Glib and superficially charming, which enhances their ability to manipulate others.
- **Indifferent to suffering**: Indifferent to others' suffering and rationalizes how others deserve to be victimized (*"They had it coming"*).
- **Violation of laws**: May repeatedly engage in behavior that results in arrest, though more sophisticated psychopaths may violate rules and laws often and avoid detection.
- **Aggressiveness**: Repeated physical fights or assaults.
- **Lack of remorse**: Unlikely to feel any genuine guilt for harming others, though they may be adept at faking it.
- **Dominance**: Seeks a sense of power by dominating others.
- **Impervious to fear**: Remains calm during dangerous situations that would be emotionally overwhelming to others.

Those high on the trait of psychopathy are masters of impression management. They know how to make others like and trust them and can often blend in as normal.

The Dark Triad/Dark Tetrad

Another model that overlaps with the personality features listed above is called the Dark Triad. This is not separate from the personality traits and their facets previously discussed. The Dark Triad is made up of the characteristics of psychopathy and narcissism with an added third construct called Machiavellianism.

The Dark Triad was initially conceptualized by Delroy Paulhus and Kevin Williams in 2002 and has since been well-studied by researchers who followed.[35]

Following are the traits described as The Dark Triad:

Machiavellianism: Machiavellianism refers to a person's tendency to treat others in a cold, calculating, manipulative, and deceptive way to achieve specific goals. A person with high Machiavellian tendencies is also very skilled at impression management.

This trait is named after Niccolo Machiavelli, the 16th-century author of the notorious book *The Prince*. This book espoused Machiavelli's views that strong rulers should be harsh with their enemies and their subjects and that glory and survival were justified by any means, even ones that were considered immoral and brutal.

By the late 16th century, "Machiavellianism" became a popular word to describe the art of being deceptive to get ahead. The following facets are included[36]:

- **Ambitions**: Only focused on own ambitions and interests.
- **Money and power**: Prioritizes money and control over relationships.
- **Charming**: Comes across as charming and confident.
- **Exploitative**: Exploits and manipulates to get ahead to achieve specific goals.
- **Deceptive**: Lies and deceives when required to meet personal goals.

- **Flattery**: Often flatters others to gain their favor.
- **Lacks principles**: Lacking appropriate principles and values.
- **Cynical**: Contemptuous of the concepts of goodness and morality.
- **Harms others**: Capable of causing others harm to achieve their means.
- **Lacks affective empathy**: Low levels of affective empathy.
- **Calculating**: Can be very patient due to calculating nature.
- **High cognitive empathy:** Good at reading social situations for the purpose of manipulation.

The Dark Triad has recently been expanded to include one additional personality trait: sadism.[37] This model is now referred to as The Dark Tetrad. Sadism is described as the pleasure derived from inflicting pain on others and is made up of the following facets[38]:

- **Humiliates others**: Through cruel and demeaning behavior.
- **Enjoys dominance**: Asserts power for pleasure and enjoyment.
- **Inflicts pain**: Intentionally inflicts physical, sexual, or psychological distress on innocent victims—experiences euphoria during the act of harming another.

Not all with sadistic traits harm others physically. Recent research reveals that behaviors like bullying, cyberstalking,[39] and toxic leadership within workplaces are examples of ways people with sadistic features inflict psychological pain on others.[40] Sadistic people simply find pleasure in causing others pain.

While the quality of sadism seems similar to psychopathy, the difference is that the psychopathic person engages in behaviors to harm others to meet a goal that will help them somehow. While they are indifferent to the harm they cause, hurting others is not the primary goal. The sadistic person harms others simply because he enjoys it. While a psychopathic person may be indifferent to another's pain, the sadist takes pleasure from witnessing it. Inducing pain may be the sole goal.

There are many similar, overlapping features between sadism, Machiavellianism, narcissism, and psychopathy.[41] Because many individuals with these traits can be highly manipulative, they often marry normal partners. Some become successful politicians, religious leaders, or salespersons. All are masters of impression management.

Bullying

The U.S. Secret Service's Threat Assessment Center (TAC) report released in March 2021 specifically examined thwarted school shooting plots between 2004 and 2018. Sixty-seven thwarted plots were identified in K–12 grades during those years; all cases involved students who made serious attempts to complete their plans. Those with inside knowledge reported the plots. One hundred perpetrators were included in the study; researchers used 43 to develop the report because there was enough information in the public domain to know some details of their lives.

Out of the 43 students studied, the report indicates that they had typically been bullied, often suffered from depression, and had stress at home. Many had trauma histories, and most were suicidal. As with other research, the TAC study states that they had exhibited behaviors that worried others well in advance of an attack phase and that early intervention saved lives.

Many of the attacks were planned for April, the anniversary month of the Columbine High School Attack. The targets were generally public schools.

Signaling Victimhood

It's a persistent belief that all mass killers have been bullied, and it's clear that many have. This has led to the belief that if we just stop bullying, mass killings will stop. This hypothesis offers a simple cause-effect narrative which can be appealing; simple narratives give us an easy way of understanding complex things, though they are only a piece of the puzzle.

Bullying is traumatic and damages kids in countless ways. As individuals and in our schools, we need to be doing everything we can to stop bullying *before* any young person is harmed. But anti-bullying programs will likely not be enough. Some researchers have specifically questioned the narrative.[42,43]

Bullying is a nearly universal experience during adolescence; it always has been. Yet never until recent history did bullying become identified as a cause for mass murder.

The news media widely spread the linear cause-effect bullying narrative at the time of the Columbine killings; it was subsequently investigated in-depth by journalist Dave Cullen, who describes it this way: "The theme is remarkably consistent: outcasts turning the tables on their bullies. Two noble souls, tortured mercilessly until they fought back, putting every American bully on notice. Avengers standing up for oppressed losers everywhere."[44] As Cullen and others have pointed out, this narrative is weak when it comes to Columbine. The Jefferson County Sheriff's Office interviewed dozens of Columbine students who knew both killers; many interviews were conducted on multiple occasions. While some friends corroborated that bullying had occurred, others who knew them well did not.[45] While disturbing (making fun of Reb in PE because he was not good in sports), specific incidents identified are not out of the range of typical high school experiences. There are also multiple accounts of both Reb and Vodka bullying and threatening others.[46] Both acknowledge in their journals that they enjoyed bullying younger students.[47]

Significantly, bullies were not targeted in the attack—most of the time, they are not.

Ultimately, it's impossible to sort out how much of a factor bullying is in most mass killers' behavior. In Peter Langman's study of 48 school shooters, he notes that only one of the 48 shooters targeted a bully. He emphasizes that bullying should not be viewed as a universal or primary cause of school shootings.

Nonetheless, bullying is a very stressful experience for children and teens. Parents and schools need to do everything they can to hinder bullying and advocate for all young people's safety. Bullying is a layer of trauma that—when combined with other factors—can increase a young person's vulnerability to mental health problems that can make the pathway to violence look appealing.

Since those who kill tend to have paranoid, narcissistic, and psychopathic traits that color their perceptions, they are extremely sensitive to perceived slights and injustices and greatly exaggerate others' adverse treatment.[48] Considering this, the bullying narrative may sometimes be amplified.[49]

Many mass killers have been bullied, and others have not. Some were both bullied *and* bullied others.[50] Some may falsely perceive themselves to be victims to justify their actions to themselves and others.[51]

Others have pointed out that the popular narrative that mass killings result from bullying can create *a cultural script that murder is an understandable response to bullying.* Thus, the narrative itself may become a template that can be adopted by an adolescent who has been bullied.[52]

Recent research also indicates that individuals with these traits can be adept at "victim signaling." This is defined as "a public and intentional expression of one's disadvantages, suffering oppression, or personal limitations." As a manipulative strategy, taking on a victim's role can be a shrewd way to enhance one's access to resources. Amplifying a troubled past for sympathy is a common manipulative strategy.[53]

Mental health clinicians can also be manipulated. In therapy, a psychopathic person will often emphasize a history of victimization to gain sympathy and color the clinician's perception.[54] Most of the time, therapists hear only the narrative of the client. Since many clients are unreliable reporters, this can result in a failure to diagnose them accurately.

A concept related to "victim signaling" is "virtue signaling." Virtue signaling is making "symbolic demonstrations that can lead observers to make favorable inferences about the signaler's moral character."[55] Saving the country from an "invasion of immigrants" is an example of attempting to reframe mass murder as a virtuous act committed by a morally superior person.

Most people have sympathy for a perpetrator who is a good person driven to his actions, which validates the mass killer's behavior as something other than what it is.[56]

Case Reviews

In looking back at the cases that have been previously discussed, we often see patterns of paranoia, narcissism, psychopathy, Machiavellianism, and sadism. Several examples are listed below.

Common to all has been the perception of themselves as victims. All accumulated grudges over a lengthy period of time, which they used to justify mass murder. All were injustice collectors.

Hypersensitive to perceived slights, injustice collectors have exaggerated perceptions of being persecuted or victimized by others and externalizing blame to other groups for any distress or problems.[57] Instead of learning to transcend slights or rejections, they obsess on plans to annihilate or torture those they have framed as offenders.

All of them loved weapons, were fixated on violence, and idolized other mass murderers who had gone before them. They wanted to be famous and make it to the top of the kill score list.

Fascinated with Nazis, Charles Manson, the Oklahoma City bomber, and other notorious mass killers, their ability to dehumanize others and their sadistic tendencies are consistent. They sought power by making others afraid.

Nearly all make attempts to manage their self-justifying narratives by creating manifestos, social media posts, or creating videos; this kind of attempt to feed a narrative to the world can be considered a press kit. Manifestos are the way they sell their story.

Most were manipulative, fooling their parents, friends, and even counselors.

Isla Vista[58]

The Isla Vista killer blamed women for his severe social problems and emotional distress. The central theme in his life was that women who did not offer him sex were victimizing him; he took no responsibility for his social deficits and therefore took no corrective action.

He kept lists of specific grievances that went back to elementary school and spent years entertaining sadistic torture fantasies of revenge against all women: "Those girls deserve to be dumped in boiling water for the crime of not giving me the attention and adoration I so rightfully deserve."

Cruelty was important. So was fame.

"Infamy," he wrote in his 137-page autobiographical manifesto, "is better than total obscurity."

The Isla Vista killer repeatedly referred to his specialness in his manifesto and the series of videos he posted on YouTube.

He considered himself "beautiful" and superior to others: "I am more than human. I am superior to them all. I am magnificent, glorious, supreme, eminent, and divine. I am the closest thing there is to a living god."

A great deal of his mental energy went into elaborate fantasies of wealth, power, and fame.

The Isla Vista killer was a master of deception. No one in his family had any inkling of his plans, interest in weapons, or violent fantasies. His parents had no idea he had ever touched a firearm.

Victims who survived his rampage mentioned his "creepy laugh" as he shot at them. He enjoyed killing.

Norway[59]

The Norwegian killer targeted the children of the dominant political party, which he hated for supporting multiculturalism. He focused paranoid fantasies on Muslim refugees that he perceived to be destroying Europe and sought out right-wing extremists to validate his paranoid thinking. These perceptions set the course of his life. He dedicated most of his mental focus to this perceived outside threat and spent a decade plotting an elaborate crusade against multiculturalism that he imagined would change the world.

Profoundly narcissistic, he considered himself a brilliant leader of modern Knight Templars, an organization that existed only in his fantasies. The Norwegian killer spent 10 years crafting the 1,518-page self-aggrandizing manifesto that he stated would be the guidebook to changing the world.

His narcissism manifested in his physical presence. He had plastic surgery to improve his facial appearance in his early 20s, became a bodybuilder, and used anabolic steroids. When undressed at the time of his booking after murdering 77 people, he assumed macho bodybuilding poses, flexing his muscles for the camera.

While he expressed his views openly online, he successfully hid them from his friends and family, who described him as "friendly and ordinary." Shortly before the murders, he visited his stepmother and told her he would do something that would "make his father proud." He created a narrative in which he was a hero.

He cited the Oklahoma City bomber as a role model and admired other neo–Nazis.

None of his friends or family members were aware of his extremist beliefs or violent plans.

Displaying an incredible sense of entitlement, he demanded special treatment after being taken into custody. After his arrest, he complained to law enforcement officers that a five-millimeter cut on his finger needed to be "treated immediately." He calmly reported that he got the cut from a piece of a victim's skull that he had shot at close range.

When imprisoned, he filed a lawsuit against Norway's government, complaining about many trivial things, including the fact that though he had been provided a PlayStation 2, he had not been upgraded to a PlayStation 3. Additional complaints suit included that his coffee had been served cold, some of his food had been cooked in a microwave, and he had been denied moisturizing lotion.

Newtown[60]

The Newtown killer at Sandy Hook Elementary School blamed society for his emotional distress and lack of competency in every significant life domain; he spent years focused on revenge fantasies and obsessively studying weapons and sadistic violence. He created the seven-foot-long spreadsheet ranking hundreds of other mass murderers and took pleasure in memorizing every detail of their crimes.

He too wanted to be famous. "Just look at how many fans you can find for all different types of mass murderers," he wrote in an online post just before murdering 20 six- and seven-year-olds and six staff members at close range. He specifically chose young children in hopes of achieving a high kill score. He knew they would not fight back.

Diagnosed as a young child on the autism spectrum, he also suffered from anxiety, obsessive-compulsive disorder, and may have developed another major mental illness. The Newton killer is an example of a person with multiple comorbid diseases, including underlying personality pathology. He started leaking his fixation on sadistic violence in the 5th grade when he created *The Big Book of Granny,* which described children's torture.

Aurora[61]

Academically accomplished, the Aurora theater killer was in a Ph.D. program in neuroscience. He had been experiencing repetitive thoughts about killing people since early adolescence.

He created a formidable, frightening appearance in selfies before the attack, after dying his hair bright-orange and wearing black contact lenses. He was theatrical and wanted to be remembered.

Despite serious mental illness, his behavior was goal-directed, well-organized, and extensively planned out. He created homemade napalm and designed elaborate booby traps around his apartment. He performed reconnaissance on possible targets and selectively chose a location where he thought he could achieve a maximum kill score. He plotted ways to limit his victims' chance of escape.

Dressed in body armor and a gas mask, he walked up to many people and shot them at close range. He stated, "I never considered how they felt about dying from their point of view."

Parkland[62]

The Parkland killer had a long history of using violence to frighten others in order to dominate them, including his mother and brother. He entertained the fantasy of being a school shooter for at least a year before the attack, a plan which he announced on social media: "All the kids will run and hide. From the wrath of my power, they will know who I am."

On the first anniversary of his high school expulsion for violence, he recorded a video on his phone describing his planned attack. He recorded another video three days later and another on Valentine's Day—the day of the attack.

After gunning down his peers, he calmly went to get a soda at Subway.

Columbine [63,64]

> "I want to tear a throat out with my own teeth like a pop can. I want to gut someone with my hand, to tear a head off and rip out the heart and lungs from the neck, to stab someone in the gut, shove it up to their heart, and yank the fucking blade out of their rib cage. I want to grab some weak little freshman and just tear them apart like a wolf, show them who is god."—Reb

A master of impression management and a straight-A student, Reb engaged in persistent fantasies of raping and torturing people. No one knew.

In the diversion program, he convinced his counselor that he was a stellar young man who was sincerely repentant for a minor criminal act and had learned from his mistake.

Both killers were released from the diversion counseling program early with glowing reviews from their counselors. Their parents had no idea they had accumulated an arsenal hidden in their bedrooms, nor that they spent a year plotting the details of what they hoped to be the greatest mass murder in history.

They laughed as they roamed the halls of their school, shooting other students in the head and throwing grenades and pipe bombs, just as they'd laughed when discussing which directors would make the story of their rampage.

When Reb held his gun to one girl's head, she begged, "Don't shoot me. I don't want to die."

He laughed. "Everyone is going to die."

"Shoot her!" Vodka yelled.

He did.

In their journals, both referred to themselves as gods.

Commonalities

From the seemingly ordinary to the almost comically diabolical, mass killers have imagined themselves as stars in their personal apocalyptic action movies.

Some imagined outside threats from immigrants or those of

different races and religions. Others fixated on women as the malevolent enemy.

They became obsessed—even addicted—to revenge fantasies, which gave them pleasure.

They obsessed, studied other mass killers, researched weapons and bombs, wrote stories, and made videos and social media posts about mass murder. In some cases, they streamed their attacks live on the internet.

They dehumanized others, were bereft of empathy, and imagined they had the power to start a race or gender war. They elevated themselves with fantasies of omnipotence. Like a vengeful Old Testament deity, they would decide who lived and who died. They would never be forgotten.

Cautions

Mass killers are not all the same, and there is no single "profile" of who will become a mass killer. The personality traits described in this chapter—particularly when occurring in combination—should be viewed as areas of psychological vulnerability that indicate a need for further assessment and intervention. Most people who display many of these traits will never engage in violence—but some may.

Treatment early in life can make a difference. Personality is most flexible in childhood and becomes less malleable over time; thus, early prevention is preferred to later intervention. The earlier mental health treatment occurs, the greater the odds it will be helpful.

If any parent notices signs that their child is fixated on gory violence or murderers, has been affected by bullying, or engages in cruel or bullying behavior with other children or animals, an experienced mental health professional should be consulted.

We have no statistics on how many potential mass murderers are interrupted early on the pathway to violence, but I have no doubt they number in the thousands.

9

Complicating Factors

Autism Spectrum Disorder,
Traumatic Brain Injury, and Trauma

We see the layers of complexity when it comes to human behavior. Many variables make us who we are and determine how we act. We all do things for reasons that are poorly understood—even by ourselves. In addition to factors such as mental illness (Chapter 7) and specific personality characteristics (Chapter 8), there have been three additional mental health conditions with speculative links to mass killings that warrant further exploration.

These factors are autistic spectrum disorder, traumatic brain injury, and childhood trauma. Since research about mass killers is often inaccurately summarized in popular media, this has sometimes led to misunderstandings about these complex conditions. In this chapter, we explore each of these conditions and any possible connection to mass killing incidents.

Autism Spectrum Disorder

The term "neurodiverse" has become common in recent years, but most people aren't quite sure what that means. "Neurodiverse" is now commonly used as a descriptor for those on the autism spectrum and relates to the differences autistic people experience due to their innate neurobiology. Autistic people experience the world in unique ways that are often hard for others to understand. Those without autism are commonly described as "neurotypical."

Like other conditions, symptoms of autism exist on a spectrum. Now known as autism spectrum disorders (ASDs), this can be described as a group of complex neurodevelopmental differences resulting in varying degrees of atypical sensory experiences, social challenges, communication difficulties, repetitive behaviors, and a narrow range of interests and activities.

These differences exist on a spectrum and show significant variation from person to person. No two people with ASD are exactly alike; many are highly dissimilar.[1]

Autism is a developmental disorder with symptoms that become apparent in infancy or early childhood. It tends to run in families, and we now understand that the causes are primarily genetic.

Though a person of any age can be diagnosed with autism, it never begins later in life. Autistic people have *always* had different ways of processing the world due to their unique neurobiology. This is apparent in studies of infants who engage with the world differently from very early in life.

Put most simply, autistic people experience differences in these three key areas:

- sensorial processing;
- social reciprocity; and
- restricted or repetitive interests and behavior.

Sensory processing differences may manifest as sensitivity to sounds, textures, lighting, or other environmental factors. An individual with autism may be overwhelmed by the noise in a restaurant or the bright fluorescent lighting in a store or classroom. They may experience odors more intensely or become nauseated by certain textures of food. They could find their clothing's fabric to be excessively scratchy, distracting, and difficult to tolerate. Small sensory details not noticed by most of us can be overwhelmingly uncomfortable for a person with autism. Because of this, they engage with the world in different ways. Being easily overwhelmed, they may withdraw from the environment to avoid uncomfortable stimulation and the emotional distress that comes with it.

This withdrawal is often mischaracterized as indifference to other people. However, autistic people are not indifferent; like everyone else, they seek connection, but the process doesn't come easily.

These sensory processing differences are at the core of why autistic people relate to others differently. The differences start in infancy.

Infants engage with their caregivers in many ways through reciprocal interactions that include gazing, smiling, and vocalizing. This is how the process of attachment develops; it's based upon social reciprocity and the connection established between each infant and his caregivers.

Prone to sensory overload, an infant with autism may be easily overstimulated by the process, which results in emotional distress and dysregulation. This distress may cause a caregiver to reduce engagement with the child to help him stay calm.

This disengagement pattern based upon sensory challenges can contribute to ongoing tendencies to withdraw when overwhelmed; an autistic person fails to develop an early foundation that allows him to connect with others naturally, something that magnifies as he gets older.

This does not mean that autistic people don't care about friendships; in fact, they crave the same connection with others that's common to us all. They don't connect in the same way as those with more typical neurobiology and thus can feel chronically misunderstood. As with other mental health conditions, those with ASD often suffer social rejection and stigmatization and may internalize shame for being different. Children with ASD are 94 percent more likely to be the victims of bullying in childhood than the neurotypical.[2]

Some children with ASD have an unusual gait or uncoordinated physical movements. They are often perceived as different from their peers, which places them at a greatly amplified risk for being singled out. The trauma of being bullied adds another layer of vulnerability to their lives.

These struggles may continue to cause an individual with ASD to withdraw from interpersonal relationships, which often leads to a preference for solitary activities.

The restricted or repetitive interests and behavior typical to those on the ASD manifest in different ways. Examples are children who have little interest in anything other than one topic, like dinosaurs or insects or space travel. They may play with only one toy repeatedly or have to build one particular object with Legos over and over again without variation. This tendency can carry over into adulthood, manifesting as an adult who seems obsessed with only one hobby or interest.

"At autism's core lies the divergence in social reciprocity," explains autism therapist and educator Barbara Avila, in her 2021 book *Seeing Autism: Connection through Understanding*:

> As children, we engage with our caregivers in quiet, relaxed environments before we are tasked with navigating more dynamic situations. Children who develop autism may become overwhelmed and need to retreat inward for neurobiological safety. The new, more complex environments (additional people, lights, sounds, smells, and touch) may feel harsh and be too much for their neurological and biological systems. Instead, they feel flooded by sensory information, so they shut down additional stimuli in favor of sameness, routine, and predictability. Instead, they feel flooded by sensory information, so they shut down additional stimuli in favor of sameness, routine, and predictability. To compensate, the child may learn to focus on things in the environment that are predictable and in their control. To calm their systems, they find rhythmic motions, line things up, or rely on other repetitive behaviors for soothing, resulting in restricted or repetitive interests of behaviors.
>
> Everything you see in autism all happens in typical development—it is a matter of extreme. Many people are somewhat sensitive to sensory stimulation but live their lives essentially unimpeded; people with autism can experience sensory sensitivities that render them unable to leave the house without noise-canceling headphones to dampen the input.

The thinking, learning, and problem-solving abilities of people with ASD can range from severely challenged to gifted. Some need a lot of help in their daily lives; others function exceptionally well. People with ASD who have no significant impairments are often referred to as "high functioning." However, this term has been criticized by many within the autism community who stress that observers have no way of knowing what internal struggles an individual is experiencing.[3]

Autism Spectrum Disorders are currently viewed from two different perspectives. The traditional medical model identifies ASD as a potentially disabling neurodevelopmental "disorder."[4] It is officially considered a developmental disability, and children with ASD qualify for special education services through the public school system, based upon the Americans with Disabilities Act.

Since the late 1990s, a self-advocacy movement has encouraged the alternate view that the autism spectrum is a normal variation of the human brain rather than a disability in need of a cure. In this contrasting view, those with ASD are referred to as "neurodiverse," and those without ASD are framed as "neurotypical."[5]

The neurodiversity perspective holds that brain differences are normal, and that any challenges that may result from ASD should not be framed as deficits. The neurodiversity view rejects the concept that people with autism are disabled, instead emphasizing that they may have strengths that are foreign to the neurotypical, such as very detailed thinking, exceptional memory, and adept analysis of complex patterns.[6] The concept of neurodiversity recognizes natural variations in the human brain that are valuable and that those who operate differently from a perceived "norm" should be valued rather than stigmatized and excluded.

This neurodiversity model emphasizes that those with ASD should take pride in their neurodiversity and be embraced for their differences. This view promotes a shift in the way services are provided to those with ASD, emphasizing individualized, person-centered goals that will help the individual live a happy and healthy life, rather than attempting to "fix" autism or attempting to make an autistic person indistinguishable from others.[7]

Some parents of children with ASD who have severe difficulties have objected to this viewpoint, feeling that it's a way of denying and minimizing the extreme challenges their children face. I think it's possible to keep both perspectives in mind and understand that there are many nuances and variations from person to person.

This self-advocacy movement has helped reduce stigma and the resulting shame and isolation that those with ASD have commonly experienced. Overall, in recent years our culture has moved toward acceptance and inclusivity of neurodiverse people. Individuals with ASD are increasingly entering the autism research community, and traditional researchers are partnering more often with autistic community-based organizations to determine how best to support ASD individuals. It is helpful to acknowledge and validate the strengths that those with ASD have, rather than solely focusing on the challenges and vulnerabilities that can come with neurodiversity.

ASD Facts

Autism spectrum disorder is a recent conceptualization in the *DSM-5* that incorporates several other conditions that used to be diagnosed separately: autistic disorder, pervasive developmental disorder, and Asperger's syndrome; thus, symptoms of ASD vary widely.[8]

There has been a significant change in the reported prevalence of ASD in recent decades. In the 1970s, the prevalence was estimated to be one in 2,500 people. Now, one in 54 children has been identified with ASD, according to the Centers for Disease Control's Autism and Developmental Disabilities Monitoring Network.[9]

This change likely reflects increased public awareness, increased screening by pediatricians and preschools, and broadened diagnostic criteria, rather than an actual increase in prevalence.[10]

Diagnosing ASD can be tricky since there is no medical test for the condition. In childhood, pediatricians observe a child's behavior and development to make a diagnosis. While ASD may be diagnosed as early as 18 months of age, many individuals with mild ASD are not diagnosed until adulthood. ASD individuals without intellectual impairments may never be diagnosed. Many older adults would meet the criteria for the ASD diagnosis but will never be screened for the condition.

ASD occurs in all racial, ethnic, and socioeconomic groups; it is four times more common among boys than girls. It has been speculated that sex hormones may influence the condition.[11]

The U.S. Centers for Disease Control defines autism spectrum disorder (ASD) as "a developmental disability that can cause significant social, communication, and behavioral challenges. There is often nothing about how people with ASD look that sets them apart from other people, but people with ASD may communicate, interact, behave, and learn in ways that are different from most other people."[12]

The CDC lists the following behaviors that may be displayed by a child with ASD[13]:

- does not point at objects to show interest (for example, not point at an airplane flying over);
- does not look at things when another person points at them;

- has trouble relating to others or not have an interest in other people at all;
- avoids eye contact and wants to be alone;
- has difficulty understanding other people's feelings or talking about their feelings;
- prefers not to be held or cuddled, or might cuddle only when they want to;
- may have a limited attachment to others;
- appears to be unaware when people talk to them but responds to other sounds;
- is very interested in people but not know how to talk, play, or relate to them;
- repeats or echos words or phrases said to them, or repeat words or phrases in place of standard language;
- has trouble expressing their needs using typical words or motions;
- does not play "pretend" games (for example, not pretend to feed a doll);
- displays hyper- or hypo-sensitivity to sensory stimulation, including lights, sounds, textures, and pain; and
- eats only a narrow range of foods, be an extremely picky eater.

Symptoms of ASD in adults may include[14]:

- difficulty interpreting what others are thinking or feeling; limitations with theory of mind;
- trouble interpreting facial expressions, body language, or social cues;
- inability to interpret nuance;
- development of intellectual skills over emotional skills;
- difficulty regulating emotion; may have rage episodes when frustrated;
- trouble keeping up a conversation;
- inflection that does not reflect feelings;
- difficulty maintaining the natural give-and-take of a conversation; prone to monologues on a favorite subject;
- tendency to engage in repetitive or routine behaviors;

- participation in a restricted range of activities;
- strict consistency to daily routines; emotional outbursts when changes occur;
- display of strong, special, sometimes idiosyncratic interests;
- tendency toward black and white thinking;
- may be perceived as emotionally cold;
- difficulty in learning from mistakes; and
- may believe that one is superior, or always right, despite evidence otherwise.

Sometimes those with ASD have difficulties with both receptive and expressive communication. "Difficulties with receptive communication" means that they may not fully understand the nuances of what another person is trying to say to them. "Difficulties with expressive language" means they have problems communicating their needs and inner experience to others.[15]

ASD, like bipolar disorder and schizophrenia, is considered to be highly heritable; it's influenced 80 percent by genetics. Research has identified more than 100 autism risk genes that manifest in many different ways, which is why we see clusters of these conditions in families. This explains how those who have been identified as having ASD may share some similarities yet still be dramatically different from one another.[16]

ASD and Violence

Violence is *not* a core feature of ASD. People with such diagnoses are much more likely to be victims of crime than perpetrators.

The idea that there is a causal link between ASD and mass killings came after media reports on several high-profile cases where perpetrators had a documented or suggested diagnosis of ASD (Isla Vista, Newtown, Charleston, and Parkland killers, among others). This caused some to speculate that people with ASD are innately dangerous. This is an erroneous conclusion, which requires deeper analysis.

Research

Current research suggests that ASD alone is *not* a risk factor for violence; instead, violence may occur in the context of a cluster of multiple additional factors that can increase an individual's vulnerability. These factors include head injury, comorbid mental illness, personality pathology, or childhood trauma history.

- A 2014 research study examining 239 incarcerated serial and mass murders found that 28 percent had "definitely, highly probable or possible ASD." Additionally, 7.4 percent of those individuals had a history of a head injury.[17]
- Mother Jones' mass shooting database examined 75 mass killers and found evidence that six (8 percent) out the 75 individuals had ASD and 16 others had "some indication of ASD." This is nearly eight times higher than the prevalence of ASD found in the general population (1.85 percent) worldwide.[18] Some view this as a conservative estimate.[19]
- The Violence Project database has identified 10 out of 177 mass shooters in the U.S. as being on the autism spectrum (5.6 percent compared to 1.85 percent of the general population).[20] There is not always enough accessible information to make a determination, so the actual number may be higher.

Since mass killings are rare events, the sample size for data analysis is too small to draw definitive conclusions; however, those with ASD do seem over-represented among mass killers compared to the general population.

Comorbid Conditions: Mechanisms and Underlying Factors

In years past, mental health clinicians tended to view autism as a diagnosis isolated from other mental health problems, a rare condition that stood entirely apart in a distinct category. That overly simplified view was incorrect. People with ASD, just like those in the neurotypical population, can have any variety of co-occurring mental health problems.[21]

We now understand that ASD occurs commonly in mild forms and is frequently comorbid with other conditions; people with ASD often experience anxiety, depression, and obsessive-compulsive disorder. A person with ASD can also have schizophrenia, bipolar disorder, or pathological personality traits. ASD can also reduce coping skills for a person with other mental health conditions, thereby amplifying their difficulties. Available research at present strongly indicates that there are multiple comorbid disorders that, when *combined* with ASD, can increase an individual's vulnerability for violent behavior.[22]

Some researchers have suggested a new diagnosis, "Criminal Autistic Psychopathy," for a small subgroup of individuals with ASD *and* psychopathic personality characteristics who have committed criminal offenses. This would help differentiate these individuals from the general population of those with ASD who will never become involved in violent crime.[23]

Another study looking at 121 adults with ASD found that compared to the adult control group, the following traits common to those with ASD could overlap with some of the characteristics and behaviors exhibited by many mass killers[24]:

- idiosyncratic areas of intense, obsessive interest and extreme focus;
- socially naïve, poor theory of mind, failure to understand social rules, misunderstanding others, misreading social cues;
- apparent difficulties with empathy or lack of concern for others;
- tendency to blame others for their distress; and
- a history of childhood trauma.

The "intense interest and obsessive focus on an idiosyncratic area of interest" associated with ASD could overlap with the obsessive preoccupations common among mass killers.[25] Spending countless hours researching Nazis, Charles Manson, and other mass murderers could be evidence of this. Years spent compiling mass murder data, creating spreadsheets, making detailed plans, writing manifestos, recording videos, studying weaponry, etc. are all behavioral patterns found in mass killers.

Some ASD individuals are more apt to see others as the cause of negative emotion or event ("other-blame") rather than understanding what they can do differently to bring a better outcome to a problem. This thinking style could contribute to injustice collecting, an exaggerated perception of one's victimization, and blaming other categories of people for one's unhappiness.[26] Most mass killers have blamed those of different religions, races, or the female gender for their distress, thereby justifying murder as righteous action.

Those who have not successfully established positive peer relationships experience social isolation, resulting in a reliance on using the internet as a primary tool for socializing. Vulnerable, isolated persons are more apt to become immersed in toxic extremist groups online, where violence is celebrated and normalized. Those with a heightened response to perceived slights and difficulty understanding what other people are thinking may also be more vulnerable to extremist views found in toxic communities on the internet. These communities can encourage members to nurse grievances and advocate for violent actions as a solution to perceived injustice.[27]

Finally, people with ASD are more likely than neurotypical people to have a history of childhood trauma (abuse by caregivers and peer bullying), often because of their neurodiverse features. Their family members may poorly understand them. Peers may perceive them to be inexplicably different. They may also have multiple other social stressors, abuse substances, and have relationship problems, all factors which escalate risks of violence in the general population, and equally so among those with ASD.[28]

Since violence is not a core feature of the neurodiverse when an individual with ASD commits violence, any comorbid conditions and social factors should be considered contributing variables.[29,30]

Interventions

School districts are now required by federal regulation to provide services for children diagnosed with ASD; however, the type of services offered is not standardized among communities. The most effective programs for children are individualized, comprehensive, and include the child's primary caregivers. Theory of mind training has been reported to increase autistic individuals' ability to understand other people's mental states, strengthen the capability to communicate, and increase the capacity to form positive relationships.[31]

These interventions are most helpful early in life and can help kids with ASD build communication and coping skills to increase their emotional resiliency and sense of success.

Parents concerned about any aspect of their child's development should consult with their pediatrician to discuss their observations. Indeed, any parent who observes social isolation or an intense preoccupation with violence should have their child assessed by a mental health professional. Whether or not they have ASD, early intervention can be a critical step in interrupting the pathway to violence.

Traumatic Brain Injury

Traumatic brain injury (TBI) is caused by a bump, jolt, or blow to the head that disrupts the brain's normal function. Not all blows to the head result in TBI. The severity of a brain injury can range from "mild" (a brief change in mental status) to "severe" (an extended period of unconsciousness or memory loss). Most TBIs that occur are mild and are commonly called concussions. They may occur with or without a loss of consciousness. Typically, a loss of consciousness indicates a more severe injury.[32]

TBI is the most significant cause of morbidity and mortality in children and young people. Unlike many other conditions, research on TBI and the long-term health consequences is extensive.[33]

TBI has been called a silent epidemic; it often flies under the radar of healthcare professionals. Many seemingly minor head injuries are never reported to physicians; thus, the impact of a head injury on an individual's subsequent behavior may never be understood.

TBI most often occurs from car accidents, falls, sports injuries, assaults, and fights. Adolescents and young men are the most at risk, and TBI is more common in those from lower socioeconomic levels.[34] The lifetime prevalence of TBI resulting in loss of consciousness is estimated to be between 8 percent and 12 percent. Even without the loss of consciousness, TBI can change the brain in multiple problematic ways.[35]

Consequences of TBI

Common effects of TBI include[36]

- memory problems;
- difficulties with attention and concentration;
- deficits in planning ability;
- impulsivity and aggression;
- poor social judgment;
- impaired decision making;
- personality changes;
- risk-taking behavior;
- emotional regulation problems;
- ADHD;
- interpersonal aggression; and
- criminality.

The prefrontal cortex, the "thinking" part of the brain, doesn't reach full maturity until age 25. Because of this, the brain is particularly vulnerable to the effects of TBI early in life, when systems for deducing emotions from facial expressions and voice are still developing. These systems are critically important for developing the theory of mind that allows one to understand and empathize with others.[37]

The effects of TBI can increase vulnerability for subsequent criminal behavior due to difficulty with regulating emotion, increased impulsivity, aggression, poor judgment, and risk-taking.[38]

Research has consistently shown that the prevalence of TBI in incarcerated adults is significantly higher in criminal offenders than in the general public. In the United States, 65 percent of incarcerated men and 72 percent of women reported a history of TBI with loss of consciousness.[39]

One of the fascinating true stories of TBI is the strange saga of Phineas Gage. In 1848 in Vermont, Gage, a foreman on a railroad construction crew, was injured when a dynamite accident blew a 13-pound iron tamping rod through the left side of his face and out the top front of his skull. The rod landed 80 feet away, along with much of his left frontal cortex.[40]

Despite his injuries, he remained conscious and only a few minutes later was sitting in an ox cart writing in his workbook. He recognized and reassured the physician who had been summoned to the scene. The wound continued to bleed for two days, followed by a virulent infection that rendered Gage semiconscious for a month. His condition was so poor that a coffin had been prepared. Nevertheless, his doctor continued treatment, and by the fifth week, the infection had resolved, and Gage had regained consciousness.[41]

Remarkably, Gage survived the horrifying brain injury, though he lost his left eye. However, in the months following the accident, his friends described him as "no longer Gage."[42]

Gage, who had been a well-liked, successful man, was followed for years by the physician who saved his life. Shortly after the accident, that doctor described him this way:

> The equilibrium, or balance, so to speak, between his intellectual faculties and animal propensities, seems to have been destroyed. His is fitful, irreverent, indulging at times in the grossest profanity (which was not previously his custom), manifesting but little deference for his fellows, impatient of restraint or advice when it conflicts with his desires, at times pertinaciously obstinate, yet capricious and vacillating, devising many plans of future operations, which are no sooner arranged than they are abandoned in turn for others appearing more feasible.[43]

Despite this, over several years, Gage gradually improved. He was eventually able to work as a stagecoach driver and was described as more appropriate in his behavior. It is thought that his remaining and undamaged right frontal cortex was able to eventually take on some of the functions of his missing left side.[44]

A brain anomaly that may have influenced a mass killer is the former Marine Corps sharpshooter in the 1966 Texas clock tower shooting. Despite his history as a childhood choir boy and an Eagle Scout (at age 12 he became the first Eagle Scout in history), this happily married man with an I.Q. of 139 inexplicably stabbed his wife and mother to death in their homes and then climbed the tower at the University of Texas to murder 16 other students.[45] He left notes with the bodies of his wife and his mother proclaiming love for them and expressing puzzlement at his actions.[46]

> I do not really understand myself these days. I am supposed to be an average, reasonable and intelligent young man. However, lately (I cannot recall when it started) I have been a victim of many unusual and irrational thoughts.
> It was after much thought that I decided to kill my wife, Kathy.... I love her dearly, and she has been as fine a wife to me as any man could ever hope to have. I cannot rationally pinpoint any specific reason for killing her. Let there be no doubt in your mind that I loved this woman with all my heart.[47]

The clock tower killer had visited multiple physicians with complaints of headaches and violent impulses the previous year. He told one psychiatrist that he was having fantasies of climbing to the top of the university clock tower and shooting people. The psychiatrist later reported that he did not take him seriously, and Gage did not return after an initial visit.[48]

Medical imaging at the time was not sufficiently advanced to obtain diagnostic scans of his brain. Thus, no cause for his symptoms could be determined.

The clock tower perpetrator's final note also requested an autopsy of his brain and that any money he had be given to a mental health foundation. At autopsy, it was discovered that he had a glioblastoma brain tumor pressing on his amygdala, the part of the brain involved in regulating emotion and aggression.[49]

Brain tumors can cause personality changes, particularly when a tumor is located in the frontal lobe. Such effects from these tumors include problems regulating one's behavior. Whether or not this tumor was a factor in the Texas clock tower murders remains a matter of speculation.

A recent study at Massachusetts General Hospital contains the first systematic review of 17 known cases where the onset of a brain lesion preceded criminal behavior. These researchers found that though the lesions were located in different brain regions, they were all part of the same functional neural network that allows neurons throughout the brain to cooperate on specific cognitive tasks.[50]

Some researchers have identified a "criminality-associated network" closely related to neural networks previously linked with moral decision making, including theory of mind and values-based decision making.[51] This network helps one appreciate how one's actions would make another person feel hurt or scared and judge the outcomes of actions as good or bad. Based upon this finding, it is speculated that problems in many parts of the brain might influence violent behavior. This possibility will continue to be studied by neuroscientists.

Questions about culpability due to brain injury are often raised in criminal cases when a perpetrator has been shown to be operating with a brain that is functionally deficient in reasoning, impulse control, and empathy. If the effects of brain trauma caused their behavior, were they acting under their own free will? Are they morally responsible for their actions? Should we view them as patients or perpetrators—or both?

An additional relevant factor in the Texas clock tower shooter's case is that he had a history of childhood trauma. He was raised in an authoritarian home with a violent, abusive father.[52] So we add that on top of the brain tumor. There can be layer upon layer of complexity.

Abuse or Psychological Trauma

Trauma is another relevant factor that can tie these problems together synergistically. Trauma can be physical, psychological, or both. It may occur in one isolated event or as a result of chronic, ongoing events in the context of one's home.

Trauma is a somewhat elastic concept because people can be impacted very differently by similar events. We all have different capacities for coping with trauma.

Psychological trauma is defined as a normal response to an experience that is deeply emotionally disturbing. Broadly speaking, many everyday life events are traumatic, including serious illnesses or injuries, a car accident, or the death of a loved one.[53] Everyone will experience some degree of trauma in life, though due to circumstances largely out of our control, some people certainly experience more than others.

Sustained trauma early in life is particularly problematic because the effects can last a lifetime. Children who are raised in abusive or neglectful environments have a very different subjective experience of life than children who have been well cared for in stable homes. Parental substance abuse, violence, harsh punishment, neglect, poverty, or homelessness are unfortunately common. This kind of chronic trauma can cause changes in the brain that affect the way a personality develops.[54]

A child's early life experiences provide the building blocks for the developing brain. In the complex epigenetics process, genes provide the blueprint for what is possible, and life experience influences and shapes how the genes manifest. Safe, stable, and nurturing relationships early in life support healthy development. However, as we know, there are myriad reasons that millions of children are raised in less-than-optimal environments.

Trauma Research

One of the most extensive investigations of childhood abuse and neglect, the Adverse Childhood Experiences study, was conducted by the CDC through the Kaiser Permanente Health Maintenance Organization from 1995 to 1997.[55]

A questionnaire about adverse childhood experiences was mailed to 13,494 adults who had completed a standardized medical evaluation through the Kaiser HMO; 9,508 responded. The specific negative childhood experiences included in the study were[56]

- physical, emotional, or sexual abuse;
- emotional or physical neglect;
- violent treatment of the mother;
- parental substance abuse;
- parental mental illness;
- parental separation/divorce; and
- incarcerated parent.

The number of categories of these adverse childhood experiences was then compared to measures of adult health status, disease, and risky adult behavior. Logistic regression was used to adjust for effects of demographic factors on the association between the cumulative number of categories of childhood trauma exposures and risk factors for the leading causes of death in adult life.

The results showed that more than half of respondents reported at least one of these traumatic adverse childhood experiences. One-fourth reported more than two categories. Persons who had experienced four or more categories of childhood trauma exposure, compared to those who had experienced none, had a 4- to 12-fold increased health risk for alcoholism, drug abuse, depression, and suicide attempt; a 2- to 4-fold increase in smoking, poor self-rated health, over 50 sexual intercourse partners, and sexually transmitted disease; and a 1.4- to 1.6-fold increase in physical inactivity and severe obesity. The number of categories of adverse childhood exposures showed a graded relationship to the presence of adult diseases, including ischemic heart disease, cancer, chronic lung disease, skeletal fractures, and liver disease. The seven categories of adverse childhood experiences were strongly interrelated, and persons with multiple types of childhood exposure were likely to have multiple health risk factors later in life.[57]

The study concluded, "We found a strong graded relationship between the breadth of exposure to abuse or household dysfunction during childhood and multiple risk factors for several of the leading causes of death in adults." Alarmingly, people who average six or more on ACE die 20 years earlier than the average American.

There have been criticisms of the study. Some feel it was too limited in scope, undercounted adverse experiences, and misrepresented social distribution. Race and ethnicity of participants were not factored in; neither was socioeconomic status. From this perspective, more relevant variables should also be assessed.[58]

Nonetheless, there is no doubt that early experience with sustained abuse or neglect changes the developing brain in harmful ways and has health consequences that can last a lifetime.

How the Brain Adapts to Trauma

The fight/flight response is the nervous system's natural response to a perceived threat and results in flooding of the stress hormones adrenaline and cortisol that affect the entire body. This system is designed to help us survive danger in the short term. However, when the threat is sustained, the developing brain makes permanent adaptations, which continue long past the traumatic events.[59]

Children who experience abuse or neglect experience changes in three different brain systems: the threat system, the reward system, and the memory system.

- Changes in the threat system result in a heightened threat sensitivity called hypervigilance. Hypervigilance can cause one to misinterpret everyday events as threatening as well misperceive others' intentions. A person with increased sensitivity to threats may be prone to paranoid thinking.
- Neglect from caregivers causes changes in the brain's reward system, which is what motivates our behavior. Over time, the brain responds less actively to positive social cues. This type of change can result in difficulties making friends and reduced motivation for social and academic achievement.
- Changes in the memory system result in difficulty remembering positive experiences since negative experiences become more prominent in the memory system. When individuals' memories are primarily negative, they have learned to expect the worst in life and fail to see positive options. Everyday memories can also become less detailed. This type of change is problematic because we all have to draw on positive past experiences to learn how to navigate new situations.

Together these brain adaptations can put children at greater risk of experiencing future mental health conditions. These traumatized children are more apt to experience learning problems, emotional dysregulation, hypersensitivity to stress, and greater impulsivity.[60]

These children have a more challenging time developing positive, trusting, intimate relationships with others. Hypersensitivity to potential threats may become a traumatized child's norm, resulting in consistent overreactions to minor slights. Some children with a history of trauma have an increased tendency to be violent with peers, which results in a cascade of additional stressful events such as disciplinary actions in school and subsequent rejection by peers.[61] Traumatized children have more significant difficulties adjusting to everyday stresses like moving to a new neighborhood or new school. Regular life is simply more daunting. Strong social and family support increases one's capacity for coping.

When we look at the many interwoven factors that make each of us unique, the layers of complexity of human behavior become evident. It is possible to be on the autism spectrum, experience a head injury, *and* suffer childhood trauma. A person can have such a history as well as a major mental illness or personality disorder. Adults with these complicated histories are over-represented in the prison population; their lives are more challenging, they experience more health problems, and they don't live as long.

But some mass killers have not experienced any of these factors. Some were exceptionally well-cared for as children, never abused, from middle-class homes with intact families. Many had no history of trauma.

Though many factors increase vulnerability, people worldwide have autism, head injuries, and trauma histories. Yet, mass killings remain predominantly unique to America.

There are yet more variables involved.

10

Racial, Ethnic, and Politically Motivated Violence

"Random violence is not detrimental to our cause, because we need to convince Americans that violence against non-whites is desirable or at least not something worth opposing anyways, because there's no way to remove a hundred million people without a massive element of violence."[1]—*The Daily Stormer*

Two patterns have shifted in recent years. Since 2014, there has been a dramatic rise in mass killings in the United States driven by extremist ideologies, and overall, these events have become deadlier.[2] Most of these attacks, including those in Europe, have been perpetrated by individuals identified as right-wing on the political spectrum.[3] All extremist killings in the United States in 2018 had links to right-wing extremism.[4] The trend has since continued. Right-wing attacks and plots accounted for over 90 percent of mass violence events between January and May in 2020.[5] In these kinds of attacks, individuals have not been targeted; instead, entire groups or communities are singled out because of something they represent to the killer.

In this chapter, we examine the issues of domestic terrorism and the patterns of extremist thinking so often evidenced by mass killers and the ways they are influenced by online culture and politics. The history of white supremacist movements is explored, along with the rise of paramilitary militias.

Increasingly, public mass killings have been labeled acts of domestic terrorism, inspired by ideologies based on racial, ethnic, religious, or gender hatred. Affiliation with such hate groups is increasing globally, and those who align with this ideology discover these groups on the internet; most devotees never actually meet in person.[6] Though most extremist-motivated mass killers act alone, their ideas are generated and inspired by these loosely organized groups.[7]

Since the 9/11 attacks on the Twin Towers, there has been a persistent myth that Islamic extremists perpetrate most terror attacks in the United States and Europe. In truth, data is clear: extreme-right attacks far outnumber those perpetrated by Islamists or by the far-left.[8]

Christchurch, New Zealand; Poway, California; Charlottesville, Virginia; Gilroy, California; Louisville, Kentucky; Pittsburgh, Pennsylvania; Oak Creek, Wisconsin; Parkland, Florida; El Paso, Texas; Munich, Germany; Paris, France; Utoya, Norway. These perpetrators, and many others, were active in online, white supremacist networks that played a role in inciting them to commit mass public killings.[9]

Defining which mass killings should be designated as terror incidents has been another area of controversy. Since research on terrorism has been done by those from diverse disciplines, there have been differing conclusions on how broadly the term "terrorism" should be defined. Some analysts emphasize that a political motive is required to meet the definition criteria, while others broaden the definition to include those with social reasons.[10]

Terrorism is defined in the Code of Federal Regulations as "the unlawful use of force and violence against persons or property to intimidate or coerce a government, the civilian population, or any segment thereof, in furtherance of political or social objectives."[11]

While not all mass killings in the United States have been committed with a clear political agenda, we see a dramatic increase in those with specific social objectives. This is particularly evident in multiple clusters of violence that have been motivated by racism and ethnic hate—primarily white supremacy—as displayed in thriving online communities.[12,13]

The reasons for this are clear if we track the pathway that leads to violence.

Extremist Ways of Thinking

Whether or not motives are political, social, or both, violent extremists share similarities with other mass killers in the five key factor areas (personal, group, community, sociopolitical, ideological).[14] Thus, extremist behavior can best be understood by examining these factors and the intersections between them. Though specific political ideologies and group affiliations frequently shift, violent extremists' common personal traits are consistent across ideologies and vary little over time.[15] These include the following extremist ways of thinking[16,17]:

- They frame themselves as defenders of righteousness, patriots, or crusaders.
- They are preoccupied with the perception of themselves as victims of persecution.
- They are paranoid and prone to conspiracy thinking.
- They are obsessed with ideological purity, no matter the ideology's content, and are unwilling to compromise or consider alternate points of view.
- They are consistently angry and often prone to fantasies of vengeance.
- They advocate violence and are often willing to die for their cause.

Though specific ideological tenets of various extremism flavors vary, the thinking patterns remain much the same; we can see numerous manifestations worldwide in modern history.[18]

Two of the most notorious domestic terrorists in the United States were the Unabomber, active from 1975 through 1995, and the Oklahoma City Bomber in 1995. The Unabomber identified as far-left on the political spectrum; the Oklahoma City Bomber identified as far-right. Despite their superficial ideological differences, their psychological processes were very similar. They were both paranoid conspiracists who were persistently angry, vengeful, obsessive, and self-righteous. Both were willing to die for their cause. Neither had empathy for others, and both viewed their crimes as virtuous. After their arrests, both had no remorse.

Politically leftwing, anarchist violence spread from Europe to the United States in the late 1800s, then died down in the 1930s when unrest diminished after the government addressed the underlying causes of income inequality and worker's rights. A notable exception to this was the Weather Underground, active in the United States in the late 1960s and 1970s, which organized in opposition to the Vietnam War. Though leftwing extremists continue to be ideologically active in certain areas, extremism's most deadly flavor in recent years has been that of far-right white supremacy. Racism has increasingly been a unifying theme for contemporary mass killers, as evidenced in their online postings and manifestos.[19]

Research analysis of white supremacists' online posts has found that anger is the prevailing emotion, and it is expressed in various ways. Among the variants of anger commonly seen is vengeance, including sadism. Users of white supremacist, online forums frequently discuss sadistic fantasies of harming, killing, mutilating, and the extermination of racial minorities.[20]

Like other flavors of potential killers, racist extremists display a paranoid thinking style and entertain bizarre notions of imaginary oppression. White supremacists misidentify the cause of their problems in life, framing personal difficulties as the inevitable result of discrimination against them for being white. This shared fallacy escalates the level of fear within the group that this "enemy," a racial or ethnic minority, seeks to harm them physically. This begins the process of creating and dehumanizing scapegoats who may soon become targets of wrath.[21]

Extremists exhibit both victim and virtue signaling, creating a false narrative that justifies their behavior in which they frame themselves as heroes. They identify as warriors for justice, inspire one another, and compete to top others' kill scores. Their attacks tend to come in waves, as high-profile killings inspire imitators.[22]

Many of these individuals drift from one iteration of extremist ideology to another, sometimes even shifting between groups with opposing ideologies. Some leftwing extremists have moved to the far-right; there have been multiple cases where a self-identified white supremacist converted to Islam and subsequently attempted to affiliate with ISIS.[23,24]

Extremism, like other aspects of human behavior, can also be viewed on a continuum. Some people buy into extremist narratives a bit, others fully. For a small number, it becomes an organizing principle of life. While most will never act out violently, those who do can be deadly. Those with narcissistic, paranoid, and psychopathic traits are most apt to engage in violence.

The critical point to understand is that, despite their rationalizations, these individuals become involved in extremist hate organizations for the social and psychological benefits they receive from the group—the ideology is just their excuse.

We all need to belong somewhere, to feel valued. Such groups provide camaraderie and justification for their anger, along with a sense of brotherhood and a place to fit in. As paranoia and sadistic urges are normalized, group members support one another in collecting injustices and sharing strategies for retribution. The progression on the pathway to violence can happen in a matter of months.

The New White Supremacy

"White supremacy" is the term used to describe various belief systems that center on the tenet that the white race is inherently superior to others and that white people should live separately from other races and ethnic groups. It encompasses the idea that social, economic, and political systems should primarily benefit those who are white, allowing them to maintain dominance over people of other races.[25]

White supremacists advance the notion that white people are genetically superior and have their own culture, superior to other cultures. As a full-fledged ideology, white supremacy is more encompassing than simple racial bigotry or prejudice.[26]

In recent years white supremacists have moved from the fringes of society into the modern mainstream. The Anti-Defamation League reports that incidents of white supremacist propaganda distributed across the country more than doubled each year from 2017 to 2019. This continued to amplify in 2020 and 2021. Their messaging has become increasingly sophisticated as racial hate is veiled behind language emphasizing patriotism. "America First" and "One nation against invasion" offer a softer invitation into the fold, which ultimately advocates genocide.[27]

Racist extremists use coded language designed to veil their motives and make racism more palatable. "White pride" and "White empowerment" put more benign spins on the ideology based upon hatred.[28]

While they may venerate Adolf Hitler and Nazi Germany as well as the defunct Confederacy of the American South, you can't tell by looking at them. Though some racists fit the trope of an older white man in a hooded Klan robe or Nazi regalia, today's racist is more apt to be an athletic college student wearing jeans and a t-shirt or a young professional in polo shirt and khakis. They can be indistinguishable from any one of our neighbors.[29]

The adherents are typically politically far-right, an ideology that encompasses ethnocentrism, xenophobia, authoritarianism, and populism. They favor a social Darwinist view of "survival of the fittest," the idea that one group of people advance in society because they are innately superior.

They are often anti-feminist, anti–Semitic, anti-gay, anti-trans, and venerate a warrior mentality.[30] They tend to celebrate traditional gender roles. Like all extremists, they are inflexible, rigid, obsessed with the purity of their beliefs, and have limited insight into their thoughts and feelings. These individuals latch on to extremist ideologies in an attempt to make sense of the world and as a way to express complex emotions.

White supremacists believe that the white race is in danger of extinction from a rise of nonwhite immigrants and that Jews are engaged in various forms of societal and political manipulation. These conspiracy theories go back hundreds of years and are rooted in a paranoid thinking style.

Violence is often advocated to achieve racial segregation, though this aspect of the movement is generally hidden from outsiders. White supremacist networks are usually informal, fluid, and overlapping and organize under different names.[31]

The recent rise of militant white supremacists in the United States and Europe has taken most of the mainstream by surprise since they have stayed under the radar of popular culture. Like the maniacal killer in the horror movie who just won't die, white supremacy keeps rising again to shock and horrify us.

The non-profit Southern Poverty Law Center (SPLC) tracks such hate groups across the country; SPLC identifies over 800 racist and anti–Semitic groups currently active in the United States.[32]

Whether they call themselves white nationalists, Oath Keepers, Atomwaffen, Ayran skinheads, the Base, Rise Above Movement (RAM), Klansmen, neo-Confederates, neo–Nazis, the alt-right, Proud

Boys, patriot militias, or any of a dozen other names that frequently morph and evolve, they fly under a common banner of disdain for those of other races and ethnicities, particularly blacks, Latinos, Jews, and Muslims.

White supremacists operate and organize online, creating cultural spaces that promote and celebrate violence. These groups use social media, online computer games, and online chat forums to recruit young men to the cause. Individuals who enter these online spaces without a specific political agenda are often influenced by those who do. Decentralized and loosely organized, these groups are difficult to track.[33]

These online recruitment tactics and the glorification of martyrdom mirror those initially developed very effectively by the Islamic State, which successfully recruited young men worldwide.[34]

In the same way, the U.S. government has sought to infiltrate ISIS, there have been many attempts by FBI undercover operatives to infiltrate white supremacist organizations. Multiple violent plots have been interrupted from this surveillance.[35]

For years multiple U.S. government agencies have identified right-wing white supremacist extremism as a severe threat, including the Department of Homeland Security in 2009,[36] West Point's Combating Terrorism Center in 2012, and the U.S. Attorney General's office in 2014.[37] This danger continues to be confirmed by current researchers from around the world.[38] Almost immediately after the election in 2021, President Joe Biden's administration made the fight against hate-based domestic extremist violence a "national priority area."[39]

In March 2021, The Department of Homeland Security (DHS) announced a $20 million grant program to help communities across the country develop innovative capabilities to combat domestic terrorism and targeted violence. Secretary of DHS Alex Mayorkas stated on the DHS website:

> Domestic violent extremism and targeted violence are two of the gravest threats facing our homeland today. Over the past few years, the United States has experienced an increasing number of targeted attacks by disaffected individuals motivated by a combination of extremist ideologies and personal grievances. This investment in local communities will help our partners develop sustainable capabilities to address an evolving threat environment, including by preventing attacks and online radicalization.

The number one U.S. think tank for defense and national security is the Center for Strategic & International Studies (CSIS). In their June 2020, report the CSIS analyzed 893 violent plots and attacks came to these conclusions: "Far right terrorism has significantly outpaced terrorism from other types of perpetrators, including from far-left networks and individuals inspired by the Islamic State and al-Qaeda. Right-wing attacks and plots account for the majority of all terrorist incidents in the United States since 1994, and the total number of right-wing attacks and plots have grown significantly during the past six years."

The CSIS report concludes that right-wing attacks and violent plots account for most incidents of mass violence in the United States and are expected to grow steadily in coming years.[40]

The FBI also identified white supremacists as the number one terror threat in the United States. Aside from major acts of violence against groups, white supremacists are behind many hate crimes against individuals. We have no accurate data on how many hate crimes actually occur in the United States since not all local police departments report data to the FBI. Many hate crimes are not designated as such by local law enforcement.[41]

Right-wing attacks are not isolated to specific parts of the country. Attacks have occurred in 42 states, Washington, D.C., Puerto Rico, and multiple European locations.[42] On January 6, 2021, a group of thousands of far-right conspiracy theorists attempted a violent insurrection at the U.S. Capitol, threatening Congress members' lives. This unprecedented attack caused shockwaves around the world which continue to reverberate.[43]

Unite the Right

Following the racially motivated Charleston church shooting in 2015, many local governments in the South were confronted by grassroots, antiracist movements demanding that Confederate monuments and statues be removed from public spaces. As part of this process, a statue of General Robert E. Lee was set to be removed from the Charlottesville, Virginia, Emancipation Park in the summer of 2017.[44]

In response to the plan to remove the statue, the newly invigorated white supremacist movement mobilized for battle. In August 2017, a national call went out online to white supremacist networks to organize a weekend event in mid–August at Charlottesville. They called this event the "Unite the Right" rally. These activists were younger, many college-age, some active-duty members of the military. Attendees traveled to Charlottesville from 35 states across the country, with the stated goal to unify the white supremacist movement and oppose removing the statue. They arrived in Charlottesville prepared for violence, which began on Friday night just before the official rally planned for the following day.[45]

Most of us watched the events unfold on network news stations. Much of the world was horrified. Who could have imagined we'd see a crowd of neo–Nazis shouting racist slogans and marching en masse in 21st-century America?

Their burning tiki torches cast an eerie light as they marched to a statue of Thomas Jefferson on the Grounds of the University of Virginia, where they were met by 30 antiracist university students who had formed a circle around the base of the statue. Violence erupted as the counter-protestors were attacked with pepper spray, clubs, flag poles, and thrown water bottles. It was only a taste of what would follow the next day.[46]

Nearby, at St. Paul's Memorial Church, a diverse crowd of 500 antiracist counter-protestors held a prayer service in response. The message they chanted was "Let's take that love to the streets."

Vehicular Attack

At sunrise on the following day, a clergy group held a morning service at another nearby church. When the service finished, many unarmed attendees and counter-protesters marched to Emancipation Park in downtown Charlottesville, where the white supremacist rally was to be held from noon to five o'clock. The massive crowd of white supremacists was already there.

The counter-protestors linked arms to face the armed white supremacists, singing "This Little Light of Mine."[47]

Skirmishes began again; pushing, shoving, and pepper spray attacks quickly escalating to rock and bottle throwing. Eventually, the crowds were dispersed by Charlottesville police, and the white supremacists began walking to another park about a mile north to continue their rally. That was when it turned deadly.[48]

A large crowd of peaceful counter-protestors were walking down a nearby street when they were approached in an intersection by a slow-moving gray Dodge Challenger. The 20-year-old driver stopped when he reached the marchers, then backed up for a block to accelerate at a higher rate of speed back toward the crowd.[49]

He plowed directly into them; bodies flew up off the hood of his car and into the air as people screamed. The driver then accelerated in reverse, hitting more marchers. One 32-year-old woman died of blunt force trauma to the chest. Thirty others were injured.[50]

Leakage from this perpetrator had been abundant, with foreshadowing everywhere. Acquaintances of the killer stated that he had been obsessed with white supremacy and Nazis since middle school. Memes and symbols of the far-right filled his social media pages, and he had a history of violence.[51] He told his mother he was attending a Donald Trump rally that day; she subsequently stated that she was unaware of his ties to white supremacy.[52]

Horrific video of the vehicular attack was spread worldwide, as Americans were forced to face the fact that violent racism still thrives beneath the surface of the supposed melting-pot of the United States.

Widely distributed video of the events in Charlottesville allowed many of the attendees to be identified by law enforcement and journalists. In partnership with *PBS Frontline*, Journalist A.C. Thompson of *ProPublica* tracked several down and publicly exposed them in the 2019 award-winning documentary film *Documenting Hate.*

Some eventually faced social consequences, including the loss of their jobs. Others were outed as members of the U.S. military and faced disciplinary action and discharge, including an 18-year-old Marine filmed repeatedly attacking counter-protestors at the rally.

Since then, decisions have been made within the white supremacist movement to guard their anonymity and avoid large public demonstrations. However, their lower public profile should not be taken to indicate that they have fallen back; their online ranks continue to swell, as attacks by solo individuals continue to be encouraged by white suprem-acist networks.[53]

Racism is alive and well and thriving in online spaces where adher-ents can easily remain anonymous.

Online Cultural Influencers

In the last two decades, the internet has revolutionized the concept of culture. Culture is no longer limited to the family we grew up in and the people who surround us in our communities. Culture has moved online through social media and platforms like YouTube; its influences are powerful and extend far outside the virtual world.

Culture teaches us our place in the world as well as our values and priorities. Culture gives meaning to our lives. It also teaches who should be feared and whom it is okay to kill.

Online communities dedicated to a single theme become closed cultural spaces where alternate points of view are screened out, making online culture particularly powerful. Nothing is censored, and only one point of view is allowed. The cloak of invisibility afforded by the inter-net enables members of these cultures to remain incognito in the outer world and thus free of fear of judgment or reprisal.[54]

The internet allows for the rapid spread of extremist ideas, which function like viruses of the mind. Coalescing in cyber-space, they spread faster online than they ever could otherwise.[55]

Groups cross-pollinate as individuals move between loosely orga-nized, decentralized groups. Influencers mainly target younger men who have military experience and those already affiliated with other hate groups.[56]

Outwardly, members of these online cultures blend into their com-munities with the appearance of normality; they may hide their extrem-ist beliefs from family members. They are likely wearing polo shirts and khakis rather than traditional Klan robes.[57]

At various times, such groups have found homes on internet sites such as 4chan, 8chan, Parler, Reddit, and secure messaging platforms like Discord, Telegram, and Gab. The choice of platforms constantly shifts, making it difficult for authorities to monitor what they are doing.

When outed on one platform, they move to another, gravitating to platforms free of gatekeepers; they go to great lengths to avoid detection.[58]

Violent "heroes" are revered. The Norwegian killer is honored by many as a warrior and saint; he's cited consistently as a source of inspiration by the far-right.[59] Many have tried to imitate him, following the guidelines for his vision of holy war as set out in his voluminous manifesto.[60] Multiple attacks have been planned on the anniversary of the Norwegian school children's massacre, including an attack on the same date in February 2020, in Munich, when a German white supremacist shot and killed nine Muslim immigrants. He posted videos online just before the attack, calling for the extermination of people from Africa, Asia, and the Middle East. Evidencing psychotic thinking, the Munich perpetrator also stated that he believed he was a victim of mind control and that he had influenced Donald Trump to focus on "America First, Buy American, Hire American."[61]

Politics of Hate

The ideas are not new. Hateful rhetoric against minority groups has long been used to mobilize a populace behind a political party by creating a common enemy and scapegoat. In the classic "us versus them" pattern, inflammatory language about racial and ethnic minorities is often used to precipitate civil war and genocide. Polarized societies with substantial economic disparities are particularly vulnerable to extremist violence and the rise of authoritarian leaders.[62]

Words matter, particularly when they come from the mouths of political leaders. What politicians say directly affects our perceptions and how we subsequently behave.[63] Political leaders have the power to polarize and divide a populace or to bring them together.

The election of Barack Obama in 2008, the nation's first Black president, spurred a dramatic resurgence of white supremacist activity.[64] Some Republican politicians whipped up the frenzy by maintaining that Obama was a Muslim with terrorist ties who was not born in the United States, despite copious documented evidence to the contrary.[65]

The backlash to Obama's election was immediate. An example was an event that occurred on the night of his election at Baylor University in Texas, where students found a noose hanging from a tree on campus. Extremists burned Obama signs in a massive bonfire nearby, and shouting matches broke out as racist extremists made violent threats to Black students and Obama supporters.[66]

The subsequent election of other politicians sympathetic to white nationalist goals further caused their numbers to swell.[67] In a data analysis going back to the 1950s, Arie Perliger, professor in the School of Criminology and Justice Studies at the University of Massachusetts Lowell, has shown a strong correlation of far-right violence with the Republican control of Congress. Extremists perceive conservative politicians as more apt to be accepting of their agenda.[68]

The election of Donald Trump in 2016, whose platform was centered on a fear of racial minorities and the plan to build a wall between the United States and Mexico, is considered a pivotal moment in the white supremacist movement.[69] Groups who had stayed in the shadows for decades suddenly felt welcomed by a president who repeatedly warned of "an invasion of illegals" and made building a giant wall to keep them out a foundation of his agenda. Such talk played upon racial anxieties and increased social tensions.[70]

Affiliations with white supremacist groups ballooned during the Trump administration. In 2017 there were beatings, shootings, and stabbings at pro–Trump rallies in Berkeley, Anaheim, Huntington Beach, Sacramento, and Portland when members of the far-right clashed with counter-protestors. Three of the four deadliest mass shootings in U.S. history occurred during the Trump administration.[71]

At a televised Florida campaign rally in May 2019 at Panama City, Trump shouted at his fans, "How do you stop these people from crossing the border?"

"Shoot them!" yelled someone in the crowd.

Trump responded with an amused smirk, "That's only in the panhandle you can get away with that stuff. Only in the panhandle."[72]

Trump was viewed as sympathetic to white supremacist goals, and he became a figurehead and rallying point to the movement. Speaking of Donald Trump, one young white supremacist stated in an interview with *ProPublica,* "He has opened up a door; it's up to us to take the initiative."[73]

The Trump administration scaled back U.S. government tracking of domestic terrorist extremist groups, a move that defied logic considering the proliferation of these groups and the clear danger they pose.[74]

The El Paso Walmart shooter posted several photos on Facebook that telegraphed his intention to kill people of color. In one image he had "liked" on Twitter, the word "T R U M P" is spelled out on the floor with nine carefully arranged guns spelling out the President's last name.[75] In his manifesto on the day of the murders, he wrote, "I'm here to stop the Hispanic invasion of Texas." This perpetrator has also been referred to as a "saint" by other white supremacists.

Countries where politicians weave hate speech into their political rhetoric subsequently experience a dramatic increase in extremist violence. Examples include Germany in the 1920s and 1930s; Argentina in the 1970s; Turkey in the late 1970s and early 1980s; Rwanda in the 1990s. Recently this has occurred in India, Poland, Russia, Colombia, Egypt, Ukraine, the Philippines, Italy, Greece, Sri Lanka, and Iraq.[76]

Most Americans never thought it would happen here.

During the Covid-19 pandemic, Trump repeatedly blamed China for the illness, often referring to it as "the China virus." As Trump spread vitriol and disinformation, discrimination against those of Asian descent soared, as did unprovoked violent attacks. Between March 2020 and March 2021, more than 3,800 hate crimes against Asian Americans were reported. Seventy percent of the victims were women.[77]

The rise in violent attacks against Asian Americans became so extreme that a subcommittee of the House Judiciary Committee had planned hearings on hate crimes against Asians just before a mass shooting in three Asian spas in Atlanta on March 16, 2021.

NPR journalist Yamiche Alcindor said to *PBS Frontline* regarding the Trump presidency, "It was the beginning of a time in American where people came to realize that America is not just a place where racist ideals can exist; it's a place where racist ideals can be fueled by the White House."[78]

The United States Military and Paramilitary Militias

All branches of the U.S. military officially maintain a zero-tolerance policy for affiliation with white supremacist groups, but this does not mean that the military is free of white supremacy.[79] Access to combat training is precious to those plotting a race war, which is the ultimate goal of the white supremacy movement. In online discussions, one white supremacist advocated for others to join the military: "The U.S. military gives great training ... you learn how to fight, and to survive."[80]

White supremacists often draw inspiration from the armed forces. Those who have "experience with firearms, explosives, and combat training share those skills with other members."[81]

Multiple participants in the Unite the Right rally were active-duty members of the military. Many who participated in the attack on the Capitol were active and former members of the military. White supremacists have recently been identified in the Army, National Guard, Marines, and Coast Guard.[82]

And they coordinate with those in other countries. In 2017 RAM traveled to Ukraine to celebrate Hitler's birthday and train with a Ukrainian National Guard's paramilitary unit—a group associated with neo–Nazism.[83]

Following the January 2021 violence at the Capitol, the first Black defense secretary underscored the need to rid the military of "racists" and "extremists."[84]

New enlistees in the U.S. military are currently screened for "aberrant thinking and behavior" in a process that involves police records checks and records for criminal convictions. Additionally, recruits are asked to sign a statement and complete a screening form to deny gang-related affiliations and associations with racist or extremist organizations.[85] It is questionable if these measures are sufficient, as many slip through the cracks.

In 2017 *Military Times* reported that 25 percent of active-duty service members surveyed said they'd had contact with white supremacists in the ranks.[86]

In 2020, the U.S. House of Representatives unanimously passed the Domestic Terrorism act, which would have allowed the Department of Defense to begin tracking and reporting white supremacist activity in the military. It would have required the initiation of a central database of investigations as well as criminal and administrative actions and the results of each. The bill did not pass the Senate.[87]

So-called "civilian militias" adopt military-speak and battle attire, often creating ragtag groups of primarily white males with murky ideologies centering on gun rights.[88] At least 25 percent of militia members were formerly in the military. Their numbers have ebbed and flowed since the 1990s but became more prominent under the Obama administration as part of the racist backlash to the first Black U.S. president's election. Some militia members became self-appointed guardians of the border between the United States and Mexico, in some cases murdering immigrants attempting to enter the United States.[89]

Militant pro-gun activists, many members of militias are insurrectionists who seek to overthrow the federal government. They were a major force in the 2021 siege of the Capitol. Framing themselves as patriots, membership in militia groups swelled dramatically under Trump. These groups frequently made a show of force at pro–Trump demonstrations, where they appeared in military attire, armed with military-style weapons and rifles.[90] On occasion, they besieged state legislatures by making a show of force demonstration and prominently flaunting their firearms at legislative meetings.[91]

There is very little coherent ideology among militia groups. Though not generally acknowledged publicly, most maintain a dedication to white supremacy and display the paranoid thinking style, xenophobia, urge to dominate, and eagerness for violence common to other far-right extremists. Most call themselves "defenders of freedom and patriots," despite their opposition to the federal government. Some have posted calls for armed conflict with law enforcement and civil war; others have attempted to align with law enforcement by offering "security services" at right-wing events.[92,93]

From 2016 to 2021, there have been multiple arrests for bomb-making as well as death threats against Democratic political candidates by those affiliated with militia groups.[94]

In May 2020, a 47-year-old militia member in Schleicher, Texas, began a personal war while live streaming video on Facebook. Ranting anti-government sentiments, he acknowledged that he suffered from anxiety and depression. Dressed in full military tactical gear, he stated, "You have a tyrannical government that sees fit to spread fear, virus nonsense, and tyrannical edicts among the people."[95] He fired his rifle at his neighbors, who called the police. He explained, "I have asked and asked and asked when we were gonna have a leader to stand up and fight against this stuff. I didn't want to be the one who has to do it. But it looks like I'm going to have to do it by myself. And that's okay. I'm okay with God. God's on my side. God knows I'm right."

He was shot and killed after firing at officers; his videos were circulated among other militia groups, where he was described as a martyr.[96]

White Supremacist Glossary

White supremacists use coded language in order to maintain a low public profile. Following are examples from the Anti-Defamation League Glossary[97]:

- **Hate crime** is a criminal act against a person or property in which the perpetrator targets victims because of a victim's race, national origin, ethnicity, sexual orientation, or gender.
- **Hate group** is an organization of those whose beliefs, activities, and purposes are primary based on a shared hostility towards of different races, ethnicities, races, gender, or sexual orientation.
- **Far-Right** (also called **the Extreme Right**) is ultra-nationalistic, racist, theocratic, chauvinistic, homophobic, anti-communist, and reactionary. They advocate for the elimination of social welfare programs. Some far-right groups state that they are patriots and advocates of the U.S. government; others seek to overthrow the government. They are generally anti-feminist and often advocate a return to traditional gender roles.
- **White Pride** is a white supremacist slogan that attempts to reframe their beliefs as a positive expression of ethnic pride while minimizing the reality that they are racists.
- **White nationalism** organizes around the principle that white people alone should inhabit and dominate Western countries. White nationalists advocate for policies to reverse changing demographics and the loss of a distinct, white majority. Ending nonwhite immigration is a top priority as well as ending multiculturalism and interracial marriages. White nationalists would like to return to an America that predates the Civil Rights Act of 1964.

- **White genocide** is a prominent conspiracy theory among white supremacists that immigration, globalism, and abortion rights are part of a larger conspiracy to exterminate white people. Many believe that "forced assimilation" is part of a Jewish plot to take over the world. Those who believe in white genocide often express concerns regarding the diminishing birth rate among whites and encourage members of their groups to procreate. These groups often promote violent action to keep the white race from "disappearing."
- **Mainstreamers** believe that infiltrating and subverting the existing political institutions is the only realistic path to white supremacist power rather than an overt race war. These individuals disguise their racist agendas and sometimes seek legitimate public office.
- **ZOG** is a white supremacist acronym for "Zionist Occupied Government," which reflects the common white supremacist belief that the U.S. government is controlled by Jews. This has resulted in white supremacist slogans such as "Smash ZOG," "Kill ZOG," or "Death to ZOG."
- **Race war** is a common white supremacist goal of an apocalyptic clash between races, sometimes called the second American Civil War, pitting whites against Blacks, Hispanics, Jews, and other minorities in a cataclysmic battle with the goal of establishing an entirely white, non–Jewish society. The concept goes back decades. Charles Manson's purpose for the murders committed by his followers was to start a race war between whites and Blacks.
- **Accelerationism** the idea that Western governments are corrupt, and as a result, white supremacists should accelerate chaos, discord, and race war through violence against racial minorities and Jews. The ultimate goal is to cause a social collapse to rebuild a white-dominated society. Accelerationists are motivated to accelerate the pace of societal collapse.
- **Boogaloo** the coded term for race war, also known as the Second American Civil War. Those promoting the war, often called Boogaloo Boys, are a subset of the paramilitary militia movement who advocate violent uprisings against the American

government and their left-wing opponents in hopes of initiating a race war. They are typically proponents of various paranoid conspiracy theories.

- **Holocaust denial** propaganda started after World War II as a form of virulent anti–Semitism. Holocaust deniers claim that the holocaust never happened or that the Nazis killed far fewer numbers of Jews.

Past to Present

> We hold these truths to be self-evident, that all men are created equal, that they are endowed by their Creator with certain unalienable Rights, that among these are Life, Liberty and the pursuit of Happiness.—*Declaration of Independence* (1776)

The United States of America is a study in contradictions. Though Thomas Jefferson authored the Declaration of Independence, he owned more than 100 slaves. Slaves accounted for one-fifth of the population in the American colonies at the time.[98]

Founded on the principles of freedom, initially, the "land of the free" was solely free for white males.

Many Americans maintain reverence for the Constitution, considering it to be close to a divine document carefully crafted by an all-wise team of founding fathers. Yet Article I of that document states that Black people are "three-fifths of a person," and Article IV requires states to return "runaway slaves" to their "owners."[99] Slavery wasn't abolished until nearly 100 years after the Constitution was ratified, and multiple states openly continued to attempt to keep Blacks from voting well into the 1960s. The Civil Rights Act of 1965 tried to change this practice but gerrymandering and voter suppression continue to this day.[100]

Racial segregation is still the norm in many parts of the country, and inequality in healthcare and education continue to have severe consequences for most Americans of color.[101]

Militant hate groups have always been active in our society, most notoriously the Ku Klux Klan. The KKK evolved as a self-identified "Christian" white supremacy group that also targeted Catholics, Jews, and other immigrants for persecution. They claimed between three and five million members in the 1920s.[102]

Membership in the Klan ebbed and flowed over the decades; it was reinvigorated during the Civil Rights Movement of the 1950s and 1960s when civil rights activists were attacked and murdered.[103]

Subsequently, federal authorities infiltrated Klan groups and arrested and prosecuted many. This government pressure led to a dramatic drop in official KKK membership in the 1970s and 1980s.[104]

By the mid–90s, 60 fragmented Klan groups remained in the United States; membership dropped to below 10,000. However, their numbers rose a decade later.[105]

The modern resurgence of white supremacy began with the Oklahoma City bombing in 1995 when 168 were killed and 680 were injured. The bomber, a 25-year-old army veteran who had studied munitions in the military, was inspired by *The Turner Diaries*, a racist novel. This book has incited thousands of other white supremacists and has been influential in at least 200 murders.[106]

The Oklahoma City bomber also displayed paranoid thinking, reportedly complaining to friends that the military had implanted a microchip in his buttocks to track him.[107]

As white supremacist activity began to proliferate on the internet, the fires of hate have only grown hotter.

In the first 10 days after Donald Trump's election in 2016, the Southern Poverty Law Center reported nine hundred bias-related incidents against minorities, in contrast to several dozen in a typical week previously. In many of these incidents, the perpetrators invoked Trump's name.[108] There were calls from white supremacy networks for attacks on the country's infrastructure. In 2017, a *ProPublica* investigation revealed that Atomwaffen Division members discussed sabotaging public water systems and taking out the California electric grid.[109] In 2019, the Base suggested its followers bomb their local power transformers.[110]

The Covid-19 pandemic of 2020–21, the unusually contentious U.S. presidential election, controversy over killings by police, and the response of the Black Lives Matter movement brought even more opportunities to spread chaos and violence. Among those vulnerable to paranoia, conspiracy theories served to increase anxiety and social unrest. In March 2020, when the Covid-19 epidemic began, online channels associated with white supremacy grew by more than 6,000 users.[111]

After Trump's repeated references to Covid-19 as "the China virus," hate crimes targeting Asian-Americans soared 150 percent from the previous year.

It was an exceptionally busy year for extremists; the FBI interrupted multiple plots in 2020 and 2021, including the following:

- In April 2020, a white supremacist planned to bomb a Missouri hospital where he believed Blacks were being treated for Covid-19. He was shot by police in a gunfight when they attempted to intercept him. In an example of ideological drift, this same perpetrator had previously planned to attack a synagogue, a mosque, or a majority-Black elementary school.[112]
- During Black Lives Matter protests in Oakland, California, in May 2020, a 32-year-old Air Force staff sergeant affiliated with the right-wing extremist group the Boogaloo Boys shot two security guards outside the federal courthouse. One was killed. He hoped that anti-racism protestors from the Black Lives Matter movement and left-wing activists, known as Antifa, would be blamed. His stated intent was to start a race war.[113]
- Multiple plots by far-right extremists who hoped to kill candidates for office, including then-candidates Joe Biden and Kamala Harris, were interrupted.[114] In one case, a 19-year-old who had searched online for Biden's home address and night-vision goggles made it to within four miles of Biden's home. He was arrested with four rifles, a 9mm handgun, explosives, books on bomb-making, and over $500,000 cash in his van. He had made multiple online posts threatening violence. In one, he stated that he was "going to do a Columbine for a while, but I think it would be better to put it towards something more memorable." He had also outlined a plan to perform a mass shooting at a mall food court.[115]
- In October 2020, the FBI arrested 14 right-wing militia members who were plotting to kidnap and "try for treason" Michigan governor Gretchen Whitmer as well as violently overthrow the state government. One extremist posted a hit list on Facebook

with lists of various government officials that should be killed. The plan had been in the works for months, and the group repeatedly met over the summer for combat drills and weapons and explosives training. One member purchased a Taser the week before the attack was to take place.[116]

- Shortly after the Capitol siege in January 2021, a 43-year-old right-wing extremist was arrested by the FBI for threatening the life of California governor Gavin Newsom. He had built five large pipe bombs and owned multiple machine guns and extensive body armor. In numerous text messages, he also suggested attacking social media companies he blamed for deplatforming Trump.[117]

These events in the United States have influenced mass killers in other countries.

New Zealand

A real-life horror movie, complete with special effects and a musical score, was live streamed to Facebook from Christchurch, New Zealand, in March 2019.

The perpetrator, a 28-year-old white supremacist, had done extensive planning. He wore a helmet with a camera mounted on his head and a military tactical vest. In a burst of innovation, the New Zealand mass killer had installed a portable audio speaker inside the vest from which he blared battle music.[118] Lyrics to one of the songs he played stated, "I am the god of hellfire!"[119]

The New Zealand killer had armed for the massacre with a semi-automatic shotgun and a military-style assault rifle. In another burst of innovation, he attached a strobe light to the end of the assault rifle to disorient his victims.[120]

The attack happened on a Friday afternoon prayer at the Al Noor Mosque in Christchurch, New Zealand. Survivors described the perpetrator as calm when he entered. The young man had rehearsed by visiting the mosque on three prior occasions, pretending to be a worshipper.[121] He was at ease during the breach and attack.

On that Friday, he was welcomed at the door by a mosque member who greeted him with "Hello, brother." This was the first man to be killed.[122]

One hundred and ninety others were inside as the killer began firing indiscriminately into the crowd. The perpetrator shot at close range; he shot many repeatedly.

The attack lasted less than five minutes.[123]

The perpetrator then drove three miles to the Linwood Islamic Center; just seven minutes after he started the first attack, he began shooting the worshippers at the second location. In total, 51 were killed and another 50 injured. Viewers saw 17 minutes of the attack on social media before moderators could remove it; in minutes, it had spread around the world on additional platforms. Some viewers described frantically trying to stop videos on their newsfeeds from auto-playing.[124]

Minutes before the attack, the New Zealand killer had emailed a 74-page manifesto titled "The Great Replacement."[125] The term refers to the core belief among white supremacists that nonwhite immigrants are replacing whites as social leaders in society and are thus guilty of "white genocide." The document was filled with anti-immigrant and anti–Muslim hate speech and neo–Nazi symbols, along with quotes from other mass killers.[126]

This perpetrator had mailed the manifesto to more than 30 recipients, including media outlets and the prime minister as well as posting it to sites online.

The New Zealand killer cited the Norwegian mass killer as his inspiration. He referred to him as "Knight," a nod to his grandiose fantasy of acting out a role as a Knight Templar. He also mentioned the Charleston church shooter by name, along with then-president Donald Trump. He stated that he saw Trump "as a symbol of renewed white identity and common purpose."[127]

He was deeply immersed in U.S. politics and indicated that his attack was aimed at an American audience. "I chose firearms for the effect it would have on social discourse, the extra media coverage they would provide and the effect it could have on the politics of the United States and thereby the political situation of the world." He stated that he'd been planning the attack for two years. One of his goals was "to incite violence, retaliation, and further divide."[128]

He was cheered on as a hero on internet sites dedicated to white nationalism.[129]

The New Zealand killer had been a bodybuilder and worked as a personal trainer; others described him as "polite and ordinary" and "a nature lover." He had no known history of mental health concerns or legal entanglements. He'd grown up in an intact family in a small town in Australia. He wrote in his manifesto, "I had a regular childhood, without any great issues."

Since then, other white supremacists have referred to him as "a saint."[130]

Just One Click

Patterns are clear. The New Zealand killer stated that he was inspired by the Norwegian killer and the Charleston killer, as were dozens of others worldwide.[131] A mass killer at a Jewish synagogue in Poway, California, in April 2019, stated he was inspired by the New Zealand killer, as did the El Paso killer in August of the same year.[132] Calls subsequently went out across the white supremacist web network praising the El Paso killer, which inspired others.[133]

And thus it goes. Copycatting and contagion continue. It is predictable.

In each case, these perpetrators were influenced by a strong online culture of hateful extremism. Despite the noble narratives they spin, their behavior's psychological motivators are the dark tetrad traits of narcissism, anger, paranoia, and sadism. Some have serious mental illnesses, but most do not. They are classic injustice collectors, signaling both victimization and virtue. They find meaning and purpose for their lives as an in-group brotherhood, crafting tales that justify violence against an out-group they have dehumanized.[134] Creating a potent fellowship of hate, they model themselves after killers who have gone before them. As mass murderers become heroes, their manifestos become guides.[135]

With the internet, they find a global audience to bring more into their fold. Hate culture is never more than just one click away.

11

Gender-Based Violence

"You girls have never been attracted to me. I don't know why you girls aren't attracted to me, but I will punish you all for it. It's an injustice, a crime, because.... I don't know what you don't see in me. I'm the perfect guy and yet you throw yourselves at these obnoxious men instead of me, the supreme gentleman."[1]—Isla Vista killer

"I don't see women as human. All they are or should be, are slaves to men. Cook, clean, and spreading legs when they're told to. Let's start beating women again."[2]—Anonymous post in an incel community

Another thread that connects many mass killers is an attitude of malevolence toward women. Many have a history of assaulting wives, girlfriends, and female family members or sharing misogynistic views in online communities dedicated to the hatred of women.[3]

The roots of this hatred are deep, and they intertwine with white supremacy. Though not every misogynist is a racist, and not every racist is a misogynist, contempt for women is often the connective tissue between both extremist groups.[4]

In this chapter, we explore the intersection of misogyny and violence.

Involuntary Celibates

One of the least understood extremist groups to have organized on the internet in recent years is the self-identified "involuntary celibates" (incels). This somewhat bizarre movement appeared online in the early 2010s and has since grown dramatically.[5]

Incels are men of all ages, mostly younger, white, and heterosexual, who define themselves by their inability to find female sexual partners. These men build a sense of fraternity in a self-sustaining online subculture based upon their perceived victimhood and a dramatically distorted sense of persecution by women.[6]

The organizing belief among those in the incel community is that they are entitled to sex just because they want it and that women are intentionally persecuting them by not offering it to them.

Commonly anxiety-ridden, incels fail to understand that sexual behavior evolves from meaningful connections with others, something that they are not very good at. Incels don't realize that women are people with personalities and emotions who have sex with men they know and like. They show a profound lack of empathy, zero insight, and a flawed theory of mind. Their sense of persecution is rooted in thinking errors.

Incels typically connect in online forums characterized by expressions of anxiety, self-pity, and anger, which they attribute to their virginal status. They share misogynistic beliefs, are self-loathing, and often racist. Many obsess over their perceived unattractiveness.

It's not uncommon for incels to also cross over to extremist white supremacy groups.[7] In the same way that racist groups coalesce and morph online, incels move from group to group on different internet platforms.

These groups provide males—mostly adolescents—with a distorted narrative that helps them make sense of their sadness and frustration and offer templates for a resolution that often involves aggression. Though not all incel communities allow users to create posts advocating violence, many do. Most of the groups are not moderated.

By reinforcing their role as victims, incels marinate in helplessness and hopelessness. Rather than supporting one another and looking for productive solutions, they focus on grievances, externalize blame, and fantasize about revenge.[8] Some joke about rape and torture.[9] This reinforces paranoia and rage, and the outlook of those in the groups can become dangerously pessimistic.

And since hate is infectious, some incels have acted out their revenge fantasies on women.[10]

It's not uncommon for group members to call for violence

against *all* sexually active people; they are angry at women, who "deny" them sex, and are also angry at men, who "steal" women from them.

While incel communities provide them with an outlet for their distress, the narrative justifies their feelings and fuels a desire for revenge. If they are depressed, anxious, and lonely, it's the fault of women—all women.

Incel "Saints"

The Isla Vista killer is often revered as a saint among incels; he's consistently mentioned as a source of inspiration. The Isla Vista killer's call for a gender war has been taken seriously among the community: "One day incels will realize their true strength and numbers, and will overthrow this oppressive feminist system. Start envisioning a world where WOMEN FEAR YOU."[11]

Intense self-loathing is rampant in incel communities. Incels, in particular, appear to have significant mental health challenges, consisting of any combination of those discussed in previous chapters. Typically, they are depressed, anxious, and socially phobic. Many have various developmental delays. Some have psychotic thinking and personality disorders. Their significant psychological problems result in a lack of the social skills that would enable them to make friends and function well in day-to-day life. Despite this, participants are usually contemptuous of any sort of mental health therapy.[12]

Though their sense of isolation is reduced through the connections they form in online groups, these virtual spaces are closed to outsiders who could offer other points of view or actual solution-focused discussion.

As with other online social communities, incels do not reveal their true identities online. It's impossible to know with certainty how many individuals are active in these groups; estimates range from the thousands to hundreds of thousands.[13]

Since 2014, there have been at least seven mass attacks perpetrated by incels, with 52 resulting deaths and many injuries.

Toronto, 2018 and 2020

Toronto, Canada, is one of the safest cities in North America. Nonetheless, it's been the location of two recent mass killings perpetrated by incels.

On a weekday morning in April 2018, a 26-year-old Canadian man rented a white Chevrolet Ryder van. Though never before physically aggressive, he'd been methodically researching mass shootings and fantasizing about mass murder for over a decade; he had come up with a plan that didn't require a gun. All he needed was a large, sturdy vehicle and a crowded downtown sidewalk.

At 1:30 in the afternoon, he was on a busy city street; sidewalks were filled with pedestrians. After accelerating through a red light, he intentionally jumped the curb and veered onto a sidewalk. Bodies flew off the hood of the van and into the air as he barreled along for several blocks. Witnesses reported that he looked directly into his victims' eyes as he smashed into them.

The Toronto van killer only stopped because one of his victims' drinks splashed over his windshield, obscuring his view.[14]

He had planned suicide by cop. Police were on the scene quickly in response to multiple 911 calls, and the driver exited the van holding his wallet as if it were a gun. "Shoot me!" he yelled at the police. Toronto law enforcement succeeded in capturing him without a shot fired.

Ten were killed and 16 injured. The youngest victim killed was 22, the oldest 94. This was the deadliest mass murder in Toronto's history.[15]

In a four-hour interview with police on the day of the attack, the van killer told Toronto detectives that he had rented the van for the specific purpose of committing the mass murder.[16]

"I felt it was time to take action and not just sit on the sidelines and just fester in my own sadness," he said. When asked how he felt about those he killed, he calmly stated, "I feel like I accomplished my mission."[17]

In a 190-page transcript of the interview with detectives, this perpetrator stated that he had a "normal childhood" and "a good relationship with his parents and brother." Still, he never had a girlfriend, and his failed interactions with women left him angry.[18]

In an eerie echo of the Isla Vista killer, he stated, "I consider myself a supreme gentleman."[19]

The Toronto perpetrator stated to detectives that he had found a community online in incel forums and that he had made contact there with two other incels who subsequently committed mass killings.[20]

Days before the killings, he had written on an incel forum that there would soon be an "incel uprising," and he encouraged others to follow suit. On the day of the attack, he made a Facebook post stating, "The incel rebellion has begun!"[21]

During his trial, a psychiatrist for the van killer's defense stated that he had been diagnosed with autism at age five. Despite having a high verbal IQ, his actual adaptive functioning was similar to that of a young child. His severe impairment in social skills translated to minimal friendships and no history of romantic relationships. The doctor concluded that he was "terrified of girls and women, had deep esoteric obsessions, and a striking absence of empathy."[22]

This perpetrator was in a special needs program in his high school. Classmates reported that he had been known to try to bite people and had been observed in hallways wringing his hands together and making meowing sounds and odd grunting noises.[23] He had been bullied and called names. Enlisting in the military only intensified his distress, where he was isolated and ridiculed during basic training and soon discharged.

He has since become revered as another saint by other incels.

Co-Occurring Diagnoses

The Toronto van killer likely has multiple mental health diagnoses, which synergistically amplified his problems.

The association of this killer's behavior with his autism diagnosis sparked understandable outrage from the neurodiversity community, who stressed that this difference alone would not account for his violent rampage. Since it is possible to be psychopathic, psychotic, *and* autistic, multiple diagnoses are likely applicable. As a reminder, those with ASD are far more likely to be victims of violence than perpetrators.[24]

Less than two years later, Toronto would see a second deadly incel attack. In February 2020, a 17-year-old armed with a machete attacked multiple people in a woman-owned erotic massage parlor. One 24-year-old woman was killed, and two others were seriously injured.[25]

The massage parlor killer stated that he was also motivated by the incel movement.[26] This was the first case of an incel-related crime to be prosecuted as an act of terrorism.[27]

Tallahassee, Florida

He had been a second lieutenant in the army, earned two master's degrees, and recently worked as a high school English teacher. He was intelligent and knew how to present well when he was motivated. Despite these apparent positive traits, the 40-year-old man was also an incel mass killer.[28]

The location was Tallahassee, Florida, which was 250 miles away from his home. On a Friday evening in 2018, the large-framed man entered a small yoga studio just as the 5:30 class was beginning. He carried a newly purchased yoga mat that still had a Walmart price sticker on it. In a black athletic bag strapped to his torso he had concealed a Glock 9mm handgun. He had driven several hours to attend this class.[29]

Approaching the studio receptionist, the man used his debit card to pay the $12 drop-in fee for the class. She would later state that she thought his manner was odd; nonetheless, she smiled at him and attempted to make him feel welcome.[30,31]

Eleven students were present; all but one were women. The sole male was a man with a slight build, a 34-year-old law school student who participated in the class with his girlfriend.[32]

The big man entered as the class started; the attendees were already in the child's pose, on their knees, foreheads to the floor with arms stretched out, palms touching the ground. He told the instructor he had a question and then fumbled in his bag to remove a set of earmuff hearing protectors. He put them on and then pulled out his 9mm Glock.[33]

He stood still for a moment, displaying the gun in the air before pointing it at the women closest to him. The other man in the room yelled, "He's got a gun!"[34]

The two women nearest to him were killed immediately. One was a 61-year-old physician, the other a 21-year-old college student. The killer then began to wildly spray the room with bullets; some students broke and ran for the door, as did the receptionist. Several were hit but managed to make it out of the room.[35]

Though the killer had 100 rounds of ammunition, his gun jammed after firing 13 shots. This was the pause that allowed a lifesaving intervention, as the slight man in the back of the room sprang into action.

The law student would later report to the *Washington Post* that though he believed he would be shot, he acted spontaneously; looking for any possible weapon in the room, he grabbed an upright vacuum and rushed the gunman.[36]

"I'm just going to hit him. He'll cock that thing back and shoot me. But I'm going to hit him." Though he slammed the big man in the head, the perpetrator didn't go down.[37]

In response, the killer swung his Glock to the side of the smaller man's face, with a blow that sent him flying backward and opened a gash over his eye. Despite this, the smaller man grabbed a broomstick and made another run at the gunman. The perpetrator inflicted another blow to his head. The student briefly lost consciousness.[38]

Though he didn't disable the killer, those few seconds allowed other students to run out the door. Police arrived in just over three minutes in response to multiple 911 calls.[39]

There appeared to be no living persons left in the room. Seconds later, the big man took one last shot, upward through his chin and into his brain. He hit the floor hard as he died.[40]

Leakage Everywhere

The Tallahassee perpetrator had a history of flagrant hostility against people of color and sexual aggression toward women going back to the eighth grade. Like mass killers before him, he left behind a copious online trail of paranoid and hateful grievances, including videos on YouTube, a personal website filled with racist and misogynistic writings, and recordings of song lyrics he'd written, recorded, and uploaded to the music sharing website Soundcloud. One song was titled "I Will Not Touch You—My Bullets Will."[41]

In the photographs and videos, he appears to be confident and smirking as he rails against interracial marriage and expresses support for white supremacy. He also stated he was part of the incel movement.[42]

His upbringing, as far as we can tell, doesn't explain the person he became. The killer was raised with two brothers in a middle-class family in a small Florida suburb. He had been a Boy Scout and served as an acolyte in the Methodist Church.[43]

After the murders, his mother told investigators that he had no mental illness history and no mental health treatment. She stated that he had trouble getting girlfriends "because his standards were impossibly high."[44]

Yet, there were dark triad traits, and they were not hidden. As a teenager, he openly admired Hitler and white supremacist groups; despite this, he was elected vice president of his high school class. He ran against a female opponent with a slogan that read in part, "We Don't Need No Woman."[45]

In high school, the Tallahassee killer wrote a 70,000-word novel called *Rejected Youth,* which is described as a revenge fantasy of a middle school boy nursing hatred of the girls who had shunned and humiliated him. The protagonist murders each girl brutally before he throws himself off a roof as the cops close in. The characters were based on his actual classmates, with names slightly changed.[46] This is a clear example of ideation and planning.

His sister-in-law reported to investigators that his family had been concerned about his potential for violence for many years. She stated that his parents slept with their bedroom door locked when he was at home.[47] A former roommate told police that people found him "weird" and that he used his large size to intimidate people.[48]

The yoga studio killer had previously been a student at Florida State University in Tallahassee and was twice arrested there. He was eventually banned from campus for groping women, all of whom had been wearing yoga pants at the time.[49] During that time, he bragged of visiting Ted Bundy's former home and the Sorority Row where Bundy had strangled women. Proudly, he stressed that Bundy had committed the murders the year he had been born.[50]

Police analyzed his internet trail and determined that he frequently sought out pornography involving yoga themes.[51]

He completed officer's school in the Army. Though he eventually earned the rank of second lieutenant, he was booted out in 2010 for "unacceptable conduct"; the charges involved inappropriate sexual contact with female soldiers.[52] For reasons that seem inexplicable, he still received an honorable discharge.

The breadcrumbs along the pathway to violence are copious in this case. In a family event at a park, he was observed touching young girls' buttocks at a water slide. He was fired from jobs for sexual harassment and was banned from bars for groping women. Generally, the victims did not press charges; in other cases, district attorneys declined to prosecute. Thus, no evidence of his conduct turned up in criminal background checks, which allowed him to become employed as a schoolteacher.[53]

While teaching high school social studies and English, he was investigated by police for touching a female student on her torso and making suggestive remarks. The case was suspended, and he taught at the school for another year before resigning. Hired for another teaching job as a substitute, he was fired for viewing porn at work.[54]

The Tallahassee killer started a Meetup.com group for singles in their 20s and 30s. Those in the group called him a Nazi. One stated, "He'd walk up and just start talking about weapons and killing people in the military, and how Hitler was right to clear the human race of gays and Jews and Blacks."[55]

Unlike many incels, he was not shy and withdrawn. He tried his hand at stand-up comedy but was fired for making racist jokes.[56]

Shortly before the murders in August 2018, the wife of an acquaintance discovered his website and was alarmed by the threatening content. She subsequently reported him to the FBI by way of their Internet tip line.

Though the tip was received, no action was taken. Threats must target a specific person or specific violent plan to be actionable by law enforcement. It was one of 731,000 such tips made that year.[57]

Senseless? Not Really

In media coverage, the motive in the yoga studio murders remained a mystery. Why would anyone target a yoga studio, and why a yoga studio 250 miles from his home? In televised news interviews, witnesses stressed the "senseless" nature of the crime.

Police investigators subsequently learned that the perpetrator had his reasons.

Five years previously, while living in Tallahassee, the yoga studio killer developed a fixation on a young woman he met at the meetup group. The two subsequently exchanged messages through Facebook messenger; they had discussed yoga in several of their conversations. Detectives noted that this young woman was in a yoga pose in her Facebook profile photo.[58]

The killer had asked her out on several dates; the young woman always declined. After he began sending her sexually suggestive messages, she responded that he was "crazy" and stated she found his messages "weird and insulting."[59]

When detectives searched his home, they found a journal in which he expressed hatred for the woman and his desire to "put it to her." They also found a map of the shopping plaza where the yoga studio was located.[60]

She was not present at the time of the murders; ironically, she had died of natural causes two years before. Apparently, the killer was unaware of this.[61]

The Tallahassee killer was an injustice collector who spent his adolescence and all of his adult life focused on hatred of women and people of color. He rarely made attempts to veil his thoughts. He was outspoken and left copious evidence of violent fantasies, including torture. He repeatedly acted on his sexually aggressive in various contexts yet never received significant consequences.[62]

Despite all, he was able to talk his way into high school teaching jobs. He was exceptionally talented at impression management when motivated.

From his journal: "If I can't find one decent female to live with, I will find many indecent females to die with. If I can't make a living, I will make a killing."[63]

Examples of Misogynistic Mass Murders

- An earlier mass murder with a documented relationship to misogyny occurred in 1975 in Ottawa, Canada.[64] An 18-year-old militia sharpshooter with an intense fixation on raping women tricked a female acquaintance into coming to his basement bedroom in this incident. After handcuffing her, raping her, and stabbing her 14 times, he went upstairs and calmly had a peanut butter sandwich prepared by his unwitting mother. Later the same day, he set the family home on fire and drove to his high school with a shotgun, where he shot six and killed two before killing himself. His mother reported that he went to church regularly and had been a diligent paperboy and worked at a pizza restaurant.

- In Montreal in 1989, a man walked into the Polytechnique engineering school with a semiautomatic rifle and shot 24 women and four men. Fourteen were killed. He then killed himself. He left a letter that stated, "I have decided to send the feminists, who have always ruined my life, back to their maker."

- Another mass murder related to gender hate occurred in Killeen, Texas, in 1991 when a gunman shot 22 people at a Luby's Cafeteria. He'd written a letter calling women "vipers." Survivors of the shooting reported that this perpetrator passed over men in the cafeteria to shoot women at point-blank range.

- In 2009 near Pittsburgh, Pennsylvania, a 48-year-old systems analyst employed at a law firm opened fire at a women's aerobics class in a gym. He killed three, injured nine, and then killed himself. A note was found inside his gym bag, indicating his hatred for women. He maintained a personal website where he had written about possibly carrying out a shooting. Over nine months, he chronicled his sexual frustration and perceived rejections by women. He wrote, "Women just don't like me. There are 30 million desirable women in the US, and I can't find one." He also posted a video of a tour of his home, which had been a homework assignment from a self-help seminar he'd recently attended on how to date women.

- In October 2015, at a community college in Roseburg, Oregon, a 26-year-old killed nine fellow students one by one and left seven wounded before killing himself.[65] He left a manifesto in which he wrote, "I have always been the most hated person in the world. Ever since I arrived in this world, I have been under siege from it. Under attack from morons and idiots … my whole life has been one lonely enterprise. And here I am, 26, with no friends, no job, no girlfriend, a virgin." The Roseburg killer then mentioned his admiration for mass killers who had gone before him, stating that they were "elite people who stand with the gods." He owned nine guns, including a semiautomatic rifle. He had gone to the shooting range with his mother, who owned her own AR-15. She stated she thought it would be a healthy mother-son activity.

- In Glendale, Arizona, in May 2020, during the Covid-19 pandemic shutdown, a 20-year-old Latino male with a semiautomatic rifle targeted couples at the Westgate shopping mall. He injured three after posting an Instagram video in which he calmly smiled at the camera and announced his name, then stated, "I'm going to be the shooter of Westgate 2020. This is to get back to mean society, so let's get this done."[66] Had the mall been filled with shoppers, there could have been many more casualties. He had previously posted multiples images on social media posing with his rifle.

- In June 2020, in Richlands, Virginia, a 23-year-old man blew off one of his hands while building a bomb meant to kill women. Investigators found notes at his residence that played out several fantasy murder scenarios targeting women, identifying "hot cheerleaders" as targets. His letter also said, "I will not back down. I will not be afraid of the consequences, no matter what. I will be heroic." He then compared himself to the Isla Vista killer.

- In March 2021, a 21-year-old white man targeted three Asian spa/massage businesses in Atlanta, where he had frequently been a customer. He killed six women of Asian descent and two other individuals who happened to be at the premises. The perpetrator had a history of extreme religiosity; high school friends stated that he had carried his Bible everywhere. Reportedly, he had a prolonged fixation with guilt and lust related to sexuality and had spent time in a religious treatment center for sex addiction. Just hours before the murders, he purchased a 9mm handgun at a local sporting goods store. Georgia has "no-wait" gun laws, which allow approval within minutes.[67]

Misogyny alone does not create a mass killer, but it can be both a gateway drug and an accelerant for those with preexisting vulnerabilities. In the case of incels, the group process they create online serves to feed their pain and rage.

We see entitlement, lack of empathy, scapegoating, paranoia, anger, sadistic fantasies, victim signaling, virtue signaling, and dehumanization—all qualities found in those on the pathway to violence. The leakage in nearly all cases was dramatic.

The Canadian Security Intelligence Service stated in 2018 that it was "increasingly preoccupied with threats from rightwing extremism, including misogynistic violence." The CSIS also noted that "many such perpetrators adopt similar tactics from political terrorists in other countries, including vehicle ramming."[68]

The Southern Poverty Law Center lists the incel movement among dangerous hate groups.[69]

Domestic Violence

Mass shootings in the United States frequently have a connection with domestic violence. Thirty-three percent of all mass killers have a documented history of violence against their wives or girlfriends.[70]

Twenty percent of the victims of domestic violence-related deaths were not the intimate partners themselves but family members, friends, neighbors, law enforcement responders, or bystanders. The danger of such a killing happening is greatest when the woman is trying to leave the relationship.[71]

- In Sutherland Springs, Texas, in 2017, a 26-year-old Air Force veteran killed 26 people and wounded 20 others in a rampage at his estranged wife's church. He fired 700 rounds in a rampage that lasted 11 minutes. Though his wife was not present at the time, her grandmother was among the dead.[72] The Sutherland Springs killer had been married twice. In 2012 he was convicted of assaulting his first wife and fracturing his toddler stepson's skull. The woman would later say that the marriage was filled with abuse and that she lived in constant fear of him. He had made threats during their marriage to kill her and her entire family. She reported, "For a whole year, he slapped me, choked me, kicked me, water-boarded me, and held a gun to my head."[73] At one point, he told her that he could bury her body where no one would find it. He also had a history of making threats to military superiors and abuse of animals, bragging that he bought dogs for target practice.[74] The Sutherland Springs killer remarried in 2014 and was separated from that wife at the time of the killings. A week before the murders, he attended a festival at the church he would target days later. He was wearing all black and reportedly acting strangely.[75] Consumed with anger about a disagreement with his mother-in-law, he began sending her threatening text messages shortly before the killings.[76]

- The man who killed 49 at the Pulse Nightclub in Orlando, Florida, in 2017 had a history of beating his wife while she was pregnant.[77]
- In Melcroft, Pennsylvania, in 2018, a gunman killed five and injured four at a car wash after his female partner left him. Among the dead were the woman and her new boyfriend.[78]
- The Dayton, Ohio, killer of nine had a long history of threatening female classmates with violence and created music seethed with anger toward women. One of those he killed was his sister.[79]

Family Annihilators

The most extreme category of domestic violence-related murders is the group of killers known as family annihilators. Though it seems incomprehensible that some men murder their entire families, this is one of the most common types of mass killing overall.[80] As with other mass killers, there are psychological patterns that can be tracked.

These perpetrators most often kill their female partners, children, or other family members in rapid succession. In many cases, they also attempt to kill first responders and sometimes take the rampage outside the home. Half of the time, they also kill themselves.[81]

These events are most often triggered by a relationship problem or separation from their partner and often in the context of disputes over child custody.[82,83] Family annihilators typically do not have a criminal history and are often described by others as "an ordinary guy."[84]

Anger and entitlement are key motivators, and the murders are an attempt to exercise power and control. Often there is an overt plan to punish the estranged partner. Through murder, this type of perpetrator communicates, "If I can't have you, no one else will." They are willing to give up their own lives to make this point.[85]

Financial problems, intoxication, and access to firearms are additional risk factors in these kinds of killings.[86]

Toxic Masculinity

What is it with men and violence? Men commit 90 percent of homicides in the United States. Ninety-three percent of incarcerated federal inmates are male.[87] Men comprise 80 percent of those arrested for violent crime and 62 percent of those arrested for property crime.[88]

The reasons for this are complex. Some blame evolution and biological gender differences, at least in part. Nonetheless, researchers agree that a major factor of male violence involves a culture that traditionally ties masculinity to violence, aggression, and sexual conquest. This comes at a high cost to all of us, regardless of our gender.

Culture teaches us what to think, how to view ourselves, and what it means to be a man or woman. Though we may collectively say that we abhor criminal violence, many other kinds of violence are celebrated. We venerate athletes in violent, competitive sports, and action movie heroes as well as outlaw anti-heroes, Navy Seals, and Marines. Successful violence has always been a source of national pride in the United States and many other countries.

In fact, in much of the world, violence is synonymous with masculinity. The world would be a very different place if male-perpetrated violence were to cease.

The American Psychological Association (APA) recently reviewed 40 years of research on masculinity and culture and found that the traditional model of masculinity causes significant harm to men and can be described as "toxic." Their researchers have defined a set of "masculine" behaviors and beliefs that include the following:

- suppressing emotions and masking distress;
- maintaining an appearance of hardness ("tough guy" behavior);
- exhibiting competitiveness and dominance;
- viewing aggression and violence as an indicator of power; and
- demonstrating yper-sexuality that dehumanizes women

Toughness is everything, while vulnerable emotions are considered weak. Emotional sensitivity and empathy are seen as "feminine" and a source of shame. The APA stresses that socializing boys to suppress their emotions in this way causes long-term damage that echoes both inwardly and outwardly. Violence becomes a way to ward off feelings of shame and replaces them with a sense of pride and control. This manifests dramatically among mass killers who compete to top one another's kill scores.

In truth, gender-related violence is perpetrated by those who have failed at healthy masculine development. They display a sense of entitlement, compare themselves to others, and tend to nurse grievances. They are prone to anger when others have what they don't. They may distort reality, collect injustices, and in some cases, plot revenge. Research has also shown that the more men adopt the toxic aspects of masculinity, the stronger their resistance to mental health treatment.[89] The APA recently created guidelines for psychological treatment of men and boys to help address these problems.[90] Of course, men immersed in toxic masculinity are the least likely among us to choose to enter psychotherapy.

In truth, masculinity is fluid and expressed differently in different cultures. Healthy men can embrace the full expression of human emotions and are comfortable with vulnerability. They have empathy for others and are naturally able to make close human connections rather than seeking conquests. These are the attachments that bring a sense of meaning and purpose to life.

Changing culture is difficult and takes time and intention. The culture surrounding boys has everything to do with the kind of men they become.

The roots of misogyny run deep, and like other forms of extremist belief, have a great deal to do with the reasons for mass killings.

12

The Conspiracy Mindset

Though conspiracy theories are common, mass killers are particularly prone to a style of thinking known as "the conspiracy mindset." In this chapter, we explore the aspects of conspiracism that are normal and those that are not and how conspiracism can veer into paranoid thinking that has the potential to fuel violent behavior. We also look more closely at the price we pay for entirely unfettered free speech.

The stories have gotten stranger and stranger over time: alien lizard people kidnapping children and drinking their blood; cannibal "Deep State" cabals secretly running the government. Though conspiracy theories have always been part of the human experience, we've seen a burgeoning in recent years, as flat–Earth proponents blend in with anti-vaxxers and those who maintain the moon landing was a hoax. As with other facets of extremism, conspiracy theories have been amplified and spread on social media.[1]

Conspiracies and Violence

Like other traits, conspiracism can also be viewed on a spectrum, ranging from mild suspiciousness about things that could be plausible to firmly held, bizarre beliefs that cannot possibly be true. While it's theoretically possible that a group rather than a lone assassin killed JFK, it is odd to believe that JFK is still alive and secretly running The Illuminati.

The reasons for this tendency originate in our neurobiological system; it serves as a protective factor. Evolution has wired us to scan the environment for potential danger.

At the mild level, conspiracy theories have little consequence in an individual's life. It's not paranoid to occasionally wonder if people at work like us or if some are talking behind our back. Sometimes a boss really is out to get us.

Moving toward the higher end of the conspiratorial spectrum into the pathological territory, we see people building cohesive groups around paranoid themes, which typically involve an evil "other" seeking to cause harm to "the good people." In this way, conspiracy theories build a sense of camaraderie among like-minded people who oppose a common enemy while building false narratives and feeding perceptual distortions.

Conspiracy theories serve to amplify hostility against other groups and seed "us versus them" thinking. When those with dark triad traits become involved with conspiracies, it leads to dehumanizing others and can become one ingredient in a recipe for violence.[2]

Dangerous conspiracism stems from the amplification of a paranoid thinking style that has become maladaptive; we find this conspiracy mindset woven into the fabric of extremism.[3]

Put most simply, the common underlying tenets of conspiracist thinking are:

- Nothing is as it seems.
- Everything happens for a reason.
- Everything is connected.

Conspiracy Detection System

Conspiracy theories are not new and are certainly not limited to the United States. Indeed, the tendency to be suspicious is part of human nature, and in past times may have served to help protect humankind from genuine threats.[4] Many hypothesize that human beings evolved through natural selection with a "conspiracy detection system" integrated into our mental structure. This system is activated by environmental cues, which could indicate an increased risk of danger. This threat system served to help keep our hunter-gatherer ancestors safe in an environment characterized by constant threats from the natural world as well as competition for resources from nearby groups.[5] As with other aspects of our information processing system, what originally started about as adaptive can become maladaptive when amplified in modern times.

No matter how logical we believe ourselves to be, emotions and certain cognitive biases play a substantial role in perceiving the world and making decisions. Since our brains are pre-wired, these influences common to all of us operate beneath the level of conscious awareness.

Conspiratorial beliefs are not grounded in analytical thinking processes. They are motivated by emotional reasoning, which is when our emotions are used to define reality apart from any basis in fact.[6] Despite this, conspiracists typically expend a great deal of energy attempting to find rationale to support their belief, often citing "research," which is nothing more than watching dozens of YouTube videos that contain false information. They are drawn to such material as they search for validation for their misperceptions.

The following are automatic cognitive processes that underlie the conspiracy mindset[7]:

- **Illusory pattern perception and errors of causality:**
  Humans automatically search for meaningful and causal patterns between stimuli they experience. This has been an essential factor in our survival as a species. Our ancestors learned to chart the days and seasons by perceiving patterns and the duration of pregnancy and cycles of crops. Understanding causal patterns allowed us to know which foods are safe to eat and which are poisonous.

  But this doesn't mean our perceptual system is infallible. Illusory pattern perception is when we erroneously connect the dots where there is actually no meaningful pattern. Errors of causality result when we perceive a cause-and-effect relationship between two events that are in fact not related.

  For example, if I wore a red shirt the day I buy a winning lottery ticket, I may interpret the "lucky red shirt" as causative. If I throw a penny in a wishing well the day I apply for a new job, I may cite the penny as a causative factor when I get the job. We avoid stepping on cracks or walking under ladders because "you just never know." We refer to this thinking as superstition, and at low levels, it's harmless. It comes naturally and makes us feel better; though illusory, it gives us a feeling of control.

- **The illusion of control:**

    The randomness of life can be anxiety-provoking. There is no end to things that can go wrong in our daily lives, from car accidents to cancer to war. We worry about our loved ones, our family members, our pets, and climate change.

    Anxiety is uncomfortable; we all seek ways to cope with it. Sometimes these coping methods are healthy, but sometimes they are not.

    Paradoxically, conspiracy theories are a common maladaptive way of coping with anxiety by implying that we can influence events over which we have no power. They give us a sense that we can organize and order our world.

    If a mysterious malevolent cabal has overtaken our government, we believe we can fight them in various ways, including taking up arms or joining militias. This is particularly dangerous when we mistake political enemies for alien lizard people or believe that an entire race or gender of people is trying to harm us or that women are conspiring against men to deny them sex.

- **Confirmation Bias:**

    Our brains constantly curate what information we pay attention to. Confirmation bias is the tendency to only pay attention to information that supports our preconceptions and existing beliefs while ignoring or automatically rejecting conflicting information.

    For example, a person who believes in ESP will keep track of instances when they were "thinking about Dad, and then the phone rang, and it was him." Yet they ignore the far more numerous times when they were thinking about Dad, and he didn't call, and when they were not thinking about Dad, and he did call.

    Confirmation bias is more robust for emotionally charged issues; it ensures that a person who is emotionally invested in a conspiracy theory only notices information that validates the conspiracy while ignoring and discounting any conflicting information.

- **Specialness:**
  Conspiracy theories are particularly seductive to those with a need to feel special since they promise "inside knowledge" that is outside the mainstream's beliefs. Only those in the inner circle, the enlightened truth-seekers, know what's *really* going on—even though their beliefs and perceptions are utterly wrong. This sense of specialness increases solidarity among members of a group who view themselves as more intelligent and more aware than everyone else. They become self-aggrandizing heroes in a life-or-death battle against evil-doers. They want to believe their group is on the side of righteousness, and by process of reciprocal reinforcement, they can convince each other of almost anything.

Human motivations common to all drive conspiratorial thinking. People are drawn to conspiracy theories because they meet psychological needs, including the drive to understand the world and feel safe and in control of our environment, and maintain a positive sense of self and social group.[8]

Simple narratives that help us "connect the dots" appeal more to an anxious mind than the uncomfortable reality of coincidence and randomness. The unpredictable nature of the world is scary. It is less threatening to believe that a natural disaster is an evil cabal's work than accepting randomness. We can arm ourselves and fight an evil cabal, but we can't control Mother Nature.

Social Factors and Crises

Conspiracy theories are heavily influenced by social factors and can be activated by social situations. They become more appealing during times of crisis and social unrest when people are anxious and more apt to feel a loss of control.[9] The sense of powerlessness becomes a driving force as people begin to perceive patterns in random noise.

Unfortunately, conspiracy theories serve to amplify fear, and frightened people are more apt to become aggressive.

Predispositions and the Conspiracy Mindset

On the extreme high end of the spectrum, belief in conspiracies correlates with a range of individual traits such as paranoia, narcissism, Machiavellianism, and insecure attachments.[10] Once again, we see familiar personality patterns of the dark triad that are found in many mass killers. While people with such predispositions will be more attracted to conspiracy theories than others, it's also possible for consistent exposure to the conspiracy narratives to *build* these tendencies in some who would not usually go down the extremist rabbit hole.

It's important to note that though conspiracy theories differ in content, the belief process's underlying psychology is the same. Many people believe in mutually incompatible conspiracy theories simultaneously, such as *"Princess Diana was murdered"* and *"Princess Diana staged her own death."*[11] The conspiracy mindset allows people to disregard facts and logic and believe almost anything. Once a conspiracy mindset is established, one conspiracy belief results in a person believing in countless other conspiracies. The single best predictor of belief in one conspiracy is a belief in a different conspiracy.[12] This is known as "fringe fluidity." Once a person has accepted one fringe belief, they readily embrace others.

Conspiracy beliefs are empirically associated with political extremism on both the far-left and far-right ends of the political spectrum[13] and contribute to the radicalization of the vulnerable in both directions.[14] As the United States has experienced an increase in political polarization and social unrest, conspiracy theories have increased accordingly.

In modern times, this common human tendency has been exploited by self-serving bad actors, from snake oil salesmen and unethical politicians to violent racists. It's been amplified by social media, which efficiently spreads the conspiracy effects through their algorithms with bots. These algorithms tend to feed people shocking content designed to maximize their engagement on the platform. One conspiracy video on YouTube leads to dozens more which then appear in the sidebar; this serves to rapidly build a massive online eco-system of the like-minded, which continues to amplify.

QAnon

Perhaps the strangest widespread conspiracy theory has involved QAnon, the movement that formed around a mysterious individual self-identified as "Q" who began initially posting messages on the online message board 4chan in 2017. These messages came to be known as "Q drops" or "breadcrumbs" and were often written in cryptic language or presented in the form of puzzles, which followers took great pride in solving. Q's initial core message was that former President Donald Trump is waging a secret war against elite Satan-worshipping pedophiles, including members of the Democratic Party, politicians, and Hollywood celebrities. As the strange story goes, these people kidnap infants and children to murder them and drink their blood.

Even though this is beyond any reasonable belief, millions of people worldwide bought into the QAnon narrative. Some have moved on to extremist violence.

QAnon adherents made up a large portion of those who stormed the U.S. Capitol in January 2021. Though it's impossible to know exact numbers, some studies assert that at least 10 percent of the U.S. population buys into at least some aspects of the QAnon conspiracy theory. A poll taken in late 2020 indicated that there is a clear split along political party lines. One in three Republicans stated that they believe that the idea that a "deep state" is secretly running the government is "mostly true"; another 23 percent say "some parts" of the conspiracy theory are true. Seventy-two percent of Democrats responded that the QAnon conspiracy is "not true at all."[15]

After the Trump presidency ended, Q-adherents began to shift their rhetoric to a blend of anti–Jewish and anti–Chinese xenophobic tropes, along with anti-vaccine disinformation and assertions about the supposed secret deep state cabal running the world.

Beliefs drive behavior, and conspiracies have consequences, even when they are entirely untrue. Conspiracies influence whether people vote, get vaccinated, take up arms to overthrow the government, or murder members of a racial or religious minority.

The FBI has designated QAnon followers as "extremists" who pose the potential for domestic terrorism. Nonetheless, in the 2020 elections, some QAnon conspiracists were elected to the U.S. Congress.

The Capitol Siege

There had been nothing like it since the war of 1812. On January 6, 2021, hundreds of right-wing extremists attempted to violently interrupt the Senate certification of the November 2020 election victory of Joseph Biden over Donald Trump. It would come to be identified as an insurrection.

There were clear reasons that this mass of people became violent that day. They were following the lead of a person with power, and people with power carry significant weight. This is particularly true when the one repetitively espousing conspiracy theories is the president of the United States.

The events unfolded as part of an organized disinformation campaign spread by the former president, who gathered a mob of thousands for a rally near the Capitol. Leakage had been apparent for months, as Trump spread disproven conspiracy theories that the opposing political party had "stolen" the election.

Trump directed the attendees to march up the street to the Capitol building, where the Senate members were meeting to ratify the vote results. He told them to "fight like hell." Believing that they were following Trump's direct orders, they did.[16]

Most called themselves patriots; some even carried Christian crosses. Many were members of civilian paramilitary militias, and they were armed with bats, stun guns, and spears. After attacking and overpowering the Capitol police, approximately 800 of them smashed their way into the Capitol building where Congress was in session.

Many insurrectionists were former military members who wore military garb and brought masses of zip-tie handcuffs into the building. Some organized in groups and were hunting for congresspersons. They chanted "Kill Mike Pence" (then vice-president), called for the speaker of the house by name, and constructed a gallows outside the building, as Congress members crouched on the floor in gas masks with doors barred in fear of their lives.

Many rioters posted photos on social media as the events unfolded and used Facebook Messenger to coordinate their attack once inside.[17] Some rioters live-streamed the events in real-time to social media.[18] When it was over, it was found that furnishings had been destroyed, desks rifled through, legislative documents stolen, and feces left smeared on the walls.[19]

A police officer was hit in the head and died later that day. One rioter was shot and killed by police as she broke through a window. Another member of the crowd was trampled to death. One hundred and forty other officers were injured during beatings; some were bludgeoned with flagpoles holding the American flag.[20] Many officers were left with severe injuries, which included the loss of an eye, loss of fingers, and brain and spinal injuries. In the weeks following the insurrection, two of those surviving officers would commit suicide.[21]

In total, five people died during the attack. It could have been worse; it also could have been prevented if the warning signs had been heeded and if preemptive action had been taken.

This was not a spontaneous event, as there was abundant evidence of advance planning. Some rioters brought maps of the Capitol building interior to find locations where lawmakers could be hiding. Pipe bombs would later be discovered in various places.[22]

Officers also found a pickup truck driven by a 70-year-old man parked nearby. Inside the truck were multiple guns, including a semi-automatic rifle, hundreds of rounds of ammunition, explosives, several machetes, camouflage smoke devices, a stun gun, a crossbow with bolts, and 11 Molotov cocktails.[23]

Many of those committing violence that day were not people one would typically associate with extremism. While many were organized and well-rehearsed for violent insurrection, others were members of the community who can be viewed as a new genre of extremists—"normal" citizens without histories of violence. Many were middle-aged business owners and people identified as soccer moms and white-collar workers whom we would consider typical middle-class people.[24]

The common theme among them was that they had been pushed in the direction of violence through bizarre conspiracy theories such as QAnon, which consumed social media during the previous four years. We know that the more a message is repeated, the more people come to believe it's true. The Capitol riot illustrates that it is possible to dramatically influence people's behavior by bombarding them with messages that heighten fear and anger, in many cases causing them to behave in uncharacteristic ways.

Many viewed former president Donald Trump as the initiator of the attempted insurrection; he consistently used inflammatory rhetoric and conspiracy theories to undermine public confidence in the 2020 election by making disproven claims of voter fraud. For weeks Trump had falsely stated that the electoral vote had been fraudulent—a statement repeatedly proven to be false in multiple courts. His rhetoric included calls for his followers to "create an army" and "fight like hell against bad people." At a nearby rally just before the insurrection, he directed the crowd to "walk down Pennsylvania Avenue" to the Congressional building to "take back the country."[25]

These actions would lead to the unprecedented case of a U.S. president being twice impeached by the House of Representatives.

The pathway to this violence began years earlier and involved concerted social media campaigns promoting bizarre conspiracy theories designed to feed paranoia. Imaginary enemies were created, as "us versus them" rhetoric was amplified to a hysterical degree. Trump signaled both false victimization and virtue. Perceptual distortions and rage grew among the far-right community as people became increasingly unhinged from reality.

Social media delivered the accelerant and the opportunity to coordinate violence. Most of it occurred in public view.

Foreshadowing and Inflammatory Language

Trump himself provided abundant foreshadowing; he was particularly adept at using language to amplify rage, thus effectively motivating others to act violently.

Decades of research show that political leaders' inflammatory language can incite violence,[26] but this has not been the norm in modern America.

Communications professor Kurt Braddock, writing in *The Conversation,* summarizes the ways that messages can cause violent behavior.[27]

- When a person encounters a message that advocates a behavior, that person will likely believe that it will have positive results. This is particularly true if the speaker of that message is liked or trusted by the message's target.
- When these messages communicate positive beliefs or attitudes about a behavior—as when our friends told us that smoking was "cool" when we were teenagers—message targets come to believe that those they care about would approve of their engaging in the behavior or would engage in the behavior themselves.
- When those messages contain language that highlights the target's ability to perform a behavior, as when a president tells raucous supporters that they have the power to overturn an election, they develop the belief that they can carry out that behavior.

Michael Humphrey, Assistant Professor of Journalism and Media Communication at Colorado State University, is a digital narrative researcher. He analyzes the stories told by politicians and how the populace is affected by them. Since Trump was an obsessive poster on Twitter, Humphrey examined Trump's tweets throughout his presidency. He has described the consistent story structure constantly repeated in the tweets and how Trump "re-scripted" the world to fit his themes.[28]

Five main themes repeated regularly:

- The authentic version of the United States is beset with invaders.
- Real Americans can see this.
- I (Trump) am uniquely qualified to stop this invasion.
- The establishment and its agents are hindering me.
- The United States is in mortal danger because of this.

Taken together over time, this formed an overall story structure that Humphrey summarizes this way: "The establishment is stopping me from protecting you against invaders." The "establishment" could be anyone—Democrats, the NFL, a media outlet, a corporation, and even Vice President Mike Pence. "The invaders" were China, the Coronavirus that first emerged there, people crossing the U.S.–Mexico border or Black Lives Matter protestors. The structure never changed. There was a danger to the nation; Trump was uniquely able to protect America, and "real" Americans righteously supported him.[29]

This messaging is consistent with the personality traits suggestive of narcissism, paranoid thinking, and classic victim and virtue signaling. With a history of decades in the television industry, Trump masterfully mobilized those with the conspiracy mindset to his advantage. It proved to be propane to extremists.

Political leaders have the power to polarize and divide a populace or to bring them together. Extremist rhetoric can motivate people to kill; it can even bring down democracy.

Trump knew how to mobilize vulnerable people by repeating a false narrative that amplified their fears and normalized a violent response. He used social media to do it, signaling false victimization as well as narcissistic virtue. He knew how to activate already angry people and amplified paranoia and anger in the vulnerable through language use. This is a proven formula for violence.

And it could have been worse. On January 15, 2021, nine days after the assault on the Capitol, FBI agents raided the home and business of a 43-year-old Napa, California, man who had an arsenal of weapons and explosives. He had made online death threats against the governor of California and had a plan to target social media companies Twitter and Facebook, who had banned Trump a week earlier for inciting violence. He also threatened to "blow up a democrat building." The Napa man stated that if Trump was not installed as president again, he planned to "go to war."[30] If he had not been interrupted, he would have been added to the list of mass killers.

Dozens of lone mass killers have been driven in part by conspiracy beliefs about those from racial, ethnic, or religious minority groups. Focusing on more than just prejudice, these groups organize around false beliefs and disinformation and build hatred that normalizes violent action. Whether white supremacists or incels, the behavior that can result affects us all.

Similarities Despite Differences

The Oklahoma City bomber distrusted the government and was obsessed with guns. He believed that the government was conspiring to disarm and enslave Americans—a belief common among opponents of gun-control and right-wing paramilitary militia groups. Yet, he had been an exemplary soldier in the U.S. military. Though he had never been a formal member of a hate group, he agreed with their ideology and was spurred to action by it.

The Unibomber, a mathematics prodigy, believed that modern technology was destroying the environment. He viewed government as a form of oppression. In the *New York Times*, his manifesto described his opposition to industrialization and his desire for a nature-centered form of anarchism.

Both identified as victims and believed they were acting virtuously.

Those with dark triad or dark tetrad traits are particularly susceptible to extreme conspiracy beliefs since they actively look for them; however, those without such strong tendencies can be pushed in that direction when repeatedly exposed to disinformation and inflammatory language.

Conspiracy theories have always existed, and they won't go away, but never before have platforms existed that facilitate their spread with such phenomenal ease. Now they are stumbled upon by people who are not even looking for them. Flawed ideas have real-world consequences, and many believe increased domestic terrorism will be in our future.[31]

"False Flags" and "Crisis Actors"

Another strange twist in the conspiracy trend that has occurred regularly since the mid–90s has been the idea that school shootings are events planned by the U.S. government to justify disarming citizens. The story goes that school shootings never really happen; instead, they are "false flag" events in which "crisis actors" are paid to pretend to be victims of the crime. In recent years such beliefs have been spread by far-right internet propagandists who traffic in peddling multiple outrageous and bizarre conspiracies involving aliens, a supposed "deep state," and other secret malevolent forces.[32]

These stories have spread due to their shocking nature, and like other conspiracies, function to help people make sense of what seems incomprehensible. At various times these false flag theories have even been peddled by prominent far-right politicians who thrive on feeding paranoia.

One of the most vocal proponents of false-flag myths is Texas conspiracist Alex Jones, who has a massive social media following. Jones was deplatformed from YouTube, Facebook, Apple, and Spotify in 2018 and is facing a civil suit for defamation and injury brought against him by parents from Sandy Hook Elementary School. Texas courts have heavily fined him, and the case continues to progress in the Texas court system.[33]

As conspiracy peddlers increasingly lose their social media platforms and are held responsible for damages caused by their behavior, we may see this particular trend slow down. Journalists and social media companies are doing a better job of exposing disinformation and de-platforming those who traffic in it.

13

Our Electronic Culture

"I'll see you on national T.V.!"—Tucson shooter, on MySpace

Culture has moved online, and we're only beginning to understand the impact on our society. This chapter explores how the news media, social media, video games, and celebrity culture intersect with incidents of mass killings.

The New Culture

Humans are social beings. We are each part of a culture, developing our identities, belief systems, and status in the social hierarchy. One of the beautiful things about humanity is how much we learn from living with each other. The flip side is that not everything we learn is good for us.

Human culture has never remained static; as people have direct contact with others who have new knowledge, skills, or different ways of thinking, norms and customs within social groups change. These changes have happened gradually and incrementally for most human history and have ultimately worked out for the better.

However, this rate of cultural change has accelerated in recent decades, in large part due to the advancement of the internet and now-ubiquitous technologies like smartphones. We're just beginning to understand the impact these new technologies have had on society. Still, it's safe to say that human culture has changed dramatically at an unprecedented rate, and not all of the effects of these changes have been beneficial.

Technology has caused people to modify most aspects of their behavior on the personal and interpersonal level. With a smartphone, a person of any age can search any imaginable topic online in just seconds, from any location. We can socialize with people of any age, gender, or belief system from all over the world, at any hour of the day or night. We meet with friends in online games without ever having to leave home or break a sweat. We can find a date, preview a restaurant, or have online sex. We can try on new identities or pretend to be someone other than who we are. We can do all this under the cloak of anonymity, and for young people, outside of parents' awareness.

Places We Don't Want to Go

Research psychologist and MIT professor Sherry Turkle has written extensively about the impact of technology on individuals, relationships, and culture. In the 90s, she focused on the potential benefits of these new ways of being and relating. She has since modified her views.

Turkle is now convinced "we have allowed technology take us places we don't want to go. We have become permanently plugged into devices that not only change what we do, they also change who we are. We relate to others differently, we relate to ourselves differently, with constant distractions that have been intentionally engineered to capture our attention and diminish our capacity for self-reflection."[1]

Turkle points out those things commonly done now which would have seemed odd in the past, such as sleeping with our smartphones. People text or shop or browse social media during work meetings or classes, thus shortening attention spans. We have come to expect constant novelty.

Families sit side by side at the dinner table, together but separate, each engaged with the devices in their hands rather than with one another. Children may sit together in groups in the same physical space, but they simultaneously stare at their separate screens rather than converse. As Turkle puts it, "We are alone, together."

Life now largely happens online. Though we used to refer to the "virtual world" as separate from the "real world," the two have now merged. Online social relationships have supplanted or replaced real-world connections for many people.

We don't become emotionally close in the same ways we used to when we made human connections by being together in the same place. The conversation has modified to short, choppy snippets of thought sent through messaging apps, becoming increasingly superficial in the process. When young people grow up communicating with one another primarily through texting, they fail to develop abilities in building deeper conversational skills and the kind of human attachments that only happen when we can attune to one another with intention.

This comes with risks. In many of these new ways of relating, we can never really be sure if we're communicating with a child or an adult, the gender they claim, or someone who is psychologically healthy. This can be risky for the vulnerable, particularly young people. Through the internet, people who would never have met find one another and form new social groups with their own values, norms, and ways of determining status. And these new groups can easily filter out others who may have different points of view, thus becoming rigid in ideologies that can be alarming.

While there have been beneficial aspects to social networking online, the not-so-beneficial elements have allowed extremist hate groups to flourish and increasingly influence the younger people who stumble into them.

Addiction

The issue of behavioral addiction to electronic video gaming has been of concern to mental health clinicians and many parents and teachers for the past 20 years.[2] With the smartphone's advent, the problem of addiction to our electronic devices has amplified and expanded. Most of us check our smartphones 150 times a day yet make very few actual phone calls; we keep them close at hand, often in a pocket, functioning as 24/7 internet browsers, game systems, and instant messaging programs that allow us the potential to be electronically connected every minute of the day to increasingly novel content.[3]

Concerns about addiction are no longer limited to the discrete amounts of time spent in a virtual gaming world from a gaming console or desktop computer. Games, and much, much more, are always at hand.

Tristan Harris is a computer scientist and ethicist who worked as a Design Ethicist at Google. He is an expert on how technology hijacks our psychological vulnerabilities. Harris has since founded the Center for Humane Technology, a nonprofit organization that focuses on consumer technology ethics.[4]

In a computer science program at Stanford University, Harris was trained in manipulative design techniques engineered into various digital platforms to make electronic media habit-forming. "There are hundreds of engineers every day whose job it is to keep you hooked," Harris stresses in his educational talks and podcast interviews. He emphasizes that the interface with electronic devices functions on the same principle of variable reward as slot machines. This reward system provides intense but momentary pleasure and is designed to produce maximum engagement from users. This is the precise mechanism of addiction. "A handful of engineers steer the behavior of billions of people," Harris says, as he explains that the goal of platform developers is to keep users engaged as much as possible.

Harris, who refers to smartphones as "the slot machine in our pockets," makes the following points[5]:

- When we pull our phone out of our pocket, we're *playing a slot machine* to see what notifications we got.
- When we refresh our email, we're *playing a slot machine* to see what new email we got.
- When we swipe down our finger to scroll the Instagram feed, we're *playing a slot machine* to see what photo comes next.
- When we swipe faces left/right on dating apps like Tinder, we're *playing a slot machine* to see if we got a match.
- When we tap the # of red notifications, we're *playing a slot machine* to what's underneath.

These techniques work. All media competes for our attention, and the companies who create the technology and content want to keep us engaged for myriad reasons. Copious amounts of our personal data are sold for marketing purposes, and advertising is embedded in the platforms we use. Engaging novel content is continuously available, increasing the pull of our attention and effectively hijacks the reward system in our brains, which is driven by the neurotransmitter dopamine. This can change the structure and function of our nervous system and alter our mood state, causing us to increase return to the device.[6] This process is the essence of behavioral addiction.

Our devices pull us out of our awareness, distracting us from our internal experience or the experience of those who are physically present with us. Without our consent, our brains are being rewired, and we are changing. The way we relate to others is changing as well.

Addiction cuts us off from ourselves and narrows our window of opportunity to engage in the environment around us. We stop enjoying other activities that would enhance and enrich life and miss opportunities for building real-world relationships and competencies.[7] Though one can be a master in a video game virtual world, this achievement does not translate into the real world.

Too much time online hampers development in countless ways. For the vulnerable, excessive online time increases the risk of veering into extremist communities. This risk is exceptionally high for children and adolescents, who are developmentally incapable of exercising wise judgment. Teens are also naturally prone to rebellion against a parent's values, just as they are apt to engage in secretive behavior.

The Culture of Social Media

> "Seems the more people you kill, the more you're in the limelight."—Roseburg, Oregon, shooter, in a blog post[8]

You can be anyone you want to be on the internet. Opportunities for creating a new digital identity are everywhere. On social media platforms, you can use a false name or often remain anonymous, and you can meet people you would never run into in your everyday life. You can learn what was previously unimaginable with just the click of a mouse.

"Social media" is the term used to describe various internet-based platforms that allow people from all over the world to connect through sharing text-based conversations, images, or a combination of the two.

Most of the time, social media helps people connect positively, but there is an underbelly that flies under the radar of many. There is no limit to the kind of content one can find online, from the positive, beautiful, and inspirational to the antisocial, dangerous, and disturbing.

Many social media platforms are visually based, like Facebook, Instagram, YouTube, Twitter, Tumblr, Snapchat, Parler, and TikTok. Others, like Reddit, Telegram, and Gab, are primarily text-based message boards. The newest platforms on the block are the audio chat apps like Clubhouse.

Text-based and image-based message boards are massive collections of forums that allow users to share content on any topic imaginable and comment on each other's posts. Reddit is one of the most highly used sites on the internet and is broken up into more than a million communities known as "subreddits," each covering a specific topic. While some sites are moderated for content, others are not. Those without moderation have sometimes become safe spaces for mass killers. This has been particularly true of imageboards.

Imageboards are a type of internet forum where anonymous users post images alongside text and discussion. Some of the more notorious imageboards have become known for hosting extremist forums—many dedicated to racial and ethnic hatred, violent misogyny, paranoid conspiracy theories, and the veneration of mass killers.

Hate groups have found homes on internet sites such as 4chan, 8chan, Parler, Reddit, and secure messaging platforms like Discord, Telegram, and Gab. The choice of platforms constantly shifts, making it difficult for authorities to monitor what they are up to. When outed on one forum, they move to another, gravitating to venues free of gatekeepers; they go to great lengths to avoid detection.[9]

8chan (later 8kun) has been known as one of the most notorious imageboards. It was developed in 2013 by then 19-year-old computer programmer Fred Brennan. Brennan created the site intending to provide a platform essentially free of content moderation. The site was made up of user-created message boards, with any decisions about content moderation left to the individual who created each board. Often, there was none. Boards were created to discuss topics such as child rape and sexualized images of minors. Links were posted to explicit child pornography hosted elsewhere. 8chan regularly hosted boards calling for racist and misogynistic violence—content that Brennan stated he personally found abhorrent, yet he defended it as the inevitable cost of free speech.[10] Over time, his views on content moderation began to evolve, as he became unable to deny the harm the imageboard was causing. In 2018 he severed ties with it.

Brennan turned 8chan over to new owner Jim Watkins and his son Ron, who became the site administrator. Though American, the Watkins operated 8chan from the Philippines, where they resided at that time.[11]

Brennan was catalyzed to action when 8chan became the digital home for multiple mass killers and those who wanted to follow their playbooks. In 2019, manifestos and messages from several mass killers were posted to 8chan, along with links to view live-streamed videos of attacks.[12] In the aftermath of the three back-to-back shootings in Dayton, El Paso, and Gilroy in late July and early August 2019, Brennan became an outspoken critic of 8chan, publicly calling for it to be shut down. The direct involvement of 8chan users in horrific acts of violence could not be denied; hate speech had moved to murder.

The Watkins were not motivated to act. 8chan was only forced to shut down when their internet infrastructure company Cloudflare refused to continue to support their site. Cloudflare's CEO said at the time that the site had been considered a "problematic user" for a long time.[13]

Struggling to find another service after being booted by Cloudflare, the Watkins briefly reincarnated 8chan under the name 8kun before eventually going defunct in 2021, following their role in the insurrection at the U.S. Capitol.[14]

8chan and 8kun were also the home of the debunked far-right QAnon conspiracy theory, also tied to extremist violence. The mysterious figure who called himself "Q" posted messages called "drops" on the boards to spur a far-right takeover of the U.S. government. Many journalists believe the Watkins were behind the Q conspiracy posts, which have now ceased, along with their imageboard.

Most recently, Telegram, Gab, Parler, and Winkim have become popular with far-right extremist groups who used the platforms to organize the insurrection attempt at the Capitol.

The social media landscape is constantly changing. When one platform fades in popularity, new ones develop and rise to the top. Official rules typically permit anyone over 13 to open an account, upload content, and gain followers. Yet, the platforms admit that millions of younger users simply lie about their age.

Online Narcissism

Children today are social media savvy, and they've learned to be performers to get attention and esteem. Obtaining followers and "likes" are seductive behavioral reinforcement, designed to keep users hooked on the process.

Not only can you have followers on YouTube or Instagram, but you can also potentially become a star. Fittingly, the celebrities of these platforms are referred to as "influencers," and they have a massive influence. Teenagers with millions of followers have channels dedicated to everything from video games to makeup and hairstyle tips to mental health topics to thousands of helpful how-to tutorials. Moving into more sinister territory, groups are dedicated to promoting anorexia (called "proana"), plastic surgery, and various forms of intentional self-harm. YouTube videos of brutal street fights, dangerous pranks, bizarre conspiracy theories, and multiple flavors of extremism can appeal to people with potentially violent tendencies.

Adolescence is the time when it's normal for parents to have diminishing influence over young people, who begin to model their behavior and values after peers; now, it's influencers on social media who teach teens how to think and behave. In a 2019 survey of 2,000 young Americans aged 13 to 38, 86 percent said they would consider becoming a social media influencer a life goal.[15]

Such easy fame comes with its consequences. Researchers have noted a dramatic upswing in the American culture's narcissistic values since the 1990s. Many social science researchers believe that the culture of social media has a lot to do with this.

Narcissistic traits include self-centeredness, entitlement, grandiosity, attention-seeking, self-deception, a drive to exert power, hypersensitivity, and over-reactions to perceived criticism. Becoming famous online can become an all-consuming addiction for some, which displaces other interests. For particularly vulnerable persons, the outcomes can be disastrous; if you can't become famous for something positive, there are always alternate paths. And in online extremist communities, people that all think the same find each other, validate each other, collectively amplify their anger, and reinforce dangerous cognitive distortions.

Cable News

Manifestos, whether written or video, are the mass killer's press kits; the news media tends to function as their microphone. By watching their broadcasts and reading their manifestos, we become their audience and provide them with a stage. Thus, mass killers have the power to terrorize an entire population of people, not just those they impact directly with bullets or a bomb.

To make sense of the interface between killers and the media, we need to understand the cable news media culture. Like that of the internet, its influence is powerful.

The way crime is reported changed dramatically in recent decades. Many can't remember a time before 24/7 news existed.

Though CNN initially took to the air in 1980, cable television news in the United States didn't fully bloom until the 1990s, as multiple profit-driven stations began to compete for international viewership. A handful of large corporations now own the major news networks that compete for the world's attention.[16]

These stations' profitability is based upon advertising revenue, which is directly linked to viewership. Thus, there is pressure to produce a constant stream of eye-catching content. While immediate access to breaking news has been helpful to society in myriad ways, there have been downsides. While outrage and terror grab the most attention, this ultimately serves to cause more problems than it solves.

Cable news is often criticized for showcasing lurid content with sensationalistic presentations designed to provoke viewers' strong emotional reactions. In the process, complex issues are reduced to interesting but superficial soundbites. Biased slant from news networks can mold viewers' thinking and behavior in multiple ways, amplifying destructive social polarization and anger. Not only do we see cultural shifts toward narcissism, we're also becoming a culture of outrage and polarization.

It's all about the ratings. The business model incentivizes sensationalism. Cable news stations are highly motivated to capture our attention and keep us watching. This is easily done with stories that trigger the fear and anger center of the brain—the amygdala. When we're exposed to frightening news, we flood with adrenaline and noradrenaline, which causes our heart rate, blood sugar levels, and blood pressure to go up. Our cognitive abilities diminish, and we're unable to process information cogently. We are in the fight, flight, or freeze response before knowing it—just from watching a story on the news.

The first station to get to the scene of a traumatic breaking news story gets the most viewers; in a rush to get the story out, factual errors are often made from less-than-credible sources. Research has shown that mass shootings are more likely than other crimes to receive extended media attention while at the same time presenting misinformation.[17]

Socially responsible journalism is often at odds with the profit-driven news media, which operates without a conscience. This kind of coverage can inadvertently propel mass killers into immediate star status as folk heroes. The Columbine killings in 1999 provide a vivid example.

The two Colorado high schoolers were acutely aware of themselves as performers; they'd been recording videos for over a year and intended to make a significant media splash by committing the largest mass murder in U.S. history. They left behind copious documentation of their intentions in the form of their journals. They self-recorded videos in which they yelled into the camera about killing people and starting a revolution. They laughed as they fantasized about Hollywood directors fighting for their stories.

And they did become famous. In the days, weeks, and months after Columbine, their names and faces loomed large on our television screens. The news coverage of the murders was constant, with replayed video footage of them walking on school grounds in their long black trench coats with their bombs and weapons stowed in duffle bags, alongside their smiling, normal-appearing senior portraits. Speculation about their personalities and motives became a national pastime as their names became known around the world.

The only prominent director to make a film about them was Michael Moore. Moore intended *Bowling for Columbine* to be a film promoting gun control, which it did. Ironically, the chilling footage of the killer's rampage that Moore integrated into his movie also became a source of inspiration to some.[18]

This led to unprecedented acts of violence worldwide in countries where such actions had been previously unknown, including England, Germany, Canada, Holland, Thailand, Brazil, and China. Researchers have termed this the "Columbine effect."[19]

No one could have paid for this kind of publicity; it directly contributed to their mythic status in a particular segment of antisocial subculture. Those who are immersed in this fandom self-identify as "Columbiners."

Columbiners

It's hard to imagine organized fandoms for mass murderers, but internet connectivity has enabled this phenomenon. The group that's been active the longest is known as "Columbiners."[20]

Columbiners connect on the internet; most of them are adolescents who were not even born when the murders happened. Yet, they continue to bond online over their obsessive infatuation with these specific killers and their crimes.

YouTube features dozens of videos of the killers, from outlaw videos they made for school projects, self-recorded videos of their target practices with friends, documentaries, and news features about them. There are clips of the killers overlaid with a musical score designed to make them appear cool. An active Reddit community is still obsessed with the Columbine killers 20 years after the event, where enthusiasts share morbid details about their autopsies, old photos and videos of the perpetrators, and any bits of trivia members discover.

Many Columbiners are teenage girls who express romantic longing for the two murderers. They commonly excuse what the killers did with the mythical narrative that they were righteous avengers striking back at bullies—a myth that has no factual basis.

Some mimic their clothing and style and romanticize their writings. Overall, they express sympathy for them as well as fascination.

At the dawn of the internet era, The Columbine killers created the cultural script—or template for behavior—which hundreds of other angry young men have attempted to follow. It's a prescription for exerting masculine power that continues to have pull to this day.

In a world connected by the internet, none of us exist in isolation. News spreads almost instantaneously around the globe. For decades research has long shown the relationship between media coverage and imitation behavior with suicide. When a suicide gets extensive media coverage, the rates of similar suicides increase—especially when the individual who dies is a famous person.

This process has been termed "social contagion," and we now see that it applies to behavior other than suicide; it has been a significant factor in mass killings.

Copycat and Contagion

Copycat and **contagion** are two distinct but closely related phenomena that have everything to do with mass killings.[21]

Copycat is identification with the specific perpetrator of a crime, an effect that can remain for months or years. This is evidenced when individuals become obsessed with the perpetrator and details of his life, identify with his grievances, and model behavior, attire, and weapons.[22]

The contagion effect is imitating a publicized violent act over subsequent days and weeks, explaining why mass killings tend to occur in clusters.[23] Teens are particularly prone to the contagion effect.

We can think of the copycat effect as providing the cultural script and the contagion effect as the viral spread.

In an analysis of hundreds of mass killings from 1997 to 2013, researchers found that another attack's probability was highest in the two weeks following a highly publicized mass killing.[24]

Mother Jones analyzed 74 plots and attacks by perpetrators claiming inspiration by Columbine. Of these, 53 plots were thwarted and

21 completed, resulting in the deaths of 89 victims and injury of 126.[25] *Mother Jones* found the following:

- The suspects planned the attack on the anniversary of Columbine.
- The goal was to outdo the Columbine body count.
- The suspects referred to the Columbine killers as heroes, idols, martyrs, or God.
- Some suspects made pilgrimages to Columbine High School.

The FBI examined 160 mass shootings committed after Columbine and found a pervasive copycat effect,[26] as did the Secret Service. Attacks were often planned in April (the month of the Columbine attack) or near the beginning or end of the school year.[27]

As of early 2021, Colorado's Northern Central region has seen at least nine mass shootings since the Columbine killings. Four major shootings have occurred within 20 miles of the high school, including the shooting in Aurora.[28]

Whether they are framed as knights, gods, avengers, or monsters, mass killers are media influencers who inspire followers. The gunman who killed 12 people at the Colorado movie theater in 2012 subsequently had a fan club on Tumblr.[29] Before the murder of nine people at an Oregon community college in 2015, the perpetrator uploaded a video to YouTube about the Newtown murders at Sandy Hook Elementary School.[30] And, we will never forget the seven-foot spreadsheet compiled by the Newtown murderer.

Video Games

Gaming is far more significant than Hollywood as a cultural influencer and moneymaker these days. Forty-three percent of all U.S. adults play video games "often or sometimes."[31] Video game sales statistics show that electronic gaming industry revenue dwarfs all other entertainment industries combined. Global film box office revenue in 2018 amounted to $41.7 billion, while the gaming market generated $151.2

billion. Despite the stereotype that most gamers are adolescents, the average age of a gamer is now 35.[32]

Enthusiasm for gaming is not limited to the United States. In many countries of the world, video games are considered a major social activity. South Korea, Japan, U.K., Italy, Germany, and Canada are examples of countries where gaming is a common cultural pastime—yet they have dramatically lower incidents of violence than the United States, and mass shootings have *never* occurred in most of them.

For years many have attempted to link violent video games and mass killings, particularly first-person shooter games. Analyzing this research is complicated and has not been without controversy. Violent video games are universally popular, and gamers are understandably quick to become defensive at allegations their hobby could cause them to become real-world killers.

Ninety-seven percent of youths between the ages of 12 and 17 play video games. While many mass killers have been avid players of violent video games, so are most young men worldwide. Women are also gamers, making up 46 percent of all players, though they are less likely to play violent first-person shooter games; 78 percent of women play nonviolent games on their smartphones.[33]

A false dichotomy has been presented: either violent video games are causing mass shootings, or they have no relevancy whatsoever. Getting to the truth isn't quite that simple, and neither of these extremes captures what's happening.

If there were a direct cause-effect process with video games and mass killings, we would see two things: far more mass killings as well as mass shootings in countries like South Korea, Canada, and Japan. This has not been the case. In fact, as gaming has ascended in popularity since the 1990s, overall rates of violent crime have gone down. However, this does not mean there is no relevancy whatsoever.

There are particular concerns about children and violent media. While most children are likely impacted in some way, violent media does not affect all children in the *same* way. Children, just like adults, have many different personalities, strengths, and vulnerabilities.

The American Psychological Association cites decades of research indicating that exposing children to a violent media clip increases their odds of aggression soon after. Major findings were as follows[34]:

- Children may become less sensitive to the pain and suffering of others.
- Children may be more fearful of the world around them.
- Children may be more likely to behave in aggressive or harmful ways toward others.

These effects are most potent when children are younger, the violence is realistic, or the violence is presented as heroic.[35]

Childhood exposure to media violence predicts higher aggression levels in young adults[36]; however, this does not translate to criminal violence. While this is both consequential and concerning, it is far from indicating a direct cause-effect relationship between violent media and mass killings. A case cannot be realistically made that playing violent video turns ordinary young people into mass murderers.

What has created confusion in the research on violent video games and their relationship to violent behavior has to do with the fact that research samples have been drawn from youthful gamers in the general population. Mass killers are not like other gamers; they represent a specific subset of gamers who have particular psychological vulnerabilities that cause them to be more dramatically impacted by violent games than their peers. Players are not all blank slates who respond in the same ways to video games. Some may play to ruminate in gory violence that feeds their sadistic fantasies; others may use the game to reduce stress by engaging in the strategy of the game. Players experience games in *qualitatively* different ways, and multiple variables come into play.[37]

We now see that violent video games have more substantial effects on kids already prone to violence. For them, violent media serves to normalize their aggressive impulses and can stoke their rage. Those individuals *do* experience a reduction in empathy from exposure to violent media and are more apt to see violence as an acceptable solution to problems.[38]

Violent video games may have a more substantial impact than violent books or films since they offer the player agency. He is not just watching or reading a story; he *becomes* an actor in the story and helps determine the outcome. The player decides who lives and who dies. This sense of power can be particularly seductive to someone who feels powerless in real life.[39]

It has also been observed that mass killers use games in different ways than regular players. Many have been obsessive players. The Norwegian killer acknowledged that at age 27, he spent one year playing World of Warcraft up to 16 hours a day from his bedroom at his mother's residence.[40] The Newtown killer spent nearly all waking hours isolated in his darkened bedroom, either gaming or researching mass killers. The Isla Vista killer had played games obsessively since early childhood, and it was a frequent source of conflict with his parents.

And then there's Parkland.

"Die, die, die," the Parkland school shooter wrote in a story in his middle school English class. His explanation: It was a line from his *Call of Duty* warfare video game booklet. Teachers were concerned that at age 12, he was spending as many as 15 hours a day playing the violent first-person shooter game. Neighbors reported that his mother struggled to limit his playing time, believing it amplified his anger problems.[41]

It's not just the games; it's the way certain players interact with certain games.

Some experiments have indicated that people become more pro-social and helpful when playing a pro-social video game and more aggressive after playing a violent game. Players of pro-social games were more likely to deescalate situations when another person was being harassed. Players of prosocial games were found to be less violent overall than those who played violent games. It's speculated that playing prosocial games affects social cognition by positively influencing players' emotions and thoughts.[42]

Rehearsal

Some mass killers have openly acknowledged that they used combat video games as a strategic rehearsal for their attacks. The Aurora theater shooter admitted that he applied military strategies that he practiced in video games during his preparation for the killings.

The Norwegian killer has described how he trained for the mass shooting by playing the computer game *Call of Duty: Modern Warfare,* a popular combat first-person-shooter game banned in Germany.

"You develop target acquisition," he said. In *Call of Duty,* he practiced shooting with a holographic aiming device used by militaries for training. "It consists of many hundreds of different tasks, and some of these tasks can be compared with an attack, for real. That's why it's used by armies around the world. It's very good for acquiring experience related to sights systems." He would use a similar holographic aiming device when he murdered 77 people, mostly schoolchildren.[43]

Displacement of Other Activities

Another critical concern long noted by therapists is the tendency for people to become so obsessed with video gaming that they stop engaging in or fail to start other everyday activities necessary for healthy development. People immersed in a virtual world while staring at a screen for hours are not moving their bodies, spending time outdoors, reading, exploring their creativity, or developing other hobbies and interests. They stop having conversations and developing relationships with people they meet in their daily lives, which can inhibit the development of necessary competencies and skills.

Excessive gaming limits healthy development in myriad ways and changes the trajectory of an individual's development. Life becomes narrow and constrained to an online world that is controlled by a manipulative system of rewards. Obsessive gaming can keep people from meeting their potential, as they develop a sense of self-worth that is entirely dependent upon their identity in the virtual world.[44]

Mods

"Mods" is the short term for modifications, which means that some games allow players to change and customize aspects of the games themselves. Game modification can enable players to create virtual environments which mirror specific locations and interests.

Much has been speculated about the Columbine killers' fascination with and dedication to the video game *Doom*. They played obsessively and made custom modifications to the game that suited their homicidal interests. Perhaps of most relevance, they created a mod of their high school, allowing them to rehearse their murder spree. Once again, they displayed leakage of what would come.

In this way, violent games may serve to function as murder simulators for a small gamers' subset.

Gamification and the Scoreboard Effect

Scores matter to mass killers. High scores bring status.

Many have noted a process of "gamification" occurring in online imageboards as people compare the "kill scores" of various mass killers, glorifying those have high scores and mocking those who don't. Would-be killers engage in one-upmanship and ego-boosting fantasies of outdoing one another. Mass killers are playing a game to win, and some make detailed posts about the best ways to stage a mass shooting, strategizing about ways to maximize their kill scores.[45]

Mass killers target school children or church groups because they realize their odds of killing many are increased with easy targets.

By emphasizing the number killed in each event, the news media unwittingly contribute to the scoreboard effect.

Masculine Domination

Violent video games focus on masculine domination themes through violence and provide the opportunity to "be someone." They can feed the narcissistic tendencies of certain vulnerable players who are more apt to become addicted. For those who play obsessively, gameplay displaces healthy social activities, reducing real-life competencies in the non-virtual world.

Some games have been specifically designed to promote racial extremism and sexual violence. In one game, the player's goal is to stalk and then rape a mother and her two daughters. The game was banned in Australia, the U.K., and Japan after public campaigns against it. It was subsequently withdrawn from the market.[46] *Battle Raper* and *Ethnic Cleansing* have similarly horrifying themes. There is even a *Super Columbine Massacre* game in which the player is in the killer's role.

While none of this may be healthy for society, it's only one piece of what's going on. Though it might be comforting to say there is a direct cause-effect relationship between video games and mass killings, it's not that simple.

Books and Movies

We are all influenced beneath our conscious awareness by the media we consume. Sometimes we're influenced positively, sometimes not, but most of us are not affected catastrophically. However, we are not all the same. Some are affected more than others. Young people who identify with violent characters in the media are more apt to become aggressive over time.[47] Having a fascination and obsession with violent media is one of the risk factors common to school shooters.

The Columbine killers could recite all the lines from the film *Natural Born Killers*; they referred to their planned attack as "going NBK."

In 1977, when he was in high school, author Stephen King wrote a book about a psychologically disturbed high school student who shoots faculty members at his school and holds his algebra class hostage. In the book's scenario, the hostage students gradually begin to identify with the killer and sympathize with him. After four school shooters cited the book as inspiration, King removed it from print in 1998.

"I pulled it because in my judgment it might be hurting people, and that made it the responsible thing to do," said King.[48]

In BookFinder.com's list of the 100 most sought-after out-of-print books of 2013, this book was ranked higher than any other novel.[49] As of 2021, copies continue to be available on Amazon, priced from $900 to $1,500.

Recommendations

When a mass killer's manifesto is published, we've allowed him to control the narrative. Providing them a platform for fame incentivizes them to kill as many as they can. Take away their microphone, and incentive diminishes.

In collaboration with the Advanced Law Enforcement Rapid Response Training Team, the FBI has developed the "Don't Name Them" campaign, which suggests minimizing naming and describing the individuals involved in mass shootings, limiting sensationalism, and refusing to broadcast shooter statements or videos.[50]

Another suggested strategy is to avoid in-depth descriptions of the shooter's rationale for engaging in the behavior. In general, people are more likely to imitate others' behaviors who they view as similar to themselves. When the media describes a purported motive for the shooting, they may inadvertently be pointing out similarities between the shooter and others. For example, saying that a shooting was revenge against bullies suggests a behavioral script to others who have experienced bullying.[51]

It is also recommended that the media reduce news coverage's duration after a mass shooting. Research has long shown that extensive media coverage following a suicide increases copycat suicides. Many legitimate news sources have attempted to modify how they cover suicides to reduce this effect.[52]

Finally, the media should avoid providing detailed, graphic accounts of the shooter's actions before, during, and after the event. Extensive details or dramatized representations serve to encourage imitation.

We have a bidirectional relationship with the media. We change in response to it; it changes in response to us. Whether we're conscious of it or not, we both influence media content and are influenced by it.

There is no doubt that the media in all its forms has played some part in the manifestation of mass murder by spreading a cultural script—a template—for behavior.

Summary

Mass killers respond to electronic media in ways that are qualitatively unique from others. What they choose to focus on and what they create indicate different thought processes. One of the Columbine killers created a computer simulation of blowing up the school in a video production class at the high school.[53]

Mass killers are overall significantly more narcissistic than other violent criminals. Their manifestos make explicitly narcissistic statements. They want their grandiose image to be remembered. There is a direct link between media attention—whether news media or social media—and narcissism.[54]

Whether they are known as knights, gods, influencers, or avengers, they inspire followers. The gunman who killed 12 people at the Colorado movie theater in 2012 subsequently had a fan club on Tumblr.[55]

There is a clear pattern. They thrive on posing with contemptuous smiles and action-hero machismo. Despite distorted and paranoid thinking, they know how to capitalize on visual exposure and understand internet fame's viral nature.

There is a cultural script in which mass killings provide a "masculine" solution to increase social status. Better to be a notorious antihero than a socially marginalized loser.[56]

Though their ideologies vary, they are all driven by a desire for power, omnipotence, and infamy. The modern media makes all these things possible by feeding narcissistic fantasies and providing a microphone.[57]

Mass killers are inspired by what they learn in the media, often attempting to turn murder into live-streamed performance art online and attain eternal-life status as folk heroes long after their deaths. Through their manifestos, they control the narrative, signal their virtue, and hope to be added to the long list of the infamous. By publicizing their propaganda, we amplify the damage due to the copycat and contagion effects.

We now know that mass killers who seek fame tend to be the deadliest offenders.[58]

Mass media has to potential to align for the public good, but this is not what's been most financially profitable. Now media can give us live-streamed, grotesque snuff films which appeal to the worst aspects of human nature.

Technology has developed faster than our ability to steer it, and we see the consequences in multiple ways.

14

Guns, Guns,
and More Guns

"A well-regulated militia, being necessary for the security of a free state, the right of people to keep and bear arms, shall not be infringed."—Second Amendment of United States Constitution

Though cultures differ superficially, human beings are essentially the same in every country. The world population shares the same strengths and vulnerabilities, the same types of fragilities and needs. We are social beings, and though we have a history of fighting over resources with people we perceive to be different from ourselves, for the most part, we express a desire to live in peace and keep our families safe. Most of us—most of the time—try to do a reasonable job of building safe communities.

Yet, there's something different about the United States, something particularly unusual for a wealthy country. Among other developed countries, it's only here that the random mass killing of strangers has become horrifyingly commonplace.

There's one key factor that's unique to America. We are awash in guns. Our civilian ownership of firearms is far higher than in any other country in the world; we protect gun rights at the expense of our children and families. And despite the consequences, there's no substantial moral alarm that in the United States, there are more guns than people.

This chapter looks at the relationship between mass killings and firearms, contrasting Second Amendment interpretations, the history of gun safety legislation, the gun lobby, and organizations active in promoting gun safety legislation.

Though mass killers may act with other weapons—bombs, knives, and even motor vehicles—guns are the most common lethal weapon of choice. And in the United States, guns are readily accessible, affordable, and easy to use. Anyone can pull the trigger on a gun, even a young child. Most mass killers don't even have to leave home to access a firearm. Guns are everywhere. Owning guns—as many as we want—is a right of citizenship.

It's impossible to examine the phenomenon of mass killings without examining the topic of guns and gun safety. In this chapter, we explore the relationship of firearms to mass killings as well as the legal history and ethical controversies involved in gun control and gun safety legislation.

There is currently no more divisive issue in the United States than that of the regulation of firearms. To explore the role of guns in America is to become immediately aware of two polarizing ideological extremes that tend to divide along political party lines: those who advocate for no gun ownership restrictions and those who do.

It's precisely this political polarization that keeps people focused on "winning" for their party rather than problem-solving about a deadly public health epidemic.

Listening to both sides, one gets the sense of people living in entirely different realities, with accordant opposing world views.

Perspective

The United States is the most heavily armed society globally, with approximately 100 guns for every 90 citizens.[1,2] Though we have only 4 percent of the world's population, we possess 31 percent of the world's guns.[3] In recent decades, firearms have become increasingly integrated into our national identity. The United States has the weakest gun laws among all developed nations, and as a consequence, the following are true:

- Americans are 25 times more likely to be killed by gun homicide than citizens of any comparable country.
- Guns are the murder weapon in 68 percent of all homicides.

- Having a gun in the home triples the risk of death by suicide; 90 percent of suicide attempts with guns are fatal; only 4 percent of suicide attempts by other methods are fatal.[4] Most people who make suicide attempts do not die—unless they use a gun. When access to firearms is limited, suicide rates decrease.
- Domestic violence victims are five times more likely to be killed when their attacker has access to a gun. On average, 53 women every month are shot by a current or former intimate partner. Over one million people are alive today who have been shot—or have been shot at—by an intimate partner.
- In over half of mass shootings, an intimate partner, former intimate partner, or other family member was also murdered before the rampage was taken outside the home.[5]
- Guns are the second leading cause of death for children under 18.

The U.S. gun death rate was 10.6 per 100,000 people in 2016. That contrasts with Canada (2.1 per 100,000) and Australia (1.0), France (2.7), Germany (0.9), and Spain (0.6). Japan has the fewest gun deaths globally, experiencing 100 or fewer gun deaths per year in a population of over 127 million.[6]

Since 1968, more Americans have been killed by gun violence than have died on all battlefields in all the wars in American history combined.[7]

From the American West's mythological gunslingers to armed war heroes and action movie stars, guns have become infused into our culture as the embodiment of masculine power. The firearm has been afforded an almost mystical status, and many believe that owning a gun is essential to ensuring their way of life.

At least three in 10 Americans own guns, and 48 percent grew up in households with guns. Among Americans who own a firearm, 66 percent own more than one, and 29 percent own five or more guns. Seventy-three percent say they cannot imagine ever living in a household without a firearm.[8]

And those numbers are increasing. At the beginning of the Covid-19 pandemic in early 2020, gun sales spiked by millions and continued to climb during the months of subsequent political unrest.[9] Gun

Violent Gun Deaths per 100,000 People per Year (2020)

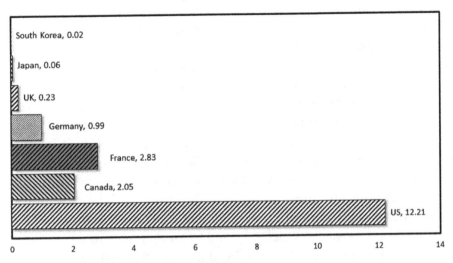

"Violent Gun Deaths Worldwide in 2020" image created by the author. Data source: World Population Review.

deaths went up accordingly. At least 19,223 lost their lives due to gun violence in 2020, a 25 percent jump from the previous year. If we add in gun deaths from suicide, the number rises to 40,000.[10]

Sixty-seven percent of Americans cite "protection" as the primary reason they have a gun; this number has risen dramatically since the 1970s. Thirty-eight percent, primarily rural residents, cite "hunting."[11]

However, this sense of protection comes with a high cost to all of us; in truth, guns kill our friends, family members, and children.

What about the defensive use of guns? Rates of self-defense gun use (SDGU) are challenging to determine and estimates of how often this occurs vary widely. Analysis of data from the National Crime Victimization Survey for 2007–2011 indicates that SDGU is seldom beneficial in reducing the likelihood of injury or property loss during an attempted crime.

Men living in rural areas are most likely to use a gun in self-defense. Out of 14,000 incidents in which the victim was present during a crime, 127 involved an SDGU. After taking protective action like calling 911, 4.2 percent of victims were injured, 38.5 percent of SDGU victims lost property, and 34.5 percent of victims who used a weapon other than a gun lost property. There is no significant better outcome from self-defense gun usage. Compared to other protective actions (calling 911), the National Crime Victimization Surveys provide little evidence that SDGU is uniquely beneficial in reducing the likelihood of injury or property loss.[12]

Most mass killers use legally purchased guns. Adolescent shooters most often use a parent's gun.[13] Firearms are readily accessible, easy to use, and affordable. In many states, anyone over the age of 18—who is not a felon or does not have a well-documented history of severe mental illness that resulted in court-ordered institutional commitment—can walk into a sporting goods store or gun show, and after a quick and cursory background check, walk out with a deadly semiautomatic weapon and associated paraphernalia.

Walmart discontinued sales of guns in 2019 following the spate of mass shootings, one of which occurred inside their El Paso store. They were vigorously attacked for this decision by the National Rifle Association, which stated, "It is shameful to see Walmart succumb to the pressure of the anti-gun elites. Lines at Walmart will soon be replaced by lines at other retailers who are more supportive of America's fundamental freedoms."

Ironically, federal laws have been more restrictive about handguns, which have historically been considered to be more likely to be used in a crime due to the ease of concealment. Though federal law states that one must be 21 to buy a handgun, an 18-year-old can buy a military-grade weapon before he is old enough to buy a beer in most states.

No matter their mental health status or criminal history, anyone can buy a gun from a private party or at a gun show in most states.

Killing with a gun is easy and requires no formal education or training. Firearms don't demand the complicated skill set of a bomb-maker.

Guns and the Law

The Second Amendment of the U.S. Constitution, established in 1791, gives Americans the right to bear arms, though the interpretation of this amendment has been fraught with controversy. As with other aspects of a document crafted 230 years ago, there are often conflicting opinions on best interpreting its application to modern times.

For the first two hundred years after it was written, the Second Amendment was largely ignored. Local gun control laws were ubiquitous in the 19th century, and many cities and states regulated firearms. Carrying any kind of weapon, guns or knives, was commonly prohibited inside city borders and outside the home. Visitors checked their guns with a law enforcement officer when they entered a town and received a token to exchange for their weapon when leaving town.[14]

Long before the availability of modern assault weapons, in the 1950s and 60s, Americans used guns primarily for hunting. A 1959 survey indicated that 60 percent of Americans favored a ban on handguns because they were more likely at the time to be used in violent crimes.

The first piece of federal gun control legislation was the 1934 National Firearms Act (NFA), which criminalized possession of unregistered sawed-off shotguns, a law that was meant to curtail gangland crimes. In 1939, the Supreme Court in *United States v. Miller* upheld the NFA. The court allowed Congress to regulate the interstate selling of sawed-off shotguns, stating that there was no evidence that a sawed-off shotgun "has some reasonable relationship to the preservation of efficiency of a well-regulated militia" and thus "we cannot say that the Second Amendment guarantees the right to keep and bear such an instrument."[15]

Following the 1963 assassination of President John Kennedy and subsequent 1968 assassinations of his brother Robert Kennedy and civil rights activist Martin Luther King, Jr., gun control legislation again become a focus. In 1968, President Lyndon Johnson urged passage of the Federal Gun Control Act (GCA).

The GCA repealed and replaced the earlier statute and added language about "destructive devices" (such as bombs), along with banning the importation of guns that have "no sporting purpose." It also imposed the mandatory age of 21 for purchasing a firearm and prohibited those with documented major mental illness and felons from buying guns.[16]

And then things changed.

The National Rifle Association (NRA) stepped in with new leadership in the late 70s and a strong push for a Second Amendment reinterpretation. At the same time, they began a concerted public relations campaign and dramatically changed their focus, emphasizing that handguns were needed for safety. No longer were guns viewed as primarily for hunting; many became convinced that guns were needed for every individual's personal protection.

Originally a gun-safety organization established in 1871, the new NRA leadership shifted to take a hardline extremist position on individual gun rights. They would soon become the most powerful gun lobby in the world as they began lobbying to remove firearms restrictions.[17] The NRA has since been a major force in American politics, with a massive budget that greatly influences legislators.[18]

As a significant donor to the Republican Party, the NRA has been a critical factor in influencing gun legislation and public perception of the need for guns.[19]

The organization has come under scrutiny for legal and ethical violations in recent years. Though their headquarters is located in Virginia, the NRA is incorporated in New York; in 2020, the New York Attorney General sued the NRA over alleged financial irregularities. Among the charges were that the leader and other executives improperly funneled millions of dollars to finance lavish personal expenses through a "significant diversion of assets." The group subsequently announced a strategic plan to restructure under bankruptcy and then reincorporate in Texas, a state known to be gun friendly.[20]

Political assassination attempts were to continue. In 1981, President Ronald Reagan and White House Press Secretary James Brady were seriously wounded in an assassination attempt by a man with severe mental illness manifesting as paranoid delusions. Reagan recovered, but Brady suffered a head wound in the attack, which left him partially paralyzed.[21]

Brady and his wife subsequently became gun control activists, founding the Brady Campaign and developing a comprehensive plan for preventing gun violence. The Bradys pushed for federal legislation requiring background checks for gun buyers, which eventually passed after an eight-year battle in the legislature. He continued gun safety efforts until his death in 2014, at the age of 73. Brady's death was ruled a homicide, caused by the shooting 33 years earlier.[22]

In 1993, President Bill Clinton signed into law the Brady Handgun Violence Prevention Act, which amended the GCA to require that background checks be completed before a gun is purchased from a licensed dealer, manufacturer, or importer. It established the National Instant

Criminal Background Check System (NICS), which the FBI maintains. This law did not cover guns sold in transactions between private parties or guns sold at gun shows.[23]

The year of 1994 brought the Violent Crime Control and Law Enforcement Act, also signed by President Clinton, which contained a subsection banning military-style semiautomatic weapons for 10 years from September 1994 to September 2004. It also banned high-capacity magazines of over 10 rounds.[24]

It is notable that during the decade when military-style semiautomatic weapons were banned, mass shooting events involving six or more victims fell 37 percent, and the number of deaths fell by 43 percent. After the ban expired, mass shooting incidents increased by 183 percent, and the number of deaths increased 239 percent.[25]

Congress did not renew the ban upon expiration, and deaths from mass shootings increased accordingly.[26]

Things shifted in the pro-gun direction under President George Bush. In 2003, the Tiahrt Amendment (proposed by Todd Tiahrt, R–Kansas) prohibited the ATF from publicly releasing data revealing where criminals purchased their firearms, stipulating that only law enforcement officers or prosecutors could access such information. This

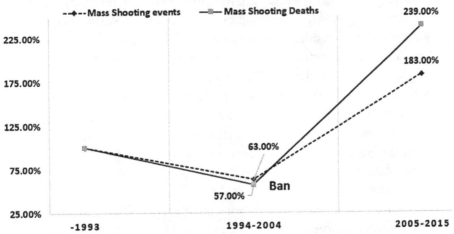

Percentage Change in Mass Shooting Events & Deaths During Assault Rifle Ban & After

"Percentage Change in Mass Shooting Events & Deaths During Assault Rifle Ban & After" image created by the author. Data source: U.S. Senate Study 2019.

amendment essentially protected retailers from public scrutiny, thus reducing their liability for acts of gun violence.[27]

Along a similar line, President Bush signed the Protection of Lawful Commerce in Arms Act in 2005, which prevented gun manufacturers from being named in federal or state civil suits by those victims of crimes committed with weapons manufactured by them.[28]

The most dramatic change happened in 2008 with a difference in the interpretation of the Second Amendment. The Supreme Court in *District of Columbia v. Heller,* in a five to four ruling, reversed a 70-year precedent by ruling that the Second Amendment term "well-regulated militia" applied to an "individual's right to possess a firearm unconnected with service in a militia." This ruling challenged the constitutionality of a 32-year-old handgun ban in Washington, D.C., stating that the ban violated the Second Amendment.[29]

Columbia v. Heller is known as the individual rights interpretation of the Second Amendment. It was controversial at the time and remained so.

In the majority opinion, Supreme Court Justice Antonin Scalia wrote, "There seems to us no doubt, on the basis of both text and history, that the Second Amendment conferred an individual right to keep and bear arms."[30]

The dissenting opinion, written by Justice John Paul Stevens, stated, "The Supreme Court would have us believe that over 200 years ago, the Framers of the Constitution made a choice to limit the tools available to elected officials wishing to regulate civilian uses of weapons.... I could not possibly conclude that the Framers made such a choice."[31]

Currently, gun laws differ significantly from state to state. Each state takes a different approach to laws that cover the sales of guns, permits, and open carry laws. Some state laws are far less restrictive than federal laws, and the Supreme Court ruled in *Printz v United States* that local law enforcement agencies are not required to enforce federal laws. Forty states have provisions that formally validate the individual rights interpretation of the Second Amendment.[32]

Data is clear that the states with the most restrictive gun laws have the lowest gun ownership and tend to have the fewest gun deaths.

There is no federal program to register guns; most states do not require any form of registration. Eight states specifically ban gun registries in any form. Only the District of Columbia, California, Maryland, New York, and Hawaii have specific registering processes. Nine states limit the size of magazines to no more than 10 rounds.[33]

Many states require permits for handguns, but not for long guns.[34] Considering the deadly potential of modern military-grade weapons, the rationale for the disparity is questionable.

Seven states and the District of Columbia have banned or attempted to ban the purchase of semiautomatic assault weapons. However, "legacy" weapons purchased before the date of the ban remain legal.[35] A motivated individual can drive across state lines to make a purchase, the Gilroy killer being a case in point.

Though the city of Boulder, Colorado, banned semiautomatic assault weapons in 2018, in March 2021, a Colorado judge struck down the law, which the NRA and other pro-gun organizations had challenged. Six days later, the Boulder mass killer purchased an assault weapon that he would use to kill 10 people who were shopping for groceries in their local King Soopers supermarket. The NRA claimed a "victory" when the ban was struck down, as did the Colorado State Shooting Association, both plaintiffs in the lawsuit against the city.[36]

In an affidavit filed shortly after the shooting, multiple individuals stated that the perpetrator talked about and played with his assault weapon in the days before the shooting. As is often the case, no one intervened.[37]

It is also common for an individual legally prohibited from buying a firearm (due to age, felon status, or institutionalization for major mental illness) to find another person to purchase for them.[38]

Background Checks and Loopholes

Many people imagine that federal background checks are comprehensive and thorough; the actual process is shockingly easy. There are major loopholes that begin with the national background check system.

The National Instant Criminal Background Check System (NICS) was instituted as part of the Brady Bill. In the NCIS process, a gun buyer presents their I.D. to the seller and fills out ATF Form 4473, asking for personal information such as social security number, citizenship, age, address, race, and criminal history, if any.[39]

The seller then submits the information to the FBI via a toll-free phone line or over the internet, and the agency checks the applicant's info against databases. The process can take as little as a few minutes and is similar to applying for a store credit card while shopping. According to the Gifford Law Center, "In at least 90% of cases, firearm background checks processed through the National Instant Criminal Background Check System are resolved immediately. The average processing time for an electronic NICS-check is less than two minutes—107 seconds to be precise."

Purchasers are asked to respond to the following questions[40]:

- Have you ever been convicted of a felony?
- Have you ever been convicted of a misdemeanor crime of domestic violence?
- Are you an unlawful user of, or addicted to, marijuana or any other depressant, stimulant, narcotic drug, or any other controlled substance?
- Are you a fugitive from justice?
- Have you ever been committed to a mental institution?

The loopholes with this system are evident; it's easy to be deceptive. The questions on criminal history and domestic violence can be fudged because not all local law enforcement agencies submit data to the FBI—which means that there is no way to flag many who fail to answer truthfully. People may also use counterfeit identification.

Another massive loophole is that many people with severe and chronic mental illness have *never* been in mental health treatment. Only a tiny fraction have ever been committed to a mental institution by order of a court. The mental illness prohibition does not apply when a person enters treatment voluntarily or is only hospitalized for short-term observation without long-term, court-ordered treatment. This bar is shockingly high. Outpatient mental health clinics and therapists in private practice do not report to the FBI about their patients. A gun seller has no way of evaluating the mental health status of a gun purchaser.

The federal government does not track nationwide gun sales, so reliable data on how many guns are sold is scarce. We do know that most mass killers use legally purchased guns.

Some states have opted to develop their own process for background checks. This may include waiting periods. For example, in Massachusetts, the state law requires that gun purchasers obtain a permit from their local police department, which conducts their own background check. This process can take weeks and requires multiple steps, including paperwork and an in-person interview. After that, the police chief has the discretion to deny the permit.

Political Battle Lines

The pattern has been consistent since 1968—Democrats tend to favor at least some types of firearm regulation, and Republicans tend to oppose them. The interpretations of the Second Amendment now tend to follow party lines, with Republicans advocating for the individual right's interpretation, and Democrats asserting that the duties of the "well-regulated militia" are fulfilled by the modern National Guard and that the Constitution does not guarantee unlimited individual rights.[41]

A 2019 survey indicated that the majority of Americans believe that gun laws should be stricter. Views differed sharply by party, with 86 percent of Democrats saying that gun laws should be more stringent, while only 31 percent of Republicans said the same. Republicans were much more likely than Democrats to state gun laws are "about right" or should be "less strict" than they are today.[42]

The individual's gun rights are the central organizing principle of the far-right militia movement, which has been embraced by many Republican politicians and some law enforcement officers. While there are individual differences among militia members, anti-government sentiments, racism, and conspiracy thinking are common. Militia members are strongly motivated by fear that a Democratic government will begin a mass confiscation of firearms, something that has never been proposed.[43]

The politicization of gun safety has impeded any progress that could have been made in the interest of public safety.

Though proposals regarding gun laws increase after every mass shooting, surprisingly, many of the proposals are to *remove* safety provisions and make it easier to get access to guns. Republican state legislatures pass significantly more gun laws that loosen restrictions, while the opposite is true in states controlled by Democrats. Republicans fall back on the "good guy with a gun" narrative, in which it's believed that a heavily armed populace will be able to stop the bad guy with a gun.[44]

As with all extremist movements, gun rights activists are fueled by paranoid imaginings in which they have become the brave protectors against a shadowy "other" who is coming for them. Allowing paranoid thinking that is divorced from the evidence to determine public policy is not in our best interest.

Las Vegas

Under current gun laws, one individual can build an arsenal fit for a small army.

In late September 2017, a 64-year-old white man checked into the Mandalay Bay Resort in Las Vegas, which overlooked the 15-acre Las Vegas Village, an event space used for outdoor music festivals. Approximately 22,000 country music fans would attend the Route 91 Harvest Music Festival there six days later on October 1.

The following information is summarized from the Las Vegas Metropolitan Police investigative report, issued on August 3, 2018.[45]

The 64-year-old white male was an obsessive professional gambler. He had planned a meticulous attack, choosing a room in the luxury hotel that afforded a view of the festival. He had scoped out several other locations adjacent to music festivals in prior months, but for reasons known only to him, settled on this event. He brought 10 large shooting-range bags with him, which he transported up to his room with the hotel luggage cart. Four days after he checked in, he added a connecting room, which provided him with twice the windows overlooking the festival.

The perpetrator had 24 firearms, mostly semiautomatic rifles with high-capacity magazines, holding up to 100 rounds each. Fourteen of the rifles were outfitted with bump stocks, which allow semiautomatic rifles to fire rapidly, essentially simulating fully automatic rifles. Some of the rifles were set up on bipods positioned to fire prolonged bursts into the crowd below and were equipped with sophisticated telescopic sites.

His planning was detailed. He had placed multiple video cameras in the hallway outside his room and inside his suite so that he could surveil the areas around him.

At 10:10 in the evening, as the festival was underway, he began firing into the crowd below. In approximately five minutes, he killed 61 and left 867 injured.

Additionally, he fired eight bullets at a large jet fuel tank at McCarran International Airport, 2,000 feet away. Two bullets struck the tank, but the fuel did not explode.

A few minutes into the attack, a hotel security guard attempted to enter the room. The gunman fired 35 shots through the door, wounding the guard who miraculously survived. Approximately 10 minutes after the gunfire started, the gunman shot himself in the head. He died instantly.

A month before the attack, the gunman had stayed in the hotel with his girlfriend. She told the Las Vegas Metropolitan Police that she observed him constantly looking out the windows of the room that overlooked the concert venue, moving from window to window to view the site from different angles.

Searching his room, officers found notes which gave more evidence of his planning. He'd written out calculations about where he needed to aim to maximize his accuracy and the actual distance to the target, his elevation, and the estimated bullet trajectory related to the line of fire. There were also laptops found in the room that contained hundreds of images of child pornography.

His car, parked in the hotel lot, contained pounds of explosives and an additional 1,600 rounds of ammunition. His plans for the explosives are unclear.

Unlike most mass killers, the Las Vegas perpetrator left no manifesto behind. His motive was initially a mystery, and the official report from the Las Vegas Metropolitan Police and the FBI released in 2018 stated: "nothing was found to indicate a motive." However, it did include speculations which included "his desire to obtain a certain amount of infamy."[46]

Since then, experts on extremist groups have cited evidence that is further suggestive of motive.

Former senior analyst at the Department of Homeland Security, Daryl Johnson, discusses these factors in his 2019 book *Hateland: A Long, Hard Look at America's Extremist Heart.*[47]

Johnson shares accounts of multiple individuals who had contact with this killer and noticed disturbing patterns. He was described as intelligent and methodical but angry and narcissistic. He was irreverent toward authority and passionately disliked the government and the tax system.

Others said he spoke of common conspiracy theories involving past events, common on the extremist far-right. These include the 51-day Waco siege between the ATF and a heavily armed religious fringe religious group in 1993, which left 76 members of the group dead,[48] as well as the 1992 incident known as the Ruby Ridge incident, when U.S. Marshals attempted to arrest a right-wing white supremacist on illegal weapons charges in Ruby Ridge, Idaho. At Ruby Ridge, two of the individual's family members were killed during a standoff with the ATF that went on for days.[49] Both events have been adopted as causes known to inflame far-right extremists, and both were spurred by issues relating to illegal guns.

A passionate advocate of individual gun rights, the Las Vegas killer stockpiled guns and associated items in his home. All were legally purchased. One individual described him as "paranoid" and "obsessive." Another person reported that they heard the perpetrator say, "Somebody has to wake up the American people. Some sacrifices have to be made."[50]

If accurate, these reports would align the Las Vegas mass killer with far-right, anti-government extremism ideologies. It's common for mass killers to believe that they are fulfilling a grand messianic vision, identifying a noble responsibility for initiating an uprising against the federal government. It's also common for violent extremists to imagine conspiracies, a thinking style indicative of paranoia. As with other mass killers, the Las Vegas perpetrator appears to have been an injustice collector.

The investigation report also stated that the perpetrator was known to exhibit minimal empathy, "primarily relating to others through a transactional lens of costs and benefits. He had a history of exploiting others through manipulation and duplicity, sometimes resulting in a cruel deprivation of their expectations without warning."[51]

The investigative report states that the killer's brother believed he was "a narcissist who only cared about people who could benefit him in some way, and needed to be important." His brother stated that he believed he would want to kill as many people as possible "because he wanted to be the best at everything," adding that both he and his brother believed they were "smarter than the majority of other people." He indicated that his brother was "detail-oriented" and would not have cared about the people he would kill. Finally, he stated that he had never displayed "anger issues" but was known to be "passive-aggressive."[52]

These qualities are consistent among those high in the traits of psychopathy and narcissism. There seems reasonable evidence of the dark triad traits of paranoia, psychopathy, and narcissism.

The report added, "His father may have influenced him." The perpetrator's father had been a convicted bank robber who went to prison in 1960.[53] Since there are also genetic factors that can contribute to psychopathy, it is possible that this killer had specific vulnerabilities for violence.

We may never have a complete picture of the details of all factors that spurred the Las Vegas killer's behavior. Still, it's a reasonable supposition based upon the evidence that contributing factors were far-right extremist views and a desire for infamy. He is not unlike other mass killers, other than the massive extent of his armory. He had enough guns to do tremendous damage.

Between 1982 and 2016, the Las Vegas killer purchased 29 firearms. Between October 2016 and September 2017, he bought over 55 guns, most of them rifles, along with multiple firearm accessories, including bump stocks.[54] The obsessive Las Vegas killer was equipped with enough guns, ammunition, and related equipment to function as a one-person army.

Gun Safety Legislation Proposals

Since the 1980s, the gun lobby has fought nearly all firearms restrictions, even though most Americans support enhancements to gun safety. The organization founded by James Brady has developed a comprehensive plan that would make a significant difference.[55]

The following are suggested guidelines for amending federal gun laws, excerpted from the Brady Comprehensive Plan:

- **Expand background checks** to all gun sales and modernize gaps and loopholes that now exist in the system.
- **Expand the category of purchasers who are prohibited from purchasing guns**. There are gaps in existing gun safety laws that allow known dangerous persons to still legally purchase guns. Though a conviction for intimate partner violence currently prohibits gun purchase, under current law, dating partners who do not share a child are not considered "intimate partners." This is known as "the boyfriend loophole." This needs to be changed so that victims of violence from dating partners can still be protected. Additionally, nothing in current law prohibits the purchase of firearms by anyone convicted of misdemeanor stalking or hate crimes. This loophole should also be closed.
- **Prevent access to assault weapons and high-capacity magazines**. Weapons of war, including military-style assault rifles and high-capacity magazines, are known for their ability to exact maximum destruction and casualties and have thus become the weapons of choice for mass killers. When used in mass shootings, they result in 47 percent more deaths. Congress should enact tighter restrictions of weapons of war and any accessories similar to bump stocks that increase semiautomatic weapons' lethality. Additionally, Americans are at risk from "ghost guns," and 3-D printed guns, which allow dangerous individuals to evade background checks by building firearms with purchased components or printing those components themselves at home. Ghost guns lack serial numbers and are thus essentially "invisible" to law enforcement. If found at a crime scene, they cannot be traced. Three-D printed guns are made entirely of plastic, rendering most modern security devices like metal detectors ineffective. **Congress should outlaw the manufacture of ghost and 3-D printed guns**.
- **Extreme risk laws** allow family members and law enforcement officers to petition a civil court to temporarily remove firearms from and prohibit their purchase by a person in the midst of

a crisis. Often family members and police officers watch as people in crisis indicate that they may be a threat to themselves and others yet are powerless to prevent them from easily and legally accessing guns. Thirteen states have enacted extreme risk protective orders or gun violence restraining order laws to counter this risk. Since self-inflicted gunshots account for the highest percentage of gun violence deaths in the country, Congress must provide grants to encourage states to pass these meaningful laws and educate the public about these protections and how best to use them.

- **Fully fund gun violence research at the CDC.** It is indisputable that gun violence is a public health epidemic in the United States. Despite rapid advances in medical technology and a heightened awareness of the gun violence crisis, gun injuries and deaths continue to rise in both rural and urban areas. Congress must provide an appropriate minimum of $50 million in committed funding for the CDC to study this epidemic over the next five years.
- **Fund local community-based programs** to break the cycle of gun violence in urban areas. Efforts should be made to mitigate the disproportionate impact of gun violence on urban environments and communities of color. Evidence-based gun violence prevention and intervention programs are proven to help break cycles of violence, and investments in these programs frequently pay for themselves several times over. Funding these programs at a federal level to ensure stable, long-term support would greatly impact stemming the plague of urban gun violence.
- **Promote safe storage and responsible gun ownership.** Easy access to a gun in the home frequently turns impulsive ideation about self-harm into a lethal event. An average of eight kids and teens are injured or killed by guns every day from causes ranging from accidents to suicides. Four and a half million kids live in homes with guns that are both unsecured and loaded. **Most school shooters have unimpeded access to guns in their homes.** (Either they use a parent's gun which they can readily access, or the gun belongs to them.)[56] Congress should pass

laws encouraging safe storage of firearms through the use of tax incentives; broadening the scope of firearms required to be sold with gun storage or safety devices; require safe storage warning be issued with the purchase of every gun; mandating magazine disconnects that render a gun inoperable when the magazine is separated from the gun; and funding or mandating research, development, and manufacturing "smart gun" technology.

- **Repeal the Protection of Lawful Commerce in Arms Act (PLCAA).** In 2005, President George Bush signed a top legislative priority of the corporate gun industry into law—the PLCAA, which provides special protection from civil lawsuits at the expense of victims of gun violence. In many cases, courts have held that PLCAA removes key incentives for the gun industry to adopt life-saving business practices and instead provides cover to irresponsible gun dealers who supply the criminal gun market. This small minority of gun dealers profits from dangerous business practices with no accountability to their victims. No other American industry enjoys such civil immunity.
- **Hold ATF accountable** for meaningful gun industry oversight. A small minority of gun industry businesses engage in reckless and illegal practices that put Americans at risk of gun violence. The ATF knows precisely who these actors are yet allow them to operate. ATF leniency for repeat and serious gun industry violators is the rule rather than the exception. Congress must exercise its oversight powers to hold the ATF accountable for failing to revoke the licenses of the worst violators in the gun industry.

Gun Buyback

Gun buyback programs have been used effectively in many U.S. cities as well as Australia. Buyback programs can be voluntary or compulsory and allow gun owners to exchange their guns with law enforcement agencies for cash or vouchers. Firearms can be exchanged "no questions asked." Multiple cities in the United States have instituted buyback programs since the 1990s.[57]

Some buyback programs differentiate what types of guns are eligible for buyback. While military-grade semiautomatic weapons are the deadliest firearm in a mass shooting event, handguns kill far more people overall. Two-thirds of gun deaths occur from suicides in which handguns were used.

Research has been mixed about how much voluntary buyback programs impact violent crime, and the science isn't yet settled. Australia presents relevant longitudinal data since their buyback program was mandatory and covered the entire country.

In 1996, a man in Port Arthur, Tasmania, used a semiautomatic rifle to kill 35 people and wound 23 others. Within two weeks, Australian legislators outlawed semiautomatic and pump-action rifles across the country. By 2001, more than 650,000 guns were exchanged and destroyed. Another buyback in 2003 resulted in the buyback of 68,000 handguns.[58]

Before the 1996 buyback, there had been 13 mass shootings in the previous 18 years. Since the buyback, there has been only one mass shooting in Australia, which occurred in 2019. Firearm deaths declined overall, including suicides. However, since suicide and homicide deaths began to decline in the mid–1990s universally, researchers have been unable to determine with clarity the full extent of the benefit of the buyback program.[59]

From a public health standpoint, buyback programs provide no risk to the community and likely offer significant benefits.

What About Self-Defense?

Though most Americans cite "protection" as the reason they have guns in their home, their own family members are most likely to be harmed by them.

A 2015 analysis of over 14,000 incidents of crime from the National Crime Victimization Surveys showed that self-defense gun use occurs in less than 1 percent of contact crimes and is *not* associated with a reduced risk of victim injury. The study concludes, "Compared to other protective actions, the National Crime Victimization Surveys provide little evidence that self-defense gun use is uniquely beneficial in reducing the likelihood of injury or property loss."[60]

The gun lobby has stated that arming more citizens would prevent would-be mass killers from engaging in murderous rampages. Some would have us arm schoolteachers, retail clerks, restaurant managers, pastors, and yoga teachers. There are multiple problems with this approach. To successfully engage a well-armed mass killer, a citizen would require specialized training and marksmanship practice to achieve basic competency. Even highly trained police officers have difficulty hitting a perpetrator in a heat-of-the-moment, unanticipated event.[61] The expectation that average citizens can effectively engage a killer in a gun battle with no harm to other bystanders is not realistic. Bystanders can easily be shot in the crossfire.

Additionally, when law enforcement officers arrive at the location of a shooting where multiple people are brandishing firearms, they have no way of differentiating the "good guy with a gun" from the "bad guy with a gun." In the aftermath of the attempt on Gabby Gifford's life, one of the bystanders had picked up the perpetrator's gun and was nearly shot by arriving police officers who mistook him for the shooter.[62]

It's questionable if having a more heavily armed populace would deter most mass killers. Since many mass killers are suicidal, they come to the location prepared to die.

It only takes one minute to kill dozens with a military-grade assault weapon.

The Weapons Effect and Priming

Our relationship with guns is complicated and fraught with emotion. Firearms also have disturbing psychological effects that happen beneath the level of conscious awareness.[63]

Multiple researchers have documented what is referred to as "the Weapons Effect," which involves the psychological process of priming. For some people, just the mere sight of a weapon or words about weapons increases aggressive thoughts and behavior.[64]

From early childhood, media scripts show us that even simple problems can be solved with shootouts. This is a significant factor in the way our culture determines how conflicts should be managed. There is a reciprocal relationship between gun culture and media violence.

Immersed in a steady stream of violent media content, we can all be primed for aggression. Some of us are more vulnerable than others. This process is amplified when news media focuses on stories and images that reinforce false narratives.

It is unlikely that the proliferation of firearms in America will diminish in the coming decades; however, improving gun safety legislation is possible and would save lives. If semiautomatic weapons were not ubiquitous, shootings that occur would not be as deadly. There is a cost-benefit analysis to be made. Are more guns really making us safer?

When the Second Amendment was written, a firearm could fire one to two rounds per minute. Now, semiautomatic weapons fire at least 45 rounds in the same 60 seconds. The world has changed in ways the founding fathers could never have imagined.

Not all Republicans have found the individual rights argument valid. In a 1991 interview on the *MacNeil/Lehrer News Hour*, former Supreme Court Chief Justice Warren Burger, a conservative, dismissed calls to reinterpret the Second Amendment as "one of the greatest pieces of fraud on the American public." Burger often stated that the "right to bear arms" belonged to the state rather than individuals.[65]

No matter how much we improve our school systems, mental health services, and crisis intervention, the most critical factor will be reducing guns' availability and proliferation.

Those who strongly believe in the individual rights interpretation of the Second Amendment are generally well-intentioned. Still, they look through a lens that shows them an altered version of reality. Imagining they are protecting their families from a dangerous other, they fail to see that their own weapons are actually the most significant risk to themselves and their loved ones.

As long as we are among the most heavily armed countries in the world, the easy accessibility to firearms will continue, as will the inevitable violence that goes with them.

We can create a better vision.

A Public Health Perspective

Anyone who has died from a firearm has died from a preventable injury. A public health approach to violence prevention focuses on improving the health and safety of all citizens by addressing underlying risk factors that increase the likelihood that any individual will become a victim or perpetrator of violence. There are four steps to the approach:

1. Define the problem through the systematic collection of information about the magnitude, scope, characteristics, and consequences of violence.

2. Establish why violence occurs, using research to determine the causes and correlates of violence, the factors that increase or decrease the risk for violence, and the factors that could be modified through interventions.

3. Find out what works to prevent violence by designing, implementing, and evaluating interventions.

4. Implement effective and promising interventions in a wide range of settings. The effects of these interventions on risk factors and the target outcome should be monitored, and their impact and cost-effectiveness should be evaluated.

We will see change if we can move into a public health perspective that focuses on problem-solving and move away from emotionally driven partisan warfare that concentrates only on punishing the other side. Irrational paranoia fueled by the gun lobby serves no one. We need informed and thoughtful legislators who are not beholden to the NRA.

The polarization and debate over gun safety legislation and the Second Amendment may not be put to rest for years if it remains within the combat zone of the contentious American two-party system.

At the very least, gun ownership must come with certain responsibilities. If guns were regulated like cars, we would see some improvement. Gun owners would be required to

- title and tag at each point of sale;
- have mandatory training in safe usage and storage, followed by written and practical tests;
- have renewals and inspections at regular intervals; and
- carry liability insurance.

Reining in the gun lobby and the paranoia it has spread can seem daunting. Complaining on social media each time there is a shooting isn't enough; we can all join and support the diligent existing organizations that have already been working to bring needed change. Collectively, we can make a difference *if* we commit to doing more than complain. We can take action.

Following are some of the highly rated non-profit organizations that are actively working in the area of gun safety:

- **Sandy Hook Promise** sandyhookpromise.org
- **Newtown Action Alliance** newtownactionalliance.org
- **Brady Campaign to Prevent Gun Violence** bradyunited.org
- **Giffords Law Center** giffords.org
- **Parkland Cares** parklandcares.org
- **Everytown for Gun Safety** everytown.org

15

What We Can Do

Clearly, it's not as simple as "Don't let the kids play *Modern Warfare*." If there were any single factor that caused mass killings, the problem would have been solved decades ago. Hopefully, we now understand that gross over-simplifications about the causes of violence won't help us solve the problem. We must break it down into manageable components and identify specific actions that can be taken.

In this chapter, we look at specific goals that will favorably impact people in all areas of development and explore specific protective factors throughout the lifespan. We examine ways to interrupt pathways that can lead to violence early—before a crisis phase is reached—as well as actions to take if we notice mental health concerns or specific red flags that can indicate potential danger.

Just as many factors contribute to the problem, many factors are to be addressed to bring positive change.

While we can't predict who will become a mass killer, we can do much to intervene with the vulnerable earlier—before they ever start down the pathway to violence. By taking a broad view, it's possible to define what humans need to develop in a healthy and prosocial manner. People who grow up to value others and see a positive purpose in life will be apt to turn away from ever viewing violence as a solution to problems.

Of course, it's far easier to identify what needs to be done than it is to do it. Change doesn't come easily; it takes focused effort and intent. But we start by creating the vision of what we're working towards because, ultimately, creating a healthier society will benefit us all. When looking through an informed and compassionate lens, we see many opportunities to bring change.

How do we build a culture where mass murder isn't viewed as a solution to one's personal problems? We start by helping people feel that life has value and is ultimately worth living.

Upstream Rather Than Downstream

We began this book by examining the impact of school lockdown drills. We still can't say with certainty if they do more good than harm. No one knows. We can say with confidence that by the time a shooter picks up a gun and drives to a targeted location, the system has already failed.

Interrupting the pathway to violence far earlier should be our primary focus because prevention early on negates the need for intervention at the final stage. There is also the legitimate concern that lockdown drills are actually teaching vulnerable children that school shootings are a normal way to vent distress or a legitimate way to enact retribution against bullies. Today's lockdown drills may be providing a template for future mass killers.

As mentioned in Chapter 2, factors from the following areas weave together to cause people to be vulnerable to committing violence[1]:

- **Personal-level factors** include psychological vulnerabilities, developmental differences, family and caregiver relationships, and trauma histories.
- **Community-level factors** include social environments such as school and work environments. Having positive, prosocial connections to a community is a robust protective factor against violence.
- **Group factors** include affiliation with specific groups, including online contacts and loosely organized communities.
- **Ideological factors** including hateful beliefs about other races and genders, and the desire to be famous.
- **Sociopolitical-level factors** include collective grievances, politics and the messaging from politicians, and influences of the media.

Each of these factors intersects. Intervening positively in one area will affect other areas in positive ways. Reviewing epigenetics—the ways our innate tendencies develop in accord with our environment—enables us to see how all these factors interweave to determine whether or not any given individual will thrive or end up on a destructive path. Genes are not about inevitabilities; they're about potentials and vulnerabilities. Environments make a difference. In that way, we are all part of the environment and can support positive social change.

Different factors carry more weight in some persons than others. Just as individuals have varying strengths, vulnerabilities, and risks, so do families and communities. Resources and opportunities continue to be decidedly unequal in the modern United States.

The Secret Service NTAC report identifies the following key findings from their research on targeted violence within schools[2]:

- Targeted school violence is preventable when communities identify warning signs and intervene.
- Schools should intervene with students before their behavior warrants legal consequences.
- Students were most motivated to plan an attack due to a grievance with a classmate.
- Other students are in the best position to notice and report concerning behaviors.

These findings essentially apply to adults outside of school settings as well.

The following are recommended actions that will benefit all of us by helping grow healthier, more resilient kids who can develop into prosocial and altruistic adults.

Growing Healthy Kids

- On the personal level, we can best help children by helping their parents. Early intervention programs for children who display developmental delays have been proven to make tremendous differences in positive outcomes in their early years that carry over the long term. Supportive services for parents and their children bring the best results and ultimately serve society as a whole.

- Well-funded and adequately staffed intervention services in the public school system should include readily accessible mental health counseling beyond that provided by the academic or vocational counseling staff. Keeping class sizes small enough so that teachers can catch signs when a child is struggling is critical. At present, teachers are often overwhelmed, over-worked, and under-supported. Teachers cannot be expected to function as therapists or to re-parent vulnerable children. We need to offer additional resources.

- Since our psychological health is every bit as important as our physical health, we need to expand public school curricula to emphasize emotional wellness, incorporating anti-racism and anti-bullying strategies. Creating an emotionally safe environment where empathy is reinforced is critical during childhood. Activities to build emotional health could be integrated into the school program from kindergarten through 12th grade, ideally by including staff with specialized mental health training. Emotional wellness has everything to do with future success in life, and emotionally stable kids will have a greater capacity to focus effectively on academic subjects and a greater tendency to behave in positive ways with others. An emotional wellness emphasis can promote and reinforce empathy, help build resiliency, and allow children to understand their emotions and behavior. By gaining communication skills, they will better understand how to seek support when they need it and be more apt to offer support to others. We *can* work to create school environments that discourage bullying and prejudice. Prompt referrals for additional mental health services should be provided when kids present with problems.

- We can help children and teens build positive networks within their schools and communities by offering social options *according to their interests*, be it music, board games, robotics, athletics, visual arts, performing arts, or creative writing. While we readily recognize that adults are not all the same, we don't

always seem to be aware that this is equally true of children
and teens. We need to value and support young peoples'
differences rather than attempt to mold them according to a
narrow template. We need to offer positive, enjoyable things that
children *can* do, rather than emphasizing what they can't.

- We need to develop more and richer after-school activities for
  kids. Most working parents are in a bind. Kids need to form deep
  and meaningful connections with both adults and their peers.
  It's through human relationships that they develop a sense of
  significance and a feeling of belonging. Excessive time alone at
  home can add to other risk factors due to the resulting isolation
  and lack of structure. For older kids, encouraging community
  service will help build compassion for others and develop a
  sense of purpose.

- For families with firearms in the home, ask that they reconsider.
  Access to weapons is a major preventable risk factor for violence.
  Most school shooters use parents' guns. Most weapons used in
  mass killings are legally purchased. When we look at suicides
  and accidental shootings, it's clear that the odds that your child
  will be hurt or killed with a home firearm are far greater than the
  odds that you will ever defend yourself against a hostile intruder.

- We need to stay mindful of how much violent media we
  allow our kids and teens to consume. While zero exposure to
  violent content may be unrealistic, it *is* possible to discourage
  movies and media where violent anti-heroes are venerated and
  romanticized. Parents and caregivers need to watch movies
  with kids and play video games *with* kids. Don't let them isolate
  themselves in their bedrooms or basements with unrestricted
  access to electronic games, movies, or the internet. Discuss with
  kids their perceptions and feelings about the media content they
  consume. Kids need adults to keep them grounded.

- Parents need to be empowered regarding the management of
  internet use in the home. We must develop parent education
  regarding the healthy management of social media from early
  childhood throughout the teen years. Few parents have the skills
  to monitor their children's online activities effectively. Many
  parents are themselves struggling with spending excessive time

online. Preschoolers with their personal iPads now spend hours on YouTube. Elementary school kids with smartphones browse social media into the wee hours of the morning, stumbling onto "influencers" who influence in only unhealthy ways as well as hate-based content. It's easy to understand why many develop a lonely and hopeless view of the world. This is also a recipe for addiction that will be very difficult to rein in down the line. The following are specific suggestions for parents regarding screen time:

1. Hold an attitude of compassion while still offering guidance and structure. Kids are under tremendous pressure from their peers to participate in far more social media and online activity than is good. Yet, they aren't mature enough to understand the risks and are not capable of self-regulating. This is why kids need parents. We must help them by offering structure.

2. Keep a clear schedule of specific times of day when screen time is allowed, with small increments of additional screen time given as an incentive and reward for good behavior. "You can have one hour of gaming time after you finish your homework" is an example.

3. Offer healthy alternatives to screen time. Rather than telling them what they can't do, emphasize other appealing activities. Develop a list of a wide variety of alternate activities they can choose from based upon their specific areas of interest. Encourage them to experiment with new things.

4. Be aware, but not authoritarian. Know where kids are going online and how online activities are monitored in their friends' homes. Talk about this with other parents. Use parental control software effectively. Since kids access the internet from multiple devices, it's not difficult for them to get around parental controls. Various tech agencies, including *PC Magazine*, rate and review parental software systems annually. If parents detect problems in this area, they should consult with a mental health counselor well-versed in problematic use of the internet. Even a healthy kid can be seduced into disturbing subcultures by the material they stumble upon online; when that happens, they are likely to be secretive about it.

5. Model healthy media use and live a balanced life with a variety of activities. We can't expect kids to know how to moderate their electronic media use when observing their parents constantly plugged into devices. Children learn what they live.

6. Discuss the ways that we can become wise consumers of media. Once parents understand how easily we can all be manipulated by toxic rhetoric found online, they will be in a better position to help their kids discern truth from untruth.

It's understandable that stressed, exhausted, and overwhelmed parents have difficulty implementing these suggestions. We need to problem-solve as a community how to best support parents in the challenging task of raising kids in our complex modern society.

We have learned that adverse childhood experiences like trauma, poverty, and abuse all increase vulnerability for future problems. By helping parents, we help kids. By helping kids, we will eventually create a safer world.

At the most basic level, we all need to have the resources and skills to build a good life. There is an intersection between mass killings and suicide since most mass killers intend to die during their attacks, or at the very least, are willing to die for their cause. The social environment we collectively create *can* make a difference by helping people see hope and a reason to live. We need to catch problems upstream rather than downstream.

Mental Health Concerns in Children/Teens

The following are the signs and symptoms that may indicate that a child or teen is experiencing mental health problems. It's essential to consult with a professional as soon as possible if any of these signs or symptoms are noticed.

- Persistent signs of sadness, loss of interest, and hopelessness.
- Making self-critical comments. Believing that one is unlikable or ugly.
- Self-harm or cutting.

- Quick to become tearful.
- Expressing wishes to be dead.
- Signs of anxiety or phobias. Fears beyond the scope of what's typical.
- Resistance to going to school.
- Failure to make friends and social isolation.
- In children, both anxiety and depression can manifest in physical symptoms, such as headaches or complaints of stomach pain.
- Extreme rage episodes; physically lashing out at others or breaking things.
- An upset child who cannot be soothed.
- Sleep problems, including trouble falling asleep, often waking, intense and frequent nightmares, or extreme over-sleeping.
- Loss of appetite, or excessive appetite.

Mental Health Concerns in Adults

The following are signs and symptoms that are common to adults experiencing mental health concerns:

- Feeling sad and self-critical.
- Experiencing a sense of worthlessness or guilt.
- Confused thinking or difficulty concentrating.
- Mood changes, including extreme irritability or euphoria.
- Avoiding friends and regular social activities.
- Hopelessness, a sense of foreshortened future.
- Sleep problems, including trouble falling asleep, staying asleep, intense nightmares, or over-sleeping.
- Loss of appetite or dramatic increase in appetite.
- Multiple physical ailments with no objective cause.
- Panic attacks, unreasonable fears, excessive worry, a sense of doom.
- Rageful outbursts or violence.
- Hearing voices or expressing odd beliefs.
- Focusing on death or thoughts of suicide.

Getting Help

Mental health therapists do much more than treat severe mental illness. They often deal with more common difficulties like stress management, building communication skills, or problems of adjustment to work or school. They can also advise family members on how to best cope with a situation when a loved one shows signs of a mental health condition. This is particularly important when a loved one has symptoms but refuses to participate in mental health treatment. Family members often need guidance.

Though it's often easy to identify when someone needs to consult with a mental health professional, it can take effort to make treatment happen. The lack of access to accessible and affordable mental health care is another public health crisis and one of the United States' most significant areas of disparity.

Those with health insurance can turn to the private sector, though mental health care providers' availability varies dramatically from place to place. Not all providers offer urgent appointments. Thus, it can take days or weeks to get an initial meeting, which is of no help to someone in crisis. Most mental health therapists have particular areas of interest and specialty—some work primarily with children and teens, others only with adults or couples. Some work more with anxiety and depression, others with family counseling. Many specialize in parenting and parent-child relationships. Interviewing at least three providers over the phone to determine if they are the best choice is helpful *before* making an appointment. Discussing the problem in advance makes it possible to ask the provider if this is something they work with and how they would see helping in this particular situation.

Some without health insurance can pay out of pocket for providers, though this is impossible for many. Most states and counties offer community mental health services available to those without health insurance, though the accessibility of these services varies from place to place. Numerous non-profit agencies provide care for mental health concerns. At the local level, schools or medical doctors can offer referrals.

It's essential to seek help promptly when someone is struggling, even when it takes effort to make it happen. Early treatment is most effective and can make a dramatic difference in the outcome. Some organizations can help find treatment resources, including:

- The **National Alliance for the Mentally Ill (NAMI)** is a national non-profit organization dedicated to offering free education and support for those with mental health conditions. NAMI provides a helpline that provides support and information on local resources around the country. Their phone number is 800–950-NAMI. They also offer a crisis service that is available by texting NAMI 741741.[3]
- The **National Suicide Prevention Lifeline** is a national network of local crisis centers that offer free, confidential, emotional support to people in suicidal crisis or emotional distress. They can provide referrals to local resources. Their helpline is staffed 24 hours a day, seven days a week, and can be accessed by calling 1–800-TALK.[4]

Accessing help is even more critical when there are amplified concerns, which are identified below. They should be considered red flags.

Amplified Concerns in Children/Teens

- Obsessive, inflexible interests, particularly when focused on gory, violent themes as evidenced by repetitive play or identification with violent villains.
- Repeatedly watching extreme violent media content.
- Writing excessively violent stories or creating morbid themes in artwork.
- Fascination with and focus on weaponry, firearms, bombs.
- Cruelty to animals or mutilating stuffed animals.
- Bullying other children, wanting to be feared by others, seeking to dominate or humiliate others.
- Making threats on social media, internet trolling, and cyberbullying.
- Fascination with fire, repeatedly playing with matches or lighters, staring at fire, starting fires.

- Fantasizing about cruelty or committing crimes.
- Attempting to manipulate or exploit others for personal gain.
- Fascination with death or expressing a desire to watch someone die.
- Fearless, not dissuaded by consequences.
- Attacking a teacher or becoming violent in a classroom.
- Extreme secretiveness, particularly about online activities.
- Extreme resistance to limits on violent media.
- Using hate speech about those of different races, genders, or ethnicities.
- Evidence of fascination with and admiration for Nazis, serial killers, or mass murderers.
- Adopting extremist narratives of victimization by "others."
- Leakage with friends or on social media. "Joking" about becoming a school shooter or murdering others.

Amplified Concerns in Adults

- Leakage, which may be as direct as preparing a manifesto, making threats or posting violent plans online, or making intimidating posts on social media.
- Hate speech or violence directed at minorities or women, whether or not there is any formal affiliation with hate groups. While most who engage in hate speech will not become violent, it's particularly concerning when hate speech is combined with anger, paranoid thinking, conspiracism, and framing oneself as a victim.
- Grandiose fantasies of oneself as a warrior or fighting a group of people perceived to be enemies.
- Implying that some sort of apocalyptic battle is coming, with hints that one is ready to die for the cause. Indicating that there is nothing to live for.
- Expressing fantasies of revenge, particularly for slights that are exaggerated or imaginary.
- Hoarding guns, ammunition, or experimenting with explosives.
- Admiration of, or fascination with, mass murderers, terrorists, or other killers.

Threat Assessment

While amplified concerns can indicate an increased vulnerability for violence, they are not all weighted equally. The threat is most significant when several of these signs occur in combination; though most people exhibiting these behaviors will not move on to commit violence, that doesn't mean these signs should be minimized or ignored.

Leakage is one of the most substantial warning signs of impending violence and should be considered a red flag. It may be bold, such as bragging to friends about specific plans, or indirect when someone inadvertently hears a rumor about another person or comes across their hit list or manifesto.

Sometimes leakage is as subtle as telling another student not to come to school on a particular day. It may be as obvious as posting a video on YouTube about a coming day of reckoning. All leakage deserves immediate intervention, though how to access resources can be confusing.

In many school districts, a process called "threat assessment" is activated when a student has exhibited signs that could indicate a risk for impending violence.

In the 1990s, the U.S. Secret Service developed the process of threat assessment after researching the violent targeting of politicians and other public figures. This model is based on the premise that specific observable behaviors can indicate impending violence, thus providing law enforcement a systematic process to identify those who exhibit these threatening behaviors and gather information to assess the risk of harm and identify a way to intervene.[5]

In 2004, the U.S. Department of Education partnered with the Secret Service to develop a guide to managing threatening situations in schools, *Enhancing School Safety Using a Threat Assessment Model.*[6] Threat assessment within schools is a prevention strategy that involves identifying student threats, determining the seriousness of the threat, developing intervention plans to protect potential victims, and intervening with the student to address underlying problems that fueled the behavior. In this model, multidisciplinary threat assessment teams are formed by school districts and typically involve members of school staff, counselors with mental health training, and members of law enforcement. Designed to be an integrated systems approach, the goal of the threat assessment process is to understand a given individual's vulnerabilities and connect them to support and resources.

In 2013, the Commonwealth of Virginia became the first state to initiate a comprehensive threat assessment policy. After the Parkland school shooting in 2017, other states passed similar laws, including Maryland, Florida, Colorado, Florida, Kentucky, Pennsylvania, Texas, Washington, and Rhode Island. While they are encouraged elsewhere, they are not currently required.[7]

The threat assessment process is critically important, though there have been criticisms of how threat assessment programs have sometimes been implemented.[8] Not all threat assessment teams are equal in skill, and the assessment process can vary widely. Some have accused teams of disproportionately targeting children of color and children with disabilities who are not threats. These children can be stigmatized and possibly even harmed when the process goes awry. Intervening effectively is a complicated and imperfect process. It's essential to keep in mind that every situation is unique and requires specialized interventions. Sensitive approaches are most apt to be beneficial, and we need uniform training and policies in all schools.

The Secret Service recommends that all schools develop comprehensive, targeted violence prevention programs, as described in their publication *Enhancing School Safety Using a Threat Assessment Model*.

While structured violence risk assessment tools in the form of checklists, guidelines, or computer software have been developed, they tend to lack empirical support; such instruments cannot accurately predict who will go on to commit violence.

Removing a Student from School Is Not a Solution

The research from the Secret Service NTAC is clear: removing a student from school based upon warning behaviors does not eliminate the risks for subsequent violence. The report cites multiple examples of students who had been expelled or transferred to other schools without additional support who planned attacks within the following year.[9] This was clearly evidenced by the Parkland perpetrator, who returned to his former high school with a gun one year after being expelled.

The Stop School Violence Act is a federal law passed in March 2018.[10] It provides annual grants to state and local education agencies through the Bureau of Justice Assistance to train school personnel, students, and law enforcement in early intervention strategies designed to prevent all forms of school violence. It also emphasizes threat assessment teams, intervention teams, and the development of anonymous reporting systems. This program also emphasizes "hardening" schools with metal detectors and security guards. This is also a voluntary program. It would be more helpful if it were universally implemented.

The national non-profit organization Sandy Hook Promise was founded by family members whose loved ones were killed at Sandy Hook Elementary School in Newtown.[11] Sandy Hook Promise has developed a four-part program offered free of charge to schools across the country through in-person and online training. As of 2021, they have worked with over 14,000 schools.

The Sandy Hook Promise programs have a unique psychological focus; they emphasize social and emotional skill development, including relationship skills, self-awareness, and responsible decision making. They incorporate lesson plans, activities, games, and discussion guides, aiming to empower student leaders to take an active role in increasing school safety and preventing different forms of violence in schools and communities.[12]

Part of the Sandy Hook Promise program includes an app for anonymous reporting for students concerned about a peer. When anonymous reporting is an option, more individuals are apt to speak up when they see or become aware of concerning events.

See Something, Say Something—Young People

There is generally a code of silence among group members, particularly teenagers who are reluctant to "snitch" on their friends. Siblings don't want to report brothers to the police. But we know in many cases of mass killings, peers were aware of leakage—often well in advance—but didn't say anything to someone who could have intervened.

Since Columbine, numerous policies have been implemented to "harden" schools around the country. These have included surveillance cameras, school resource officers, metal detectors, and restricting campus entrances. Some have questioned how much these practices serve to prevent school rampages; some of these practices were already in place at Columbine High School at the time of the killings. Sandy Hook Elementary School had a very sophisticated security system that didn't stop the killer. Some have speculated that while they reduce parents' anxiety, school hardening measures should not be viewed as a complete solution. While the benefits of school resource officers have been debated, the Secret Service NTAC report on threat assessment stresses that school resource officers play an essential role in violence prevention. In one-third of the cases of their study of thwarted school attacks, the reports about a student showing warning signs were made to the school resource officer.[13]

What *is* strongly associated with preempting mass killings in schools has been students willing to break the code of silence by speaking up and reporting signs of impending violence to school staff or their parents. Students are most likely to guard the secrets of close friends; those who report leakage are more apt to have peripheral knowledge of warning behaviors.[14] We will never know how many tragedies have been averted because someone said something, but it's likely they number in the hundreds.

Researchers have studied what helps students decide to come forward and tell. Strong, positive relationships between school staff and students have been associated with an increased willingness of students to report. When students care about their school, trust the teachers and administrators, and feel supported and involved, they are more likely to act protectively. It is also crucial that options for anonymous reporting be readily available and widely known.[15]

Ironically, when schools have adopted harsh, punitive discipline policies, the code of silence may be strengthened by creating an environment that discourages students from revealing concerns due to fear of punishment.[16]

When trusting relationships have been built between kids and adults in a positive school environment, it's far more likely that those who see something will say something.[17]

See Something, Say Something—Adults

The process of intervening can be decidedly more complex with adults. While the principle of "see something, say something" still applies, it's harder to know how to make an effective report, and follow-up action is proven to be more complicated. People are unsure where to make a report, often assuming a mental health professional or law enforcement agency to be the best resource. At this point, both are appropriate—a therapist may be helpful for concerns that aren't imminent threats, law enforcement for concerns that seem to be. The best outcomes generally result when there is a partnership between law enforcement and mental health providers who collaborate in a threat assessment process.

Law enforcement personnel are not typically trained in assessing mental health conditions and certainly can't be expected to understand all other personal characteristics that can be contributing factors in an individual's potential for violence. We tend to expect too much from officers beyond the scope of their education, training, and experience.

The public has long been under the impression that mental health clinicians can easily and accurately assess the risk of future violence in any given individual. This is simply not true. The process of assessment is exceedingly complicated, and there is no checklist or diagnostic test that allows a therapist to predict anyone's future behavior.

Most perpetrators have not been in mental health treatment, and even when they have, those with manipulative tendencies can be adept at giving false impressions. Therapists cannot read minds; they are only aware of what an individual chooses to tell them.

Even when mental health therapists have concerns about the potential for violence in an individual they are working with, the law dramatically limits what actions they can take. The reasons for this are complicated.

Consider the following case examples:

- Both Columbine killers had been in mandated counseling through the probation department before their rampage. Due to their finesse with impression management, they convinced the counselors that they were of no risk of future criminality.

They were released early from the counseling program, with positive reviews. Mental health counselors can't read minds, and *perpetrators with manipulative traits know how to mislead.*

- The Parkland killer had severe mental health problems for most of his life and had years of specialized therapy. His propensity for aggression was well-documented in school and at home, including threats made to his mother and brother. There were multiple contacts by law enforcement over the years, but the police were limited by law with what actions they could take. While his mental health therapy may have served to mitigate the risk of mass violence while receiving treatment, he opted out of all treatment when he turned 18. *Adults cannot legally be forced into treatment other than in exceptionally rare situations.*

- The Aurora killer told three mental health professionals at his college that he couldn't stop fantasizing about murder. However, he didn't share any *specific* plans or the fact that he'd been accumulating weapons, making detailed plans, and researching target locations. He'd been fantasizing about killing others for years. Though the clinicians were alarmed and attempted to intervene, privacy laws state that they can't make reports to police unless they have *specific* details about a client's plans. Before the attack, his primary therapist contacted his mother at the final therapy session. She reported that her son had always been odd, but she knew of no imminent threats. The clinician also contacted the university threat assessment team, who were unable to determine any impending danger. Their investigation was dropped as soon as the perpetrator left the campus. While mental health therapists do have "duty to warn" obligations, the law states that duty to warn laws only apply when an event is *imminent,* and a target is *identified* in a *specific* plan. *Developing more threat assessment options in cases where mental health clinicians have reasonable suspicions of potential dangerousness would increase public safety.* Mental health clinicians need legal options to coordinate with law enforcement agencies when there is reasonable concern about violence, even if a specific target is not identified to them verbally.

- In several cases, law enforcement had been contacted about leakage and red flags from specific individuals, but current procedures limit how much they can do and what actions they can take. The Isla Vista killer's mother requested law enforcement intervention weeks before his killing spree after discovering some of his disturbing videos on YouTube. Though officers performed a cursory welfare check with a brief visit to his home, they never reviewed the YouTube videos that prompted his mother's report. In the killer's manifesto, he stated that his plans would have been thwarted if the officers had searched his home and found his writings and guns. This perpetrator was also adept at impression management. Critical details were missed during a quick and superficial conversation. A better assessment would have included an advanced review of the disturbing videos. *Improved threat assessment procedures are needed that involve reviewing social media posts.*

- A man with severe and chronic mental illness shot 18 people during the attempted assassination of Gabby Giffords in Tucson. He had been extremely psychotic for years. His parents, friends, and all who had contact with him at his community college were aware of this. He frightened people. Multiple reports were to campus police, who visited his parents to discuss the problems. The question has been asked, "Why wasn't he committed to a mental hospital *before* he became violent?"

There is a general misunderstanding about involuntary commitment in the United States. No one can be involuntarily committed just because they are severely mentally ill or because they engage in behavior that others find bizarre and intimidating. Involuntary commitment laws are very restrictive and allow the state to intervene only under the most extreme circumstances. *No one can legally lose their right to freedom just because someone else is suspicious of them.* All citizens in the United States are protected from unjustified confinement. Commitment to a mental hospital, even for evaluation, is considered a violation of civil rights that requires that an individual meet extremely stringent criteria, as specified by law.

All states and the District of Columbia have laws authorizing civil commitment to locked mental health facilities for psychiatric evaluation as a *crisis* response when there is significant evidence that a person is suspected of being of *imminent danger* to themselves or others. Laws state that a person can only be held for a maximum of 72-hours when there is a *clear and imminent danger.* This is a very high bar to meet, even for a severely mentally ill person. Even if involuntarily hospitalized, the individual can be released any time during those 72 hours if they state that they have no plans to harm themselves or anyone. This is very easy to assert, even for a potentially dangerous individual.

If a person has been determined by mental health staff to continue to meet criteria for commitment after 72 hours, the state can petition a judge for an order to hold the person for an additional period of time, but the standards for this vary from state to state.[18] Again, the bar is exceptionally high, and the vast majority of people are not held beyond 72 hours.

These facilities are generally under-funded with disturbingly limited capacity to serve the needs of the community. Thus, there is an incentive to release as many people as possible to free up space. We recall that the Tucson killer was polite, even shaking the police officer's hand when pulled over on a traffic violation on the morning of the murders. He gave no indication of his plans and didn't seem threatening. *Current laws regarding involuntary commitments for mental health holds are very limited in scope.*

There are additional complications. Most individuals with severe mental illness do not believe they are mentally ill (anosognosia). Thus, they refuse treatment. Additionally, *mental health symptoms are often episodic,* so a person may appear fine during an interview that happens to catch them on a good day. *Intentional deception is the norm for mass killers.* Combining these factors with existing laws and practices, it's easy to see how difficult it is to intervene with adults effectively.

Improving the System

Once we understand the weaknesses in the current system, we can set goals for strategic changes. I propose the following suggestions:

- *Develop standardized anonymous reporting resources.* The state of Colorado Attorney General's office has instituted a program called *Safe2Tell*, which allows any individual to make an anonymous report statewide by use of the phone, web, or mobile app. Reports can be made 24-hours a day whenever one perceives a threat to their safety or the safety of others. The agency reports that during the 2018–2019 school years 19,861 tips were received.[19] This highlights the need for adequate resources to investigate when tips are made.

- *Expand law enforcement prevention and intervention strategies, and mental health holds.* There is a strong movement in the country to partner mental health clinicians *with* law enforcement, rather than expecting the police to intervene in situations that can best be evaluated by those with expertise in mental health assessment. By developing more *standardized and comprehensive procedures for threat assessment* when reports are made, fewer potentially dangerous persons will likely fall through the cracks. It is more likely that a mental health clinician will pick up on subtle signs of dangerousness that police officers may miss.

- *Adequately fund and staff the local mental health facilities* where individuals are held once an involuntary hold has been initiated. There should never be an incentive to release potentially dangerous people due to overcrowding. These programs should also provide follow-up outreach care, perhaps from a partnering organization, once people are released.

- *Expand local crisis intervention services.* The Violence Project reports that 80 percent of mass killers evidenced some signs of being in a crisis before their attacks. Making crisis intervention services easily accessible at the community level could interrupt some who may be moving toward violence.

- Law enforcement agencies need to develop strategies to *review social media evidence* when a tip is given since social media is now one of the primary sources for leakage.

Imminent threats require an immediate call to local law enforcement as well as the FBI tip line. If someone indicates they will show up with guns at a political rally or school event, 911 should be contacted immediately. We can never assume that anyone is joking. See something, say something.

The Media and Internet

The now defunct imageboard 8chan has been just one of the popular online communities for racism and violent extremism. Just moments before the El Paso shooter murdered shoppers in Walmart, he posted his manifesto on 8chan. In the manifesto, he encouraged his "brothers" to spread his message. Several other mass killers did the same.

During the New Zealand mosque murders, the killer live-streamed to Facebook, posting links on 8chan. Users followed and responded in real-time, as it was happening. This contributes to the copycat and contagion effects.

There is a bidirectional effect with the media. We influence the media, and the media influences us. It's a complicated relationship to untangle.

Modern media companies are operated by profit, not conscience. They have proven they do not act in accord with what's most helpful to society. These companies have immense power to facilitate the spread of false realities, increase polarization, and fuel the growth of hate-filled online communities that advocate violence. While those with hateful agendas have always existed, never before have they been able to spread their messages with such ease.

Algorithms spread misinformation, disinformation, and conspiracy theories on social media that create feedback loops promoting extremist ideologies, grievances, and paranoia. People immersed in these feedback loops become more extreme without realizing it. This is a significant factor in the spread of domestic terrorism, which experts believe will continue to simmer in the years ahead.

Since social media has developed into a major influence on culture, there has been a rising insistence that tech companies follow ethical editorial standards and initiate self-policing through improved content moderation. It's an issue of public safety.

Content Moderation

On several occasions, Congress has held hearings with the CEOs of major tech companies to stress that they must act to curb the promotion and amplification of false, harmful, and misleading content—or face more regulation from the government. In March 2021, 12 attorneys general from across the United States called on Facebook and Twitter to remove anti-vaccine disinformation, citing that just 12 accounts were responsible for 65 percent of the anti-vaccine content across social media. Those accounts particularly targeted people of color.[20]

The debate of if and when government should step in to regulate media content in the interest of public safety has gone on for decades. If media companies can be held to reasonable, ethical standards, it negates the need for government intervention. Like Facebook and Twitter, the larger companies have begun to move in the direction of enhancing moderation efforts.

The issue of content moderation often spurs opposition due to arguments against inhibiting free expression.

Fred Brennan, the software developer and technology leader who founded the massively popular 8chan in 2013 when he was 19 years old, was initially motivated to create a public space free of content moderation in the interest of "free speech"; he has since changed his mind. He now regrets starting it. After 8chan was directly linked with the series of mass killings, he became disgusted with the site and severed all ties. Brennan became an outspoken critic of 8chan, stating in media interviews, "Shut it down."[21]

In a recent interview for the 2021 HBO documentary *Q: Into the Storm,* Brennan said, "Free speech was a sacred American value—I never really questioned that. That was the kind of mentality I opened 8chan with. But you can't go three years as 8chan's administrator seeing the reality of totally free speech without having your faith in this sacred concept shaken a bit."[22]

The virtual world has real-world consequences. As a 19-year-old, Brennan didn't understand that. He does now.

As recently identified by Facebook's Mark Zuckerberg, action can be taken in three areas[23]:

- Holding internet companies accountable for having specific systems and procedures in place for monitoring harmful content.
- Requiring companies to meet specific performance targets when it comes to content that violates their policies.

- Requiring companies to restrict specific harmful forms of speech, even if the speech is not illegal.

Social media activity has been proven to move offline and affect real-world behavior, sometimes in deadly ways. These companies need to be held to a reasonable standard of ethics that supports public safety.

Deplatforming is when internet companies remove certain accounts and individuals from their platforms. After the Capitol insurrection, all major social media companies deplatformed multiple individuals, including Donald Trump, along with many far-right hate groups. Facebook also began deplatforming communities and blocking posts that spread disinformation about Covid-19. Deplatforming, when there are risks to public safety, should continue to be supported.[24]

Social bots are a type of automated software agents that mimic human users. Bots proliferate on social media sites and are typically used by bad actors to create an army of false personas working to spread hate speech and disinformation. Among other harmful effects, bots have spread the news of mass shooter events contributing to contagion. Bots have been a significant factor in recent political elections and the spread of conspiracy theories.

Russia has strategically used bots to amplify social problems in the United States to increase the political polarization and social instability that feed extremism. It is estimated that up to 15 percent of active Twitter accounts may be social bots. Of all tweeted links to popular websites, 66 percent appear to have characteristics of an automated bot rather than human users.[25] Considering the viral spread of disinformation and extremist rhetoric, we need to hold social media companies responsible for removing such bots and fake accounts from their platforms.

We must continue to ask that cable news companies report targeted mass violence incidents but practice the "Don't Name Them" policy. This has the power to reduce copycatting and contagion dramatically. News organizations should report the relevant facts but should not contribute to turning perpetrators into celebrities. In a rush to be the first to report "breaking news," it's also essential that they take the time to check facts before reporting to the public thoroughly.

Monitoring Violent Websites

Those who originally developed the internet could never have imagined its vast influence. It has benefited users worldwide in countless ways and has more power for good than any other media form. While the benefit we achieve from the internet shouldn't be diminished, we can't discount that it has also enabled dangerous antisocial behaviors from pedophilia and human trafficking to genocide and public mass killings.

One way to confront the potential harm is by encouraging the monitoring of sites that embolden and empower those who seek to harm or exploit others. This does not mean attempting to monitor the entire internet; instead, we ask law enforcement agencies to observe activity on hazardous sites, so that intervention actions can be taken when warranted.

Some website hosting services have banned hate groups from their servers. After the 2021 Capitol insurrection, Amazon suspended the social media site Parler from its web-hosting service. Parler has refused to moderate any content on its platform and was used by thousands of people in planning the Capitol insurrection. Amazon stated that Parler represented "a very real risk to public safety."[26]

It is acknowledged increased monitoring will result in some hate groups relocating to the "dark web," where it's far more challenging to monitor them. The dark web refers to the part of the internet that is not indexed by search engines and thus intentionally hidden. In a 2016 study, researchers Daniel Moore and Thomas Rid of King's College in London found that 57 percent of dark web sites hosted illicit material. This rose to 77 percent in 2019.[27]

Trafficking in drugs, guns, child pornography, stolen credentials, stolen credit card numbers, bank login credentials, and more can be found on the dark web. Computer hackers can even be hired, and hate groups proliferate.

The National Institute of Justice has developed and supported training programs to raise awareness, instruct law agencies to investigate criminal activity on the dark web, and equip special investigation units.[28] These efforts should be universally encouraged.

Support Prosocial Entertainment

We can all be mindful of the kind of media we consume, particularly what we allow young children to absorb. If we collectively begin to turn away from films and television that celebrate violent, racist, and misogynistic content, it will no longer be profitable. If we bring it into our homes, it will continue to sink its teeth into the young and vulnerable. It's important to remember that kids are not all the same. And some are more vulnerable to these influences than others.

At the very least, we must emphasize to parents the risk to kids from highly violent and antisocial media content; we can all turn away from entertainment that equates masculine power with violence, domination, and misogyny. Kids absorb everything they experience, and these harmful messages become internalized as their view of reality and their beliefs about themselves.

By supporting prosocial entertainment, more prosocial content will be created.

The Power of Positive Relationships

One of the most substantial protective factors against violence and other antisocial behavior is rooted in the power of human relationships. Deep and positive human connections have everything to do with the kind of people we become and the lives we lead.[29]

Our minds are always intensely influenced by our relationships with others, though for the most part, this happens beneath the level of our conscious awareness. We are all impacted far more by the quality of our relationships than we realize—and this includes online connections.

This is supported by science. Interpersonal Neurobiology (IPNB) is the interdisciplinary science of the relational underpinnings of the human mind. IPNB defines the "mind" as emerging from a relational process occurring *between* people as they interact. Through a process called "neuroplasticity," to some degree, our minds are reshaped by experiences as well as our relationships with others.[30]

Clinical professor of psychiatry at UCLA Dan Siegel coined the term "interpersonal neurobiology" in the 1990s. The theory evolved out of multiple science areas, including neuroscience, biology, anthropology, linguistics, physics, and psychology. IPNB has been revolutionary in helping us understand the development of the human mind and the power of relationships across the lifespan.[31]

Early human development theories were based upon the premise that our minds were formed in early childhood and were not significantly changed after that. We now realize it's far more complicated. Though the initial process is established in childhood through relationships with our caregivers, mind development doesn't stop there; relationships continue to remain impactful for the duration of our lives. As our relationships change, so do our nervous systems in an evolving process that continues into adulthood.[32]

These changes can go in both positive and negative directions. Healthy relationships are critical to developing a healthy mind, and painful or abusive relationships can hurt us. Psychological pain is coded in the brain in a process similar to physical pain and increases our vulnerability to psychological and other health problems.

IPNB stresses that profoundly positive interpersonal connections help keep us mentally healthy and serve as protective factors against mental health problems as well as antisocial behavior. Healthy relationships have the power to heal; this is a crucial component in psychotherapy and other healing practices.

Rising Out of Hatred

Journalist Eli Saslow's 2018 book, *Rising Out of Hatred: The Awakening of a Former White Nationalist*, tells the remarkable story of Derek Black, the white nationalist son of the founder of Stormfront, the largest racist hate group website and community. Derek, an avowed white nationalist, was the prodigy of his father, Don Black. Derek was steeped in racism for his entire life; his godfather was David Duke, the infamous KKK grand wizard.[33]

Derek was homeschooled from 3rd grade through high school and steeped in white supremacist philosophy. As a teenager, Derek ran his own racist website and launched a 24-hour white nationalist online radio network. He had his own white supremacist radio show, which aired five nights a week and advocated for America to be a whites-only country, with minorities forced to leave.

The movement's stated goal was to infiltrate mainstream politics, and Derek won a local election as a Republican in Florida. He was known as precocious, thoughtful, polite, and intellectual. As stated on the radio, his goal was to "normalize those white nationalist ideas that already fit so neatly within the divides of modern society. Most white people don't want to be called racists, but they do want to make sure their culture and their position in society isn't going to be undermined." Derek stated, "People are just waiting for white candidates to come along who are brave enough to talk about these things, and when that happens, whites will go streaming to the polls."

Derek planned to rise through local politics and eventually lead a media company, with the hope of packing the Supreme Court with justices who would overturn the Fourteenth Amendment: "My life goals were essentially to overturn our social order and replace it."

Things changed when Derek Black went to college. For the first time in his life, he would be surrounded by people who did not think like his family.

Though he tried to keep his beliefs under cover during school hours, he was eventually outed as a white supremacist. It was then that a group of Orthodox Jewish students intentionally befriended him and began including him in their weekly Shabbat dinners. Derek got to know them on a deeply personal level.

After months of dialogue with his new Jewish friends, Derek became increasingly confused about what he believed and began inventing excuses to get out of his radio show. He stopped posting on Stormfront, and spent a lot of time alone, thinking, and he fell in love with a Jewish girl. Eventually, Derek Black publicly renounced white nationalism. His family subsequently rejected him.

He now speaks out against racism.

Derek was profoundly changed by the positive relationships he made outside the insular world of his upbringing. Thousands of others echo this process.

Former white supremacist leader Christian Piccolino is now a peace advocate who chronicled his journey into and out of the movement in his 2020 book *Breaking Hate: Confronting the New Culture of*

Extremism. Piccolino was a member of the neo–Nazi movement for over a decade, eventually becoming the leader of a notoriously violent Chicago skinhead group. He now leads the Free Radicals Project, a global extremism prevention network.[34]

Piccolino describes a phase of "pre-radicalization" in which those with traumas and multiple psychological vulnerabilities seek out maladaptive solutions to their pain. This corresponds with the early stages of the pathway to violence.

It's easy for people with particular vulnerabilities to initially find solace in membership in hate groups, who manipulate the fragile with carefully orchestrated messages of belonging. Piccolino describes the search for identity, community, and purpose common among adolescents. Hate becomes normalized in the group bonding process, as people desperate for human connection discover camaraderie online and begin to reinforce grievances.

White supremacist ideology offers a comforting identity that becomes a source of pride, while the underlying traumas and losses are never addressed. As thinking errors are enforced, and scapegoats identified, grievances escalate. Violence is presented as a reasonable solution to the grievances. Rage builds over time—some progress down the pathway to violence.

In his book, Christian Piccolino states that the way out is through relationships:

> Establishing a link requires building rapport and trust through non-confrontational and meaningful interactions that challenge existing narratives—but that does not directly address ideology—and foster an environment free from fear of judgment, emotional repercussion, or shame. Building this bridge first is of utmost importance, even if progress appears implausible or negligible at first. Force yourself to see an imperfect human being instead of the hateful persona they want you to see.[35]

It's an uncomfortable truth that the phenomenon of mass killings has arisen from our culture. Collectively, we celebrate violence, venerate warriors, and conflate aggression with power and masculinity with dominance. We are seduced by the adrenaline of "breaking news," even though much of what is reported is inaccurate or biased. We allow ourselves to be shaped by forces that don't have our best interests in mind. The internet has become a de facto parent, teaching children that becoming famous is everything and that any attention is better than no attention. The most impactful sex education now comes from porn sites devoid of any sense of interpersonal connection between human beings. Our political system is fractious, polarized, dramatic, and volatile; it feeds a palpable undercurrent of anger, distrust, and paranoia. Then, to top it off, we allow the proliferation of easily accessible weapons of war yet act surprised when a young man picks up a gun to follow a clear cultural script that we've all had a part in creating.

We need to be our best selves to help our children become their best selves. We can start in our own homes and move outward to our communities on local, state, and federal levels. We need legislative leaders who understand these things, people who are compassionate, honest, and committed to solving problems that directly impact public health.

Prevention before the first step on the pathway to violence is the most protective action we can take. Solid, nurturing, healthy relationships are the very best medicine—this is what helps change brains in prosocial ways.

We can all work proactively to learn to listen so people will talk and talk so people will listen. Heart-to-heart connections are everything, and when we view our world through this lens, none of us are powerless to make a difference.

And if we see something, we will say something.

Afterword

"When we try to pick out anything by itself, we find it hitched to everything else in the universe."—John Muir

I often wish I had a magic wand to fix people's lives or psychic powers that enabled me to read minds. It seems that the general public expects mental health clinicians to be that powerful. When it comes to mass killings, however, the most we can offer is clarification on the pathways that lead to violence and suggestions on how to intervene at various points. All the while, we do our best to catch developing problems upstream before anyone is ever hurt. While none of those things are magic, they can be powerful.

Mason

He was only 15 but six feet tall, with a shock of light brown hair that hung into his eyes. He shuffled when he walked into my office; glaring, he refused to shake my hand. That's not unusual behavior for a teenager mandated to go to therapy.

I explicitly permitted him to hate being there. "Nobody likes to be forced to talk to a therapist," I said. "It sucks. I'd be pissed off too. After all, I'm someone you don't even know, and they want you to talk to me about very personal things."

Mason hadn't wanted to come to see me, but the high school principal hadn't given him a choice. Mason had written a note about "going Columbine" that his ex-girlfriend found and gave to the school counselor. He'd been sent home that day after his mother was called in for a conference. He wasn't welcome back at the school until "corrective action" had been taken. Seeing me was part of the mandated corrective action.

No formal threat assessment had been done. The school didn't have a team set up for that, but they did realize that Mason was a kid at risk. I often get referrals from them in similar situations.

And he was at risk. Mason was depressed and angry and admitted he had been thinking about death for over a year. Though he wasn't making *specific* plans to harm anyone, he entertained thoughts of dying dramatically and was becoming fascinated with the idea of notoriety. Mason wanted to be noticed; he wanted his life to matter.

On that first visit, I made conversation about how complicated it can be to be a teenager; how most of us feel it's hard to fit in. He took a deep breath and looked at me for the first time. Once he started talking, he didn't stop.

One of the first things we discussed was whether or not Mason had access to a gun. Fortunately, he did not.

Mason lived with his divorced mother, who was overworked and underpaid. Mom loved him and meant well, but her attunement capacity was limited; she didn't have the resources to spare. Though they lived in close quarters, they were not emotionally intimate.

Their relationship had been strained for years, and no other family members were involved with their lives. Mason's father had been arrested for domestic violence, and his parents had divorced when he was two years old. Dad left town, and Mason never heard from him again.

Nothing about Mason looked "crazy." At the end of our first visit, he agreed to see me weekly. As I got to know him in the coming weeks, it was clear that he didn't have psychopathic or sadistic tendencies. Still, he seemed to be developing a paranoid thinking style, magnifying slights and quick to assume the worst about others. Though he wasn't psychotic, he was accumulating grievances. In the typical teen way, Mason wasn't good at seeing nuance or understanding context. He was looking at the world through a dystopian lens.

After many years of being on his own after school, he'd retreated into the virtual world of video games and online imageboards; he had no other hobbies or interests. He spent a lot of time ruminating on the unfairness of his life and people who hadn't treated him right and then blowing things virtually up in the gaming world.

Mason was also angry at women. He'd had one girlfriend, a relationship of three months duration. Though brief, he'd attached to her intensely and had been quick to fantasize about marrying her. When she abruptly broke up with him for another guy, he'd started harboring revenge fantasies. His anger at her was starting to generalize to all women.

Mason was a vulnerable kid and was at risk. He was collecting grievances, his thinking style was starting to move in unhealthy directions, and he needed help to keep from spiraling down. There was no way of knowing with any certainty what things would look like for him downstream.

I work hard to make an emotional connection with clients. Particularly with teens at risk, I take an active approach to treatment. It's critical to address the context in which they live, the personal, group, and community factors, including their family, school, and surrounding culture. After all, I would only have one hour a week to spend with Mason, and my power to directly impact his life was minimal. But if we could change Mason's environment in positive ways, Mason would have greater odds of growing into the best version of himself.

For the next two years, we worked together, and I also met with his mother monthly to help her learn better ways to communicate with him. She desperately needed support with parenting.

During this time, we were able to make multiple adjustments in the systems that made up Mason's world. Though he couldn't put it into words, he yearned for healthy attachments with supportive adults. The large high school he attended was contributing to his isolation; he was lost in the crowd. Though people surrounded him, he wasn't connected there. I suggested to his mother and the school counselor that he transfer to the small community continuation school, which had an entirely different structure and just a handful of kids in each class.

The continuation school was based upon an independent study model, and students spent time in classrooms with a small number of students, developing close bonds with the teachers. Though there is often a bias against such programs—that they are for criminally-oriented or for "losers"—I have found that most teens with vulnerabilities do far better in a small program where they can form healing attachments. Like other vulnerable kids, Mason thrived there. His thinking patterns and perception began to change.

He became close to several students and teachers. He learned to play chess, and one teacher sponsored a chess club that allowed the students to participate in chess tournaments with other school districts. Mason was a strong player, and he enjoyed it. He also became interested in drawing, and to his surprise, discovered he was quite talented. He even began writing poetry and short stories.

Mason began to feel like he mattered because he was connected with many people who were invested in him. As he developed a sense of competency in something outside the world of video games, he saw a new world of possibilities. He no longer fantasized about suicide or "going Columbine."

Mason made a special request for me to attend the small graduation ceremony when he completed 12th grade at age 17. Since I am careful about maintaining boundaries with my clients and keeping our contact within the office, this is not something I would typically do. But in this case, I knew it meant a lot to him, and it seemed that the most ethical choice was to show up.

As I sat on the metal folding chair in the small assembly room, I listened as each of the 10 graduating students spoke from the podium. Mason was quietly eloquent as he thanked his mother and me for supporting him through school.

I'm not sure where Mason is today. I last heard from him a few years ago when he was working with a wildlife organization in the Pacific Northwest. I don't know everything about how Mason developed as an adult, but I know he didn't become a criminal. He grew into a good man. I am relieved to say I'm not worried about him.

There is a cost to all of us who live in a country where gun violence and the risk of mass killings are part of our daily lives. Collectively, each event touches all of us with trauma; it affects how we move through the world.

There are millions of Masons in our country. And it's never too late to take protective action.

One of the persistent myths dispelled early in this book is "there's nothing we can do." This is not true. There is much we can do, but we have to choose to do it. We can start with just one thing—and then add another.

Chapter Notes

Chapter 1

1. German Lopez, "2018 Was by Far the Worst Year on Record for Violence in Schools," *Vox News*, December 10, 2018, https://www.vox.com/2018/12/10/18134232/gun-violence-schools-mass-shootings.

2. "Reports," *The Gun Violence Archive*, https://www.gunviolencearchive.org/.

3. Patty Nieberg, Thomas Peipert, and Colleen Slevin, "Colorado Suspect Got Assault Weapon 6 Days Before Shooting," *AP News*, March 22, 2021, https://apnews.com/article/colorado-supermarket-shooting-10-dead-3da92f0d3db65afdb373cc6bb534a711.

4. Institute of Medicine and National Research Council, *From Neurons to Neighborhoods: The Science of Early Childhood Development* (Washington, D.C.: The National Academies Press, 2000), https://doi.org/10.17226/9824.

5. "Understanding Anxiety in Children and Teens: 2018 Children's Mental Health Report," *Child Mind Institute*, 2018, https://childmind.org/our-impact/childrens-mental-health-report/2018report/.

6. Jillian Peterson, "How to Prevent School Shootings," *The Violence Project*, https://www.theviolenceproject.org.

7. "How Does Play Therapy Work?" *Play Therapy International*, 2020, http://playtherapy.org/Helping-Children/About-Play-Therapy.

8. Anya Kemenetz, "Two Big Teachers Unions Call for Rethinking Student Involvement in Lockdown Drills," *National Public Radio*, February 11, 2020, https://www.npr.org/2020/02/11/804468827/2-big-teachers-unions-call-for-rethinking-student-involvement-in-lockdown-drills.

9. Eileen Williamson, "When Active Shooter Drills Scare the Children They Hope to Help," *The New York Times*, September 4, 2019, https://www.nytimes.com/2019/09/04/us/politics/active-shooter-drills-schools.html.

10. Anya Kemenetz, "Two Big Teachers Unions Call for Rethinking Student Involvement in Lockdown Drills," *National Public Radio*, February 11, 2020, https://www.npr.org/2020/02/11/804468827/2-big-teachers-unions-call-for-rethinking-student-involvement-in-lockdown-drills.

11. Amy Nutt, "Why Kids and Teens May Face Far More Anxiety These Days," *The Washington Post*, May 10, 2018, https://www.washingtonpost.com/news/to-your-health/wp/2018/05/10/-why-kids-and-teens-may-face-far-more-anxiety-these-days/.

12. Bruce S. McEwen, "Effects of Stress on the Developing Brain," *Cerebrum* 2011 (September-October 2011): 14, https://www.ncbi.nlm.nih.gov/pmc/articles/PMC3574783/.

13. Robert Sapolsky, *Behave: The Psychology of Humans at Our Best and Our Worst* (New York: Penguin, 2017).

14. Abigail Hess, "50% of Teachers Say They've Considered Quitting," *CNBC*, August 9, 2019, https://www.cnbc.com/2019/08/09/50percent-of-teachers-surveyed-say-theyve-considered-quitting-teaching.html.

15. Hasan Abdeel, "Hate Crime Violence Hits 16-year High, FBI Reports," *The New York Times*, November 3, 2019, https://www.nytimes.com/2019/11/12/us/hate-crimes-fbi-report.html.

16. "Quick Look: 277 Active Shooter Incidents in the United States from 2000 to 2018," *Federal Bureau of Investigation*, 2018, https://www.fbi.gov/about/partnerships/-office-of-partner-engagement/active-shooter-incidents-graphics.

17. United States Department of Homeland Security, "FBI Foils Neo-Nazi Plot to Blow Up Missouri Hospital," *Homeland Security Newswire*, March 27, 2020, http://www.homelandsecuritynewswire.com/-dr20200327-fbi-foils-neo-nazi-plot-to-blow-up-missouri-hospital.

18. "Mass Shootings: Definitions and Trends," *Gun Policy in America*, The Rand Corporation, March 2, 2018, https://www.rand.org/research/gun-policy/analysis/essays/mass-shootings.html.

19. "Mass Shootings," *Gun Policy in America*.

20. Jillian Peterson and James Densley, "Reports," *The Violence Project*, https://theviolenceproject.org.

21. Mark Follman, Gavin Aronson, and Deanna Pan, "U.S. Mass Shootings, 1982–2020: Data from Mother Jones' Investigation," *Mother Jones*, February 26, 2020, https://www.motherjones.com/politics/2012/12/mass-shootings-mother-jones-full-data/.

22. Peterson and Densley, "Reports."

23. Jeremy Bernfeld, "Introducing: Guns and America," *Guns and America*, September 4, 2018, https://gunsandamerica.org/.

24. Peterson and Densley, "Reports."

25. "Active Shooter Resources," *Federal Bureau of Investigation, Office of Partner Resources*, https://www.fbi.gov/about/partnerships/office-of-partner-engagement/active-shooter-resources.

26. National Threat Assessment Center, "Averting Targeted School Violence," United States Secret Service, March 30, 2021, https://www.documentcloud.org/documents/20533588-usss-averting-targeted-school-violence-2021.

27. Arnold Arluke, Adam Lankford, and Eric Madfis, "Harming Animals and Massacring Humans: Characteristics of Public Mass and Active Shooters Who Abused Animals," *Behavioral Sciences and the Law* 36, no. 6 (November 2018): 739–751, http://doi.org/ 10.1002/bsl.2385.

28. "Mass Shootings," *Gun Policy in America*.

29. Paul H. Blackman et al., eds., *The Varieties of Homicide and Its Research: Proceedings of the 1999 Meeting of the Homicide Research Working Group* (Quantico, VA: Federal Bureau of Investigation Academy, 1999).

30. J. Reid Meloy and Alan R. Felthous, "Serial and Mass Homicide," *Behavioral Sciences and the Law* 22, no. 3 (May/June 2004): 289–290, https://onlinelibrary.wiley.com/toc/10990798/22/3.

31. Robert J. Morton and Mark A. Hilts, "Serial Murder: Multidisciplinary Perspective for Investigators," *Federal Bureau of Investigation Behavior Analysis Unit*, https://www.fbi.gov/stats-services/publications/serial-murder.

32. Adam Lankford, "A Comparative Analysis of Suicide Terrorists and Rampage, Workplace, and School Shooters in the United States From 1990 to 2010," *Homicide Studies* 17, no. 3 (August 2013): 255–74. https://doi.org/10.1177/1088767912462033,

33. Charles Montaldo, "Mass Murderers, Spree, and Serial Killers," *Thoughtco.com*, June 23, 2019, https://www.thoughtco.com/defining-mass-spree-and-serial-killers-973123.

34. Alia E. Dastagir, "Mass Killers and Misogyny: The Violent Ideology We Can't Ignore," *USA Today*, August 8, 2019, https://www.usatoday.com/story/news/nation/2019/08/0.6/shooting-ohio-dayton-el-paso-texas-shooter-gilroy-california/1924532001/

35. Dave Cullen, *Columbine* (New York: Hachette, 2010).

36. Nick Rennison, "What is the Origin of the Phrase 'Going Postal,' Meaning 'Going Berserk'?," *History Extra*, September 16, 2009, https://www.historyextra.com/period/modern/what-is-the-origin-of-the-phrase-going-postal-meaning-going-berserk/.

37. Jeff Tolvin, "What Drives Individuals to Kill Their Coworkers?" *Rutgers University*, January 30, 2015, https://phys.org/news/2015-01-individuals-co-workers.html.

38. Cullen, *Columbine*.

39. Chris Canape, "What the Deadliest Mass Shooters Have in Common," *Axios*, September 7, 2019, https://www.axios.com/deadliest-mass-shootings-common-4211bafd-da85–41d4-b3b2-b51ff61e7c86.html.

40. Mitch Smith, "Inside a Deadly American Summer," *The New York Times,* September 21, 2019, https://www.nytimes.com/interactive/2019/09/21/us/summer-mass-shootings.html.

41. Alex Stone, "Gilroy Garlic Festival Shooting: Santino William Legan, 19, Identified as Gunman Who Allegedly Killed Three People," *ABC News,* July 29, 2019, https://abcnews.go.com/U.S./active-shooter-incident-garlic-festival-california/story?id=64624542.

42. Matthew Ormseth, "Disturbing Portrait Emerges of Gilroy Garlic Festival Shooter," *Los Angeles Times,* July 30, 2019, https://www.latimes.com/california/story/2019-07-29/gilroy-garlic-festival-shooting-suspect.

43. Jay Syzdlowski, "Santino William Legan: Gilroy Shooter from Boxing Loving Family," *USA Today,* July 29, 2019, https://www.usatoday.com/story/news/nation/2019/07/29/santino-willian-legan-lagan-picture-rifle-might-makes-right/1860828001/.

44. Tim Arango, "Minutes Before El Paso Killings Hate-Filled Manifesto Appears Online," *The New York Times,* August 3, 2019, https://www.nytimes.com/2019/08/03/us/patrick-crusius-el-paso-shooter-manifesto.html.

45. Bill Hutchinson, "Family of Alleged Gunman in El Paso Massacre Claims He was Influenced by People We Don't Know," *ABC News,* August 7, 2019, https://abcnews.go.com/U.S./family-alleged-gunman-el-paso-massacre-claims-influenced/story?id=64825925.

46. Lois Beckett, "It Can Happen Again: America's Long History of Attacks Against Latinos," *The Guardian,* August 9, 2019, https://www.theguardian.com/us-news/2019/aug/14/it-can-happen-again-americas-long-history-of-attacks-against-latinos.

47. Will Garbe, "Dayton Shooting: Oregon District Gunman Left Decade of Red Flags," *Dayton Daily News,* August 9, 2019. https://www.daytondailynews.com/news/crime—law/dayton-shooting-oregon-district-gunman-left-decade-red-flags/E5UoTI8To1CJDaWUndXBlO/.

48. Daniel Neuhauser, "Dayton Shooter Was in a Pornogrind Band That Released Songs About Raping and Killing Women," *Vice News,* August 6, 2019, https://www.vice.com/en_us/article/j5yekp/exclusive-dayton-shooter-was-in-a-pornogrind-band-that-released-songs-about-raping-and-killing-women.

49. Kris Maher, "Portrait of Dayton Shooter: 'Uncontrollable Urges' and Violent Talk Couched as Jokes," *The Wall Street Journal,* August 6, 2019, https://www.wsj.com/articles/dayton-shooter-recalled-for-uncontrollable-urges-and-violent-statements-couched-as-jokes-11565122531.

50. Will Garbe, "Dayton Shooter Obsessed with Killing," *Dayton Daily News,* August 4, 2019, https://www.daytondailynews.com/news/local/-new-details-dayton-shooter-obsessed-with-killing-bellbrook-classmates-say/uCuyd2JeZzo70NDgArsqOI/.

51. Jane Ward, "What Is Forensic Psychology?" *American Psychological Association,* September 2013, https://www.apa.org/ed/precollege/psn/2013/09/forensic-psychology.

52. Adam Lankford and James Silver, "Why Have Mass Public Shootings Become More Deadly? Assessing How Perpetrators' Motives and Methods Have Changed Over Time," *Criminology & Public Policy* 19, no. 1 (December 2019): 37–60, https://doi.org/10.1111/1745–9133.12472.

53. Jennifer Johnston and Andrew Joy, "Mass Media and the Social Contagion Effect," *Presentation to the American Psychological Association Western New Mexico University,* August 4, 2016, https://www.apa.org/news/press/releases/2016/08/-media-contagion-effect.pdf.

54. Jillian Peterson and James Densley, "Five Types of Mass Shooters." *Los Angeles Times,* November 14, 2019, https://www.latimes.com/opinion/story/2019-11–14/the-five-types-of-mass-shooters.

55. Cullen, *Columbine.*

56. Lois Beckett, "It Can Happen Again: America's Long History of Attacks Against Latinos," *The Guardian,* August 15, 2019, https://www.theguardian.com/us-news/2019/aug/14/it-can-happen-again-americas-long-history-of-attacks-against-latinos.

57. "Lynching in America: Confronting the Legacy of Racial Terror," *Equal Justice Initiative Report 3rd Edition,* https://lynchinginamerica.eji.org/report/.

58. Ying Liu, "Asian Americans Top

Threat Target for Harassment During Pandemic," The Conversation, *GoErie* March 30, 2021, https://www.goerie.com/story/opinion/columns/2021/04/06/-asian-americans-top-target-threats-and-harassment-during-pandemic/7065932 002/.

59. Abdeel Hassan, "Hate Crime Violence Hits 16-year High, FBI Reports," *The New York Times*, November 13, 2019, https://www.nytimes.com/2019/11/12/us/-hate-crimes-fbi-report.html.

60. Alena Schor, "Reports of White Supremacist Propaganda More Than Doubled Last Year," *Time Magazine*, February 12, 2020, https://www.yahoo.com/news/-reports-white-supremacist-propaganda-more-080425623.html.

61. Sarah Weinman, "Massacre on 9th and Main," *Buzfeed News*, March 24, 2016, https://www.buzzfeed.com/sarahweinman/-how-a-forgotten-1903-killing-spree-became-the-first-modern-m.

62. Katrina Gulliver, "Why We Have Forgotten the Worst School Attack in U.S. History," History, *Time*, February 26, 2018, https://time.com/4492872/kehoe-attack-history.

63. Patrick Sauer, "The Story of the First Mass Murder in U.S. History," *The New York Times*, October 14, 2018, https://www.smithsonianmag.com/history/story-first-mass-murder-us-history-180956927/.

64. "Biography of Charles Whitman," *Biography*, August 8, 2019, https://www.biography.com/political-figure/charleswhitman.

65. Sapolsky, "Behave."

66. Lankford and Silver, "Why Have Mass Public Shootings."

67. Lankford and Silver, "Why Have Mass Public Shootings."

68. Peterson and Densley, "Five Types of Mass Shooters."

Chapter 2

1. Sarah Bast and Victoria DeSimone, *Youth Violence Prevention in the United States: Examining International Terrorists, Domestic Terrorists, School Shooters, and Gang Members*. Report. Center for Strategic and International Studies (2019): i–ii, https://www.jstor.org/stable/resrep22584.1.

2. Jillian K. Peterson and James A. Densley, "The Violence Project Database of Mass Shootings in the United States, 1966–2019," *The Violence Project*, https://www.theviolenceproject.org/mass-shooter-database/.

3. Alice Marwick and Becca Lewis, "The Online Radicalization We're Not Talking About," Intelligencer, *New York Magazine*, May 18, 2017, https://nymag.com/intelligencer/2017/05/the-online-radicalization-were-not-talking-about.html.

4. Peter Langman, *School Shooters: Understanding High School, College, and Adult Perpetrators* (Lanham, MD: Rowman & Littlefield, 2015).

5. Bast and DeSimone, *Youth Violence Prevention*.

6. Dave Cullen, *Columbine* (New York: Hachette, 2010).

7. Cullen, *Columbine*.

8. Cullen, *Columbine*.

9. Cullen, *Columbine*.

10. Cullen, *Columbine*.

11. Peterson and Densley, "The Violence Project."

12. Peterson and Densley, "The Violence Project."

13. Tara Law, "Navy Veteran Survived Las Vegas Shooting Only to Be Killed in The Borderline Bar 1 Year Later," *Time*, November 9, 2018, https://time.com/5450351/tel-orfanos-survived-las-vegas-shooting-killed-borderline/.

14. Dalvin Brown, "'Fact Is I Had No Reason to Do It': Thousand Oaks Killer Posted to Instagram During Massacre," *USA Today*, November 10, 2018, https://www.usatoday.com/story/news/nation/2018/11/10/thousand-oaks-shooting-gunman-posted-instagram-during-bar-massacre/1958013002/.

15. Doug Stanglin, "'This Is Not Happening Again': Three Who Survived Gilroy Garlic Festival Also Survived Las Vegas in 2017," *USA Today*, August 1, 2019, https://www.usatoday.com/story/news/nation/2019/08/01/gilroy-garlic-festival-3-also-survived-las-vegas-shooting/1887837001/.

16. Peter Langman, *School Shooters: Understanding High School, College, and Adult Perpetrators* (Lanham, MD: Rowman & Littlefield, 2015).

17. Peterson and Densley, "The Violence Project."

18. Peterson and Densley, "The Violence Project."

19. Peterson and Densley, "The Violence Project."

20. Peterson and Densley, "The Violence Project."

21. Peterson and Densley, "The Violence Project."

22. Peterson and Densley, "The Violence Project."

23. Peterson and Densley, "The Violence Project."

24. Bast and DeSimone, *Youth Violence Prevention.*

25. Joseph McEllistrem, "Affective and Predatory Violence: A Bimodal Classification System of Human Aggression and Violence," *Aggression and Violent Behavior* 10, no. 1 (2004): 1–30, https://doi.org/10.1016/j.avb.2003.06.002.

26. J. Reid Meloy, "Predatory Violence During Mass Murder," *Journal of Forensic Sciences* 42, no. 2 (March 1997): 326–329, https://doi.org/10.1520/JFS14122J.

27. McEllistrem, "Affective and Predatory Violence."

28. R.J. Blair, "Considering Anger from a Cognitive Neuroscience Perspective," *Wiley Interdisciplinary Review Cognitive Science* 3, no. 1 (January 2012): 65–74, https://doi.org/10.1002/wcs.154.

29. Reid, "Predatory Violence During Mass Murder."

30. Blair, "Considering Anger."

31. J. Reid Meloy, Angela Book, Ashley Hosker-Field, Methot-Jones, Tabitha, and Jennifer Roters, "Social, Sexual and Violent Predation: Are Psychopathic Traits Evolutionarily Adaptive?" *Violence and Gender* 5, no. 3 (September 12, 2018): 153–165, http://doi.org/10.1089/vio.2018.0012.

32. T.R. Gregg and A. Siegel, A. "Brain Structures and Neurotransmitters Regulating Aggression in Cats: Implications for Human Aggression," *Progress in NeuroPsychopharmacology & Biological Psychiatry* 25, no. 1 (January 2001): 91–140, https://doi.org/10.1016/s0278–5846(00)00150–0.

33. Gregg and Siegel, "Brain Structures and Neurotransmitters."

34. Liz Berg, "Comparing Predatory Versus Affective Violence and Examining Early Life Stress as a Risk Factor," *Writing Excellence Award Winners,* Paper 37 (2014), http://soundideas.pugetsound.edu/writing_awards/37.

35. McEllistrem, "Affective and Predatory Violence."

Chapter 3

1. Mary Ellen O'Toole, "The Dangerous Injustice Collector: Behaviors of Someone Who Never Forgets, Never Forgives, Never Lets Go, and Strikes Back!" *Violence and Gender* 1, no. 3 (September 19, 2014): 97–99, https://doi.org/10.1089/vio.2014.1509.

2. O'Toole, "The Dangerous Injustice Collector."

3. Andre Simons and J. Reid Meloy, "Foundations of Threat Assessment and Management," in Vincent B. Van Hasselt and Michael L. Bourke (eds.), *Handbook of Behavioral Criminology* (Champaign, IL: Springer, 2017).

4. Simons and Meloy, "Foundations of Threat Assessment."

5. Office of the District Attorney, County of Santa Barbara, *Public Report on Officer-Involved Shooting of Elliot Rodger by Santa Barbara County Deputy Sheriffs on May 23, 2014,* September 4, 2015, https://www.countyofsb.org/da/msm_county/documents/PublicReportonOfficerInvolvedShootingofElliotRodgerbySheriffDeputiesonMay23_2014.PDF.

6. Office of the District Attorney, County of Santa Barbara, *Public Report.*

7. Office of the District Attorney, County of Santa Barbara, *Public Report.*

8. Elliot Rodger, *Retribution: The Final Video,* https://www.youtube.com/watch?v=0TgeR_SFNB8&t=390s.

9. Elliot Rodger, *My Twisted World: The Story of Elliot Rodger,* schoolshooters.info.

10. Rodger, *My Twisted World.*

11. James Silver, John Horgan, and Paul Gill, "Foreshadowing Targeted Violence: Assessing Leakage of Intent by Public Mass Murderers," *Aggression and Violent Behavior* 38 (2018): 94–100, https://doi.org/10.1016/j.avb.2017.12.002.

12. Office of the District Attorney, County of Santa Barbara, *Public Report.*

13. Office of the District Attorney, County of Santa Barbara, *Public Report.*

14. Office of the District Attorney, County of Santa Barbara, *Public Report.*

15. Office of the District Attorney, County of Santa Barbara, *Public Report.*

16. ABC News, "Father Relives Day Elliot Rodger Went on Rampage," *20/20,* June 28, 2014, https://abcnews.go.com/2020/video/father-relives-day-elliot-rodger-rampage-24346090.

17. Office of the District Attorney, County of Santa Barbara, *Public Report.*

18. Rodger, *My Twisted World.*

19. Rodger, *My Twisted World.*

20. ABC News, "Father Relives Day."

21. Rodger, *My Twisted World.*

22. Office of the District Attorney, County of Santa Barbara, *Public Report.*

23. Rodger, *My Twisted World.*

24. Office of the District Attorney, County of Santa Barbara, *Public Report.*

25. Rodger, *Retribution.*

26. Laura Begley Bloom, "Ranked: The 20 Happiest Countries in the World," *Forbes*, March 20, 2020, https://www.forbes.com/sites/laurabegleybloom/2020/03/20/-ranked-20-happiest-countries-2020/#108724c78503.

27. Bruce Bawer, "The Islamization of Oslo," *The City Journal*, January 24, 2018, https://www.city-journal.org/html/-islamization-oslo-15686.html.

28. Anders Behring Breivik, *2083—A European Declaration of Independence*, from *Public Intelligence*, July 22, 2012, https://publicintelligence.net/anders-behring-breiviks-complete-manifesto-2083-a-european-declaration-of-independence/.

29. Asne Seierstad, *One of Us: The Story of Anders Breivik and the Massacre in Norway* (New York: Farrar, Straus & Giroux, 2015).

30. Seierstad, *One of Us.*

31. Seierstad, *One of Us.*

32. Seierstad, *One of Us.*

33. Breivik, *2083.*

34. Breivik, *2083.*

35. Breivik, *2083.*

36. Breivik, *2083.*

37. Breivik, *2083.*

38. Seierstad, *One of Us.*

39. "Anders Behring Breivik: Norway Court Finds Him Sane," *BBC News*, August 24, 2012, https://www.bbc.com/news/world-europe-19365616.

Chapter 4

1. Langman, "Shocked Beyond Belief."

2. Andre Simons and J. Reid Meloy, "Foundations of Threat Assessment and Management," in Vincent B. Van Hasselt and Michael L. Bourke (eds.), *Handbook of Behavioral Criminology* (Champaign, IL: Springer, 2017).

3. Simons and Meloy, "Foundations."

4. Peter Langman, "Elliot Rodger: An Analysis," *The Journal Campus Behavioral Intervention* 2 (2014): 5–19, https://doi.org/10.17732/JBIT2014/1.

5. Anders Behring Breivik, *2083—A European Declaration of Independence*, from *Public Intelligence*, July 22, 2012, https://publicintelligence.net/anders-behring-breiviks-complete-manifesto-2083-a-european-declaration-of-independence/.

6. Simons and Meloy, "Foundations."

7. Stephen J. Sedensky III, *Report of the State's Attorney for the Judicial District of Danbury on the Shootings at Sandy Hook Elementary School and 36 Yogananda Street, Newtown Connecticut on December 14, 2012*, November 25, 2013, https://doi.org/10.13016/f6u6-o0p4.

8. Peter Langman, "The Enigma of Adam Lanza's Mind and Motivations for Murder," *The Journal of Campus Behavioral Intervention* 3 (2015): 1–11.

9. Stephen J. Sedensky III, *Report of the State's Attorney.*

10. Stephen J. Sedensky III, *Report of the State's Attorney.*

11. Matthew Lysiak, *Newtown: An American Tragedy* (New York: Gallery Books, 2013).

12. Lysiak, *Newtown.*

13. Lysiak, *Newtown.*

14. Lysiak, *Newtown.*

15. Stephen J. Sedensky III, *Report of the State's Attorney.*

16. Stephen J. Sedensky III, *Report of the State's Attorney.*

17. Stephen J. Sedensky III, *Report of the State's Attorney.*

18. Stephen J. Sedensky III, *Report of the State's Attorney.*

19. Stephen J. Sedensky III, *Report of the State's Attorney.*

20. Lysiak, *Newtown.*

21. Stephen J. Sedensky III, *Report of the State's Attorney.*

22. Stephen J. Sedensky III, *Report of the State's Attorney.*

23. Connecticut Office of the Child Advocate, *Shooting at Sandy Hook Elementary School: Report of the Office of the Child Advocate*, State of Connecticut, November 21, 2014, https://portal.ct.gov/oca.

24. Stephen J. Sedensky III, *Report of the State's Attorney.*

25. Eric Madfis, "In Search of Meaning: Are School Rampage Shootings Random

and Senseless Violence?" *The Journal of Psychology* 151, no. 1 (January 2, 2017): 21–35, DOI: 10.1080/00223980.2016.1196161.

26. Lysiak, *Newtown.*

27. Lysiak, *Newtown.*

28. Connecticut Office of the Child Advocate, *Shooting at Sandy Hook.*

29. Andrew Solomon, "The Reckoning: The Father of the Sandy Hook Killer Searches for Answers," *The New Yorker,* March 10, 2014, https://www.newyorker.com/magazine/2014/03/17/the-reckoning.

30. Connecticut Office of the Child Advocate, *Shooting at Sandy Hook.*

31. Connecticut Office of the Child Advocate, *Shooting at Sandy Hook.*

32. Connecticut Office of the Child Advocate, *Shooting at Sandy Hook.*

33. Connecticut Office of the Child Advocate, *Shooting at Sandy Hook.*

34. Stephen J. Sedensky III, *Report of the State's Attorney.*

35. Solomon, "The Reckoning."

36. Langman, "The Enigma."

37. Connecticut Office of the Child Advocate, *Shooting at Sandy Hook.*

38. Connecticut Office of the Child Advocate, *Shooting at Sandy Hook.*

39. Connecticut Office of the Child Advocate, *Shooting at Sandy Hook.*

40. Lysiak, *Newtown.*

41. Connecticut Office of the Child Advocate, *Shooting at Sandy Hook.*

42. Solomon, "The Reckoning."

43. Connecticut Office of the Child Advocate, *Shooting at Sandy Hook.*

44. Connecticut Office of the Child Advocate, *Shooting at Sandy Hook.*

45. Connecticut Office of the Child Advocate, *Shooting at Sandy Hook.*

46. Solomon, "The Reckoning."

47. Connecticut Office of the Child Advocate, *Shooting at Sandy Hook.*

48. Connecticut Office of the Child Advocate, *Shooting at Sandy Hook.*

49. Connecticut Office of the Child Advocate, *Shooting at Sandy Hook.*

50. Connecticut Office of the Child Advocate, *Shooting at Sandy Hook.*

51. Connecticut Office of the Child Advocate, *Shooting at Sandy Hook.*

52. Connecticut Office of the Child Advocate, *Shooting at Sandy Hook.*

53. Connecticut Office of the Child Advocate, *Shooting at Sandy Hook.*

54. Connecticut Office of the Child Advocate, *Shooting at Sandy Hook.*

55. Lysiak, *Newtown.*

56. Connecticut Office of the Child Advocate, *Shooting at Sandy Hook.*

57. Lysiak, *Newtown.*

58. Peter Langman, "Shocked Beyond Belief: Complete Threads," www.schoolshooters.info, July 7, 2020.

59. Langman, "The Enigma."

60. Connecticut Office of the Child Advocate, *Shooting at Sandy Hook.*

61. Connecticut Office of the Child Advocate, *Shooting at Sandy Hook.*

62. Connecticut Office of the Child Advocate, *Shooting at Sandy Hook.*

63. Connecticut Office of the Child Advocate, *Shooting at Sandy Hook.*

64. Solomon, "The Reckoning."

65. Lysiak, *Newtown.*

66. Connecticut Office of the Child Advocate, *Shooting at Sandy Hook.*

67. Langman, "Shocked Beyond Belief."

68. Lysiak, *Newtown.*

69. Lysiak, *Newtown.*

70. Lysiak, *Newtown.*

71. Stephen J. Sedensky III, *Report of the State's Attorney.*

72. Connecticut Office of the Child Advocate, *Shooting at Sandy Hook.*

73. Solomon, "The Reckoning."

74. Lysiak, *Newtown.*

75. Lysiak, *Newtown.*

76. Langman, "Shocked Beyond Belief."

77. Connecticut Office of the Child Advocate, *Shooting at Sandy Hook.*

78. Peter Langman, "Miscellaneous Writings by Adam Lanza: Lovebound," www.schoolshooters.info, July 7, 2020, https://schoolshooters.info/sites/default/files/Lovebound.pdf.

79. Langman, "Shocked Beyond Belief."

80. Langman, "Shocked Beyond Belief."

81. Asne Seierstad, *One of Us: The Story of Anders Breivik and the Massacre in Norway* (New York: Farrar, Straus & Giroux).

82. Seierstad, *One of Us.*

83. Langman, "Shocked Beyond Belief."

84. Jon Lender, "Chimp Owner, in Month Before She Died, Told Lawyer of Her Odd Life with Travis," *Hartford Courant,* August 9, 2012, https://www.courant.com/news/connecticut/hc-xpm-2012-08-09-hc-words-of-chimp-owner-0810-20120809-story.html.

85. Langman, "Shocked Beyond Belief."

86. Langman, "Shocked Beyond Belief."

87. Langman, "The Enigma."

88. Connecticut Office of the Child Advocate, *Shooting at Sandy Hook.*

89. Madfis, "In Search of Meaning."

Chapter 5

1. Molly Amman, Karie A. Gobson, and Matthew Bowlin, "Making Prevention a Reality: Identifying, Assessing, and Managing the Threat of Targeted Attacks," Federal Bureau of Investigation, https://www.fbi.gov/file-repository/making-prevention-a-reality.pdf/view, accessed July 26, 2020.

2. Amman, Gobson, and Bowlin, "Making Prevention."

3. "Aurora, Colo., Theater Shooting Timeline Facts," *KABC-TV*, July 26, 2012, https://abc7.com/archive/8743134/.

4. Miguel Bustillo, Shelly Banjo, and Tamara Audi, "Theater Rampage Jolts Nation," *The Wall Street Journal*, July 21, 2012, https://www.wsj.com/articles/SB10008723963904444643045775382926047050.

5. William H. Reid, *A Dark Night in Aurora* (New York: Skyhorse, 2018).

6. "Aurora, Colo.," *ABC News.*

7. William Bennet, "Aurora Heroes: Three Who Gave Their Lives," *CNN,* July 29, 2012, https://www.cnn.com/2012/07/25/opinion/bennett-aurora-three.

8. "Aurora, Colo.," *ABC News.*

9. Keith Coffman, "Colorado Police Officer Say Movie Theater Gunman Was Very Calm," *Reuters*, April 30, 2015, https://www.reuters.com/article/us-usa-shooting-denver/colorado-police-officer-says-movie-theater-gunman-was-very-calm-idUKKBN0NL26U20150430.

10. Reid, *A Dark Night in Aurora.*

11. Reid, *A Dark Night in Aurora.*

12. Reid, *A Dark Night in Aurora.*

13. Reid, *A Dark Night in Aurora.*

14. Sara Burnett and Jessica Fender, "Aurora Shooting Suspect Left Apartment Booby Trapped," *The Denver Post*, July 20, 2012, https://www.denverpost.com/2012/07/20/aurora-shooting-suspect-left-apartment-booby-trapped-music-blaring-2/.

15. Jack Healy, "Colorado Killer James Holmes Notes: Detailed Plans vs. a Whole Lot of Crazy," *The New York Times,* May 28, 2015, https://www.nytimes.com/2015/05/29/us/james-holmess-notebook-and-insanity-debate-at-aurora-shooting-trial.html.

16. Healy, "Colorado Killer James Holmes Notes."

17. Reid, *A Dark Night in Aurora.*

18. Michelle Castillo, "Colorado Shooter Purchased Guns Legally from Three Different Stores," *CBS News*, July 5, 2016, https://www.cbsnews.com/news/colo-shooter-purchased-guns-legally-from-3-different-stores/.

19. Reid, *A Dark Night in Aurora.*

20. Castillo, "Colorado Shooter."

21. Reid, *A Dark Night in Aurora.*

22. David Wagner, "Holmes Took Cell-Phone Selfies with Black Contacts, Guns, and Tongue Out," *The Atlantic*, January 9, 2013, https://www.theatlantic.com/national/archive/2013/01/holmes-took-cell-phone-selfies-black-contacts-guns-and-tongue-out/319702/.

23. Calum Patton, "Florida Shooting Suspect Nikolas Cruz Called Himself 'Annihilator' in Social Media Posts and Was Obsessed with Guns," *Newsweek*, February 15, 2018, https://www.newsweek.com/florida-shooting-suspect-nikolas-cruz-called-himself-annihilator-social-media-807908.

24. Patton, "Florida Shooting Suspect."

25. Theresa Seiger, "Uber Driver: Nikolas Cruse 'Seemed Just Like a Normal Person," *Cox Media Group*, April 4, 2018, https://www.ajc.com/news/national/uber-driver-nikolas-cruz-said-was-going-music-class-seemed-like-just-normal-person/GpWwe8IcXSW4qO8Rqs58IM/.

26. Michelle Mark, Kieren Corcoran, and David Choi, "This Timeline Shows Exactly How the Parkland Shooting Unfolded," *Business Insider*, February 14, 2019, https://www.businessinsider.com/-timeline-shows-how-the-parkland-florida-school-shooting-unfolded-2018-2.

27. Brittany Wallman, et al., "School Shooter Nikolas Cruz: A Lost and Lonely Killer," *Sun-Sentinel*, July 24, 2018, https://www.sun-sentinel.com/local/broward/parkland/florida-school-shooting/fl-florida-school-shooting-nikolas-cruz-life-20180220-story.html.

28. Paul Murphy, "Exclusive: Group Chat Messages Show School Shooter Obsessed with Race, Violence, and Guns," *CNN*, Feb-

ruary 17, 2018, https://www.cnn.com/2018/02/16/us/exclusive-school-shooter-instagram-group/index.html.

29. Murphy, "Exclusive: Group Chat."

30. Murphy, "Exclusive: Group Chat."

31. James Michael, "Parkland's Nikolas Cruz Made Chilling Videos before Shooting: 'You're All Going to Die,'" *USA Today*, May 30, 2018, https://www.usatoday.com/story/news/2018/05/30/parkland-killer-video-im-going-next-school-shooter/657774002/.

32. Michael, "Parkland's Nikolas Cruz Made Chilling Videos."

33. Curt Devine and Jose Pagliery, "Sheriff Says He Got 23 Calls about Shooter's Family, but Records Show More," *CNN*, February 27, 2018, https://www.cnn.com/2018/02/27/us/parkland-shooter-cruz-sheriff-calls-invs/index.html.

34. Megan O'Matz and Travis Scott, "Nikolas Cruz' Journey: A Timeline of a Troubled Youth through the Schools," *Sun Sentinel*, February 27, 1018.

35. Nicholas Nehamas, "'School Shooter in the Making': All the Times Authorities Were Warned About Nikolas Cruz," *Miami Herald*, February 23, 2018, https://www.miamiherald.com/news/local/community/broward/article201684874.html.

36. Nehamas, "School Shooter in the Making."

37. Kevin Drum, "How Many Threats Can the FBI Evaluate on a Daily Basis?" *Mother Jones*, February 18, 2018, https://www.motherjones.com/kevin-drum/2018/02/how-many-threats-can-the-fbi-evaluate-on-a-daily-basis/.

38. Megan O'Matz, "Mental Health Provider Had Long History with Parkland Shooter. Was Agency Negligent?" *Sun-Sentinel*, January 16, 2019, https://www.sun-sentinel.com/local/broward/parkland/florida-school-shooting/fl-ne-henderson-cruz-civil-suit-20190116-story.html.

39. O'Matz and Scott, "Nikolas Cruz' Journey."

40. O'Matz and Scott, "Nikolas Cruz' Journey."

41. O'Matz, "Mental Health Provider."

42. "Columbine Tapes," Jefferson County Sheriff Department, https://www.youtube.com/watch?v=NZdVtnksBHs, accessed July 28, 2020.

43. "Columbine Tapes," Jefferson County Sheriff Department.

44. David Cullen, *Columbine*. New York: Hatchett Book Group, 2010.

45. Murder Diaries, Dylan Klebold, and Eric Harris, *The Journals of Dylan Klebold and Eric Harris: Columbine Killers Diaries* (Google Books, 2019).

46. Cullen, *Columbine*.

47. Cullen, *Columbine*.

48. Peter Langman, "Desperate Identities: A Bio-Psycho-Social Analysis of Perpetrators of Mass Violence," *Criminology and Public Policy* 19, no. 1 (2019): 1–24, https://schoolshooters.info/sites/default/files/Desperate_Identities.pdf.

49. Murder Diaries, Klebold, and Harris, *The Journals*.

50. Cullen, *Columbine*.

51. Peter Langman, *Why Kids Kill: Inside the Minds of School Shooters* (Basingstoke: Palgrave Macmillan, 2009).

52. Cullen, *Columbine*.

53. Peter Langman, *Why Kids Kill*.

54. Peter Langman, *Why Kids Kill*.

55. Cullen, *Columbine*.

56. Cullen, *Columbine*.

57. Peter Langman, "Eric Harris' Diversion Documents," *schoolshooters.info*, https://schoolshooters.info/sites/default/files/eric-harris-diversion.pdf.

58. Murder Diaries, Klebold, and Harris, *The Journals*.

59. Murder Diaries, Klebold, and Harris, *The Journals*.

60. Murder Diaries, Klebold, and Harris, *The Journals*.

61. Peter Langman, *School Shooters* (Lanham, MD: Rowman & Littlefield, 2015).

62. Cullen, *Columbine*.

63. Murder Diaries, Klebold, and Harris, *The Journals*.

64. Murder Diaries, Klebold, and Harris, *The Journals*.

65. Murder Diaries, Klebold, and Harris, *The Journals*.

66. Cullen, *Columbine*.

67. Murder Diaries, Klebold, and Harris, *The Journals*.

68. Cullen, *Columbine*.

69. Cullen, *Columbine*.

70. "Columbine Tapes," Jefferson County Sheriff Department.

71. Cullen, *Columbine*.

72. Cullen, *Columbine*.

73. Sue Klebold and Andrew Solomon, *A Mother's Reckoning: Living in the Aftermath of Tragedy* (New York: Crown, 2016).

74. "Columbine Tapes," Jefferson County Sheriff Department.

Chapter 6

1. Dave Cullen, *Columbine* (New York: Hachette, 2010).

2. Dave Grossman, *On Killing: The Psychological Cost of Learning to Kill in War and Society* (New York: Back Bay Books, 1996).

3. Dave Grossman and Laurel Christianson, *On Combat: The Psychology and Physiology of Deadly Conflict in War and in Peace* (Mascoutah, IL: Killology Research Group, 2012).

4. S.L.A. Marshall and Samuel Lyman Atwood, *Men Against Fire: The Problem of Battle Command* (Norman: University of Oklahoma Press, 2000).

5. Marshall and Lyman, *Men Against Fire*.

6. Marshall and Lyman, *Men Against Fire*.

7. Megan L. Healy and Murray Grossman, "Cognitive and Affective Perspective-Taking: Evidence for Shared and Dissociable Anatomical Substrates," *Frontiers in Neurology* 6 (June 2018).

8. Healy and Grossman, "Cognitive and Affective Perspective-Taking."

9. Healy and Grossman, "Cognitive and Affective Perspective-Taking."

10. Michele Poletti, Ivan Enrici, and Mauro Adenzato, "Cognitive and Affective Theory of Mind in Neurodengerative Diseases: Neuropsychological, Neuroanatomical and Neurochemical Levels," *Neuroscience & Biobehavioral Reviews* 36, no. 9 (October 2012): 2147–2164.

11. Helen Riess, "The Science of Empathy," *Journal of Patient Experience* 4, no. 2 (2017): 74–77.

12. Robert Sapolsky, *Behave: The Psychology of Humans at Our Best and Our Worst* (New York: Penguin, 2017).

13. Healy and Grossman, "Cognitive and Affective Perspective-Taking."

14. Institute of Medicine and National Research Council, *From Neurons to Neighborhoods: The Science of Early Childhood Development* (Washington, D.C.: The National Academies Press, 2000), https://doi.org/10.17226/9824.

15. Institute of Medicine and National Research Council, *From Neurons*.

16. Institute of Medicine and National Research Council, *From Neurons*.

17. Institute of Medicine and National Research Council, *From Neurons*.

18. Institute of Medicine and National Research Council, *From Neurons*.

19. Institute of Medicine and National Research Council, *From Neurons*.

20. Institute of Medicine and National Research Council, *From Neurons*.

21. Mary Gordon, *The Roots of Empathy: Changing the World Child by Child* (New York: The Experiment, LLC, 2009).

22. Li Dandan, et al., "Comparing the Ability of Cognitive and affective Theory of Mind in Adolescent Onset Schizophrenia," *Neuropsychiatric Disease and Treatment* 13 (March 27, 2017): 937–945, https://noi.org/10.2147/NDT.S128116.

23. Marco Iacoboni, *Mirroring People* (New York: Picador, 2008).

24. Iacoboni, *Mirroring People*.

25. Iacoboni, *Mirroring People*.

26. Iacoboni, *Mirroring People*.

27. Riess, "The Science of Empathy."

28. Iacoboni, *Mirroring People*.

29. Albert Bandura, "Moral Disengagement in the Perpetration of Inhumanities," *Personality and Social Psychology Review* 3, no. 3 (August 1999): 193–209.

30. Bandura, "Moral Disengagement."

31. Murder Diaries, Dylan Klebold and Eric Harris, *The Journals of Dylan Klebold and Eric Harris: Columbine Killers Diaries* (Google Books, 2019).

32. Riess Helen, "The Science of Empathy."

33. Riess Helen, "The Science of Empathy."

34. Riess Helen, "The Science of Empathy."

35. Riess Helen, "The Science of Empathy."

36. Dustin Waters and Kevin Sullivan, "Dylann Roof Guilty on 33 Counts of Federal Hate Crimes for Charleston Church Shooting," *The Washington Post*, December 15, 2016, https://www.washingtonpost.com/national/dylann-roof-guilty-on-33-counts-of-federal-hate-crimes-for-charleston-church-shooting/2016/12/15/-0bfad9e4-c2ea-11e6-9578-0054287507db_story.html.

37. Department of Justice, U.S. Attorney's Office. District of South Carolina, *Attorney General Lynch Statement Following*

the *Federal Grand Jury Indictment Against Dylann Storm Roof,* July 22, 2015, https://www.justice.gov/opa/pr/attorney-general-lynch-statement-following-federal-grand-jury-indictment-against-dylann-storm.

38. "Dylan Roof Had a 'Cold and Hateful Heart' in Charleston Church Shooting," *CBS News,* December 7, 2016, https://www.cbsnews.com/news/dylann-roof-death-penalty-trial-charleston-church-shooting/.

39. Waters and Sullivan, "Dylann Roof Guilty."

40. Waters and Sullivan, "Dylann Roof Guilty."

41. Waters and Sullivan, "Dylann Roof Guilty."

42. Waters and Sullivan, "Dylann Roof Guilty."

43. Waters and Sullivan, "Dylann Roof Guilty."

44. "Dylan Roof Had a 'Cold and Hateful Heart,'" *CBS News.*

45. Waters and Sullivan, "Dylann Roof Guilty."

Chapter 7

1. Jill Peterson and James Densley, "The Violence Project Database of Mass Shootings in the United States, 1966–2019," *The Violence Project,* last modified 2020, accessed June 1, 2020. https://www.theviolenceproject.org/mass-shooter-database/.

2. James Silver, Andre Simons, and Sarah Craun, "A Study of Pre-Attack Behaviors of Active Shooters in the United States Between 2000 and 2013," Federal Bureau of Investigation, June 2018, https://www.fbi.gov/file-repository/pre-attack-behaviors-of-active-shooters-in-us-2000–2013.pdf/view.

3. National Institutes of Health, *Information About Mental Illness and the Brain,* Biological Sciences Curriculum Study, NIH Curriculum Supplement Series (Bethesda, MD: National Institutes of Health, 2007). https://www.ncbi.nlm.nih.gov/books/NBK20369/.

4. Steven K. Hoge, "Competence to Stand Trial: An Overview," *Indian Journal of Psychiatry* 58, Suppl. 2 (2016):S187–S190, https://doi.org/10.4103/0019–5545.196830.

5. Robert Sapolsky, *Behave: The Psychology of Humans at Our Best and Our Worst* (New York: Penguin, 2017).

6. Sapolsky, *Behave.*

7. National Institutes of Health, *Information About Mental Illness.*

8. National Institutes of Health, *Information About Mental Illness.*

9. National Institutes of Health, *Information About Mental Illness.*

10. National Institutes of Health, *Information About Mental Illness.*

11. National Institutes of Health, *Information About Mental Illness.*

12. National Institutes of Health, *Information About Mental Illness.*

13. Sapolsky, *Behave.*

14. Sapolsky, *Behave.*

15. Sapolsky, *Behave.*

16. Sapolsky, *Behave.*

17. Kristen L. Syme and Edward H. Hagen, "Mental Health Is Biological Health: Why Tackling 'Diseases of the Mind' Is an Imperative for Biological Anthropology in the 21st Century," *American Journal of Physical Anthropology* 171, no. S70 (May 2020): 87–117, https://doi.org/10.1002/ajpa.23965.

18. Robert Sapolsky, *Why Zebras Don't Get Ulcers* (New York: Henry Holt, 1994).

19. Syme and Hagen, "Mental Health Is Biological Health."

20. National Institutes of Health, *Information About Mental Illness.*

21. Syme and Hagen, "Mental Health Is Biological Health."

22. DJ Jaffe, "What Is Serious Mental Illness and What is Not?" *mentalillnesspolicy.org,* https://mentalillnesspolicy.org/serious-mental-illness-not/.

23. National Institutes of Health, *Information About Mental Illness.*

24. National Institutes of Health, *Information About Mental Illness.*

25. The American Psychiatric Association, *Diagnostic and Statistical Manual of Mental Disorders, Fifth Edition (DSM-5)* (Washington, D.C.: American Psychiatric Association Publishing, 2013).

26. The American Psychiatric Association, *DSM-5.*

27. Arusha Farahani and Christoph U. Correll, "Are Antipsychotics or Antidepressants Needed for Psychotic Depression? A Systematic Review and Meta-Analysis of Trials Comparing Antidepressant or Antipsychotic Monotherapy with Combination Treatment," *Journal of Clinical Psychiatry* 73, no. 4 (April 2012): 486–496, https://doi.org/10.4088/JCP.11r07324.

28. The American Psychiatric Association, *DSM-5.*

29. The American Psychiatric Association, *DSM-5.*

30. The American Psychiatric Association, *DSM-5.*

31. Liam S. Carroll and Michael J. Owen, "Genetic Overlap Between Autism, Schizophrenia, and Bipolar Disorder," *Genome Medicine* 1, no. 10 (October 30, 2009): 102, https://doi.org/10.1186/gm102.

32. Carroll and Owen, "Genetic Overlap."

33. "2011 Tucson Shooting," *FBI Records: The Vault,* https://vault.fbi.gov/2011-tucson-shooting.

34. William H. Reid, *A Dark Night in Aurora* (New York: Skyhorse, 2018).

35. "2011 Tucson Shooting," *FBI Records.*

36. "2011 Tucson Shooting," *FBI Records.*

37. Reid, *A Dark Night in Aurora.*

38. Gabrielle Giffords and Mark Kelly, *Enough* (New York: Scribner, 2014).

39. Sam Quinones, "Jared Lee Loughner's Parents Alone with Their Anguish," *Los Angeles Times,* January 11, 2011, https://www.latimes.com/archives/la-xpm-2011-jan-10-la-na-0111-loughner-parents-20110111-story.html.

40. John Cloud, "The Troubled Life of Jared Loughner," *Time,* January 15, 2011, http://content.time.com/time/magazine/article/0,9171,2042358,00.html.

41. Tim Steller, "Suspect Had Troubled Job History," *Arizona Daily Star,* January 13, 2011, https://tucson.com/news/local/-suspect-had-troubled-job-history/article_a57b6492-6e34-5ffd-ac73-ea17ee720238.html.

42. Nick Bauman, "Exclusive: Loughner Friend Explains Alleged Gunman's Grudge Against Giffords," *Mother Jones,* January 10, 2011, https://www.motherjones.com/politics/2011/01/jared-lee-loughner-friend-voicemail-phone-message/.

43. Mark Memmott, "Loughner's Parents Said to Be Devastated; Very Private," *National Public Radio,* January 11, 2011, https://www.npr.org/sections/thetwo-way/2011/01/11/132829508/loughners-parents-said-to-be-devastated-very-private.

44. Tim Steller, "Loughner's Friends, Teachers, Tell of Descent into Madness," *Arizona Daily Star,* January 15, 2011, https://tucson.com/news/local/loughners-friends-teachers-tell-of-descent-into-madness/-article_390c68dd-1c30-5c34-bb74-c4d7ec8e55ec.html.

45. Steller, "Loughner's Friends."

46. Justin Blum and Drew Armstrong, "Loughner's 'Dark Personality' Eluded Health Scrutiny," *Bloomberg News,* January 11, 2011, https://www.bloomberg.com/news/articles/2011-01-14/loughner-s-dark-personality-eluded-mental-health-scrutiny-before-rampage.

47. David Von Drehle, "The Real Lesson of the Tucson Tragedy," *Time,* January 13, 2011, http://content.time.com/time/magazine/article/0,9171,2042360-3,00.html.

48. Stellar, "Loughner's Friends."

49. Leslie Eaton, Daniel Gilbert, and Ann Zimmerman, "Tucson Shooter's Downward Spiral," *The Wall Street Journal,* January 13, 2011, https://www.wsj.com/articles/SB10001424052748703889204576078331279621622.

50. "2011 Tucson Shooting," *FBI Records.*

51. Reid, *A Dark Night in Aurora.*

52. Reid, *A Dark Night in Aurora.*

53. Reid, *A Dark Night in Aurora.*

54. "2011 Tucson Shooting," *FBI Records.*

55. Giffords and Kelly, *Enough.*

56. "2011 Tucson Shooting," *FBI Records.*

57. "2011 Tucson Shooting," *FBI Records.*

58. Reid, *A Dark Night in Aurora.*

59. Giffords and Kelly, *Enough.*

60. Giffords and Kelly, *Enough.*

61. Norman Ghiasi, Yusra Azhar, and Jasbir Singh, *Psychiatric Illness and Criminality* (Treasure Island, FL: Stat Pearls Publishing, 2020).

62. Devin Dwyer, et al., "Parents of Jared Loughner Say They Don't Understand What Prompted Rampage," *ABC News,* January 10, 2011, https://abcnews.go.com/U.S./jared-loughners-family-remains-imposed-isolation-tucson-shooting/story?id=12587114.

63. Silver, Simons, and Craun, *A Study of the Pre-Attack Behavior.*

Chapter 8

1. Institute of Medicine and National Research Council, *From Neurons to Neigh-*

borhoods: *The Science of Early Childhood Development* (Washington, D.C.: The National Academies Press, 2000), https://doi.org/10.17226/9824.

2. Institute of Medicine and National Research Council, *From Neurons.*

3. Institute of Medicine and National Research Council, *From Neurons.*

4. Institute of Medicine and National Research Council, *From Neurons.*

5. Robert Sapolsky, *Behave: The Psychology of Humans at Our Best and Our Worst* (New York: Penguin, 2017).

6. Sapolsky, *Behave.*

7. Sapolsky, *Behave.*

8. Sapolsky, *Behave.*

9. Oliver P. John, Laura P. Naumann, and Christopher J. Soto, "Paradigm Shift to the Integrative Big Five Trait Taxonomy: History, Measurement, and Conceptual Issues," in O.P. John, R.W. Robins, and L.A. Pervins (eds.), *Handbook of Personality Theory and Research*, 3d ed. (New York: Guilford, 2008).

10. Christopher J. Soto, et al., "Age Differences in Personality Traits from 10 to 65: Big Five domains and facets in a large cross-sectional sample," *Journal of Personality and Social Psychology* 100, no. 2 (February 2011): 330–348, https://doi.org/10.1037/a0021717.

11. Floyd H. Allport and Gordon W. Allport, "Personality Traits: Their Classification and Measurement," *The Journal of Abnormal Psychology and Social Psychology* 16, no. 1 (1921), https://doi.org/10.1037/h0069790.

12. Raymond B. Cattell, *The Scientific Use of Factor Analysis in Behavioral and Life Sciences* (New York: Plenum, 1978).

13. Cattell, *The Scientific Use.*

14. Timothy J. Trull and Thomas A. Widiger, "Dimensional Models of Personality: The Five Factor Model and the DSM-5," *Dialogues in Clinical Neuroscience* 15, no. 2 (June 2013): 134–46, https://doi.org/10.31887/DCNS.2013.15.2/ttrull.

15. John, Naumann, and Soto, "Paradigm Shift."

16. Thomas A. Widiger, "The DSM-5 Dimensional Model of Personality Disorder: Rationale and Empirical Support," *Journal of Personality Disorder* 25, no. 2 (2011): 222–34, https://doi.org/10.1521/pedi.2011.25.2.222.

17. Takakuni Suzuki, at al., "DSM-5 Alternative Personality Disorder Model Traits as Maladaptive Extreme Variants of the Five-Factor Model: An Item-Response Theory Analysis," *Journal Abnormal Psychology* 124, no. 2 (May 2015): 343–345, https://doi.org/10.1037/abn0000035.

18. W. John Livesley, "A Framework for Integrating Dimensional and Categorical Classifications of Personality Disorder," *Journal of Personality Disorders* 21, no. 2 (April 2007): 199–224, https://doi.org/10.1521/pedi.2007.21.2.199.

19. The American Psychiatric Association, *Diagnostic and Statistical Manual of Mental Disorders, Fifth Edition (DSM-5)* (Washington, D.C.: American Psychiatric Association Publishing, 2013).

20. The American Psychiatric Association, *DSM-5.*

21. Brent W. Roberts and Wendy F. DelVecchio, "The Rank-Order Consistency of Personality Traits from Childhood to Old Age: A Quantitative Review of Longitudinal Studies," *Psychological Bulletin* 126, no. 1 (2000): 3–25, https://psycnet.apa.org/doi/10.1037/0033–2909.126.1.3.

22. Elisabeth M. Laurenssen, et al., "Diagnosis of Personality Disorders in Adolescents: A Study Among Psychologists," *Child and Adolescent Psychiatry and Mental Health* 7, no. 3 (February 11, 2013): 3, https://doi.org/10.1186/1753–2000-7-3.

23. The American Psychiatric Association, *DSM-5.*

24. The American Psychiatric Association, *DSM-5.*

25. Andrew Skodol, "Dimensional-Categorical Approach to Assessing Personality Disorder Pathology," *UpToDate*, August 1, 2018, https://www.uptodate.com/contents/dimensional-categorical-approach-to-assessing-personality-disorder-pathology.

26. Thomas A. Widiger, "Dimensional Models of Personality Disorder," *World Psychiatry* 6, no. 2 (June 2007): 79–83, https://www.ncbi.nlm.nih.gov/pmc/articles/PMC2219904/.

27. Timothy J. Trull and Thomas A. Widiger, "Dimensional-Categorical Approach to Assessing Personality Disorder Pathology," *Dialogues in Clinical Neuroscience* 15, no. 2 (June 2013): 135–136, https://doi.org/10.31887/DCNS.2013.15.2/ttrull. Dimensional models of personality: the five-factor model and the *DSM-5*

28. Michael H. Stone, "Mass Murder, Mental Illness, and Men," *Violence and Gender* 2, no. 1 (March 12, 2015): 51–86, https://doi.org/10.1089/vio.2015.0006.

29. Debra Cassens Weiss, "Mass Murderers Often Have These Personality Distortions," *ABA Journal*, April 8, 2015, https://www.abajournal.com/news/article/mass_murderers_often_have_these_personality_distortions.

30. Allen J. Frances, "Dimensional Diagnosis of Personality—Not Whether, but When and Which," *Psychological Inquiry 4, no. 2* (1993): 110–11, https://doi.org/10.1207/s15327965pli0402_7.

31. Trull and Widiger, "Dimensional Models of Personality."

32. The American Psychiatric Association, *DSM-5*.

33. The American Psychiatric Association, *DSM-5*.

34. Robert D. Hare, *Without Conscience: The Disturbing World of the Psychopaths Among Us* (New York: Guilford, 1993).

35. Delroy L. Paulus and Kevin M. Williams, "The Dark Triad of Personality: Narcissism, Machiavellianism, and Psychopathy," *Journal of Research in Personality* 36, no. 6 (December 2002): 556–63, https://doi.org/ 10.1016/S0092–6566(02)00505–6.

36. Delroy L. Paulus, et al., "Screening for Dark Personalities: The Short Dark Tetrad," *European Journal of Psychological Assessment* (2020), http://dx.doi.org/10.1027/1015–5759/a000602.

37. L.L. Johnson, R.A. Plouffe, D.H. Saklofske, "Subclinical Sadism and the Dark Triad: Should There be a Dark Tetrad?" *Journal of Individual Differences* 40, no. 3 (January 2018): 127–133, https://doi.org/ 10.1027/1614–0001/a000284.

38. Paulus, et al., "Screening for Dark Personalities."

39. William Brown, Sana Hazraty, and Marek Palasinki, "Examining the Dark Tetrad and Its Link to Cyberbullying," *Cyberpsychology, Behavior, and Social Networking* 22, no. 8 (August 2019): 552–57, https://doi.org/ 10.1089/cyber.2019.0172.

40. Mitch Van Geel, et al., "Which Personality Traits Are Related to Traditional Bullying and Cyberbullying? A Study with the Big Five, Dark Triad, and Sadism," *Personality and Individual Differences* 106 (February 1, 2017): 231–35, https://doi.org/10.1016/j.paid.2016.10.063.

41. Paulus, et al., "Screening for Dark Personalities."

42. Daniel P. Mears, Melissa Moon, and Angela J. Thielo, "Columbine Revisited: Myths and Realities about the Bullying-School Shootings Connection," *Victims and Offenders* 12, no. 6 (November 2017): 939–55, https://doi.org/ 10.1080/ 15564886.2017.1307295.

43. Donald G. Dutton, Katherine R. White, and Dan Fogarty, "Paranoid Thinking in Mass Shooters," *Aggression and Violent Behavior* 18, no. 5 (September-October 2013): 548–53, https://doi.org/10.1016/j.avb.2013.07.012.

44. Dave Cullen, *Columbine* (New York: Hachette, 2010).

45. Peter Langman, "Jefferson County Sheriff's Office Official Columbine Report," *schoolshooters.info*, https://schoolshooters.info/sites/default/files/jcso_official_columbine_report_0.pdf.

46. Peter Langman, "JCSO Columbine Documents Organized by Theme," *schoolshooters.info*, https://schoolshooters.info/sites/default/files/jcso_docs_by_theme_1.6_0.pdf.

47. Murder Diaries, Dylan Klebold, and Eric Harris, *The Journals of Dylan Klebold and Eric Harris: Columbine Killers Diaries.* Google Books: 2019.

48. Dutton, White, and Fogarty, "Paranoid Thinking in Mass Shooters."

49. Dutton, White, and Fogarty, "Paranoid Thinking in Mass Shooters."

50. Mears, Moon, and Thielo, "Columbine Revisited."

51. Dutton, White, and Fogarty, "Paranoid Thinking in Mass Shooters."

52. Jenni Raitanen, Sandberg Sveinung, and Atte Oksanen, "The Bullying-School Shooting Nexus: Bridging Master Narratives of Mass Violence with Personal Narratives of Social Exclusion," *Deviant Behavior* 40, no. 1 (2019): 96–109, https://doi.org/10.1080/01639625.2017.1411044.

53. Ekin Ok, et al., "Signaling Virtuous Victimhood as Indicators of Dark Triad Personalities," *Journal of Personality and Social Psychology: Personality Processes and Individual Differences*, July 2, 2020, http://dx.doi.org/10.1037/pspp0000329.

54. Hare, Robert D. "Without Conscience."

55. Ok, et al., "Signaling Virtuous Victimhood."

56. Ok, et al., "Signaling Virtuous Victimhood."

57. Dutton, White, and Fogarty, "Paranoid Thinking in Mass Shooters."

58. Elliot Rodger, *My Twisted World: The Story of Elliot Rodger, schoolshooters.info.*

59. Ann Scierstad, *One of Us* (New York: Farrar, Strauss, & Giroux, 2013).

60. Lysiak, *Newtown.*

61. William H. Reid, *A Dark Night in Aurora* (New York: Skyhorse, 2018).

62. Dave Cullen, *Parkland: Birth of a Movement* (London: Riverrun, 2019).

63. Dave Cullen, *Columbine* (New York: Hachette, 2010).

64. Langman, *Jefferson County Sheriff's Report.*

Chapter 9

1. Centers for Disease Control and Prevention, "What Is Autism Spectrum Disorder?" March 25, 2020, https://www.cdc.gov/ncbddd/autism/facts.html.

2. Laurie A. Sperry and David C. Gavisk, "Violence and ASD," *Encyclopedia of Autism Spectrum Disorders*, https://doi.org/10.1007/978-1-4614-6435-8_102129-1.

3. Centers for Disease Control and Prevention, "What Is Autism Spectrum Disorder?"

4. The American Psychiatric Association, *Diagnostic and Statistical Manual of Mental Disorders, Fifth Edition (DSM-5)* (Washington, D.C.: American Psychiatric Association Publishing, 2013).

5. Christina Nicolaidis, "What Can Physicians Learn from the Neurodiversity Movement?" *Virtual Mentor* 14, no. 6 (June 14, 2012): 503–10, https://doi.org/ 10.1001/virtualmentor.2012.14.6.oped1-1206.

6. Nicolaidis, "What Can Physicians Learn."

7. Nicolaidis, "What Can Physicians Learn."

8. The American Psychiatric Association, *DSM-5.*

9. Centers for Disease Control and Prevention, "What Is Autism Spectrum Disorder?"

10. Sperry and Gavisk, "Violence and ASD."

11. Donna M. Werling and Daniel H. Geschwind, "Sex Differences in Autism Spectrum Disorders." *Current Opinion in Neurology* 26, no. 2 (April 2013): 145–53, https://doi.org/10.1097/WCO.0b013e32835ee548.

12. Centers for Disease Control and Prevention, "What Is Autism Spectrum Disorder?"

13. Centers for Disease Control and Prevention, "What Is Autism Spectrum Disorder?"

14. Janice Rodden, "What Does Autism Spectrum Disorder Look Like in Adults," *Additude*, October 11, 2019, https://www.additudemag.com/autism-spectrum-disorder-in-adults/.

15. Sperry and Gavisk, "Violence and ASD."

16. Liam S. Carroll and Michael J. Owen, "Genetic Overlap between Autism, Schizophrenia, and Bipolar Disorder," *Genome Medicine* 1, no. 102 (October 30, 2009), https://doi.org/10.1186/gm102.

17. Clare S. Allely, et al., "Neurodevelopmental and Psychosocial Risk Factors in Serial Killers and Mass Murderers," *Aggression and Violent Behavior* 19, no 3 (May/June 2014): 288–301, https://doi.org/10.1016/j.avb.2014.04.004.

18. Mark Follman, Gavin Aronsen, and Deanna Pan, "U.S. Mass Shootings, 1982–2020: Data from Mother Jones' Investigation," April 16, 2021, https://www.motherjones.com/politics/2012/12/mass-shootings-mother-jones-full-data/.

19. C.S. Allely, et al., "Violence Is Rare in Autism: When It Does Occur, Is It Sometimes Extreme?" *The Journal of Psychology* 151, no. 1 (2017): 46–68, https://doi.org/10.1080/00223980.2016.11759988.

20. Jillian Peterson and James Densley, *The Violence Project Database*, https://www.theviolenceproject.org/mass-shooter-database/.

21. Sperry and Gavisk, "Violence and ASD."

22. Stewart S. Newman and Mohammed Ghaziuddin, "Violent Crime in Asperger Syndrome: The Role of Psychiatric Comorbidity," *Journal of Autism and Developmental Disorders* 38, no. 10 (November 2008): 1848–52, https://doi.org/ 10.1007/s10803-008-0580-8.

23. Allely, et al., "Violence Is Rare in Autism."

24. Allely, et al., "Violence Is Rare in Autism."

25. Allely, et al., "Violence Is Rare in Autism."

26. Allely, et al., "Violence Is Rare in Autism."

27. Brendan Borrell, "Radical Online Communities and Their Toxic Allure for Autistic Men," *Spectrum: Autism Research News*, May 13, 2020, https://www.spectrum news.org/features/deep-dive/radical-online-communities-and-their-toxic-allure-for-autistic-men/.

28. Allely, et al., "Violence Is Rare in Autism."

29. Lee E. Wachtel and Edward Shorter, "Autism Plus Psychosis: A 'One-Two Punch' Risk for Tragic Violence?" *Medical Hypotheses* 81, no. 3 (September 2013): 404–09, https://doi.org/10.1016/j.mehy.2013.05.032.

30. Newman and Ghaziuddin, "Violent Crime in Asperger Syndrome."

31. Xin Wei, et al., "Special Education Services Received by Students with Autism Spectrum Disorders from Preschool Through High School," *Journal of Special Education* 48, no. 3 (November 2014): 167–79, https://doi.org/10.1177/0022466913483576.

32. Centers for Disease Control and Prevention, *Surveillance Report of Traumatic Brain Injury-Related Emergency Department Visits, Hospitalizations, and Deaths—United States*, U.S. Department of Health and Human Services. 2014, https://www.cdc.gov/traumaticbraininjury/pdf/TBI-Surveillance-Report-FINAL_508.pdf.

33. Thomas W. McAllister, "Neurobiological Consequences of Traumatic Brain Injury," *Dialogues in Clinical Neuroscience* 13, no. 3 (September 2011): 287–300, https://doi.org/10.31887/DCNS.2011.13.2/tmcallister.

34. Centers for Disease Control and Prevention, *Surveillance Report.*

35. Huw Williams, et al., "Traumatic Brain Injury: A Potential Cause of Violent Crime?" *Lancet Psychiatry* 5, no. 10 (October 2018): 836–44, https://doi.org/ 10.1016/S2215-0366(18)30062-2.

36. Williams, et al., "Traumatic Brain Injury."

37. Williams, et al., "Traumatic Brain Injury."

38. Williams, et al., Traumatic Brain Injury."

39. Williams, et al., "Traumatic Brain Injury."

40. Robert Sapolsky, *Behave: The Psychology of Humans at Our Best and Our Worst* (New York: Penguin, 2017).

41. Kieran O. Driscoll and Paul Leach, "'No Longer Gage': An Iron Bar Through the Head, Early Observations of Personality Change After Injury to the Prefrontal Cortex," *BMJ Clinical Research* 317, no. 7174 (December 19, 1998): 1673–1674, https://doi.org/10.1136/bmj.317.7174.1673a.

42. Driscoll and Leach, "'No Longer Gage.'"

43. Henry Jacob Bigelow, "Dr. Harlow's Case of Recovery from the Passage of an Iron Bar through the Head," *Journal of the Medical Sciences* 16, no. 39 (July 1850): 13–22, https://collections.countway.harvard.edu/onview/index.php/items/show/25403.

44. Bigelow, "Dr. Harlow's Case of Recovery."

45. "Austin Texas. Police Department Records of the Charles Whitman Mass Murder Case," Austin, Texas, Public Library.

46. Gary M. Lavergne, *A Sniper in the Tower: The Charles Whitman Murders* (Denton: University of North Texas Press, 1997).

47. Charles Whitman, "Whitman Letter," The Whitman Archives, *Austin American-Statesman*, August 1, 2019, https://www.statesman.com/photogallery/TX/201908 01/NEWS/801009999/PH/1.

48. "Austin Texas. Police Department Records," Austin, Texas, Public Library.

49. "Austin Texas. Police Department Records," Austin, Texas, Public Library.

50. Ryan Darby, et al., "Lesion Network Localization of Criminal Behavior," *Proceedings of the National Academy of Sciences of the United States of America* 115, no. 3 (January 18, 2017): 601–06, https://doi.org/10.1073/pnas.1706587115.

51. Darby, et al., "Lesion Network Localization."

52. "Austin Texas. Police Department Records," Austin, Texas, Public Library.

53. The American Psychiatric Association, *DSM-5.*

54. Michael D. DeBellis and Abigail A.B. Zisk, "The Biological Effects of Childhood Trauma," *Child and Adolescent Psychiatric Clinics of North America* 23, no. 2 (February 16, 2014): 185–222, https://doi.org/10.1016/j.chc.2014.01.002.

55. Vincent J. Felliti, et al., "Relationship of Child Abuse and Household Dysfunction to Many Leading Causes of Death in Adults," *American Journal of*

Preventive Medicine 14, no. 4 (May 1, 1998): 245–58, https://doi.org/ 10.1016/ s0749-3797(98)00017-8.

56. Felliti, et al., "Relationship of Child Abuse."

57. Felliti, et al., "Relationship of Child Abuse."

58. Craig A. McEwen and Scout F. Gregerson, "A Critical Assessment of the Adverse Childhood Experiences Study at Twenty Years," *American Journal of Preventive Medicine* 56, no. 6 (June 2019): 790–94, https://doi.org/ 10.1016/j. amepre.2018.10.016.

59. DeBellis and Zisk, "The Biological Effects of Childhood Trauma."

60. DeBellis and Zisk, "The Biological Effects of Childhood Trauma."

61. DeBellis and Zisk, "The Biological Effects of Childhood Trauma."

Chapter 10

1. Michael Edison Hayden, "White Nationalists Praise El Paso Attack and Mock the Dead," Hatewatch, *Southern Poverty Law Center*, August 4, 2019, https:// www.splcenter.org/hatewatch/2019/08/04/-white-nationalists-praise-el-paso-attack-and-mock-dead.

2. Jillian Peterson and James Densley, *The Violence Project*, https://www. theviolenceproject.org.

3. Jacob Aasland Ravendal and Tore Bjørgo, "Investigating Terrorism from the Extreme Right: A Review of Past and Present Research." *Perspectives in Terrorism* 12, no. 6 (December 2018): 5–22, https://www. sv.uio.no/c-rex/english/news-and-events/news/2019/special-issue.html.

4. Anti-Defamation League, *Murder and Extremism in the United States in 2018*, Center on Extremism Report, *Anti-Defamation League*, January 2019, https://www.adl. org/murder-and-extremism-2018.

5. Seth G. Jones, Catrina Doxsee, and Nicholas Harrington, *The Escalating Terrorism Problem, Center for Strategic and International Studies*, June 17, 2020, https://csis-website-prod.s3.amazonaws. com/s3fs-public/publication/200612_ Jones_DomesticTerrorism_v6.pdf.

6. David Neiwart, *Alt-America—The Rise of the Radical Right in the Age of Trump* (New York: Verso, 2017).

7. Arie Perliger, *American Zealots: Inside*

Right-Wing Domestic Terrorism (New York: Columbia University Press, 2020).

8. Ravendal and Bjørgo, "Investigating Terrorism."

9. Hayden, "White Nationalists."

10. Ravendal and Bjørgo, "Investigating Terrorism."

11. Federal Bureau of Investigation, "Terrorism: 2002–2005," U.S. Department of Justice.

12. Neiwart, *Alt-America*.

13. Jones, Doxsee, and Harrington, *The Escalating Terrorism Problem*.

14. Sarah Bast and Victoria DeSimone, *Youth Violence Prevention in the United States: Examining International Terrorists, Domestic Terrorists, School Shooters, and Gang Members, Center for Strategic and International Studies*, September 2019, https://csis-website-prod.s3.amazonaws. com/s3fs-public/publication/190925_ISP_ YouthViolence_WEB_v3.pdf.

15. Best and DeSimone, *Youth Violence*.

16. Adam Lankford, "A Comparative Analysis of Suicide Terrorists and Rampage, Workplace, and School Shooters in the United States from 1990 to 2010," *Homicide Studies* 17, no. 3 (August 2013): 255–274, https://doi.org/10.1177/108876791246 2033.

17. Quassim Cassam, "Why Extremism Is a Question of Psychology, Not Politics," *New Statesman*, February 18, 2020, https://www.newstatesman.com/2020/02/-why-extremism-question-psychology-not-politics.

18. Nils Bockler, et al., "Same but Different? Developmental Pathways to Demonstrative Targeted Attacks—Qualitative Case Analyses of Adolescent and Young Adult Perpetrators of Targeted School Attacks and Jihadi Terrorist Attacks in Germany," *International Journal of Developmental Science* 12, nos. 1–2 (September 5, 2018): 5–24, https://doi.org/10.3233/DEV-180255.

19. Ravendal and Bjørgo, "Investigating Terrorism."

20. Keyona Summers, "From Hate Speech to Hate Crimes: UNLV Sociologist on How Interacting in Online White Supremacy Networks Can Convert Hateful Words into Real Violence," University of Nevada, Las Vegas, October 2, 2019, https://www.unlv.edu/news/ release/hate-speech-hate-crimes.

21. Simon Gottschalk, "Accelerators,

Amplifiers, and Conductors: A Model of Tertiary Deviance in Online White Supremacist Networks," *Deviant Behavior* 41, no. 7 (March 9, 2020): 841–55, https://doi.org/10.1080/01639625.2020.1734746.

22. Gottschalk, "Accelerators, Amplifiers, and Conductors."

23. Tim Stelloh, "Neo-Nazi Turned Muslim Charged with Killing Roommates Who 'Disrespected Faith,'" *NBC News*, May 22, 2017, https://www.nbcnews.com/news/us-news/neo-nazi-turned-muslim-charged-killing-roommates-who-disrespected-faith-n763251.

24. State of New Jersey, Office of Homeland Security and Preparedness, "Domestic Extremists Embrace Foreign Terrorist Ideologies," June 24, 2019, https://www.njhomelandsecurity.gov/media/-podcast-domestic-extremists-embrace-foreign-terrorist-ideologies.

25. Peter Simi and Robert Futrell, *American Swastika: Inside the White Power Movement's Hidden Spaces of Hate* (Lanham, MD: Rowman & Littlefield, 2015).

26. Simi and Futrell, *American Swastika*.

27. Anti-Defamation League, *Murder and Extremism*.

28. Elana Schor, "Reports of White Supremacist Propaganda More Than Doubled Again Last Year, Anti-Defamation League Says," *Time*, February 12, 2020, https://autos.yahoo.com/reports-white-supremacist-propaganda-more-080425623.html.

29. Simi and Futrell, *American Swastika*.

30. Simi and Futrell, *American Swastika*.

31. Simi and Futrell, *American Swastika*.

32. "Hate Map: 2019," *Southern Poverty Law Center*, https://www.splcenter.org/hate-map.

33. Neiwart, *Alt-America*.

34. Simi and Futrell, *American Swastika*.

35. Simi and Futrell, *American Swastika*.

36. U.S. Department of Homeland Security, "Rightwing Extremism: Current Economic and Political Climate Fueling Resurgence in Radicalization and Recruitment," *Federation of American Scientists*, April 7, 2009, https://fas.org/irp/eprint/rightwing.pdf.

37. U.S. Department of Homeland Security, "Rightwing Extremism."

38. Ravendal and Bjørgo, "Investigating Terrorism."

39. Department of Homeland Security, "DHS Makes $20 Million in Funding Available for Targeted Violence and Terrorism Prevention Grants," March 24, 2021, https://www.dhs.gov/news/2021/03/24/dhs-makes-20-million-funding-available-targeted-violence-and-terrorism-prevention.

40. Jones, Doxsee, and Harrington, *The Escalating Terrorism Problem*.

41. Peter Aldhous, "The Cities Where the Cops See No Hate," *Buzzfeed*, December 13, 2018, https://www.buzzfeednews.com/article/peteraldhous/hate-crimes-miami-police-irving-syracuse.

42. Jones, Doxsee, and Harrington, *The Escalating Terrorism Problem*.

43. Jones, Doxsee, and Harrington, *The Escalating Terrorism Problem*.

44. Debbie Lord, "What Happened at Charlottesville: Looking Back at the Rally That Ended in Death," *The Atlanta Journal-Constitution*, August 13, 2019, https://www.ajc.com/news/national/-what-happened-charlottesville-looking-back-the-anniversary-the-deadly-rally/fPpnLrbAtbxSwNI9BEy93K/.

45. Lord, "What Happened at Charlottesville."

46. Lauren Hansen, "48 Hours in Charlottesville," *The Week*, August 12, 2017, https://theweek.com/captured/718250/48-hours-charlottesville.

47. Hansen, "48 Hours in Charlottesville."

48. Hansen, "48 Hours in Charlottesville."

49. Brett Barrouquere, "Virginia Judge Hands Down Life Sentence, Plus 419 Years, in Case of James Alex Fields, Jr., Calls Attack an Act of 'Terror,'" *Hatewatch*, Southern Poverty Law Center, July 15, 2019, https://www.splcenter.org/hatewatch/2019/07/15/-virginia-judge-hands-down-life-sentence-plus-419-years-case-james-alex-fields-jr-calls.

50. Barrouquere, "Virginia Judge Hands Down Life Sentence."

51. Bob Strickly, et al., "911 Calls, Records Reveal Tumultuous Past for Accused Charlottesville Driver, Family," *The Cincinnati Enquirer*, August 15, 2017, https://www.cincinnati.com/story/news/local/-northern-ky/2017/08/14/mom-previously-accused-charlottesville-driver-james-alex-fields-jr-beating-her/566078001/.

52. Joe Ruiz, "Ohio Man Charged with Murder in Fatal Car Attack on Anti-White

Nationalist March," *NPR*, August 13, 2017, https://www.kqed.org/news/11611615/ohio-man-charged-with-murder-in-fatal-car-attack-on-anti-white-nationalist-march.

53. Jones, Doxsee, and Harrington, *The Escalating Terrorism Problem*.

54. Gottschalk, "Accelerators, Amplifiers, and Conductors."

55. Simi and Futrell, *American Swastika*.

56. Simi and Futrell, *American Swastika*.

57. Neiwart, *Alt-America*.

58. Simi and Futrell, *American Swastika*.

59. Friederike Wegener, "The Globalisation of Right-Wing Copycat Attacks," *Global Network on Extremism and Technology*, March 16, 2020, https://gnet-research.org/2020/03/16/the-globalisation-of-right-wing-copycat-attacks/.

60. Wegener, "The Globalisation."

61. Philip Oltermann, "Hanau Attack Gunman Railed Against Ethnic Minorities Online," *The Guardian*, February 20, 2020, https://www.theguardian.com/world/2020/feb/20/hanau-gunman-tobias-rathjen-railed-against-ethnic-minorities-online.

62. James Piazza, "When Politicians Use Hate Speech, Political Violence Increases," *The Conversation*, September 28, 2020, https://theconversation.com/when-politicians-use-hate-speech-political-violence-increases-146640.

63. Piazza, "When Politicians Use Hate Speech."

64. Neiwart, *Alt-America*.

65. Max Fisher, "Poll: 54% of Republicans Say That, 'Deep Down,' Obama Is a Muslim," *Vox*, February 25, 2015, https://www.vox.com/2015/2/25/8108005/obama-muslim-poll.

66. Neiwart, *Alt-America*.

67. Neiwart, *Alt-America*.

68. Perliger, *American Zealots*.

69. Neiwart, *Alt-America*.

70. Neiwart, *Alt-America*.

71. Clare Hill, "The One Trump Record He Doesn't Want You to Talk About: An Unprecedented Number of Mass Shootings," *Independent*, November 5, 2020, https://www.independent.co.uk/news/world/americas/us-election-2020/trump-mass-shootings-usa-2020-election-biden-guns-nra-b1424716.html.

72. Rachel Scott and Will Seakin, "Trump Team Defends Him on Twitter," *ABC News*, May 9, 2019, https://abcnews.go.com/Politics/trump-team-defends-

president-twitter-supporter-shouts-shoot/story?id=62928006.

73. A.C. Thompson, Ali Winston, and Jake Hanrahan, "Ranks of Notorious Hate Group Include Active-Duty Military," *ProPublica*, May 3, 2018, https://www.propublica.org/article/atomwaffen-division-hate-group-active-duty-military.

74. Vera Bergengruen and W.J. Hennigan, "'We Are Being Eaten from Within.' Why American Is Losing the Battle Against White Nationalist Terrorism," *Time*, August 8, 2019, https://time.com/5647304/white-nationalist-terrorism-united-states/.

75. Lois Beckett and Sam Levin, "El Paso Shooting: 21-Year-Old Suspect 'Posted Anti-Immigrant Manifesto,'" *The Guardian*, August 4, 2019, https://www.theguardian.com/us-news/2019/aug/03/el-paso-shooting-21-year-old-suspect-in-custody-as-officials-investigate-possible-hate.

76. Piazza, "When Politicians Use Hate Speech."

77. Alisha Haridasani Gupta, "In Her Words: The Atlanta Shootings," *The New York Times*, May 19, 2021, https://supscrib.com/message/7fe734b8–19e0–4f04-bf67-d0b656f73a78-a7feaf73–6dd1–543f-9731–0a7f483eebb1/in-her-words-atlanta-shootings.

78. Michael Kirk, dir., "Trump's American Carnage," *Frontline*, Season 2021, Episode 10, January 26, 2021, https://www.pbs.org/wgbh/frontline/film/trumps-american-carnage/.

79. Thompson, Winston, and Hanrahan, "Ranks of Notorious Hate Group."

80. Thompson, Winston, and Hanrahan, "Ranks of Notorious Hate Group."

81. Simi and Futrell, *American Swastika*.

82. Thompson, Winston, and Hanrahan, "Ranks of Notorious Hate Group."

83. Ali Winston and A.C. Thompson, "American Hate Group Looks to Make Allies in Europe," *ProPublica*, July 5, 2018, https://www.pbs.org/wgbh/frontline/article/american-hate-group-looks-to-make-allies-in-europe/.

84. Phil Stewart and Idress Ali, "Pentagon Stumped by Extremism in Ranks Orders Stand-Down in Next 60 Days," *Reuters*, February 3, 2021, https://www.reuters.com/article/us-usa-biden-pentagon-extremism/pentagon-stumped-by-extremism-in-ranks-orders-stand-down-in-next-60-days-idUSKBN2A335W.

85. Thompson, Winston, and Hanrahan, "Ranks of Notorious Hate Group."

86. Thompson, Winston, and Hanrahan, "Ranks of Notorious Hate Group."

87. Max Brantley, "Condemn White Supremacist Terrorists? Not the U.S. Senate," *Arkansas Times*, October 2, 2020, https://arktimes.com/arkansas-blog/2020/10/02/-condemn-white-supremacist-terrorists-not-the-u-s-senate.

88. Neiwart, *Alt-America.*

89. Neiwart, *Alt-America.*

90. Neiwart, *Alt-America.*

91. Paul Egan, "Paramilitaries? Terrorists? What Should Militia Groups be Called?" *Detroit Free Press*, October 10, 2020, https://www.freep.com/story/news/local/michigan/2020/10/10/whitmer-michigan-militias-terrorists/5935823002/.

92. Neiwart, *Alt-America.*

93. Perliger, *American Zealots.*

94. Neiwart, *Alt-America.*

95. "Donny Leak Facebook Live Stream," *YouTube*, May 14, 2020.

96. "DPS Confirms Suspect Killed in Standoff Near Menard County Line," *The Eldorado Success*, May 14, 2020, https://myeldorado.net/Content/Default/News/Article/DPS-Confirms-Suspect-Killed-in-Standoff-Near-Menard-County-Line/-3/9/921.

97. "Defining Extremism: A Glossary of White Supremacist Terms, Movements, and Philosophies," *Anti-Defamation League*, https://www.adl.org/education/resources/-glossary-terms/defining-extremism-white-supremacy.

98. "The Constitution and Slavery," *Constitutional Rights Foundation,* https://www.crf-usa.org/black-history-month/the-constitution-and-slavery.

99. "The Constitution and Slavery," *Constitutional Rights Foundation.*

100. Carl Skutsch, "The History of White Supremacy in America," *Rolling Stone*, August 19, 2017, https://www.rollingstone.com/politics/politics-features/the-history-of-white-supremacy-in-america-205171/.

101. Skutsch, "The History of White Supremacy in America."

102. Neiwart, *Alt-America.*

103. Neiwart, *Alt-America.*

104. Neiwart, *Alt-America.*

105. Neiwart, *Alt-America.*

106. Simi and Futrell, *American Swastika.*

107. Jonathan Chait, "It's Getting a Little Chippy." *The New Republic*, April 28, 2010, https://newrepublic.com/article/74699/its-getting-little-chippy.

108. Perliger, *American Zealots.*

109. Thompson, Winston, and Hanrahan, "Ranks of Notorious Hate Group."

110. Thompson, Winston, and Hanrahan, "Ranks of Notorious Hate Group."

111. Billy Perrigo, "White Supremacist Groups Are Recruiting with Help from Coronavirus and a Popular Messaging App," *Time*, April 8, 2020, https://time.com/5817665/coronavirus-conspiracy-theories-white-supremacist-groups/.

112. Perrigo, "White Supremacist Groups."

113. Katie Shepherd, "An Officer Was Gunned Down—The Killer Was a Boogaloo Boy Using Peaceful Nearby Protests as Cover, Feds Say," *The Washington Post*, June 17, 2020, https://www.washingtonpost.com/nation/2020/06/17/boogaloo-steven-carrillo/.

114. Timothy Bella, "A 19-Year-Old with a Van Full of Guns and Explosives Plotted to Assassinate Biden, Federal Officials Say," *The Washington Post*, October 23, 2020, https://www.washingtonpost.com/nation/2020/10/23/biden-treisman-assassination-plot/.

115. Bella, "A 19-Year-Old."

116. Nicholas Bogel-Burroughs, Sheila Dewan, and Kathleen Gray, "FBI Says Michigan Anti-Government Group Plotted to Kidnap Governor Gretchen Whitmer," October 8, 2020, https://www.nytimes.com/2020/10/08/us/gretchen-whitmer-michigan-militia.html.

117. Richard Winton, "Extremist Accused of Plotting to Attack Newsom: A Dangerous Nazi Sympathizer or a 'Mouthy Drunk'?" *Los Angeles Times*, January 29, 2021, https://www.latimes.com/california/story/2021-01-29/extremist-accused-of-plotting-to-attack-newsom-a-dangerous-nazi-sympathizer-or-a-mouthy-drunk.

118. Steve Hendrix and Michael Miller, "Let's Get This Party Started: New Zealand Killing Suspect Narrated His Killing Rampage," *The Washington Post*, March 15, 2019, https://www.washingtonpost.com/local/lets-get-this-party-started-new-zealand-gunman-narrated-his-chilling-rampage/2019/03/15/fb3db352-4748-11e9-90f0-0ccfeec87a61_story.html.

119. Kevin Roose, "A Mass Murder Of, and For, the Internet," *The New York Times*, March 15, 2019, https://www.nytimes.com/2019/03/15/technology/facebook-youtube-christchurch-shooting.html.

120. Hendrix and Miller, "Let's Get This Party Started."

121. Lizzie Dearden, "Revered as a Saint by Online Extremists, How the Christchurch Killer Inspired Copycat Killers around the World," *The Independent*, August 24, 2019, https://www.independent.co.uk/news/world/australasia/brenton-tarrant-christchurch-shooter-attack-el-paso-norway-poway-a9076926.html.

122. Dearden, "Revered as a Saint."

123. "Mosque Attacks Timeline: 18 Minutes from First Call to Arrest," *Radio New Zealand*, April 7, 2019, https://www.rnz.co.nz/news/national/387248/mosque-attacks-timeline-18-minutes-from-first-call-to-arrest.

124. Dearden, "Revered as a Saint."

125. "Mosque Attacks Timeline," *Radio New Zealand*.

126. Dearden, "Revered as a Saint."

127. "New Zealand Mosque Attacks Suspect Praised Trump in Manifesto," *Al Jazeera*, March 16, 2019, https://www.aljazeera.com/news/2019/3/16/new-zealand-mosque-attacks-suspect-praised-trump-in-manifesto.

128. Hendrix and Miller, "Let's Get This Party Started."

129. Zack Beauchamp, "Accelerationism: The Obscure Idea Inspiring White Supremacist Killers Around the World," *Vox*, November 18, 2019, https://www.vox.com/the-highlight/2019/11/11/20882005/accelerationism-white-supremacy-christchurch.

130. Dearden, "Revered as a Saint."

131. Dearden, "Revered as a Saint."

132. Dearden, "Revered as a Saint."

133. Gottschalk, "Accelerators, Amplifiers, and Conductors."

134. Simi and Futrell, *American Swastika*.

135. J.M. Berger, "*The Dangerous Spread of Extremist Manifestos*," The Atlantic, February 26, 2019.

Chapter 11

1. Elliot Rodger, *Retribution: The Final Video*, https://www.youtube.com/watch?v=0TgeR_SFNB8&t=390s.

2. Jesselyn Cook, "A Toxic 'Brotherhood': Inside Incels' Dark Online World," *Huffington Post*, July 26, 2018, https://www.huffpost.com/entry/incel-toxic-brotherhood-online-misogyny_n_5b490e5fe4b0bc69a7873ff0.

3. Julie Bosman, Kate Taylor, and Tim Arango, "A Common Trait Among Mass Killers: Hatred Toward Women," *The New York Times*, August 10, 2019, https://www.nytimes.com/2019/08/10/us/mass-shootings-misogyny-dayton.html.

4. "When Women are the Enemy: The Intersection of Misogyny and White Supremacy," *Anti-Defamation League*, https://www.adl.org/resources/reports/when-women-are-the-enemy-the-intersection-of-misogyny-and-white-supremacy.

5. Zack Beauchamp, "Incel, the Misogynist Ideology That Inspired the Deadly Toronto Attack, Explained," *Vox*, April 25, 2018, https://www.vox.com/world/2018/4/25/17277496/incel-toronto-attack-alek-minassian.

6. Beauchamp, "Incel, the Misogynist Ideology."

7. Steve Hendrix, "He Always Hated Women, Then He Decided to Kill Them," *The Washington Post*, June 7, 2019, https://www.washingtonpost.com/graphics/2019/local/yoga-shooting-incel-attack-fueled-by-male-supremacy/?utm_term=.84aede149a37&tid=sm_tw.

8. Beauchamp, "Incel, the Misogynist Ideology."

9. Amanda Taub, "On Social Media's Fringes, Growing Extremism Targets Women," *The New York Times*, May 9, 2018, https://www.nytimes.com/2018/05/09/world/americas/incels-toronto-attack.html.

10. Beauchamp, "Incel, the Misogynist Ideology."

11. Rodger, *Retribution*.

12. Aja Romano, "What a Woman-Led Incel Support Group Can Teach Us About Men and Mental Health," *Vox*, June 20, 2018, https://www.vox.com/2018/6/20/17314846/incel-support-group-therapy-black-pill-mental-health.

13. Zoe Williams, "'Raw Hatred': Why the Incel Movement Targets and Terrorizes Women," *The Guardian*, April 25, 2018, https://www.theguardian.com/world/2018/apr/25/raw-hatred-why-incel-movement-targets-terrorises-women.

14. Bryan Passifiume, Kevin Connor,

and Jane Stevenson, "10 Dead, 15 Wounded When Van Hits Pedestrians Near Yonge and Finch," *Toronto Sun*, April 23, 2018, https://torontosun.com/news/local-news/-multiple-pedestrians-struck-by-van-on-yonge-st.

15. Amanda Coletta, "Man Accused of Killing 10 in Toronto Van Attack Told Police His 'Mission' Was 'Accomplished,'" *The Washington Post*, September 27, 2019, https://www.washingtonpost.com/world/the_americas/-man-accused-of-killing-10-in-toronto-van-attack-told-police-his-mission-was-accomplished/2019/09/27/d5152a44-e161-11e9-be7f-4cc85017c36f_story.html.

16. Coletta, "Man Accused of Killing 10."

17. Coletta, "Man Accused of Killing 10."

18. Coletta, "Man Accused of Killing 10."

19. Coletta, "Man Accused of Killing 10."

20. Coletta, "Man Accused of Killing 10."

21. Jennifer Wright, "Why Incels Hate Women," *Harper's Bazaar*, April 27, 2018, https://www.harpersbazaar.com/culture/politics/a20078774/what-are-incels/.

22. Liam Casey, "Alek Minassian Was Never Aggressive to Others Before the Attack," *The Star*, November 30, 2020, https://www.thestar.com/news/canada/2020/11/30/alek-minassian-was-never-aggressive-to-others-before-van-attack-court-hears.html.

23. Jeremy Grimaldi, "Alleged Attacker Alek Minassian May Have Mental Health Issues," *Richmond Hill Liberal*, April 24, 2018, https://www.toronto.com/news-story/8566082-update-alleged-attacker-alek-minassian-may-have-mental-health-issues/.

24. Grimaldi, "Alleged Attacker."

25. "Police Treating Attack at Toronto Massage Parlour as Act of Incel Terrorism," *BNO News*, May 19, 2020, https://bnonews.com/index.php/2020/05/deadly-attack-at-toronto-massage-parlour-treated-as-incel-terrorism/.

26. "Police Treating Attack," *BNO News*.

27. Bruce Hoffman, Jacob Ware, and Ezra Shapiro, "Assessing the Threat of Incel Violence," *Studies in Conflict and Terrorism*" 43, no. 7: 565–587, https://doi.org/10.1080/1057610X.2020.1751459.

28. Tallahassee Police Department, "CIB Supplemental Report: Investigative Summary," November 2, 2018, https://www.talgov.com/uploads/public/documents/tpd/supplemental_report.pdf.

29. Hendrix, "He Always Hated Women."

30. Hendrix, "He Always Hated Women."

31. Tallahassee Police Department, "CIB Supplemental Report."

32. Tallahassee Police Department, "CIB Supplemental Report."

33. Hendrix, "He Always Hated Women."

34. Hendrix, "He Always Hated Women."

35. Tallahassee Police Department, "CIB Supplemental Report."

36. Tallahassee Police Department, "CIB Supplemental Report."

37. Hendrix, "He Always Hated Women."

38. Tallahassee Police Department, "CIB Supplemental Report."

39. Tallahassee Police Department, "CIB Supplemental Report."

40. Tallahassee Police Department, "CIB Supplemental Report."

41. Tallahassee Police Department, "CIB Supplemental Report."

42. Tallahassee Police Department, "CIB Supplemental Report."

43. Hendrix, "He Always Hated Women."

44. Tallahassee Police Department, "CIB Supplemental Report."

45. Hendrix, "He Always Hated Women."

46. Hendrix, "He Always Hated Women."

47. Tallahassee Police Department, "CIB Supplemental Report."

48. Tallahassee Police Department, "CIB Supplemental Report."

49. Tallahassee Police Department, "CIB Supplemental Report."

50. Tallahassee Police Department, "CIB Supplemental Report."

51. Tallahassee Police Department, "CIB Supplemental Report."

52. Tallahassee Police Department, "CIB Supplemental Report."

53. Tallahassee Police Department, "CIB Supplemental Report."

54. Tallahassee Police Department, "CIB Supplemental Report."

55. Tallahassee Police Department, "CIB Supplemental Report."

56. Tallahassee Police Department, "CIB Supplemental Report."

57. Tallahassee Police Department, "CIB Supplemental Report."

58. Tallahassee Police Department, "CIB Supplemental Report."

59. Tallahassee Police Department, "CIB Supplemental Report."

60. Tallahassee Police Department, "CIB Supplemental Report."

61. Tallahassee Police Department, "CIB Supplemental Report."

62. Tallahassee Police Department, "CIB Supplemental Report."

63. Tallahassee Police Department, "CIB Supplemental Report."

64. Claire Turenne Sjolander, "The Killers among Us: School Shootings and the Militarization of Childhood," 217–326, in J. Marshall Beier (ed.), *The Militarization of Childhood* (New York: Palgrave Macmillan, 2011).

65. Rick Anderson, "'Here I Am, 26, with No Friends, No Job, No Girlfriend': Shooter's Manifesto Offers Clues to 2015 Oregon College Rampage," *Los Angeles Times*, September 23, 2017, https://www.latimes.com/nation/la-na-school-shootings-2017-story.html.

66. Eliott McLaughlin, Andy Rose, and Konstantin Toropin, "Suspect in Arizona Shooting Wanted to Target Couples, Prosecutor Says," *CNN*, May 20, 2020, https://www.cnn.com/2020/05/20/us/westgate-arizona-shooting/index.html.

67. Scott Reinhard, "8 Dead in Atlanta Spa Shootings, With Fears of Anti-Asian Bias," *The New York Times*, March 19, 2021, https://www.nytimes.com/live/2021/03/17/us/shooting-atlanta-acworth.

68. Coletta, "Man Accused of Killing 10."

69. Southern Poverty Law Center, "Hatewatch," https://www.splcenter.org/hatewatch.

70. Jillian Peterson and James Densley, *The Violence Project*, https://www.theviolenceproject.org.

71. Sharon G. Smith, Katherine A. Fowler, and Phyllis H. Niolon, "Intimate Partner Homicide and Corollary Victims in 16 States: National Violent Death Reporting System, 2003–2009," *American Journal of Public Health* 104, no. 3 (March 2014): 461–66, https://doi.org/ 10.2105/AJPH.2013.301582.

72. Edgar Sandoval and Terence Cullen, "Texas Massacre Survivors Say Gunman Devin Kelley Became Enraged by Scared Children During Church Shooting," *New York Daily News*, November 8, 2017, https://www.nydailynews.com/news/national/survivors-texas-massacre-recalls-moments-gunman-entered-church-article-1.3616562.

73. "Texas Church Gunman's Ex-Wife Tells Inside Edition: He Just Had a Lot of Demons," *My San Antonio*, November 13, 2017, https://www.mysanantonio.com/news/local/texas/article/Tessa-Brennaman-devin-patrick-kelley-shooting-12349127.php.

74. Kirk Mitchell, "Gunman Who Killed 26 People in Texas Cited for Cruelty to Animals in Colorado," *The Denver Post*, November 6, 2017, https://www.denverpost.com/2017/11/06/texas-shooting-devin-patrick-kelley-colorado-arrest/.

75. Emily Schmall, "Parishioners: Gunman Acted Oddly Week Before Sutherland Springs Church Attack," *The Denver Post*, November 10, 2017, https://www.denverpost.com/2017/11/10/sutherland-springs-church-shooting-gunman-acted-oddly/.

76. Schmall, "Parishioners: Gunman Acted Oddly."

77. Bosman, Taylor, and Arango, "A Common Trait."

78. Amy Wang, "Jealousy and Obsession May Have Led Carwash Shooting Suspect to Kill Four, Relatives Say," *The Washington Post*, January 30, 2018, https://www.washingtonpost.com/news/post-nation/wp/2018/01/29/jealousy-and-obsession-may-have-led-carwash-shooting-suspect-to-kill-four-relatives-say/.

79. Bosman, Taylor, and Arango, "A Common Trait."

80. Justin Benton, "Familicide: Experts Say Family Murder-Suicides, Though Rare, Are Most Common Mass Killing," *San Francisco Examiner*, June 20, 2007.

81. Marieke Liem, et al., "The Nature and Prevalence of Familicide in the United States, 2000–2009," *Journal of Family Violence* 28, no. 4 (2013): 351–358, https://doi.org/10.1007/s10896-013-9504-2.

82. "Family Annihilation: Fathers Who Kill Their Children," *BBC News*, April 25, 2013, https://www.bbc.com/news/uk-england-22213942.

83. Linda C. Karlsson, et al., "Familicide: A Systematic Literature Review," *Trauma, Violence, & Abuse* 22, no. 1 (January 1, 2021): 83–98, https://doi.org/10.1177/1524838018821955.

84. Melissa Hogenboom, "Criminologists Identify Family Killer Characteristics," BBC News, August 14, 2013.

85. BBC News, "Family Annihilation: Fathers Who Kill Their Children," April 25, 2013.

86. Karlsson, et al., "Familicide."

87. Federal Bureau of Prisons, "Inmate Gender," December 5, 2020, https://www.bop.gov/about/statistics/statistics_inmate_gender.jsp.

88. Jeffery T. Walker and Sean Maddan, *Understanding Statistics for the Social Sciences, Criminal Justice, and Criminology* (New York: Jones & Bartlett, 2013).

89. Omar Yousaf, Aneka Popat, and Myra S. Hunter, "An Investigation of Masculinity Attitudes, Gender, and Attitudes toward Psychological Help-Seeking," *Psychology of Men & Masculinity* 16, no. 2 (2015): 234–237, https://doi.org/10.1037/a0036241.

90. American Psychological Association, *APA Guidelines for Psychological Practice with Boys and Men*, August 2018, http://www.apa.org/about/policy/psychological-practice-boys-men-guidelines.pdf.

Chapter 12

1. Jan-Willem Van Prooijen and Karen M. Douglas, "Belief in Conspiracy Theories: Basic Principles of an Emerging Research Domain," *European Journal of Social Psychology* 48, no. 7 (December 2018): 879–908, https://doi.org/10.1002/ejsp.2530.

2. Karen M. Douglas, Robbie M. Sutton, and Aleksandra Cichocka, "The Psychology of Conspiracy Theories," *Current Directions in Psychological Science* 26, no. 6 (June 2017): https://doi.org/10.1177%2F0963721417718261.

3. Van Prooijen and Douglas, "Belief in Conspiracy Theories."

4. Douglas, Sutton, and Cichocka, "The Psychology of Conspiracies."

5. Van Prooijen and Douglas, "Belief in Conspiracy Theories."

6. Van Prooijen and Douglas, "Belief in Conspiracy Theories."

7. Van Prooijen and Douglas, "Belief in Conspiracy Theories."

8. Douglas, Sutton, and Cichocka, "The Psychology of Conspiracies."

9. Van Prooijen and Douglas, "Belief in Conspiracy Theories."

10. Van Prooijen and Douglas, "Belief in Conspiracy Theories."

11. Van Prooijen and Douglas, "Belief in Conspiracy Theories."

12. Van Prooijen and Douglas, "Belief in Conspiracy Theories."

13. Jan-Willem Van Prooijen, Andre P. Krouwel, and Thomas V. Pollet, "Political Extremism Predicts Belief in Conspiracy Theories," *Social Psychology and Personality Science* 1, no. 9 (January 12, 2015): 1–9, https://doi.org/10.1177%2F1948550614567356.

14. Van Prooijen and Douglas, "Belief in Conspiracy Theories."

15. Tommy Beer, "Majority of Republicans Believe the QAnon Conspiracy Theory Is Partly or Mostly True, Survey Finds," *Forbes*, September 2, 2020, https://www.forbes.com/sites/tommybeer/2020/09/02/-majority-of-republicans-believe-the-qanon-conspiracy-theory-is-partly-or-mostly-true-survey-finds/?sh=22cc5cbb5231.

16. Lauren Leatherby, et al., "How a Presidential Rally Turned Into a Capitol Rampage," *The New York Times*, January 12, 2021, https://www.nytimes.com/interactive/2021/01/12/us/capitol-mob-timeline.html.

17. Leatherby, "How a Presidential Rally Turned."

18. Leatherby, "How a Presidential Rally Turned."

19. Fabiola Cineas, "Whiteness Is at the Core of the Insurrection," *Vox*, January 8, 2021, https://www.vox.com/2021/1/8/22221078/us-capitol-trump-riot-insurrection.

20. Leatherby, "How a Presidential Rally Turned."

21. Cristina Marcos, "Second Officer Dies by Suicide Following Capitol Attack," *The Hill*, January 27, 2021, https://thehill.com/homenews/house/536189-second-police-officer-dies-by-suicide-after-capitol-attack.

22. Leatherby, "How a Presidential Rally Turned."

23. Rich Schapiro, "Off the Grid, Heavily Armed, and Radicalized: He's a Law Enforcement Nightmare," *NBC News*, January 17, 2021, https://www.nbcnews.com/news/us-news/grid-heavily-armed-radicalized-he-s-law-enforcement-nightmare-n1254510.

24. Robert A. Pape and Kevin Ruby, "The Capitol Rioters Aren't Like Other Extremists," *The Atlantic*, February 2, 2021, https://www.theatlantic.com/ideas/archive/2021/02/the-capitol-rioters-arent-like-other-extremists/617895/

25. Kurt Braddock, "Impeachment Trial: Research Spanning Decades Shows Language Can Incite Violence," *The Conversation*, February 5, 2021, https://theconversation.com/impeachment-trial-research-spanning-decades-shows-language-can-incite-violence-154615.

26. Braddock, "Impeachment Trial."

27. Braddock, "Impeachment Trial."

28. Michael Humphrey, "I Analyzed All of Trump's Tweets to Find Out What He Was Really Saying," *The Conversation*, February 8, 2021, https://theconversation.com/i-analyzed-all-of-trumps-tweets-to-find-out-what-he-was-really-saying-154532.

29. Humphrey, "I Analyzed All of Trump's."

30. Kevin Courtney, "FBI: Ian Rogers Threatened 'Going to War' If Trump Is Removed from Office," *Napa Valley Register*, Jan, 31, 2021, https://napavalleyregister.com/news/local/fbi-ian-rogers-threatened-going-to-war-if-trump-is-removed-from-office/article_b10ca7b3–6c57–5e56-aabf-03172a71aadd.html.

31. Stephen Marche, "The Insurrection Has Not Yet Happened. But It's Coming," *The Globe and Mail*, January 15, 2021, https://www.theglobeandmail.com/opinion/article-the-insurrection-has-not-yet-happened-but-its-coming/.

32. Michael Rocque and Stephanie Kelly-Romano, "Why Do Mass Shootings Spawn Conspiracy Theories?" *The Conversation*, February 21, 2021, https://theconversation.com/why-do-mass-shootings-spawn-conspiracy-theories-155017.

33. Daniel Trotta, "Infowars Founder Who Claimed Sandy Hook Shooting Was a Hoax Ordered to Pay $100,000," *Reuters*, December 31, 2019, https://www.reuters.com/article/us-texas-lawsuit-alex-jones/-infowars-founder-who-claimed-sandy-hook-shooting-was-a-hoax-ordered-to-pay-100000-idUSKBN1YZ1BB.

Chapter 13

1. Sherry Turkle, "Connected, but Alone?" *TED*, Apr. 3, 2012, https://www.youtube.com/watch?v=t7Xr3AsBEK4.

2. Neils Clark and P. Shavaun Scott, *Game Addiction: The Experience and the Effects.* (Jefferson, NC: McFarland, 2009).

3. Tristan Harris, "How Technology Is Hijacking Your Mind—from a Magician and Google Design Ethicist," *Thrive Global*, May 18, 2016, https://medium.com/thrive-global/how-technology-hijacks-peoples-minds-from-a-magician-and-google-s-design-ethicist-56d62ef5edf3.

4. "Who We Are," *Center for Humane Technology*, 2021, https://www.humanetech.com/who-we-are#work.

5. Harris, "How Technology Is Hijacking Your Mind."

6. Clark and Scott, *Game Addiction.*

7. Clark and Scott, *Game Addiction.*

8. Erica Good and Benedict Carey, "Mass Killings Are Seen as a Kind of Contagion," *The New York Times*, October 7, 2015, https://www.nytimes.com/2015/10/08/science/mass-killers-often-rely-on-past-perpetrators-blueprints.html.

9. Pete Simi and Robert Futrell, *American Swastika: Inside the White Power Movement's Hidden Spaces of Hate* (Lanham, MD: Rowman & Littlefield, 2010).

10. Rob Arthur, "We Analyzed More Than 1 Million Comments on 4chan. Hate Speech Has Spiked by 40% There since 2015," *Vice News*, July 10, 2019, https://www.vice.com/en/article/d3nbzy/we-analyzed-more-than-1-million-comments-on-4chan-hate-speech-there-has-spiked-by-40-since-2015.

11. Timothy McLaughlin, "The Weird, Dark History of 8chan," *Wired*, August 6, 2019, https://www.wired.com/story/the-weird-dark-history-8chan/.

12. April Glaser, "8chan Is a Normal Part of Mass Shootings Now," *Slate*, August 4, 2019, https://slate.com/technology/2019/08/el-paso-8chan-4chan-mass-shootings-manifesto.html.

13. Makena Kelly, "Cloudflare to Revoke 8chan's Service, Opening the Fringe Website Up for DDoS Attacks," *The Verge*, August 4, 2019, https://www.theverge.com/2019/8/4/20754310/cloudflare-8chan-fredrick-brennan-ddos-attack.

14. McLaughlin, "The Weird, Dark History of 8chan."

15. *The Influencer Report: Engaging Gen Z and Millennials, Morning Consult*, 2020, https://morningconsult.com/wp-content/uploads/2019/11/The-Influencer-Report-Engaging-Gen-Z-and-Millennials.pdf.

16. Nickie Louise, "These Six Corporations Control 90% of the Media Outlets in America," *Tech Startups*, September 18, 2020, https://techstartups.

com/2020/09/18/6-corporations-control-90-media-america-illusion-choice-objectivity-2020/.

17. Michael Rocque and Grant Duwe, "Rampage Shootings: An Historical, Empirical, and Theoretical Overview," *Current Opinion in Psychology* 19 (February 2018): 28–33, https://10.1016/j.copsyc.2017.03.025.

18. Pierre Thomas, et al., "Columbine Shootings' Grim Legacy: More than 50 School Attacks, Plots," *ABC News*, October 7, 2014, https://abcnews.go.com/U.S./columbine-shootings-grim-legacy-50-school-attacks-plots/story?id=26007119.

19. Jack Levin and Eric Madfis, "School Rampage in International Perspective: The Salience of Cumulative Strain Theory," in Nils Böckler, et al. (eds.), *School Shootings: International Research, Case Studies, and Concepts for Prevention* (New York: Springer-Verlag, 2013).

20. Krishna Andavolu, "The Allure of Columbine Fandom," *Vice News Tonight*, May 2020, https://video.vice.com/en_us/video/the-allure-of-columbine-fandom/5e693c03fbf62c7c394f3285.

21. Bram van der Meer, J. Reid Meloy, and Jens Hoffmann, "The Adult Mass Murderer in Europe and North America," available at http://drreidmeloy.com/wp-content/uploads/2017/08/ATAP2017.pdf, accessed December 28, 2020.

22. van der Meer, Meloy, and Hoffmann, "The Adult Mass Murderer."

23. Sherry Towers, et al., "Contagion in Mass Killings and School Shootings," *PLoS ONE* 10, no. 7 (July 2, 2015): e0117259, https://doi.org/ 10.1371/journal.pone.0117259.

24. van der Meer, Meloy, and Hoffmann, "The Adult Mass Murderer."

25. Mark Follman, et al., "The True Cost of Gun Violence in America," *Mother Jones*, April 15, 2015, https://www.motherjones.com/politics/2015/04/true-cost-of-gun-violence-in-america/.

26. Pete Blair and Katherine Schweit, "A Study of Active Shooter Incidents in the United States Between 2000 and 2013," U.S. Department of Justice, Federal Bureau of Investigation, September 16, 2013, *National Center for Campus Public Safety*, https://nccpsafety.org/assets/files/library/Active_Shooter_Incidents_Between_2000_and_2013.pdf.

27. National Threat Assessment Center, *Averting Targeted School Violence*, United States Secret Service, March 31, 2021, https://www.documentcloud.org/documents/20533588-usss-averting-targeted-school-violence-2021.

28. Teo Armus, Timothy Bella, and Alex Horton, "Days After an Assault Weapons Ban Was Lifted in Boulder, a Community Grieves Another Mass Shooting in America," *The Washington Post*, March 23, 2021, https://www.washingtonpost.com/nation/2021/03/23/guns-boulder-shooting-assault-weapons-ban/.

29. Good and Carey, *Mass Killings*.

30. Good and Carey, *Mass Killings*.

31. Aaron Warnick, "Video Games and Health: Sorting Science from Popular Beliefs—Many Believe Games Cause Gun Violence," *The Nation's Health*, October 2019, https://www.thenationshealth.org/content/49/8/1.2.

32. G. Dautovic, "The Rise of the Virtual Empire: Video Game Industry Statistics for 2020," *Fortunly*, March 4, 2020, https://fortunly.com/statistics/.

33. Dautovic, "The Rise of the Virtual Empire."

34. "Violence in the Media: Psychologists Study Potential Harmful Effects," *American Psychological Association*, November 2013, https://www.apa.org/action/resources/research-in-action/protect.

35. Robert Sapolsky, *Behave: The Psychology of Humans at Our Best and Our Worst* (New York: Penguin, 2017).

36. Craig A. Anderson, et al., "Violent Video Game Effects on Aggression, Empathy, and Prosocial Behavior in Eastern and Western Countries: A Meta-Analytic Review," *Psychology Bulletin* 136, No. 2 (March 2010): 151–73, https://doi.org/10.1037/a0018251.

37. Christopher J. Ferguson, Nicholas David Bowman, and Rachel Kowert, "Is the Link Between Games and Aggression More about the Player, Less about the Game?" in Peter Sturmey (ed.), *The Wiley Handbook of Violence and Aggression* (New York: John Wiley and Sons, 2017), https://doi.org/10.1002/9781119057574.whbva036.

38. *Grand Theft Childhood*? https://www.grandtheftchildhood.com/GTC/Home.html.

39. Clark and Scott, *Game Addiction*.

40. Helen Pidd, "Anders Breivik 'Trained' for Shooting Attacks by Playing *Call of Duty*," *Reuters*, April 19, 2012, https://www.theguardian.com/world/2012/apr/19/anders-breivik-call-of-duty.

41. Megan O'Matz, "Violent Video Games May Have Primed the Parkland School Shooter," *Florida Sun-Sentinel*, April 29, 2019, https://www.sun-sentinel.com/local/broward/parkland/florida-school-shooting/fl-ne-nikolas-cruz-mental-health-services-20190425-story.html.

42. Tobias Greitmeyer and Sylvia Osswald, "Prosocial Video Games Reduce Aggressive Cognitions," *Journal of Experimental Social Psychology* 45, no. 4 (July 2009): 896, https://doi.org/10.1016/j.jesp.2009.04.005.

43. Pidd, "Anders Breivik 'Trained.'"

44. Clark and Scott, *Game Addiction*.

45. "Charlie Warzel Interview," *PBS NewsHour*, August 4, 2019.

46. Marissa Meli, "The Most Controversial Video Games," *Ugo*, July 19, 2011, http://www.ugo.com/games/most-controversial-video-games-six-days-in-fallujah.html.

47. Kyle Gamache, Judith Platania, and Matt Zaitchik, "An Examination of the Individual and Contextual Characteristics Associated with Active Shooter Events," *Open Access Journal of Forensic Psychology* 7 (2015), https://docs.rwu.edu/fcas_fp/203/.

48. Cory Adwar, "This Stephen King Novel Will Never Be Printed Again after It Was Tied to School Shootings," *Business Insider*, April 1, 2014, https://www.businessinsider.com/school-shootings-drove-stephen-king-to-take-rage-off-shelves-2014-3.

49. Adwar, "This Stephen King Novel."

50. James N. Meindl and Jonathan W. Ivy, "Mass Shootings: The Role of the Media in Promoting Generalized Imitation," *American Journal of Public Health* 107, no. 3 (March 2017): 368–70, https://doi.org/10.2105/AJPH.2016.303611.

51. Meindl and Ivy, "Mass Shootings."

52. Meindl and Ivy, "Mass Shootings."

53. Peter Langman, "JCSO Columbine Documents Organized by Theme: Eric's and Dylan's Activities and Friends," *schoolshooters.info*, https://schoolshooters.info/sites/default/files/jcso_docs-by_theme_1.5.pdf.

54. Brad J. Bushman, "Narcissism, Fame Seeking, and Mass Shootings," *America Behavioral Scientist* 62, no. 2 (February 2018): 229–41, https://doi.org/10.1177/0002764217739660.

55. Good and Carey, *Mass Killings*.

56. Mark Follman, "How the Media Inspires Mass Shooters, and 7 Ways News Outlets Can Help Prevent Copycat Attacks," *Mother Jones*, October 6, 2015, https://www.motherjones.com/politics/2015/10/-media-inspires-mass-shooters-copycats/.

57. Marissa A. Harrison and Thomas G. Bowers, "Autogenic Massacre as a Maladaptive Response to Status Threat," *The Journal of Forensic Psychiatry and Psychology* 21, no. 6 (2010): 916–32, https://psycnet.apa.org/doi/10.1080/14789949.2010.506618.

58. Adam Lankford and Eric Madfis, "Don't Name Them, Don't Show Them, but Report Everything Else: A Pragmatic Proposal for Denying Mass Killers the Attention They Seek and Deterring Future Offenders," *American Behavioral Scientist* 62, no. 2 (September 5, 2017): 260–79, https://doi.org/10.1177/0002764217730854.

Chapter 14

1. "Small Arms Survey Reveals: More Than One Billion Firearms in the World." *Small Arms Survey*, June 18, 2018, http://www.smallarmssurvey.org/fileadmin/docs/Weapons_and_Markets/Tools/Firearms_holdings/SAS-Press-release-global-firearms-holdings.pdf.

2. "Small Arms Survey Reveals," *Small Arms Survey*.

3. John Gramlich and Katherine Schaeffer, "7 Facts About Guns in the U.S.," *Pew Research Center*, October 22, 2019, https://www.pewresearch.org/fact-tank/2019/10/22/facts-about-guns-in-united-states/.

4. Andrew Anglemyer, Tara Horvath, and George Rutherford, "The Accessibility of Firearms and Risk for Suicide and Homicide Victimization Among Household Members: A Systematic Review and Meta-Analysis," *Annals of Internal Medicine*, January 21, 2014, https://doi.org/10.7326/M13-1301.

5. "Guns and Violence Against Women: America's Uniquely Lethal Intimate Partner Violence Problem," *Everytown for Gun Safety*, October 17, 2019, last updated April 23, 2021, https://everytownresearch.org/report/guns-and-violence-against-women-

americas-uniquely-lethal-intimate-partner-violence-problem/.

6. Moshen Naghavi, et al., "Global Mortality from Firearms, 1990–2016," *Journal of the American Medical Association* 320, no. 8 (August 28, 2018): 792–814, https://doi.org/10.1001/jama.2018.10060.

7. Louis Jacobson, "More Americans Killed by Guns Since 1968 Than in All U.S. Wars, Columnist Nicholas Kristof Writes," *PolitiFact*, August 27, 2015, https://www.politifact.com/factchecks/2015/aug/27/-nicholas-kristof/more-americans-killed-guns-1968-all-wars-says-colu/.

8. Gramlich and Schaeffer, "7 Facts."

9. Phillip B. Levine and Robin McKnight, "Three Million More Guns: The Spring 2020 Hike in Firearm Sales," *Brookings*, July 13, 2020, https://www.brookings.edu/blog/up-front/2020/07/13/three-million-more-guns-the-spring-2020-spike-in-firearm-sales/.

10. "Fact Sheet: Thousands of Preventable Gun Suicides," *Everytown for Gun Safety*, June 10, 2020, https://everytownresearch.org/report/thousands-of-preventable-gun-suicides-a-collateral-covid-19-public-health-crisis/.

11. Gramlich and Schaeffer, "7 Facts."

12. David Hemenway and Sara J. Solnick, "The Epidemiology of Self-Defense Gun Use: Evidence from the National Crime Victimization Surveys 2007–2011," *Preventive Medicine* 79 (October 2015): 22–27, https://doi.org/10.1016/j.ypmed.2015.03.029.

13. Mark Follman, Gavin Aronsen, and Deanna Pan, "A Guide to Mass Shootings in America," *Mother Jones*, February 26, 2020, https://www.motherjones.com/politics/2012/07/mass-shootings-map/.

14. Matt Jancer, "Gun Control Is as Old as the Old West," *Smithsonian Magazine*, February 5, 2018, https://www.smithsonianmag.com/history/gun-control-old-west-180968013/.

15. Sarah Gray, "Here's a Timeline of the Major Gun Control Laws in America," *Time*, April 30, 2019, https://time.com/5169210/us-gun-control-laws-history-timeline/.

16. Sarah Gray, "Here's a Timeline of Gun Control Laws."

17. Michael Waldman, "How the NRA Rewrote the Second Amendment," *Politico*, May 20, 2014, https://www.politico.com/magazine/story/2014/05/nra-guns-second-amendment-106856.

18. Waldman, "How the NRA Rewrote."

19. Waldman, "How the NRA Rewrote."

20. Brian Mittendorf and Sarah Webber, "The NRA Declares Bankruptcy: 5 Questions Answered," *The Conversation*, January 22, 2021, https://theconversation.com/the-nra-declares-bankruptcy-5-questions-answered-153423.

21. "History of Brady," *Brady United*, 2019, https://www.bradyunited.org/history.

22. "History of Brady," *Brady United*.

23. Gray, "Here's a Timeline."

24. Gray, "Here's a Timeline."

25. U.S. Senate Committee on the Judiciary, "Studies: Gun Massacre Deaths Dropped During Assault Weapons Ban, Increased After Expiration," *Committee on the Judiciary*, U.S. Senate, September 24, 2019, https://www.judiciary.senate.gov/press/dem/releases/studies-gun-massacre-deaths-dropped-during-assault-weapons-ban-increased-after-expiration.

26. U.S. Senate Committee on the Judiciary, "Studies: Gun Massacre Deaths."

27. Gray, "Here's a Timeline."

28. Gray, "Here's a Timeline."

29. Gray, "Here's a Timeline."

30. "District of Columbia v. Heller," *Legal Information Institute*, Cornell Law School, June 26, 2008, https://www.law.cornell.edu/supremecourt/text/07-290.

31. "District of Columbia v. Heller," *Legal Information Institute*.

32. "Gun Laws by State: The Complete Guide," *Guns to Carry*, 2020, https://www.gunstocarry.com/gun-laws-state/.

33. "Gun Laws by State: The Complete Guide," *Guns to Carry*.

34. "Gun Laws by State: The Complete Guide," *Guns to Carry*.

35. "Gun Laws Save Lives," *Giffords Law Center to Prevent Gun Violence*, 2021, https://giffords.org/lawcenter/gun-laws/.

36. Tio Armus, Timothy Bella, and Alex Horton, "Days After an Assault Weapons Ban Was Lifted in Boulder, a Community Grieves Another Mass Shooting.in America: It Hurts," *The Washington Post*, March 23, 2021, https://www.washingtonpost.com/nation/2021/03/23/guns-boulder-shooting-assault-weapons-ban/.

37. Armus, Bella, and Horton, "Days After."

38. "Gun Laws Save Lives," *Giffords Law Center to Prevent Gun Violence.*

39. Criminal Justice Information Services, "National Instant Criminal Background Check System (NICS)," *Federal Bureau of Investigation*, https://www.fbi.gov/services/cjis/nics.

40. Criminal Justice Information Services, "National Instant."

41. "District of Columbia v. Heller," *Legal Information Institute.*

42. Gramlich and Schaeffer, "7 Facts."

43. Gregory S. Schneider, "In Va., Gun-Control Fight Gives Rise to Movement for County-Approved Militias," *The Washington Post*, October 31, 2020, https://www.washingtonpost.com/local/virginia-politics/virginia-gun-control-armed-militias/2020/10/30/5709aa86–17c4–11eb-82db-60b15c874105_story.html.

44. Christopher Poliquin, "Gun Control Fails Quickly in Congress Following Each Mass Shooting, but States Often Act—Including to Loosen Gun Laws," *The Conversation*, March 27, 2021, https://theconversation.com/gun-control-fails-quickly-in-congress-after-each-mass-shooting-but-states-often-act-including-to-loosen-gun-laws-157746.

45. Joseph Lombardo, "LVMPD Criminal Investigative Report of the 1 October Mass Casualty Shooting," *Las Vegas Metropolitan Police Department*, August 3, 2018, https://www.lvmpd.com/en-us/Documents/1-October-FIT-Criminal-Investigative-Report-FINAL_080318.pdf.

46. Lombardo, "LVMPD Criminal Investigative Report."

47. Daryl Johnson, *Hateland: A Long, Hard Look at America's Extremist Heart* (New York: Prometheus, 2019).

48. Catherine Wessinger, "The Death of 76 Branch Davidians in 1993 Could Have Been Avoided—So Why Didn't Anyone Care?" *The Conversation*, April 13, 2018, https://theconversation.com/the-deaths-of-76-branch-davidians-in-april-1993-could-have-been-avoided-so-why-didnt-anyone-care-90816.

49. Jason Wilson, "Ruby Ridge 1992: The Day the American Militia Movement Was Born," *The Guardian*, August 26, 2017.

50. Johnson, *Hateland.*

51. Lombardo, "LVMPD Criminal Investigative Report."

52. Lombardo, "LVMPD Criminal Investigative Report."

53. Lombardo, "LVMPD Criminal Investigative Report."

54. Lombardo, "LVMPD Criminal Investigative Report."

55. "A Comprehensive Approach to Preventing Gun Violence, 116th Congress," *Brady United Against Gun Violence*, 2020, https://brady-static.s3.amazonaws.com/globals/BradyPolicyApproach.pdf.

56. National Threat Assessment Center, *Averting Targeted School Violence: A U.S. Secret Service Analysis of Plots Against Schools, United States Secret Service*, March 31, 2021, https://www.documentcloud.org/documents/20533588-usss-averting-targeted-school-violence-2021.

57. Clark Merrefield, "Gun Buybacks: What the Research Says," *The Journalist's Resource*, January 9, 2020, https://journalistsresource.org/health/gun-buybacks-what-the-research-says/.

58. Merrefield, "Gun Buybacks."

59. Merrefield, "Gun Buybacks."

60. Hemenway and Solnick, "The Epidemiology."

61. A. Nieuwenhuys and R. Oudejans, "Effects of anxiety on handgun shooting behavior of police officers: A pilot study." Anxiety Stress Coping. 2010;23(2):225–33. doi: 10.1080/10615800902977494. PMID: 19462309.

62. Gabrielle Giffords and Mark Kelly, *Enough* (New York: Scribner, 2014).

63. Arthur L. Kellermann, et al., "Gun Ownership as a Risk Factor for Homicide in the Home," *New England Journal of Medicine* 329, no 15 (October 7, 1993): 1084–1091, https://doi.org/10.1056/NEJM199310073291506.

64. Bruce D. Bartholow, et al., "Interactive Effects of Life Experience and Situational Cues on Aggression: The Weapons Priming Effect in Hunters and Nonhunters," *Journal of Experimental Social Psychology* 41, no. 1 (January 2005): 48–60, https://doi.org/10.1016/j.jesp.2004.05.005.

65. Joan Biskupic, "Guns: A Second (Amendment) Look," *The Washington Post*, May 10, 1995, https://www.washingtonpost.com/wp-srv/national/longterm/supcourt/stories/courtguns051095.htm.

Chapter 15

1. Sarah Best and Victoria DeSimone, *Youth Violence Prevention in the United States: Examining International Terrorists, Domestic Terrorists, School Shooters, and Gang Members* (Washington, D.C.: Center for Strategic and International Studies, 2019).

2. National Threat Assessment Center, *Averting Targeted School Violence: A U.S. Secret Service Analysis of Plots Against Schools, United States Secret Service*, March 31, 2021, https://www.documentcloud.org/documents/20533588-usss-averting-targeted-school-violence-2021.

3. *National Alliance for the Mentally Ill*, 2021, https://www.nami.org/Home/.

4. *National Suicide Prevention Lifeline*, 2021, https://suicidepreventionlifeline.org/.

5. National Threat Assessment Center, *Averting Targeted School Violence.*

6. United States Secret Service and United States Department of Education, *Threat Assessment in Schools: A Guide to Managing Threatening Situations and Creating Safe School Environments*, July 2004, https://www2.ed.gov/admins/lead/safety/threatassessmentguide.pdf.

7. "Threat Assessment and Reporting," SchoolSafety.gov, https://www.schoolsafety.gov/prevent/threat-assessment-and-reporting.

8. Miriam Rollin, "Here's How 'Threat Assessments' May Be Targeting Vulnerable Students," *Education Post*, December 12, 2019, https://educationpost.org/heres-how-threat-assessments-may-be-targeting-vulnerable-students/.

9. United States Secret Service and United States Department of Education, *The Final Report and Findings of the Safe School Initiative: Implications for the Prevention of School Attacks in the United States*, July 2004, https://www2.ed.gov/admins/lead/safety/preventingattacksreport.pdf.

10. "H.R. 4909 (115th): STOP School Violence Act of 2018," *GovTrack*, April 24, 2021, https://www.govtrack.us/congress/bills/115/hr4909.

11. "Know the Signs. Save Lives," *Sandy Hook Promise*, 2020, https://www.sandyhookpromise.org/our-programs/program-overview/.

12. "Know the Signs. Save Lives," *Sandy Hook Promise.*

13. National Threat Assessment Center, *Averting Targeted School Violence.*

14. United States Secret Service and United States Department of Education, *The Final Report and Findings.*

15. United States Secret Service and United States Department of Education, *The Final Report and Findings.*

16. Beverly E. Kingston, et al., "Building Schools' Readiness to Implement a Comprehensive Approach to School Safety," *Clinical Child and Family Psychology Review* 21, no. 4 (December 2018): 433–49, https://doi.org/ 10.1007/s10567-018-0264-7.

17. United States Secret Service and United States Department of Education, *The Final Report and Findings.*

18. "Know the Laws in Your State," *Treatment Advocacy Center*, 2018, https://www.treatmentadvocacycenter.org/component/content/article/183-in-a-crisis/-1596-know-the-laws-in-your-state.

19. "Submit an Anonymous Report," *safe2tell Colorado*, District Attorney of Colorado, https://www.Safe2tell.org.

20. Salvador Rodriguez, "12 Attorneys General Call on Facebook and Twitter to Remove Anti-Vaxxers from Their Services," *CNBC*, March 24, 2021, https://www.cnbc.com/2021/03/24/attorneys-general-call-on-facebook-and-twitter-to-remove-anti-vaxxers-off-their-services.html.

21. Kevin Roose, "'Shut the Site Down,' Says the Creator of 8chan, a Megaphone for Gunman," *The New York Times*, August 4, 2019, https://www.nytimes.com/2019/08/04/technology/8chan-shooting-manifesto.html.

22. *Q: Into the Storm*, HBO, March 2021, https://www.hbo.com/q-into-the-storm.

23. Monika Bickert, "Charting a Way Forward: Online Content Regulation," *Facebook*, February 2020, https://about.fb.com/regulations/.

24. Danny Crichton, "The Deplatforming of President Trump," *TechCrunch*, January 29, 2021, https://techcrunch.com/2021/01/09/the-deplatforming-of-a-president/.

25. Stefan Wojcik, et al., "Bots in the Twittersphere," *Pew Research Center*, April 9, 2018, https://www.pewresearch.org/internet/2018/04/09/bots-in-the-twittersphere/.

26. Stephen Shankland, Edward Moyer, and Ian Sherr, "Parler Offline Following

Amazon, Apple, Google bans over Capitol Violence Content," *CNet*, January 11, 2021, https://www.cnet.com/news/amazon-apple-google-ban-parler-app-over-violent-content-around-capitol-attack/.

27. Darren Guccione, "What is the Dark Web? How to Access it and What You'll Find," *The State of Cybersecurity*, November 18, 2020, https://www.csoonline.com/article/3249765/what-is-the-dark-web-how-to-access-it-and-what-youll-find.html.

28. National Institute of Justice, "Taking on the Dark Web: Law Enforcement Experts ID Investigative Needs," *National Institute of Justice,* June 15, 2020. https://nij.

ojp.gov/topics/articles/taking-dark-web-law-enforcement-experts-id-investigative-needs.

29. Daniel Siegel, *The Developing Mind: How Relationships and the Brain Interact to Shape Who We Are*, 3d ed. (New York: Guilford, 2020)

30. Siegel, *The Developing Mind.*

31. Siegel, *The Developing Mind.*

32. Siegel, *The Developing Mind.*

33. Eli Saslow, *Rising Out of Hatred* (New York: Anchor, 2018).

34. Christian Picciolini, *Breaking Hate* (New York: Hachette, 2020).

35. Picciolini, *Breaking Hate.*

Bibliography

ABC News. "Aurora, Colo., Theater Shooting Timeline Facts." *KABC-TV,* July 26, 2012. https://abc7.com/archive/8743134/.

ABC News. "Father Relives Day Elliot Rodger Went on Rampage." *20/20,* June 28, 2014. https://abcnews.go.com/2020/video/father-relives-day-elliot-rodger-rampage-24346090.

Abdeel, Hasan. "Hate Crime Violence Hits 16-Year High, FBI Reports." *The New York Times,* November 3, 2019. https://www.nytimes.com/2019/11/12/us/hate-crimes-fbi-report.html.

Adwar, Cory. "This Stephen King Novel Will Never Be Printed Again after It Was Tied to School Shootings." *Business Insider,* April 1, 2014. https://www.businessinsider.com/school-shootings-drove-stephen-king-to-take-rage-off-shelves-2014-3.

Aldhous, Peter. "The Cities Where the Cops See No Hate." *Buzzfeed,* December 13, 2018. https://www.buzzfeednews.com/article/peteraldhous/hate-crimes-miami-police-irving-syracuse.

Allely, Clare S., Helen Minnis, Lucy Thompson, Philip Wilson, and Christopher Gillberg. "Neurodevelopmental and Psychosocial Risk Factors in Serial Killers and Mass Murderers." *Aggression and Violent Behavior* 19, no. 3 (May/June 2014): 288–301. https://doi.org/10.1016/j.avb.2014.04.004.

Allely, Clare S., P. Wilson, H. Minnis, L. Thompson, E. Yaksic, and C. Gillberg. "Violence Is Rare in Autism: When It Does Occur, Is It Sometimes Extreme?" *The Journal of Psychology* 151, no. 1 (2017): 46–68. https://doi.org/10.1080/00223980.2016.1175998.

Allport, Floyd H., and Gordon W. Allport. "Personality Traits: Their Classification and Measurement." *The Journal of Abnormal Psychology and Social Psychology* 16, no. 1 (1921). https://doi.org/10.1037/h0069790.

The American Psychiatric Association. *Diagnostic and Statistical Manual of Mental Disorders, Fifth Edition (DSM-5).* Washington, D.C.: American Psychiatric Association Publishing, 2013.

The American Psychological Association. *APA Guidelines for Psychological Practice with Boys and Men,* August 2018. http://www.apa.org/about/policy/psychological-practice-boys-men-guidelines.pdf.

Amman, Molly, Karie A. Gobson, and Matthew Bowlin. "Making Prevention a Reality: Identifying, Assessing, and Managing the Threat of Targeted Attacks." *FBI.* https://www.fbi.gov/file-repository/making-prevention-a-reality.pdf/view.

Andavolu, Krishna. "The Allure of Columbine Fandom." *Vice News Tonight,* May 2020. https://video.vice.com/en_us/video/the-allure-of-columbine-fandom/5e693c03fbf62c7c394f3285.

"Anders Behring Breivik: Norway Court Finds Him Sane." *BBC News,* August 24, 2012. https://www.bbc.com/news/av/world-europe-19375965.

Anderson, Craig A. "Violent Video Game Effects on Aggression, Empathy, and Prosocial Behavior in Eastern and Western Countries: A Meta-Analytic Review." *Psychology Bulletin* 136, no. 2 (March 2010): 151–73, https://doi.org/10.1037/a0018251.

Anderson, Rick. "'Here I Am, 26, with No Friends, No Job, No Girlfriend': Shooter's Manifesto Offers Clues to 2015 Oregon College Rampage." *Los Angeles Times,* September 23, 2017. https://www.latimes.com/nation/la-na-school-shootings-2017-story.html.

Anglemyer, Andrew, Tara Horvath, and George Rutherford. "The Accessibility of Firearms and Risk for Suicide and Homicide Victimization Among Household Members: A Systematic Review and Meta-Analysis." *Annals of Internal Medicine,* January 21, 2014. https://doi.org/10.7326/M13–1301.

Anti-Defamation League. "Defining Extremism: A Glossary of Terms, Movements, and Philosophies." https://www.adl.org/education/resources/glossary-terms/defining-extremism-white-supremacy.

Anti-Defamation League. "Murder and Extremism in the United States in 2018." *Center on Extremism Report,* January 2019. https://www.adl.org/murder-and-extremism-2018.

Arango, Tim. "Minutes Before El Paso Killings Hate-Filled Manifesto Appears Online." *The New York Times,* August 3, 2019. https://www.nytimes.com/2019/08/03/us/patrick-crusius-el-paso-shooter-manifesto.html.

Arluke, Arnold, Adam Lankford, and Eric Madfis. "Harming Animals and Massacring Humans: Characteristics of Public Mass and Active Shooters Who Abused Animals." *Behavioral Science Law* 36, no. 6 (November 2018): 739–51. https://doi.org/10.1002/bsl.2385.

Armus, Tio, Timothy Bella, and Alex Horton. "Days After an Assault Weapons Ban Was Lifted in Boulder, a Community Grieves Another Mass Shooting.in America: It Hurts." *The Washington Post,* March 23, 2021. https://www.washingtonpost.com/nation/2021/03/23/guns-boulder-shooting-assault-weapons-ban/.

Arthur, Rob. "We Analyzed More Than 1 Million Comments on 4chan. Hate Speech Has Spiked by 40% There Since 2015." *Vice News,* July 10, 2019. https://www.vice.com/en/article/d3nbzy/we-analyzed-more-than-1-million-comments-on-4chan-hate-speech-there-has-spiked-by-40-since-2015.

"Austin Texas. Police Department Records of the Charles Whitman Mass Murder Case." Austin, Texas, Public Library.

Avila, Barbara. *Seeing Autism: Connection through Understanding.* Portland, OR: Synergy Books, 2021.

Bandura, Albert. "Moral Disengagement in the Perpetration of Inhumanities." *Personality and Social Psychology Review* 3, no. 3 (1999): 193–209. https://doi.org/10.1207/s15327957pspr0303_3.

Barrouquere, Brett. "Virginia Judge Hands Down Life Sentence, Plus 419 Years, in Case of James Alex Fields, Jr., Calls Attack an Act of 'Terror.'" Hatewatch, *Southern Poverty Law Center,* July 15, 2019. https://www.splcenter.org/hatewatch/2019/07/15/virginia-judge-hands-down-life-sentence-plus-419-years-case-james-alex-fields-jr-calls.

Bartholow, Bruce D., Craig A. Anderson, Nicholas L. Carnagey, and Arlin James Benjamin, Jr. "Interactive Effects of Life Experience and Situational Cues on Aggression: The Weapons Priming Effect in Hunters and Nonhunters." *Journal of Experimental Social Psychology* 41, no. 1 (January 2005): 48–60. https://doi.org/10.1016/j.jesp.2004.05.005.

Bast, Sarah, and Victoria DeSimone. *Youth Violence Prevention in the United States: Examining International Terrorists, Domestic Terrorists, School Shooters, and Gang Members.* Report. Center for Strategic and International Studies (2019): i–ii. https://www.jstor.org/stable/resrep22584.1.

Bauman, Nick. "Exclusive: Loughner Friend Explains Alleged Gunman's Grudge Against Giffords." *Mother Jones,* January 10, 2011. https://www.motherjones.com/politics/2011/01/jared-lee-loughner-friend-voicemail-phone-message/.

Bawer, Bruce. "The Islamazation of Oslo." *The City Journal,* January 24, 2018. https://www.city-journal.org/html/islamization-oslo-15686.html.

Beauchamp, Zack. "Accelerationism: The Obscure Idea Inspiring White Supremacist Killers Around the World." *Vox,* November 18, 2019. https://www.vox.com/the-highlight/2019/11/11/20882005/accelerationism-white-supremacy-christchurch.

Beauchamp, Zack. "Incel, the Misogynist Ideology That Inspired the Deadly Toronto Attack, Explained." *Vox,* April 25, 2018. https://www.vox.com/world/2018/4/25/17277496/incel-toronto-attack-alek-minassian.

Beckett, Lois. "It Can Happen Again: America's Long History of Attacks Against Latinos." *The Guardian,* August 9, 2019. https://www.theguardian.com/us-news/2019/aug/14/it-can-happen-again-americas-long-history-of-attacks-against-latinos.

Beckett, Lois, and Sam Levin. "El Paso Shooting: 21-Year-Old Suspect 'Posted Anti-Immigrant Manifesto.'" *The Guardian,* August 4, 2019. https://www.theguardian.com/us-news/2019/aug/03/el-paso-shooting-21-year-old-suspect-in-custody-as-officials-investigate-possible-hate.

Beer, Tommy. "Majority of Republicans Believe the QAnon Conspiracy Theory Is Partly or Mostly True, Survey Finds." *Forbes,* September 2, 2020. https://www.forbes.com/sites/tommybeer/2020/09/02/majority-of-republicans-believe-the-qanon-conspiracy-theory-is-partly-or-mostly-true-survey-finds/?sh=22cc5cbb5231.

Begley Bloom, Laura. "Ranked: The 20 Happiest Countries in the World." *Forbes,* March 20, 2020. https://www.forbes.com/sites/laurabegleybloom/2020/03/20/ranked-20-happiest-countries-2020/#108724c78503.

Bella, Timothy. "A 19-Year-Old with a Van Full of Guns and Explosives Plotted to Assassinate Biden, Federal Officials Say." *The Washington Post,* October 23, 2020. https://www.washingtonpost.com/nation/2020/10/23/biden-treisman-assassination-plot/.

Bennett, William. "Aurora Heroes: Three Who Gave Their Lives." *CNN,* July 29,2012. https://www.cnn.com/2012/07/25/opinion/bennett-aurora-three.

Berg, Liz. "Comparing Predatory Versus Affective Violence and Examining Early Life Stress as a Risk Factor." *Writing Excellence Award Winners.* Paper 37 (2014). http://soundideas.pugetsound.edu/writing_awards/37.

Bergengruen, Vera, and W.J. Hennigan. "Why America is Losing the Battle Against White Nationalist Terrorism." *Time,* August 8, 2019. https://time.com/5647304/white-nationalist-terrorism-united-states/.

Bernfeld, Jeremy. "Introducing: Guns and America." *Guns and America,* September 4, 2018. https://gunsandamerica.org/story/18/09/04/introducing-guns-america/.

Berton, Justin. "Familicide? Experts Say Family Murder-Suicide Often Related to the Father's Financial Worries." *SFGate,* June 20, 2007. https://www.sfgate.com/crime/article/Behind-dad-s-slaying-of-family-FAMILICIDE-2585684.php.

Bickert, Monika. "Charting a Way Forward: Online Content Regulation." *Facebook,* February 2020. https://about.fb.com/regulations/.

Bigelow, Henry Jacob. "Dr. Harlow's Case of Recovery from the Passage of an Iron Bar through the Head." *Journal of the Medical Sciences* 16, no. 39 (July 1850): 13–22. https://collections.countway.harvard.edu/onview/index.php/items/show/25403.

"Biography of Charles Whitman." *Biography,* August 8, 2019. https://www.biography.com/political-figure/charles-whitman.

Biskupic, Joan. "Guns: A Second (Amendment) Look." *The Washington Post,* May 10, 1995. https://www.washingtonpost.com/wp-srv/national/longterm/supcourt/stories/courtguns051095.htm.

Blackman, Paul H., Vanessa Levrier Leggett, Brittawni Lee Olson, and John P. Jarvis. "The Varieties of Homicide and its Research: Proceedings of the 1999 Meeting of the Homicide Research Working Group." Washington, D.C.: Federal Bureau of Investigation, 2000. https://doi.org/10.1.1.28.9125.

Blair, Pete, and Katherine Schweit. "A Study of Active Shooter Incidents in the United States between 2000 and 2013." U.S. Department of Justice, Federal Bureau of Investigation, September 16, 2013, *National Center for Campus Public Safety.* https://nccpsafety.org/assets/files/library/Active_Shooter_Incidents_Between_2000_and_2013.pdf.

Blair, R.J. "Considering Anger from a Cognitive Neuroscience Perspective." *Wiley Interdisciplinary Review Cognitive Science* 3, no. 1 (January/February 2012): 65–74. https://doi.org/10.1002/wcs.154.

Blum, Justin, and Drew Armstrong. "Dark Personality Eluded Health Scrutiny." *Bloomberg News,* January 11, 2011. https://www.bloomberg.com/news/articles/2011-01-14/loughner-s-dark-personality-eluded-mental-health-scrutiny-before-rampage.

Bockler, Nils, Vincenz Leuschner, Andreas Zick, and Herbert Scheithaur. "Same but Different? Developmental Pathways to Demonstrative Targeted Attacks—Qualitative Case Analyses of Adolescent and Young Adult Perpetrators of Targeted School Attacks and Jihadi Terrorist Attacks in Germany." *International Journal of Developmental Science* 12, nos. 1–2 (September 5, 2018): 5–24. https://doi.org/ 10.3233/DEV-180255.

Bogel-Burroughs, Nicholas, Shaila Dewan, and Kathleen Gray. "FBI Says Anti-Government Group Plotted to Kidnap Gov. Gretchen Whitmer." *The New York Times,* October 8, 2020. https://www.nytimes.com/2020/10/08/us/gretchen-whitmer-michigan-militia.html.

Borrell, Brendan. "Radical Online Communities and Their Toxic Allure for Autistic Men." *Spectrum: Autism Research News,* May 13, 2020. https://www.spectrumnews.org/features/deep-dive/radical-online-communities-and-their-toxic-allure-for-autistic-men/.

Bosman, Julie, Kate Taylor, and Tim Arango. "A Common Trait Among Mass Killers: Hatred Toward Women." *The New York Times,* August 10, 2019. https://www.nytimes.com/2019/08/10/us/mass-shootings-misogyny-dayton.html.

Braddock, Kurt. "Impeachment Trial: Research Spanning Decades Shows Language Can Incite Violence." *The Conversation,* February 5, 2021. https://theconversation.com/impeachment-trial-research-spanning-decades-shows-language-can-incite-violence-154615.

Brantley, Max. "Condemn White Supremacist Terrorists? Not the U.S. Senate." *Arkansas Times,* October 2, 2020. https://arktimes.com/arkansas-blog/2020/10/02/condemn-white-supremacist-terrorists-not-the-u-s-senate.

Breivik, Anders Behring. *2083—A European Declaration of Independence,* July 22, 2012. https://publicintelligence.net/anders-behring-breiviks-complete-manifesto-2083-a-european-declaration-of-independence/.

Brown, Dalvin. "'Fact Is I Had No Reason to Do It': Thousand Oaks Killer Posted to Instagram During Massacre." *USA Today,* November 10, 2018. https://www.usatoday.com/story/news/nation/2018/11/10/thousand-oaks-shooting-gunman-posted-instagram-during-bar-massacre/1958013002/.

Brown, William, Sana Hazraty, and Marek Palasinki. "Examining the Dark Tetrad and Its Link to Cyberbullying." *Cyberpsychology, Behavior, and Social Networking* 22, no. 8 (August 2019): 552–57. https://doi.org/ 10.1089/cyber.2019.0172.

Burnett, Sara, and Jessica Fender. "Aurora Shooting Suspect Left Apartment 'Booby Trapped,' Music Blaring." *The Denver Post,* July 20, 2012. https://www.denverpost.com/2012/07/20/aurora-shooting-suspect-left-apartment-booby-trapped-music-blaring-2/.

Bushman, Brad J. "Narcissism, Fame Seeking, and Mass Shootings." *America Behavioral Scientist* 62, no. 2 (February 2018): 229–41. https://doi.org/10.1177/0002764217739660.

Bustillo, Miguel, Shelly Banjo, and Tamara Audi. "Theater Rampage Jolts Nation." *The Wall Street Journal,* July 21, 2012. https://www.wsj.com/articles/SB10000872396390444464304577538292604705890.

Canape, Chris. "What the Deadliest Mass Shooters Have in Common." *Axios,* September 7, 2019. https://www.axios.com/deadliest-mass-shootings-common-4211bafd-da85-41d4-b3b2-b51ff61e7c86.html.

Carroll, Liam S., and Michael J. Owen. "Genetic Overlap Between Autism, Schizophrenia, and Bipolar Disoder." *Genome Medicine* 1, no. 10 (October 30, 2009): 102. https://doi.org/10.1186/gm102.

Casey, Liam. "Alek Minassian Was Never Aggressive to Others before the Attack." *The Star,* November 30, 2020. https://www.thestar.com/news/canada/2020/11/30/alek-minassian-was-never-aggressive-to-others-before-van-attack-court-hears.html.

Cassam, Quassim. "Why Extremism is a Question of Psychology, Not Politics." *New Statesman,* February 18, 2020. https://www.newstatesman.com/2020/02/why-extremism-question-psychology-not-politics.

Castillo, Michelle. "Colorado Shooter Purchased Guns Legally from Three Different Stores." *CBS News,* July 5, 2016. https://www.cbsnews.com/news/colo-shooter-purchased-guns-legally-from-3-different-stores/.

Cattell, Raymond B. *The Scientific Use of Factor Analysis in Behavioral and Life Sciences.* New York: Plenum, 1978.

CBS News. "Dylann Roof Had a 'Cold and Hateful Heart' in Charleston Church Shooting." *Mountain News WYMT,* December 7, 2016. https://www.wymt.com/content/news/Dylann-Roof-had-cold-and-hateful-heart-during-Charleston-church-shooting-prosecutor-says-405510965.html.

Centers for Disease Control and Prevention. *Surveillance Report of Traumatic Brain*

Injury-Related Emergency Department Visits, Hospitalizations, and Deaths—United States. U.S. Department of Health and Human Services, 2014. https://www.cdc.gov/traumaticbraininjury/pdf/TBI-Surveillance-Report-FINAL_508.pdf.

Centers for Disease Control and Prevention. "What Is Autism Spectrum Disorder?" March 25, 2020. https://www.cdc.gov/ncbddd/autism/facts.html.

Chait, Jonathan. "It's Getting a Little Chippy." *The New Republic,* April 28, 2010. https://newrepublic.com/article/74699/its-getting-little-chippy.

"Charlie Warzel Interview." *PBS NewsHour,* August 4, 2019. https://www.pbs.org/video/how-online-extremism-experts-saw-the-capitol-riot-coming-1610823088/.

Cineas, Fabiola. "Whiteness Is at the Core of the Insurrection." *Vox,* January 8, 2021. https://www.vox.com/2021/1/8/22221078/us-capitol-trump-riot-insurrection.

Clark, Neils, and P. Shavaun Scott. *Game Addiction: The Experience and the Effects.* Jefferson, NC: McFarland, 2009.

Cloud, John. "The Troubled Life of Jared Loughner." *Time.* January 15, 2011. http://content.time.com/time/magazine/article/0,9171,2042358,00.html.

Coffman, Keith. "Colorado Police Officer Says Movie Theater Gunman Was 'Very Calm.'" *Reuters,* April 30, 2015. https://www.reuters.com/article/us-usa-shooting-denver/colorado-police-officer-says-movie-theater-gunman-was-very-calm-idUKKBN0NL26U20150430.

Coletta, Amanda. "Man Accused of Killing 10 in Toronto Van Attack Told Police His 'Mission' Was 'Accomplished.'" *The Washington Post,* September 27, 2019. https://www.washingtonpost.com/world/the_americas/man-accused-of-killing-10-in-toronto-van-attack-told-police-his-mission-was-accomplished/2019/09/27/d5152a44-e161-11e9-be7f-4cc85017c36f_story.html.

"Columbine Tapes." Jefferson County Sheriff Department. Accessed July 28, 2020. https://www.youtube.com/watch?v=NZdVtnksBHs.

"A Comprehensive Approach to Preventing Gun Violence, 116th Congress." *Brady United Against Gun Violence,* 2020, https://brady-static.s3.amazonaws.com/globals/BradyPolicyApproach.pdf.

The Constitutional Rights Foundation. "The Constitution and Slavery." 2021. https://www.crf-usa.org/black-history-month/the-constitution-and-slavery.

Cook, Jesslyn. "A Toxic 'Brotherhood': Inside Incels' Dark Online World." *Huffington Post,* July 26, 2018. https://www.huffpost.com/entry/incel-toxic-brotherhood-online-misogyny_n_5b490e5fe4b0bc69a7873ff0.

Courtney, Kevin. "FBI: Ian Rogers Threatened 'Going to War' If Trump Is Removed from Office." *Napa Valley Register,* January 31, 2021. https://napavalleyregister.com/news/local/fbi-ian-rogers-threatened-going-to-war-if-trump-is-removed-from-office/article_b10ca7b3-6c57-5e56-aabf-03172a71aadd.html.

Crichton, Danny. "The Deplatforming of President Trump." *TechCrunch,* January 29, 2021. https://techcrunch.com/2021/01/09/the-deplatforming-of-a-president/.

Criminal Justice Information Services. "National Instant Criminal Background Check System (NICS)." *Federal Bureau of Investigation.* https://www.fbi.gov/services/cjis/nics.

Cullen, Dave. *Columbine.* New York: Hachette, 2010.

Cullen, Dave. *Parkland: Birth of a Movement.* London: Riverrun, 2019.

Darby, Ryan, Andreas Horn, Fiery Cushman, and Michael D. Fox. "Lesion Network Localization of Criminal Behavior." *Proceedings of the National Academy of Sciences of the United States of America* 115, no. 3 (January 18, 2017): 601–06. https://doi.org/10.1073/pnas.1706587115.

Dastagir, Alia E. "Mass Killers and Misogyny: The Violent Ideology We Can't Ignore." *USA Today,* August 8, 2019. https://www.usatoday.com/story/news/nation/2019/08/06/shooting-ohio-dayton-el-paso-texas-shooter-gilroy-california/1924532001/.

Dautovic, G. "The Rise of the Virtual Empire: Video Game Industry Statistics for 2020." *Fortunly,* March 4, 2020. https://fortunly.com/statistics/.

Dearden, Lizzie. "Revered as a Saint by Online Extremists: How Christchurch Shooter Inspired Copycat Terrorists Around the World." *The Independent,* August 24, 2019. https://www.independent.co.uk/news/world/australasia/brenton-tarrant-christchurch-shooter-attack-el-paso-norway-poway-a9076926.html.

DeBellis, Michael D., and Abigail A.B. Zisk. "The Biological Effects of Childhood Trauma." *Child and Adolescent Psychiatric Clinics of North America* 23, no. 2 (February 16, 2014): 185–222, https://doi.org/10.1016/j.chc.2014.

Department of Homeland Security. "DHS Makes $20 Million in Funding Available for Targeted Violence and Terrorism Prevention Grants." March 24, 2021. https://www.dhs.gov/news/2021/03/24/dhs-makes-20-million-funding-available-targeted-violence-and-terrorism-prevention.

Department of Homeland Security. "Rightwing Extremism: Current Economic and Political Climate Fueling Resurgence in Radicalization and Recruitment." April 2009. https://fas.org/irp/eprint/rightwing.pdf.

Department of Justice, U.S. Attorney's Office. District of South Carolina. "Attorney General Lynch Statement Following the Federal Grand Jury Indictment Against Dylann Storm Roof," *U.S. Department of Justice,* July 22, 2015. https://www.justice.gov/opa/pr/attorney-general-lynch-statement-following-federal-grand-jury-indictment-against-dylann-storm.

Devine, Curt, and Jose Pagliery. "Sheriff Says He Got 23 Calls About Shooter's Family, but Records Show More." *CNN,* February 27, 2018. https://www.cnn.com/2018/02/27/us/parkland-shooter-cruz-sheriff-calls-invs/index.html.

"District of Columbia v. Heller." *Legal Information Institute,* Cornell Law School, June 26, 2008, https://www.law.cornell.edu/supremecourt/text/07-290.

"Donny Leak Facebook Live Stream." *YouTube,* May 14, 2020.

Douglas, Karen M., Robbie M. Sutton, and Aleksandra Cichocka. "The Psychology of Conspiracy Theories." *Current Directions in Psychological Science* 26, no. 6 (June 2017). https://doi.org/10.1177%2F0963721417718261.

"DPS Confirms Suspect Killed in Standoff Near Menard County Line." *The Eldorado Success,* May 14, 2020. https://myeldorado.net/Content/Default/News/Article/DPS-Confirms-Suspect-Killed-in-Standoff-Near-Menard-County-Line/-3/9/921.

Driscoll, Kieran O., and John Paul Leach. "No Longer Gage: An Iron Bar Through the Head, Early Observations of Personality Change After Injury to the Prefrontal Cortex." *BMJ.* 1998 Dec 19; 317(7174): 1673–1674. https://dx.doi.org/10.1136%2Fbmj.317.7174.1673a.

Drum, Kevin. "How Many Threats Can the FBI Evaluate on a Daily Basis?" *Mother Jones,* February 18, 2018. https://www.motherjones.com/kevin-drum/2018/02/how-many-threats-can-the-fbi-evaluate-on-a-daily-basis/.

Dutton, Donald G., Katherine R. White, and Dan Fogarty. "Paranoid Thinking in Mass Shooters." *Aggression and Violent Behavior* 18, no. 5 (September-October 2013): 548–53. https://doi.org/10.1016/j.avb.2013.07.012.

Dwyer, Devin, Tonya Kerr, Josey Crews, and Emily Friedman. "Parents of Jared Loughner Say They 'Don't Understand' What Prompted Rampage." *ABC News,* January 10, 2011. https://abcnews.go.com/US/jared-loughners-family-remains-imposed-isolation-tucson-shooting/story?id=12587114.

Eaton, Leslie, Daniel Gilbert, and Ann Zimmerman. "Suspect's Downward Spiral." *The Wall Street Journal,* January 13, 2011. https://www.wsj.com/articles/SB10001424052748703889204576078331279621622.

Egan, Paul. "Paramilitaries? Terrorists? What Should Militia Groups Be Called?" *Detroit Free Press,* October 10, 2020. https://www.freep.com/story/news/local/michigan/2020/10/10/whitmer-michigan-militias-terrorists/5935823002/.

Equal Justice Initiative. "Lynching in America: Confronting the Legacy of Racial Terror." *Equal Justice Initiative Report 3rd Edition.* Accessed March 10, 2020. https://lynchinginamerica.eji.org/report/.

"Eric Harris's Diversion Documents." Schoolshooters.info, 2021. https://schoolshooters.info/eric-harriss-diversion-documents.

"Fact Sheet: Thousands of Preventable Gun Suicides." *Everytown for Gun Safety,* June 10, 2020. https://everytownresearch.org/report/thousands-of-preventable-gun-suicides-a-collateral-covid-19-public-health-crisis/.

"Family Annihilation: Fathers Who Kill Their Children." *BBC News,* April 25, 2013. https://www.bbc.com/news/uk-england-22213942.

Farahani, Arusha, and Christoph U. Correll. "Are Antipsychotics or Antidepressants Needed for Psychotic Depression? A Systematic Review and Meta-Analysis of Trials Comparing Antidepressant or Antipsychotic Monotherapy with Combination Treatment." *Journal of Clinical Psychiatry* 73, no. 4 (April 2012):486–496. https://doi.org/10.4088/JCP.11r07 324.

Federal Bureau of Investigation. "Active Shooter Resources." About, *Federal Bureau of Investigation, Office of Partner Engagement.* https://www.fbi.gov/about/partnerships/office-of-partner-engagement/active-shooter-resources.

Federal Bureau of Investigation. "Quick Look: 277 Active Shooter Incidents in the United States from 2000 to 2018." About, *Federal Bureau of Investigation,* 2018. https://www.fbi.gov/about/partnerships/office-of-partner-engagement/active-shooter-incidents-graphics.

Federal Bureau of Investigation. "Terrorism 2002/2005." Stats & Services, *Federal Bureau of Investigation.* https://www.fbi.gov/stats-services/publications/terrorism-2002–2005.

Federal Bureau of Investigation. *2011 Tucson Shooting. FBI Records: The Vault.* https://vault.fbi.gov/2011-tucson-shooting.

Federal Bureau of Prisons. "Inmate Gender." About, *Federal Bureau of Prisons,* December 5, 2020. https://www.bop.gov/about/statistics/statistics_inmate_gender.jsp.

Felliti, Vincent J., Robert F. Anda, Dale Nordenberg, David F. Williamson, Alison M. Spitz, Valerie Edwards, Mary P. Koss, and James S. Marks. "Relationship of Child Abuse and Household Dysfunction to Many Leading Causes of Death in Adults." *American Journal of Preventive Medicine* 14, no. 4 (May 1, 1998): 245–58. https://doi.org/ 10.1016/ s0749–3797(98)00017–8.

Ferguson, Christopher J., Nicholas David Bowman, and Rachel Kowert. "Is the Link Between Games and Aggression More about the Player, Less about the Game?," in *The Wiley Handbook of Violence and Aggression,* Peter Sturmey, ed. New York: John Wiley and Sons, 2017. https://doi.org/10.1002/9781119057574.whbva036.

Fisher, Max. "Poll: Majority of Americans Say That Deep Down, Obama Is a Muslim." *Vox,* February 25, 2015. https://www.vox.com/2015/2/25/8108005/obama-muslim-poll.

Follman, Mark. "How the Media Inspires Mass Shooters, and 7 Ways News Outlets Can Help Prevent Copycat Attacks." *Mother Jones,* October 6, 2015. https://www.motherjones.com/politics/2015/10/media-inspires-mass-shooters-copycats/.

Follman, Mark, Gavin Aronsen, and Deanna Pan. "A Guide to Mass Shootings in America." *Mother Jones,* February 26, 2020. https://www.motherjones.com/politics/2012/07/mass-shootings-map/.

Follman, Mark, Gavin Aronsen, and Deanna Pan. "U.S. Mass Shootings, 1982–2020: Data from Mother Jones' Investigation." *Mother Jones,* April 16, 2021, https://www.motherjones.com/politics/2012/12/mass-shootings-mother-jones-full-data/.

Follman, Mark, Julia Lurie, Jaeah Lee, and James West. "The True Cost of Gun Violence in America." *Mother Jones,* April 15, 2015. https://www.motherjones.com/politics/2015/04/true-cost-of-gun-violence-in-america/.

Frances, Allen J. "Dimensional Diagnosis of Personality—Not Whether, but When and Which." *Psycholological Inquiry* 4, no. 2 (1993): 110–11. https://doi.org/10.1207/s15327965pli0402_7.

Gamache, Kyle, Judith Platania, and Matt Zaitchik. "An Examination of the Individual and Contextual Characteristics Associated with Active Shooter Events." *Open Access Journal of Forensic Psychology* 7 (2015). https://docs.rwu.edu/fcas_fp/203/.

Garbe, Will. "Dayton Shooting: Oregon District Gunman Left Decade of Red Flags." *Dayton Daily News,* August 9, 2019. https://www.daytondailynews.com/news/crime—law/dayton-shooting-oregon-district-gunman-left-decade-red-flags/E5UoTI8To1CJDaWUndXBlO/.

Ghiasi, Norman, Yusra Azhar, and Jasbir Singh. "Psychiatric Illness and Criminality." *Stat Pearls,* June 23, 2020. https://www.statpearls.com/ArticleLibrary/viewarticle/27969.

Giffords, Gabrielle, and Mark Kelly. *Enough.* New York: Scribner, 2014.

Glaser, April. "8chan Is a Normal Part of Mass Shootings Now." *Slate,* August 4, 2019. https://slate.com/technology/2019/08/el-paso-8chan-4chan-mass-shootings-manifesto.html.

Good, Erica, and Benedict Carey. "Mass Killings Are Seen as a Kind of Contagion." *The New*

York Times, October 7, 2015. https://www.nytimes.com/2015/10/08/science/mass-killers-often-rely-on-past-perpetrators-blueprints.html.

Gordon, Mary. *Roots of Empathy: Changing the World Child by Child.* Markham, ON, Canada: Thomas Allen & Son, 2012.

Gottschalk, Simon. "Accelerators, Amplifiers, and Conductors: A Model of Tertiary Deviance in Online White Supremacist Networks." *Deviant Behavior* 41, no. 7 (March 9, 2020): 841–55. https://doi.org/10.1080/01639625.2020.1734746.

Gramlich, John, and Katherine Schaeffer. "7 Facts About Guns in the U.S." *Pew Research Center,* October 22, 2019. https://www.pewresearch.org/fact-tank/2019/10/22/facts-about-guns-in-united-states/.

Grand Theft Childhood? https://www.grandtheftchildhood.com/GTC/Home.html.

Gray, Sarah. "Here's a Timeline of the Major Gun Control Laws in America." *Time,* April 30, 2019. https://time.com/5169210/us-gun-control-laws-history-timeline/.

Gregg, Thomas R., and A. Siegel. "Brain Structures and Neurotransmitters Regulating Aggression in Cats: Implications for Human Aggression." *Progress in NeuroPsychopharmacology & Biological Psychiatry* 25, no. 1 (January 2001): 91–140. https://doi.org/10.1016/s0278-5846(00)00150-0.

Greitmeyer, Tobias, and Sylvia Osswald. "Prosocial Video Games Reduce Aggressive Cognitions." *Journal of Experimental Social Psychology* 45, no. 4 (July 2009): 896, https://doi.org/10.1016/j.jesp.2009.04.005.

Grimaldi, Jeremy. "Alleged Attacker Alek Minassian May Have Mental Health Issues." *Richmond Hill Liberal,* April 24, 2018. https://www.toronto.com/news-story/8566082-update-alleged-attacker-alek-minassian-may-have-mental-health-issues/.

Grossman, Dave. *On Killing: The Psychological Cost of Learning to Kill in War and Society.* New York: Back Bay Books, 1996.

Grossman, Dave, and Laurel Christianson. *On Combat: The Psychology and Physiology of Deadly Conflict in War and in Peace.* Mascoutah, IL: Warrior Science Publications, 2012.

Guccione, Darren. "What Is the Dark Web? How to Access It and What You'll Find." *The State of Cybersecurity,* November 18, 2020. https://www.csoonline.com/article/3249765/what-is-the-dark-web-how-to-access-it-and-what-youll-find.html.

Gulliver, K. "Why Have we Forgotten the Worst School Attack in U.S. History?" *Time,* February 26, 2018. https://time.com/4492872/kehoe-attack-history/.

"Gun Laws by State: The Complete Guide." *Guns to Carry,* 2020. https://www.gunstocarry.com/gun-laws-state/.

"Gun Laws Save Lives." *Giffords Law Center to Prevent Gun Violence,* 2021. https://giffords.org/lawcenter/gun-laws/.

"Guns and Violence Against Women: America's Uniquely Lethal Intimate Partner Violence Problem." *Everytown for Gun Safety,* October 17, 2019, last updated April 23, 2021. https://everytownresearch.org/report/guns-and-violence-against-women-americas-uniquely-lethal-intimate-partner-violence-problem/.

Gupta, Alisha Haridasani. "In Her Words: The Atlanta Shootings." *The New York Times,* May 19, 2021. https://supscrib.com/message/7fe734b8-19e0-4f04-bf67-d0b656f73a78-a7feaf73-6dd1-543f-9731-0a7f483eebb1/in-her-words-atlanta-shootings.

Hare, Robert D. *Without Conscience: The Disturbing World of the Psychopaths Among Us.* New York: The Guilford Press, 1993.

Harris, Tristan. "How Technology Is Hijacking Your Mind—from a Magician and Google Design Ethicist." *Thrive Global,* May 18, 2016. https://medium.com/thrive-global/how-technology-hijacks-peoples-minds-from-a-magician-and-google-s-design-ethicist-56d62ef5edf3.

Harrison, Marissa A., and Thomas G. Bowers. "Autogenic Massacre as a Maladaptive Response to Status Threat." *The Journal of Forensic Psychiatry and Psychology* 21, no. 6 (2010): 916–32. https://psycnet.apa.org/doi/10.1080/14789949.2010.506618.

Healy, Jack. "Colorado Killer James Holmes Notes: Detailed Plans vs. 'a Whole Lot of Crazy.'" *New York Times,* May 28, 2015. https://www.nytimes.com/2015/05/29/us/james-holmes-notebook-and-insanity-debate-at-aurora-shooting-trial.html.

Healy, Megan L., and Murray Grossman. "Cognitive and Affective Perspective-Taking:

Evidence for Shared and Dissociable Anatomical Substrates." *Frontiers in Neurology* 9 (June 25, 2018). https://doi.org/10.3389/fneur.2018.00491.

Hemenway, David, and Sara J. Solnick. "The Epidemiology of Self-Defense Gun Use: Evidence from the National Crime Victimization Surveys 2007–2011." *Preventive Medicine* 79 (October 2015): 22–27. https://doi.org/10.1016/j.ypmed.2015.03.029.

Hendrix, Steve. "He Always Hated Women, Then He Decided to Kill Them." *The Washington Post*, June 7, 2019. https://www.washingtonpost.com/graphics/2019/local/yoga-shooting-incel-attack-fueled-by-male-supremacy/?utm_term=.84aede149a37&tid=sm_tw.

Hendrix, Steve, and Michael Miller. "'Let's Get This Party Started': New Zealand Killing Suspect Narrated His Killing Rampage." *The Washington Post*, March 15, 2019. https://www.washingtonpost.com/local/lets-get-this-party-started-new-zealand-gunman-narrated-his-chilling-rampage/2019/03/15/fb3db352–4748–11e9–90f0–0ccfeec87a61_story.html.

Hess, Abigail. "50% of Teachers Say They've Considered Quitting." *CNBC*, August 9, 2019. https://www.cnbc.com/2019/08/09/50percent-of-teachers-surveyed-say-theyve-considered-quitting-teaching.html.

Hill, Clare. "The One Trump Record He Doesn't Want You to Talk About: An Unprecedented Number of Mass Shootings." *The Independent*, November 5, 2020. https://www.independent.co.uk/news/world/americas/us-election-2020/trump-mass-shootings-usa-2020-election-biden-guns-nra-b1424716.html.

"History of Brady." *Brady United*, 2019. https://www.bradyunited.org/history.

Hoffman, Bruce, Jacob Ware, and Ezra Shapiro. "Assessing the Threat of Incel Violence." *Studies in Conflict and Terrorism* 43, no. 7: 565–587, https://doi.org/10.1080/10576 10X.2020.1751459.

Hoge, Steven K. "Competence to Stand Trial: An Overview." *Indian Journal of Psychiatry* 58, Supplement 2 (December 2016): S187–S190. https://dx.doi.org/10.4103%2F0019-5545.196830. *BBC News*, August 14, 2013.

Hogenboom, Melissa. "Criminologists Identify Family Killer Characteristics." *BBC News*, August 15, 2013. https://www.bbc.com/news/science-environment-23686913.

Homeland Security Newswire. "FBI Foils Neo-Nazi Plot to Blow Up Missouri Hospital." *U.S. Department of Homeland Security*, March 27, 2020. http://www.homelandsecuritynewswire.com/dr20200327-fbi-foils-neo-nazi-plot-to-blow-up-missouri-hospital.

"H.R. 4909 (115th): STOP School Violence Act of 2018." *GovTrack*, April 24, 2021. https://www.govtrack.us/congress/bills/115/hr4909.

Humphrey, Michael. "I Analyzed All of Trump's Tweets to Find Out What He Was Really Saying." *The Conversation*, February 8, 2021. https://theconversation.com/i-analyzed-all-of-trumps-tweets-to-find-out-what-he-was-really-saying-154532.

Hutchinson, Bill. "Family of Alleged Gunman in El Paso Massacre Claims He Was Influenced by People We Don't Know." *ABC News*, August 7, 2019. https://abcnews.go.com/US/family-alleged-gunman-el-paso-massacre-claims-influenced/story?id=64825925.

Iacoboni, Marco. *Mirroring People*. New York: Picador, 2008.

The Influencer Report: Engaging Gen Z and Millennials. Morning Consult, 2020. https://morningconsult.com/wp-content/uploads/2019/11/The-Influencer-Report-Engaging-Gen-Z-and-Millennials.pdf.

Institute of Medicine and National Research Council. *From Neurons to Neighborhoods: The Science of Early Childhood Development*. Washington, D.C.: The National Academies Press, 2000. https://doi.org/10.17226/9824.

Jacobson, Louis. "More Americans Killed by Guns Since 1968 Than in All U.S. Wars, Columnist Nicholas Kristof Writes." *PolitiFact*, August 27, 2015. https://www.politifact.com/factchecks/2015/aug/27/nicholas-kristof/more-americans-killed-guns-1968-all-wars-says-colu/.

Jaffe, DJ. "What Is 'Serious Mental Illness' and What Is Not?" *MentalIllnessPolicy.Org*, September 2017. https://mentalillnesspolicy.org/serious-mental-illness-not/.

Jancer, Matt. "Gun Control Is as Old as the Old West." *Smithsonian Magazine*, February 5, 2018. https://www.smithsonianmag.com/history/gun-control-old-west-180968013/.

"JCSO Columbine Documents Organized by Theme." Schoolshooters.info. https://schoolshooters.info/sites/default/files/jcso_docs_by_theme_1.6_0.pdf.

"Jefferson County Sheriff's Office Official Columbine Report." Schoolshooters.info. https:// schoolshooters.info/sites/default/files/jcso_official_columbine_report_0.pdf.

John, Oliver P., Laura P. Naumann, and Christopher J. Soto. "Paradigm Shift to the Integrative Big Five Trait Taxonomy: History, Measurement, and Conceptual Issues," in O.P. John, R.W. Robins, and L.A. Pervins, eds., *Handbook of Personality Theory and Research*, 3rd Edition. New York: Guilford, 2008.

Johnson, Daryl. *Hateland: A Long, Hard Look at America's Extremist Heart.* New York: Prometheus Books, 2019.

Johnson, Laura, Rachel A. Plouffe, and Don Saklofske. "Subclinical Sadism and the Dark Triad: Should There be a Dark Tetrad?" *Journal of Individual Differences* 40, no. 3 (January 2018): 127–133, https://doi.org/ 10.1027/1614–0001/a000284.

Johnston, Jennifer, and Andrew Joy. "Mass Media and the Social Contagion Effect." *Presentation to the American Psychological Association Western New Mexico University.* August 4, 2016. https://www.apa.org/news/press/releases/2016/08/media-contagion-effect.pdf.

Jones, Seth G., Catrina Doxsee, and Nicholas Harrington. "The Escalating Terrorism Problem in the United States." *The Center for Strategic and International Studies,* June 17, 2020. https://www.csis.org/analysis/escalating-terrorism-problem-united-states.

Karlsson, Linda C., Jan Antfolk, Hanna Putkonen, Sabine Amon, João da Silva Gerreiro, Vivienne de Vogel, Sandra Flynn, and Ghitta Weizmann-Henelius. "Familicide: A Systematic Literature Review." *Trauma, Violence, & Abuse* 22, no. 1 (January 1, 2021): 83–98. https:// doi.org/10.1177/1524838018821955.

Kellermann, Arthur L., Frederick P. Rivara, Norman B. Rushforth, Joyce G. Banton, Donald T. Reay, Jerry T. Francisco, Ana B. Locci, Janice Prodzinski, Bela B. Hackman, and Grant Somes. "Gun Ownership as a Risk Factor for Homicide in the Home." *New England Journal of Medicine* 329, no. 15 (October 7, 1993): 1084–1091. https://doi.org/ 10.1056/ NEJM199310073291506.

Kelly, Makena. "Cloudflare to Revoke 8chan's Service, Opening the Fringe Website Up for DDoS Attacks." *The Verge,* August 4, 2019. https://www.theverge.com/2019/8/4/20754310/ cloudflare-8chan-fredrick-brennan-ddos-attack.

Kemenetz, Anya. "Two Big Teachers Unions Call for Rethinking Student Involvement in Lockdown Drills." *National Public Radio.* Accessed February 2, 2020. https://www. npr.org/2020/02/11/804468827/2-big-teachers-unions-call-for-rethinking-student-involvement-in-lockdown-drills.

Kingston, Beverly, Sabrina Arredondo Mattson, Allison Dymnicki, Elizabeth Spier, Monica Fitzgerald, Kimberly Shipman, Sarah Goodrum, William Woodward, Jody Wit, Karl G. Hill, and Delbert Elliott. "Building Schools' Readiness to Implement a Comprehensive Approach to School Safety." *Clinical Child and Family Psychology Review* 21, no. 4 (December 2018): 433–49. https://doi.org/ 10.1007/s10567–018–0264–7.

Klebold, Sue, and Andrew Solomon. *A Mother's Reckoning: Living in the Aftermath of Tragedy.* New York: Crown, 2016.

"Know the Laws in Your State." *Treatment Advocacy Center,* 2018. https://www. treatmentadvocacycenter.org/component/content/article/183-in-a-crisis/1596-know-the-laws-in-your-state.

"Know the Signs. Save Lives." *Sandy Hook Promise,* 2020. https://www.sandyhookpromise. org/our-programs/program-overview/.

Langman, Peter. "Desperate Identities: A Bio-Psycho-Social Analysis of Perpetrators of Mass Violence." *Criminal Public Policy* 19, no. 1 (February 2020): 61–84. https://doi. org/10.1111/1745–9133.12468.

Langman, Peter. "Elliot Rodger: An Analysis." *The Journal of the National Behavioral Intervention Team.* https://cdn.nabita.org/website-media/nabita.org/wordpress/wp-content/ uploads/2016/02/JBIT2014_Article-1.pdf.

Langman, Peter. "The Enigma of Adam Lanza's Mind and Motivations for Murder." *The Journal of Campus Behavioral Intervention* 3 (2015): 1–11. http://dx.doi.org/10.17732/JBIT2015/1.

Langman, Peter. *School Shooters: Understanding High School, College, and Adult Perpetrators.* Lanham, MD: Rowman & Littlefield, 2015.

Langman, Peter. *School Shooters.* Lanham, MD: Rowman & Littlefield, 2015.

Langman, Peter. *Why Kids Kill: Inside the Minds of School Shooters.* Basingstroke: Palgrave Macmillan, 2009.

Lankford, Adam. "A Comparative Analysis of Suicide Terrorists and Rampage, Workplace, and School Shooters in the United States From 1990 to 2010." *Homicide Studies: An Interdisciplinary & International Journal* 17, no. 3 (October 12, 2012): 255–74. https://psycnet.apa.org/doi/10.1177/1088767912462033.

Lankford, Adam, and Eric Madfis. "Don't Name Them, Don't Show Them, but Report Everything Else: A Pragmatic Proposal for Denying Mass Killers the Attention They Seek and Deterring Future Offenders." *American Behavioral Scientist* 62, no. 2 (September 5, 2017): 260–79. https://doi.org/10.1177/0002764217730854.

Lankford, Adam, and James Silver. "Why Have Public Mass Shootings Become More Deadly? Assessing How Perpetrators' Motives and Methods Have Changed Over Time." *Criminology & Public Policy* 19, no. 1 (December 2019): 37–60. https://doi.org/10.1111/1745–9133.12472.

Laurenssen, Elisabeth Martina Petronella, Joost Hutsebaut, Dine Jerta Feenstra, Jan Jurgen Van Busschbach, and Patrick Luyten. "Diagnosis of Personality Disorders in Adolescents: A Study Among Psychologists." *Child and Adolescent Psychiatry and Mental Health* 7, no. 3 (February 11, 2013): 3. https://doi.org/10.1186/1753–2000-7-3.

Lavergne, Gary M. *A Sniper in the Tower: The Charles Whitman Murders.* Denton: University of North Texas Press, 1997.

Law, Tara. "Navy Veteran Survived Las Vegas Shooting Only to Be Killed in the Borderline Bar 1 Year Later." *Time,* November 9, 2018. https://time.com/5450351/tel-orfanos-survived-las-vegas-shooting-killed-borderline/.

Leatherby, Lauren, Arielle Ray, Anjali Singhvi, Christiaan Triebert, Derek Watkins, and Haley Willis. "How a Presidential Rally Turned into a Capitol Rampage." *The New York Times,* January 12, 2021. https://www.nytimes.com/interactive/2021/01/12/us/capitol-mob-timeline.html.

Lender, Jon. "Chimp Owner, in Month Before She Died, Told Lawyer of Her Odd Life with Travis." *Hartford Courant,* August 9, 2012. https://www.courant.com/news/connecticut/hc-xpm-2012–08–09-hc-words-of-chimp-owner-0810–20120809-story.html.

Levin, Jack, and Eric Madfis. "School Rampage in International Perspective: The Salience of Cumulative Strain Theory." In *School Shootings: International Research, Case Studies, and Concepts for Prevention,* Nils Böckler, et al., eds. New York: Springer-Verlag, 2013.

Levine, Phillip B., and Robin McKnight. "Three Million More Guns: The Spring 2020 Hike in Firearm Sales." *Brookings,* July 13, 2020. https://www.brookings.edu/blog/upfront/2020/07/13/three-million-more-guns-the-spring-2020-spike-in-firearm-sales/.

Li, Dandan, Xiaosi Li, Fenqiong Yu, Xingui Chen, Long Zhang, Dan, Li, Qiang Wei, Qing Zhang, Chunyan Zhu, and Kai Wang. "Comparing the Ability of Cognitive and Affective Theory of Mind in Adolescent Onset Schizophrenia." *Neuropsychiatric Disease and Treatment* 13 (March 27, 2017): 937–45. https://doi.org/10.2147/ndt.s128116.

Liem, Marieke, Jack Levin, Curtis Holland, and James Alan Fox. "The Nature and Prevalence of Familicide in the United States, 2000–2009." *Journal of Family Violence* 28, no. 4 (2013): 351–358. https://doi.org/10.1007/s10896–013–9504–2.

Liu, Ying. "Asian Americans Top Threat Target for Harassment During Pandemic." *The Conversation,* March 30, 2021. https://theconversation.com/asian-americans-top-target-for-threats-and-harassment-during-pandemic-158011.

Livesley, W. John. "A Framework for Integrating Dimensional and Categorical Classifications of Personality Disorder." *Journal of Personality Disorders* 21, no. 2 (April 2007): 199–224. https://doi.org/10.1521/pedi.2007.21.2.199.

Lombardo, Joseph. "LVMPD Criminal Investigative Report of the 1 October Mass Casualty Shooting." *Las Vegas Metropolitan Police Department,* August 3, 2018. https://www.lvmpd.com/en-us/Documents/1-October-FIT-Criminal-Investigative-Report-FINAL_080318.pdf.

Lopez, German. "2018 Was by Far the Worst Year on Record for Violence in Schools." *Vox News,* December 10, 2018. https://www.vox.com/2018/12/10/18134232/gun-violence-schools-mass-shootings.

Lord, Debbie. "What Happened at Charlottesville: Looking Back at the Rally That Ended in Death." *Atlanta Journal News,* August 13, 2019. https://www.ajc.com/news/national/what-happened-charlottesville-looking-back-the-anniversary-the-deadly-rally/fPpnLrbAtbxSwNI9BEy93K/.

Louise, Nickie. "These Six Corporations Control 90% of the Media Outlets in America." *Tech Startups,* September 18, 2020. https://techstartups.com/2020/09/18/6-corporations-control-90-media-america-illusion-choice-objectivity-2020/.

Lysiak, Matthew. *Newtown: An American Tragedy.* New York: Gallery Books, 2013.

Madfis, Eric. "In Search of Meaning: Are School Rampage Shootings Random and Senseless Violence?" *The Journal of Psychology* 151, no. 1 (June 28, 2016): 21–35. https://doi.org/10.1080/00223980.2016.1196161.

Maher, Kris. "Portrait of Dayton Shooter: 'Uncontrollable Urges' and Violent Talk Couched as Jokes." *The Wall Street Journal,* August 6, 2019. https://www.wsj.com/articles/dayton-shooter-recalled-for-uncontrollable-urges-and-violent-statements-couched-as-jokes-11565122531.

Marche, Stephen. "The Insurrection Has Not Yet Happened. But It's Coming." *The Globe and Mail,* January 15, 2021. https://www.theglobeandmail.com/opinion/article-the-insurrection-has-not-yet-happened-but-its-coming/.

Marcos, Cristina. "Second Officer Dies by Suicide Following Capitol Attack." *The Hill,* January 27, 2021. https://thehill.com/homenews/house/536189-second-police-officer-dies-by-suicide-after-capitol-attack.

Mark, Michelle, Kieren Corcoran, and David Choi. "This Timeline Shows Exactly How the Parkland Shooting Unfolded." *Business Insider,* February 14, 2019. https://www.businessinsider.com/timeline-shows-how-the-parkland-florida-school-shooting-unfolded-2018-2.

Marshall, S.L.A., and Samuel Lyman Atwood. *Men Against Fire: The Problem of Battle Command.* Norman: University of Oklahoma Press, 2000.

Marwick, Alice, and Becca Lewis. "The Online Radicalization We're Not Talking About." *Intelligencer, New York Magazine,* May 18, 2017. https://nymag.com/intelligencer/2017/05/the-online-radicalization-were-not-talking-about.html.

McAllister, Thomas W. "Neurobiological Consequences of Traumatic Brain Injury." *Dialogues in Clinical Neuroscience* 13, no. 3 (September 2011): 287–300. https://doi.org/10.31887/DCNS.2011.13.2/tmcallisterNeurobiological consequences of traumatic brain injury.

McEllistrem, Joseph. "Affective and Predatory Violence: A Bimodal Classification System of Human Aggression and Violence." *Aggression and Violent Behavior* 10, no. 1 (2004): 1–30. https://doi.org/10.1016/j.avb.2003.06.002.

McEwen, Bruce S. "Effects of Stress on the Developing Brain." *Cerebrum* September-October 2011 (September 21, 2011): 14. https://www.ncbi.nlm.nih.gov/pmc/articles/PMC3574783/.

McEwen, Craig A., and Scout F. Gregerson. "A Critical Assessment of the Adverse Childhood Experiences Study at Twenty Years." *American Journal of Preventive Medicine* 56, no. 6 (June 2019): 790–94. https://doi.org/ 10.1016/j.amepre.2018.10.016.

McLaughlin, Elliott, Andy Rose, and Konstantin Toropin. "Suspect in Arizona Shooting Wanted to Target Couples, Prosecutor Says." *CNN,* May 20, 2020.

McLaughlin, Timothy. "The Weird, Dark History of 8chan." *Wired,* August 6, 2019. https://www.wired.com/story/the-weird-dark-history-8chan/.

Mears, Daniel P., Melissa Moon, and Angela J. Thielo. "Columbine Revisited: Myths and Realities about the Bullying-School Shootings Connection." *Victims and Offenders* 12, no. 6 (November 2017): 939–55. https://doi.org/ 10.1080/15564886.2017.1307295.

Meindl, James N., and Jonathan W. Ivy. "Mass Shootings: The Role of the Media in Promoting Generalized Imitation." *American Journal of Public Health* 107, no. 3 (March 2017): 368–70. https://doi.org/10.2105/AJPH.2016.303611.

Meli, Marissa. "The Most Controversial Video Games." *Ugo,* July 19, 2011. http://www.ugo.com/games/most-controversial-video-games-six-days-in-fallujah.html.

Meloy, J. Reid. "Predatory Violence During Mass Murder." *Journal of Forensic Sciences* 42, no. 2 (March 1997): 326–329. https://doi.org/10.1520/JFS14122J.

Meloy, J. Reid, and Alan R. Felthous. "Serial and Mass Homicide." *Behavioral Sciences and the Law* 22 (May/June, 2004): 289–290. https://onlinelibrary.wiley.com/toc/10990798/22/3.

Meloy, J. Reid, Angela Book, Ashley Shoker-Field, Tabitha Methot-Jones, and Jennifer Roters. "Social, Sexual and Violent Predation: Are Psychopathic Traits Evolutionarily Adaptive?" *Violence and Gender* 5, no. 3 (September 12, 2018): 153–165. http://doi.org/10.1089/vio.2018.0012.

Memott, Mark. "Loughner's Parents Said to Be 'Devastated'; Very Private." *NPR*, January 11, 2011. https://www.npr.org/sections/thetwo-way/2011/01/11/132829508/loughners-parents-said-to-be-devastated-very-private.

Merrefield, Clark. "Gun Buybacks: What the Research Says." *The Journalist's Resource*, January 9, 2020. https://journalistsresource.org/health/gun-buybacks-what-the-research-says/.

Michael, James. "Parkland's Nikolas Cruz Made Chilling Videos before Shooting: 'You're All Going to Die.'" *USA Today*, May 30, 2018. https://www.usatoday.com/story/news/2018/05/30/parkland-killer-video-im-going-next-school-shooter/657774002/.

"Miscellaneous Writings by Adam Lanza: 'Lovebound.'" Schoolshooters.info. Accessed July 7, 2020. https://schoolshooters.info/sites/default/files/Lovebound.pdf.

Mitchell, Kirk. "Gunman Who Killed 26 People in Texas Cited for Cruelty to Animals in Colorado." *The Denver Post*, November 6, 2017. https://www.denverpost.com/2017/11/06/texas-shooting-devin-patrick-kelley-colorado-arrest/.

Mittendorf, Brian, and Sarah Webber. "The NRA Declares Bankruptcy: 5 Questions Answered." *The Conversation*, January 22, 2021. https://theconversation.com/the-nra-declares-bankruptcy-5-questions-answered-153423.

Montaldo, Charles. "Mass Murderers, Spree, and Serial Killers." *Thoughtco.com*, June 23, 2019. https://www.thoughtco.com/defining-mass-spree-and-serial-killers-973123.

Morton, Robert J., and Mark A. Hilts. "Serial Murder: Multidisciplinary Perspective for Investigators." *Federal Bureau of Investigation, Behavior Analysis Unit*. https://www.fbi.gov/stats-services/publications/serial-murder.

"Mosque Attacks Timeline: 18 Minutes from First Call to Arrest." *Radio New Zealand*, April 7, 2019. https://www.rnz.co.nz/news/national/387248/mosque-attacks-timeline-18-minutes-from-first-call-to-arrest.

Murder Diaries, Dylan Klebold, and Eric Harris. *The Journals of Dylan Klebold and Eric Harris: Columbine Killers Diaries*. Google Books, 2019.

Murphy, Paul. "Exclusive: Group Chat Messages Show School Shooter Obsessed with Race, Violence, and Guns." *CNN*, February 17, 2018. https://www.cnn.com/2018/02/16/us/exclusive-school-shooter-instagram-group/index.html.

Naghavi, Moshen, et al. "Global Mortality from Firearms, 1990–2016." *Journal of the American Medical Association* 320, no. 8 (August 28, 2018): 792–814. https://doi.org/10.1001/jama.2018.10060.

National Alliance for the Mentally Ill, 2021. https://www.nami.org/Home/.

National Institute of Justice. "Taking on the Dark Web: Law Enforcement Experts ID Investigative Needs." *National Institute of Justice*, June 15, 2020. https://nij.ojp.gov/topics/articles/taking-dark-web-law-enforcement-experts-id-investigative-needs.

National Institutes of Health. *Biological Sciences Curriculum Study*. NIH Curriculum Supplement Series. Bethesda, MD: National Institutes of Health, 2007.

National Research Council Institute of Medicine. "From Neurons to Neighborhoods: The Science of Early Childhood Development." Washington, D.C.: National Academy Press, 2000.

National Suicide Prevention Lifeline. 2021. https://suicidepreventionlifeline.org/.

National Threat Assessment Center. *Averting Targeted School Violence. U.S. Secret Service*, March 31, 2021. https://www.documentcloud.org/documents/20533588-usss-averting-targeted-school-violence-2021.

Nehamas, Nicholas. "School Shooter in the Making: All the Times Authorities Were Warned About Nikolas Cruz." *Miami Herald*, February 23, 2018. https://www.miamiherald.com/news/local/community/broward/article201684874.html.

Neiwert, David. *Alt-America—The Rise of the Radical Right in the Age of Trump*. New York: Verso, 2017.

Neuhauser, Daniel. "Dayton Shooter was in a Pornogrind Band That Released Songs about Raping and Killing Women." *Vice News*. August 6, 2019. https://www.vice.com/en_us/ article/j5yekp/exclusive-dayton-shooter-was-in-a-pornogrind-band-that-released-songs-about-raping-and-killing-women.

"New Zealand Mosque Attacks Suspect Praised Trump in Manifesto." *Al Jazeera*, March 16, 2019. https://www.aljazeera.com/news/2019/3/16/new-zealand-mosque-attacks-suspect-praised-trump-in-manifesto.

Newman, Stewart S., and Mohammed Ghaziuddin. "Violent Crime in Asperger Syndrome: The Role of Psychiatric Comorbidity." *Journal of Autism and Developmental Disorders* 38, no. 10 (November 2008): 1848–52. https://doi.org/ 10.1007/s10803–008–0580–8.

Nicolaidis, Christina. "What Can Physicians Learn from the Neurodiversity Movement?" *Virtual Mentor* 14, no. 6 (June 14, 2012): 503–10. https://doi.org/ 10.1001/virtualmentor.2012.14.6. oped1–1206.

Nieberg, Patty, Thomas Peipert, and Colleen Slevin. "Colorado Suspect Got Assault Weapon 6 Days Before Shooting." *Associated Press*, March 22, 2021. https://apnews.com/ article/colorado-supermarket-shooting-10-dead-3da92f0d3db65afdb373cc6bb534a711.

Nieuwenhuys, Arne, and Raôul R.D. Oudejans. "Effects of Anxiety on Handgun Shooting Behavior of Police Officers: A Pilot Study." *Anxiety Stress Coping* 23, no. 2 (2010): 225–33. http://dx.doi.org/10.1080/10615800902977494.

Nutt, Amy. "Why Kids and Teens May Face Far More Anxiety These Days." *The Washington Post*, May 10, 2018. https://www.washingtonpost.com/news/to-your-health/ wp/2018/05/10/why-kids-and-teens-may-face-far-more-anxiety-these-days/.

Office of the Child Advocate. *Shooting at Sandy Hook Elementary School: Report of the Office of the Child Advocate*. State of Connecticut, Office of Governmental Accountability, November 21, 2014. https://portal.ct.gov/-/media/OCA/SandyHook11212014pdf.pdf.

Office of the District Attorney, County of Santa Barbara. *Public Report on Officer-Involved Shooting of Elliot Rodger by Santa Barbara County Deputy Sheriffs on May 23, 2014. County of Santa Barbara*, September 4, 2015. https://www.countyofsb.org/da/msm_county/ documents/PublicReportonOfficerInvolvedShootingofElliotRodgerbySheriffDeputieson May23_2014.PDF.

Office of the State's Attorney Judicial District of Danbury. *Shootings at Sandy Hook Elementary School and 36 Yogananda Street, Newtown Connecticut on December 14, 2012. State of Connecticut*, November 25, 2013. https://portal.ct.gov/-/media/OCA/ SandyHook11212014pdf.pdf.

Ok, Ekin, Yi Qian, Brendan Strejcek, and Karl Aquino. "Signaling Virtuous Victimhood as Indicators of Dark Triad Personalities." *Journal of Personality and Social Psychology: Personality Processes and Individual Differences*, July 2, 2020. http://dx.doi.org/10.1037/ pspp0000329.

Oltermann, Philip. "Hanau Attack Gunman Railed Against Ethnic Minorities Online." *The Guardian*, February 20, 2020. https://www.theguardian.com/world/2020/ feb/20/hanau-gunman-tobias-rathjen-railed-against-ethnic-minorities-online.

O'Matz, Megan. "Mental Health Provider had Long History with Parkland Shooter. Was Agency Negligent?" *South Florida Sun-Sentinel*, January 16, 2019. https://www.sun-sentinel.com/local/broward/parkland/florida-school-shooting/fl-ne-henderson-cruz-civil-suit-20190116-story.html.

O'Matz, Megan. "Violent Video Games May Have Primed the Parkland School Shooter." *South Florida Sun-Sentinel*, April 29, 2019. https://www.sun-sentinel.com/local/broward/parkland/ florida-school-shooting/fl-ne-nikolas-cruz-mental-health-services-20190425-story.html.

O'Matz, Megan, and Travis Scott. "Nikolas Cruz' Journey: A Timeline of a Troubled Youth through the Schools." *South Florida Sun-Sentinel*, February 27, 1018. https://www.sun-sentinel.com/local/broward/parkland/florida-school-shooting/fl-florida-school-shooting-bcps-timeline-20180227-story.html.

Ormseth, Matthew. "Disturbing Portrait Emerges of Gilroy Garlic Festival Shooter." *Los Angeles Times*, July 30, 2019. https://www.latimes.com/california/story/2019–07–29/gilroy-garlic-festival-shooting-suspect.

O'Toole, Mary Ellen. "The Dangerous Injustice Collector: Behaviors of Someone Who Never

Forgets, Never Forgives, Never Lets Go, and Strikes Back." *Violence and Gender* 1, no. 3 (2014): 97–99. https://psycnet.apa.org/doi/10.1089/vio.2014.1509.

Pape, Robert A., and Kevin Ruby. "The Capitol Rioters Aren't Like Other Extremists." *The Atlantic*, February 2, 2021. https://www.theatlantic.com/ideas/archive/2021/02/the-capitol-rioters-arent-like-other-extremists/617895/.

Passifiume, Bryan, Kevin Connor, and Jane Stevenson. "10 Dead, 15 Wounded When Van Hits Pedestrians Near Yonge and Finch." *Toronto Sun*, April 23, 2018. https://torontosun.com/news/local-news/multiple-pedestrians-struck-by-van-on-yonge-st.

Patton, Calum. "Florida Shooting Suspect Nikolas Cruz Called Himself 'Annihilator' in Social Media Posts and Was Obsessed with Guns." *Newsweek*, February 15, 2018. https://www.newsweek.com/florida-shooting-suspect-nikolas-cruz-called-himself-annihilator-social-media-807908.

Paulus, Delroy L., and Kevin M. Williams. "The Dark Triad of Personality: Narcissism, Machiavellianism, and Psychopathy." *Journal of Research in Personality* 36, no. 6 (December 2002): 556–63. https://doi.org/ 10.1016/S0092–6566(02)00505–6.

Paulus, Delroy L., Erin E. Buckels, Paul D. Trapnell, and Daniel N. Jones. "Screening for Dark Personalities: The Short Dark Tetrad." *European Journal of Psychological Assessment* (2020). http://dx.doi.org/10.1027/1015–5759/a000602.

PBS. "Trump's American Carnage." *Frontline*, January 26, 2921. https://www.pbs.org/wgbh/frontline/film/trumps-american-carnage/.

Perliger, Arie. "American Zealots: Inside Right-Wing Domestic Terrorism." New York: Columbia University Press, 2020.

Perrigo, Billy. "White Supremacist Groups Are Recruiting with Help from Coronavirus and a Popular Messaging App." *Time*, April 8, 2020. https://time.com/5817665/coronavirus-conspiracy-theories-white-supremacist-groups/.

Peterson, Jillian K., and James A. Densley. "The Violence Project Database of Mass Shootings in the United States, 1966–2019." *The Violence Project*. Last modified 2020. Accessed June 1, 2020. https://www.theviolenceproject.org/mass-shooter-database/.

Peterson, Jillian K., and James Densley. "Five Types of Mass Shooters." *Los Angeles Times*, November 14, 2019. https://www.latimes.com/opinion/story/2019–11–14/the-five-types-of-mass-shooters.

Piazza, James. "When Politicians Use Hate Speech, Political Violence Increases." *The Conversation*, September 28, 2020. https://theconversation.com/when-politicians-use-hate-speech-political-violence-increases-146640.

Picciolini, Christian. *Breaking Hate*. New York: Hachette, 2020.

Pidd, Helen. "Anders Breivik 'Trained' for Shooting Attacks by Playing *Call of Duty*." *Reuters*, April 19, 2012. https://www.theguardian.com/world/2012/apr/19/anders-breivik-call-of-duty.

Play Therapy International. "Helping Children: About Play Therapy." *Play Therapy International*. Accessed June 1, 2020. http://playtherapy.org/Helping-Children/About-Play-Therapy.

Poletti, Michele, Ivan Enrici, and Mauro Adenzato. "Cognitive and Affective Theory of Mind in Neurodegenerative Diseases: Neuropsychological, Neuroanatomical, and Neurochemical Levels." *Neuroscience & Biobehavioral Reviews* 36, no. 9 (October 2012): 2147–2164. https://doi.org/ 10.1016/j.neubiorev.2012.07.004.

"Police Treating Attack at Toronto Massage Parlour as Act of Incel Terrorism." *BNO News*, May 19, 2020. https://bnonews.com/index.php/2020/05/deadly-attack-at-toronto-massage-parlour-treated-as-incel-terrorism/.

Poliquin, Christopher. "Gun Control Fails Quickly in Congress Following Each Mass Shooting, but States Often Act—Including to Loosen Gun Laws." *The Conversation*, March 27, 2021. https://theconversation.com/gun-control-fails-quickly-in-congress-after-each-mass-shooting-but-states-often-act-including-to-loosen-gun-laws-157746.

Q: Into the Storm. HBO, March 2021. https://www.hbo.com/q-into-the-storm.

Quinones, Sam. "Jared Lee Loughner's Parents along with Their Anguish." *Los Angeles Times*, January 11, 2011. https://www.latimes.com/archives/la-xpm-2011-jan-10-la-na-0111-loughner-parents-20110111-story.html.

Raitanen, Jenni, Sandberg Sveinung, and Atte Oksanen. "The Bullying-School Shooting Nexus: Bridging Master Narratives of Mass Violence with Personal Narratives of Social Exclusion." *Deviant Behavior* 40, no. 1 (2019): 96–109. https://doi.org/10.1080/01639625.2 017.1411044.

The Rand Corporation. "Mass Shootings: Definitions and Trends." *Gun Policy in America, The Rand Corporation,* March 2, 2018. https://www.rand.org/research/gun-policy/ analysis/essays/mass-shootings.html.

Ravendal, Jacob Aasland, and Tore Bjorgo. "Investigating Terrorism from the Extreme Right: A Review of Past and Present Research." *Perspectives in Terrorism, Center for Terrorism and Security Studies* 12, no 6 (December 2018): 5–22. http://urn.nb.no/URN:NBN:no-70987.

Reid, William H. *A Dark Night in Aurora.* New York: Skyhorse, 2018.

Reinhard, Scott. "8 Dead in Atlanta Spa Shootings, With Fears of Anti-Asian Bias." *The New York Times,* March 19, 2021. https://www.nytimes.com/live/2021/03/17/us/shooting-atlanta-acworth.

Rennison, Nick. "What Is the Origin of the Term 'Going Postal'?" *History Extra,* September 16, 2009. Accessed March 1, 2020. https://www.historyextra.com/period/modern/what-is-the-origin-of-the-phrase-going-postal-meaning-going-berserk/.

"Reports." *The Gun Violence Archive.* Accessed June 1, 2020. https://www.gunviolencearchive. org/.

Riess, Helen. "The Science of Empathy." *Journal of Patient Experience* 4, no. 2 (May 9, 2017): 74–77. https://doi.org/10.1177%2F2374373517699267.

Roberts, Brent W., and Wendy F. DelVecchio. "The Rank-Order Consistency of Personality Traits from Childhood to Old Age: A Quantitative Review of Longitudinal Studies." *Psychological Bulletin* 126, no. 1 (2000): 3–25. https://psycnet.apa.org/ doi/10.1037/0033-2909.126.1.3.

Rocque, Michael, and Grant Duwe. "Rampage Shootings: An Historical, Empirical, and Theoretical Overview." *Current Opinion in Psychology* 19 (February 2018): 28–33. https://10.1016/j.copsyc.2017.03.025.

Rocque, Michael, and Stephanie Kelly-Romano. "Why Do Mass Shootings Spawn Conspiracy Theories?" *The Conversation,* February 21, 2021. https://theconversation. com/why-do-mass-shootings-spawn-conspiracy-theories-155017.

Rodden, Janice. "What Does Autism Spectrum Disorder Look Like in Adults." *Additude,* October 11, 2019. https://www.addituedemag.com/autism-spectrum-disorder-in-adults/.

Rodger, Elliot. *My Twisted World: The Story of Elliot Rodger.* Schoolshooters.info. https:// schoolshooters.info/sites/default/files/rodger_my_twisted_world.pdf.

Rodger, Elliot. *Retribution: The Final Video.* https://www.youtube.com/watch?v=0TgeR_ SFNB8&t=390s.

Rodriguez, Salvador. "12 Attorneys General Call on Facebook and Twitter to Remove Anti-Vaxxers from Their Services." *CNBC,* March 24, 2021. https://www.cnbc. com/2021/03/24/attorneys-general-call-on-facebook-and-twitter-to-remove-anti-vaxxers-off-their-services.html.

Rollin, Miriam. "Here's How 'Threat Assessments' May Be Targeting Vulnerable Students." *Education Post,* December 12, 2019. https://educationpost.org/heres-how-threat-assessments-may-be-targeting-vulnerable-students/.

Romano, Aja. "What a Woman-Led Incel Support Group Can Teach Us About Men and Mental Health." *Vox,* June 20, 2018. https://www.vox.com/2018/6/20/17314846/incel-support-group-therapy-black-pill-mental-health.

Roose, Kevin. "A Mass Murder Of, and For, the Internet." *The New York Times,* March 15, 2019. https://www.nytimes.com/2019/03/15/technology/facebook-youtube-christchurch-shooting.html.

Roose, Kevin. "'Shut the Site Down,' Says the Creator of 8chan, a Megaphone for Gunman." *The New York Times,* August 4, 2019. https://www.nytimes.com/2019/08/04/technology/ 8chan-shooting-manifesto.html.

Ruiz, Joe. "Ohio Man Charged with Murder in Fatal Car Attack on Anti-White Nationalist March." *The Two Way,* NPR, August 13, 2017. https://www.npr.org/sections/thetwo-way/ 2017/08/13/543176250/charlottesville-attack-james-alex-fields-jr.

Sandoval, Edgar, and Terence Cullen. "Texas Massacre Survivors Say Gunman Devin Kelley Became Enraged by Scared Children During Church Shooting." *New York Daily News,* November 8, 2017. https://www.nydailynews.com/news/national/survivors-texas-massacre-recalls-moments-gunman-entered-church-article-1.3616562.

Sapolsky, Robert. *Behave: The Psychology of Humans at Our Best and Our Worst.* New York: Penguin, 2017.

Sapolsky, Robert. *Why Zebras Don't Get Ulcers.* New York: Henry Holt, 1994.

Saslow, Eli. *Rising Out of Hatred.* New York: Anchor Books, 2018.

Sauer, Patrick. "The Story of the First Mass Murder in U.S. History." *The New York Times,* October 14, 2018. https://www.smithsonianmag.com/history/story-first-mass-murder-us-history-180956927/.

Schapiro, Rich. "Off the Grid, Heavily Armed, and Radicalized: He's a Law Enforcement Nightmare." *NBC News,* January 17, 2021. https://www.nbcnews.com/news/us-news/grid-heavily-armed-radicalized-he-s-law-enforcement-nightmare-n1254510.

Schmall, Emily. "Parishioners: Gunman Acted Oddly Week Before Sutherland Springs Church Attack." *The Denver Post,* November 10, 2017. https://www.denverpost.com/2017/11/10/sutherland-springs-church-shooting-gunman-acted-oddly/.

Schneider, Gregory S. "In Va., Gun-Control Fight Gives Rise to Movement for County-Approved Militias." *The Washington Post,* October 31, 2020. https://www.washingtonpost.com/local/virginia-politics/virginia-gun-control-armed-militias/2020/10/30/5709aa86-17c4-11eb-82db-60b15c874105_story.html.

Schor, Alena. "Reports of White Supremacist Propaganda More Than Doubled Last Year." *Time,* February 12, 2020. https://www.yahoo.com/news/reports-white-supremacist-propaganda-more-080425623.html

Scott, Rachel, and Will Seakin. "Trump Team Defends President on Twitter After Supporter Shouts 'Shoot' Migrants at Border." *ABC News,* May 9, 2019. https://abcnews.go.com/Politics/trump-team-defends-president-twitter-supporter-shouts-shoot/story?id=62928006.

Seierstad, Asne. *One of Us: The Story of Anders Breivik and the Massacre in Norway.* New York: Farrar, Straus and Giroux, 2013.

Seiger, Theresa. "Uber Driver: Nikolas Cruse 'Seemed Just Like a Normal Person.'" *Cox Media Group,* April 4, 2018. https://www.ajc.com/news/national/uber-driver-nikolas-cruz-said-was-going-music-class-seemed-like-just-normal-person/GpWwe8IcXSW4qO8Rqs58IM/.

Shankland, Stephen, Edward Moyer, and Ian Sherr. "Parler Offline Following Amazon, Apple, Google Bans over Capitol Violence Content." *CNet,* January 11, 2021. https://www.cnet.com/news/amazon-apple-google-ban-parler-app-over-violent-content-around-capitol-attack/.

Shepherd, Katie. "An Officer Was Gunned Down—The Killer Was a 'Boogaloo Boy' Using Peaceful Nearby Protests as a Cover." *The Washington Post,* June 17, 2020. https://www.washingtonpost.com/nation/2020/06/17/boogaloo-steven-carrillo/.

"'Shocked Beyond Belief': Complete Threads." Schoolshooters.info. Accessed July 7, 2020. https://schoolshooters.info/shocked-beyond-belief-complete-threads.

Siegel, Daniel. *The Developing Mind: How Relationships and the Brain Interact to Shape Who We Are,* 3rd edition. New York: Guilford, 2020.

Silver, James, Andre Simons, and Sarah Craun. "A Study of Pre-Attack Behaviors of Active Shooters in the United States Between 2000 and 2013." *Federal Bureau of Investigation,* Documents. https://www.fbi.gov/file-repository/pre-attack-behaviors-of-active-shooters-in-us-2000-2013.pdf/view.

Silver, John P., J. Horgan, and Paul Gill. "Foreshadowing Targeted Violence: Assessing Leakage of Intent by Public Mass Murderers." *Aggression and Violent Behavior* 38 (December 2017): 94–100. http://dx.doi.org/10.1016/j.avb.2017.12.002.

Simi, Pete, and Robert Futrell. *American Swastika: Inside the White Power Movement's Hidden Spaces of Hate.* Lanham, MD: Rowman & Littlefield, 2010.

Simons, Andre, and J. Reid Meloy. "Foundations of Threat Assessment and Management." In Vincent B. Van Hasselt and Michael L. Bourke, eds., *Handbook of Behavioral Criminology.* Champaign, IL: Springer, 2017.

Sjolander, Claire Turenne. "The Killers among Us: School Shootings and the Militarization of Childhood." In J. Marshall Beier, ed., *The Militarization of Childhood*. New York: Palgrave Macmillan, 2011.

Skodol, Andrew. "Dimensional-Categorical Approach to Assessing Personality Disorder Pathology." *UpToDate*, August 1, 2018. https://www.uptodate.com/contents/dimensional-categorical-approach-to-assessing-personality-disorder-pathology.

Skutsch, Carl. "The History of White Supremacy in America." *Rolling Stone*, August 19, 2017. https://www.rollingstone.com/politics/politics-features/the-history-of-white-supremacy-in-america-205171/.

"Small Arms Survey Reveals: More Than One Billion Firearms in the World." *Small Arms Survey*, June 18, 2018. http://www.smallarmssurvey.org/fileadmin/docs/Weapons_and_Markets/Tools/Firearms_holdings/SAS-Press-release-global-firearms-holdings.pdf.

Smith, Mitch. "Inside a Deadly American Summer." *The New York Times*, September 21, 2019. https://www.nytimes.com/interactive/2019/09/21/us/summer-mass-shootings.html

Smith, Sharon G., Katherine A. Fowler, and Phyllis H. Niolon. "Intimate Partner Homicide and Corollary Victims in 16 States: National Violent Death Reporting System, 2003–2009." *American Journal of Public Health* 104, no. 3 (March 2014): 461–66. https://doi.org/10.2105/AJPH.2013.301582.

Solomon, Andrew. "The Reckoning: The Father of the Sandy Hook Killer Searches for Answers." *The New Yorker*, March 10, 2014. https://www.newyorker.com/magazine/2014/03/17/the-reckoning.

Soto, Christopher J., Samuel D. Gosling, and Oliver John. "Age Differences in Personality Traits from 10 to 65: Big Five Domains and Facets in a Large Cross-Sectional Sample." *Journal of Personality and Social Psychology* 100, no. 2 (February 2011): 330–348. https://doi.org/10.1037/a0021717.

Southern Poverty Law Center. *Hatewatch*. https://www.splcenter.org/hatewatch.

Southern Poverty Law Center. "White Nationalists Praise El Paso Attack and Mock the Dead." *Hatewatch*, August 4, 2019. https://www.splcenter.org/hatewatch/2019/08/04/white-nationalists-praise-el-paso-attack-and-mock-dead.

Sperry, Laurie A., and David C. Gavisk. "Violence and ASD." *Encyclopedia of Autism Spectrum Disorders*: 1–6. https://doi.org/10.1007/978-1-4614-6435-8_102129-1.

Stanglin, Doug. "'This Is Not Happening Again': Three Who Survived Gilroy Garlic Festival Also Survived Las Vegas in 2017." *USA Today*, August 1, 2019. https://www.usatoday.com/story/news/nation/2019/08/01/gilroy-garlic-festival-3-also-survived-las-vegas-shooting/1887837001/.

State of New Jersey, Office of Homeland Security and Preparedness. "Domestic Extremists Embrace Foreign Terrorist Ideologies," May 28, 2019. https://www.njhomelandsecurity.gov/media/podcast-domestic-extremists-embrace-foreign-terrorist-ideologies.

Steller, Tim. "Loughner's Friends, Teachers, Tell of Descent into Madness." *Arizona Daily Star*, January 15, 2011. https://tucson.com/news/local/loughners-friends-teachers-tell-of-descent-into-madness/article_390c68dd-1c30-5c34-bb74-c4d7ec8e55ec.html.

Steller, Tim. "Suspect Had Troubled Job History." *Arizona Daily Star*, January 13, 2011. https://tucson.com/news/local/suspect-had-troubled-job-history/article_a57b6492-6e34-5ffd-ac73-ea17ee720238.html.

Stelloh, Tim. "Neo-Nazi Turned Muslim Charged with Killing Roommates Who 'Disrespected Faith.'" *NBC News*, May 22, 2017. https://www.nbcnews.com/news/us-news/neo-nazi-turned-muslim-charged-killing-roommates-who-disrespected-faith-n763251.

Stewart, Phil, and Idress Ali. "Pentagon, Stumped by Extremism in Ranks, Orders Stand-Down in Next 60 Days." *Reuters*, February 3, 2021. https://www.reuters.com/article/us-usa-biden-pentagon-extremism/pentagon-stumped-by-extremism-in-ranks-orders-stand-down-in-next-60-days-idUSKBN2A335W.

Stone, Alex. "Gilroy Garlic Festival Shooting: Santino William Legan, 19, Identified as Gunman Who Allegedly Killed Three People." *ABC News*, July 29, 2019. https://abcnews.go.com/US/active-shooter-incident-garlic-festival-california/story?id=64624542.

Stone, Michael H. "Mass Murder, Mental Illness, and Men." *Violence and Gender* 2, no. 1 (March 12, 2015): 51–86. https://doi.org/10.1089/vio.2015.0006.

Strickly, Bob, Sarah Brookbank, Chris Graves, and Chris Mayhew. "911 Calls, Records Reveal Tumultuous Past for Accused Charlottesville Driver, Family." *The Cincinnati Enquirer,* August 15, 2017. https://www.cincinnati.com/story/news/local/northern-ky/2017/08/14/mom-previously-accused-charlottesville-driver-james-alex-fields-jr-beating-her/566078001/.

"Submit an Anonymous Report." *safe2tell Colorado,* District Attorney of Colorado. https://www.Safe2tell.org.

Summers, Keyona. "From Hate Speech to Hate Crimes: UNLV Sociologist on How Interacting in Online White Supremacy Networks Can Convert Hateful Words into Real Violence." University of Nevada, Las Vegas, News Center, October 2, 2019. https://www.unlv.edu/news/release/hate-speech-hate-crimes.

Syme, Kristen L., and Edward H. Hagen. "Mental Health Is Biological Health: Why Tackling 'Diseases of the Mind' Is an Imperative for Biological Anthropology in the 21st Century." *American Journal of Physical Anthropology* 171, Issue S70 (May 2020): 87–117. https://doi.org/10.1002/ajpa.23965.

Syzdlowski, Jay. "Santino William Legan: Gilroy Shooter from Boxing Loving Family." *USA Today,* July 29, 2019. https://www.usatoday.com/story/news/nation/2019/07/29/santino-willian-legan-lagan-picture-rifle-might-makes-right/1860828001/.

Takakuni, Suzuki, Douglas B. Samuel, Shandell Pahlen, and Robert F. Krueger. "DSM-5 Alternative Personality Disorder Model Traits as Maladaptive Extreme Variants of the Five-Factor Model: An Item-Response Theory Analysis." *Journal Abnormal Psychology* 124, no. 2 (May 2015): 343–345. https://doi.org/10.1037/abn0000035.

Tallahassee Police Department. "CIB Supplemental Report: Investigative Summary." *Tallahassee Government,* November 2, 2018. https://www.talgov.com/uploads/public/documents/tpd/supplemental_report.pdf.

Taub, Amanda. "On Social Media's Fringes, Growing Extremism Targets Women." *The New York Times,* May 9, 2018. https://www.nytimes.com/2018/05/09/world/americas/incels-toronto-attack.html.

"Texas Church Gunman's Ex-Wife Tells Inside Edition: He Just Had a Lot of Demons." *My San Antonio,* November 13, 2017. https://www.mysanantonio.com/news/local/texas/article/Tessa-Brennaman-devin-patrick-kelley-shooting-12349127.php.

Thomas, Pierre, Mike Levine, Jack Cloherty, and Jack Date. "Columbine Shootings' Grim Legacy: More than 50 School Attacks, Plots." *ABC News,* October 7, 2014, https://abcnews.go.com/US/columbine-shootings-grim-legacy-50-school-attacks-plots/story?id=26007119.

Thompson, A.C., Ali Winston, and Jake Hanrahan. "Ranks of Notorious Hate Group Include Active-Duty Military." *Propublica,* May 3, 2018. https://www.propublica.org/article/atomwaffen-division-hate-group-active-duty-military.

"Threat Assessment and Reporting." SchoolSafety.gov. https://www.schoolsafety.gov/prevent/threat-assessment-and-reporting.

Tolvin, Jeff. "What Drives Individuals to Kill Their Coworkers?" *Phys.org,* January 30, 2015. https://phys.org/news/2015-01-individuals-co-workers.html.

Towers, Sherry, Andres Gomez-Lievano, Maryam Khan, Anuj Mubayi, and Carlos Castillo-Chavez. "Contagion in Mass Killings and School Shootings." *PLoS ONE* 10, no. 7 (July 2, 2015). https://doi.org/ 10.1371/journal.pone.0117259.

Trotta, Daniel. "Infowars Founder Who Claimed Sandy Hook Shooting Was a Hoax Ordered to Pay $100,000." *Reuters,* December 31, 2019. https://www.reuters.com/article/us-texas-lawsuit-alex-jones-infowars-founder-who-claimed-sandy-hook-shooting-was-a-hoax-ordered-to-pay-100000-idUSKBN1YZ1BB.

Trull, Timothy J., and Thomas A. Widiger. "Dimensional Models of Personality: The Five Factor Model and the DSM-5." *Dialogues in Clinical Neuroscience* 15, no. 2 (June 2013): 135–46. https://dx.doi.org/10.31887%2FDCNS.2013.15.2%2Fttrull.

Trull, Timothy J., and Thomas A. Widiger. "Dimensional-Categorical Approach to Assessing Personality Disorder Pathology." *Dialogues in Clinical Neuroscience* 15, no. 2 (June 2013): 135–136. https://doi.org/10.31887/DCNS.2013.15.2/trull.

Turkle, Sherry. "Connected, but Alone?" *TED,* April 3, 2012. https://www.youtube.com/watch?v=t7Xr3AsBEK4.

"Understanding Anxiety in Children and Teens: 2018 Children's Mental Health Report." *Child Mind Institute,* accessed June 1, 2020. https://childmind.org/our-impact/childrens-mental-health-report/2018report/.

United States Secret Service and United States Department of Education. *The Final Report and Findings of the Safe School Initiative: Implications for the Prevention of School Attacks in the United States.* July 2004. https://www2.ed.gov/admins/lead/safety/preventingattacksreport.pdf.

United States Secret Service and United States Department of Education, *Threat Assessment in Schools: A Guide to Managing Threatening Situations and Creating Safe School Environments,* July 2004. https://www2.ed.gov/admins/lead/safety/threatassessmentguide.pdf.

U.S. Senate Committee on the Judiciary. "Studies: Gun Massacre Deaths Dropped During Assault Weapons Ban, Increased After Expiration." *Committee on the Judiciary,* U.S. Senate, September 24, 2019. https://www.judiciary.senate.gov/press/dem/releases/studies-gun-massacre-deaths-dropped-during-assault-weapons-ban-increased-after-expiration.

van der Meer, Bram, J. Reid Meloy, and Jens Hoffmann. "The Adult Mass Murderer in Europe and North America." Accessed December 28, 2020. http://drreidmeloy.com/wp-content/uploads/2017/08/ATAP2017.pdf.

Van Geel, Mitch, Anouk Goemans, Fatih Toprak, and Paul Vedder. "Which Personality Traits Are Related to Traditional Bullying and Cyberbullying? A Study with the Big Five, Dark Triad, and Sadism." *Personality and Individual Differences* 106 (February 1, 2017): 231–35. https://doi.org/10.1016/j.paid.2016.10.063.

Van Prooijen, Jan-Willem, and Karen M. Douglas. "Belief in Conspiracy Theories: Basic Principles of an Emerging Research Domain." *European Journal of Social Psychology* 48, no. 7 (December 2018): 879–908. https://doi.org/10.1002/ejsp.2530.

Van Prooijen, Jan-Willem, Andre P. Krouwel, and Thomas V. Pollet. "Political Extremism Predicts Belief in Conspiracy Theories." *Social Psychology and Personality Science* 1, no. 9 (January 12, 2015): 1–9. https://doi.org/10.1177%2F1948550614567356.

"Violence in the Media: Psychologists Study Potential Harmful Effects." *American Psychological Association,* November 2013. https://www.apa.org/action/resources/research-in-action/protect.

Von Drehle, David. "The Real Lesson of the Tucson Tragedy." *Time,* January 13, 2011. http://content.time.com/time/magazine/article/0,9171,2042360,00.html.

Wachtel, Lee E., and Edward Shorter. "Autism Plus Psychosis: A 'One-Two Punch' Risk for Tragic Violence?" *Medical Hypotheses* 81, no. 3 (September 2013): 404–09. https://doi.org/10.1016/j.mehy.2013.05.032.

Wagner, David. "Holmes Took Cell-Phone Selfies with Black Contacts, Guns, and Tongue Out." *The Atlantic,* January 9, 2013. https://www.theatlantic.com/national/archive/2013/01/holmes-took-cell-phone-selfies-black-contacts-guns-and-tongue-out/319702/.

Waldman, Michael. "How the NRA Rewrote the Second Amendment." *Politico,* May 20, 2014. https://www.politico.com/magazine/story/2014/05/nra-guns-second-amendment-106856.

Walker, Jeffery T., and Sean Maddan. *Understanding Statistics for the Social Sciences, Criminal Justice, and Criminology.* New York: Jones & Bartlett, 2013.

Wallman, Brittany, Paula McMahon, Megan O'Matz, and Susannah Bryan. "School Shooter Nikolas Cruz: A Lost and Lonely Killer." *South Florida Sun-Sentinel,* July 24, 2018. https://www.sun-sentinel.com/local/broward/parkland/florida-school-shooting/fl-florida-school-shooting-nikolas-cruz-life-20180220-story.html.

Wang, Amy. "Jealousy and Obsession May Have Led Carwash Shooting Suspect to Kill Four, Relatives Say." *The Washington Post,* January 30, 2018. https://www.washingtonpost.com/news/post-nation/wp/2018/01/29/jealousy-and-obsession-may-have-led-carwash-shooting-suspect-to-kill-four-relatives-say/.

Ward, Jane. "What is Forensic Psychology?" *American Psychological Association,* September 2013. https://www.apa.org/ed/precollege/psn/2013/09/forensic-psychology.

Warnick, Aaron. "Video Games and Health: Sorting Science from Popular Beliefs—Many Believe Games Cause Gun Violence." *The Nation's Health,* October 2019. https://www.thenationshealth.org/content/49/8/1.2.

Waters, Dustin, and Kevin Sullivan. "Dylann Roof Guilty on 33 Counts of Federal Hate

Crimes for Charleston Church Shooting." *The Washington Post,* December 15, 2016. https://www.washingtonpost.com/national/dylann-roof-guilty-on-33-counts-of-federal-hate-crimes-for-charleston-church-shooting/2016/12/15/0bfad9e4-c2ea-11e6–9578–0054287507db_story.html.

Wegener, Friederike. "The Globalisation of Rightwing Copycat Attacks." *Global Network on Extremism and Technology,* March 16, 2020. https://gnet-research.org/2020/03/16/the-globalisation-of-right-wing-copycat-attacks/.

Weinman, Sarah. "Massacre on 9th and Main." *Buzzfeed News,* March 24, 2016. https://www.buzzfeed.com/sarahweinman/how-a-forgotten-1903-killing-spree-became-the-first-modern-m.

Weiss, Debra Cassens. "Mass Murderers Often Have These Personality Distortions." *ABA Journal,* April 8, 2015. https://www.abajournal.com/news/article/mass_murderers_often_have_these_personality_distortions.

Werling, Donna M., and Daniel H. Geschwind. "Sex Differences in Autism Spectrum Disorders." *Current Opinion in Neurology* 26, no. 2 (April 2013): 145–53. https://doi.org/10.1097/WCO.0b013e32835ee548.

Wessinger, Catherine. "The Death of 76 Branch Davidians in 1993 Could Have Been Avoided—So Why Didn't Anyone Care?" *The Conversation,* April 13, 2018. https://theconversation.com/the-deaths-of-76-branch-davidians-in-april-1993-could-have-been-avoided-so-why-didnt-anyone-care-90816.

"When Women Are the Enemy: The Intersection of Misogyny and White Supremacy." *Anti-Defamation League.* https://www.adl.org/resources/reports/when-women-are-the-enemy-the-intersection-of-misogyny-and-white-supremacy.

Whitman, Charles. "Whitman Letter." The Whitman Archives, *Austin American-Statesman,* August 1, 2019. https://www.statesman.com/photogallery/TX/20190801/NEWS/801009999/PH/1.

Widiger, Thomas A. "Dimensional Models of Personality Disorder." *World Psychiatry* 6, no. 2 (June 2007): 79–83. https://www.ncbi.nlm.nih.gov/pmc/articles/PMC2219904/.

Widiger, Thomas A. "The DSM-5 Dimensional Model of Personality Disorder: Rationale and Empirical Support." *Journal of Personality Disorder* 25, no. 2 (2011): 222–34, https://doi.org/ 10.1521/pedi.2011.25.2.222.

Williams, W. Huw, Prathiba Chitsabesan, Seena Fazel, Tom McMillan, Nathan Hughes, Michael Personage, and James Tonks. "Traumatic Brain Injury: A Potential Cause of Violent Crime?" *Lancet Psychiatry* 5, no. 10 (October 2018): 836–44. https://doi.org/ 10.1016/S2215–0366(18)30062–2.

Williams, Zoe. "'Raw Hatred': Why the Incel Movement Targets and Terrorizes Women." *The Guardian,* April 25, 2018. https://www.theguardian.com/world/2018/apr/25/raw-hatred-why-incel-movement-targets-terrorises-women.

Williamson, Eileen. "When Active Shooter Drills Scare the Children They Hope to Help." *The New York Times,* September 4, 2019. https://www.nytimes.com/2019/09/04/us/politics/active-shooter-drills-schools.html.

Wilson, Jason. "Ruby Ridge 1992: The Day the American Militia Movement Was Born." *The Guardian,* August 26, 2017. https://www.theguardian.com/us-news/2017/aug/26/ruby-ridge-1992-modern-american-militia-charlottesville.

Winston, Ali, and A.C. Thompson. "American Hate Group Looks to Make Allies in Europe." *ProPublica,* July 5, 2018. https://www.pbs.org/wgbh/frontline/article/american-hate-group-looks-to-make-allies-in-europe/.

Winton, Richard. "Extremist Accused of Plotting to Attack Newsome: A Dangerous Nazi Sympathizer or a Mouthy Drunk?" *Los Angeles Times,* January 29, 2021. https://www.latimes.com/california/story/2021–01–29/extremist-accused-of-plotting-to-attack-newsom-a-dangerous-nazi-sympathizer-or-a-mouthy-drunk.

Wojcik, Stefan, Solomon Messing, Aaron Smith, Lee Rainie, and Paul Hitlin. "Bots in the Twittersphere." *Pew Research Center,* April 9, 2018. https://www.pewresearch.org/internet/2018/04/09/bots-in-the-twittersphere/.

Wright, Jennifer. "Why Incels Hate Women." *Harper's Bazaar,* April 27, 2018.https://www.harpersbazaar.com/culture/politics/a20078774/what-are-incels/.

Xin Wei, Mary Wagner, Elizabeth R.A. Christiano, Paul Shattuck, and Jennifer W. Yu. "Special Education Services Received by Students with Autism Spectrum Disorders from Preschool through High School." *Journal of Special Education* 48, no. 3 (November 2014): 167–79, https://doi.org/10.1177/0022466913483576.

Yousaf, Omar, Aneka Popat, and Myra S. Hunter. "An Investigation of Masculinity Attitudes, Gender, and Attitudes Toward Psychological Help-Seeking." *Psychology of Men & Masculinity* 16, no. 2 (2015): 234–237. https://doi.org/10.1037/a0036241.

Index

adolescence 46, 123, 135, 136, 140, 141, 150, 155, 211, 240
Adverse Childhood Experiences 174, 175, 284
affective violence 40, 43
Alcindor, Yamiche 191
Allport, Gordon 137
American Psychological Association 216, 246
amygdala 41, 43, 100, 107, 119, 172, 242
anti-bullying 149, 281
anxiety 1, 9, 11, 51, 71, 100, 107, 111, 113, 119, 120, 123, 140, 154, 167, 190, 193, 197, 203, 222, 285, 286, 292
Asian 8, 12, 25, 36, 47, 52, 191, 213
assessment 2, 16, 34, 68, 69, 79, 126, 128, 131, 137, 140, 142, 149, 157, 289, 295, 297, 308
ATF 131, 261, 263, 268, 272
Atlanta 191, 213
attachment 102, 104, 160, 164, 217, 224, 235, 309
Aurora 12, 80, 83, 94, 155, 245, 248, 294
Austin 27
autism 3, 67, 68, 70, 71, 77, 104, 105, 117, 127, 144, 154, 158, 160, 162, 163, 165, 166, 167, 169, 177, 206

background checks 93, 210, 260, 263, 265, 270
Bath 26
behavioral addiction 235, 237
bipolar disorder 115, 117, 122, 125, 127, 140, 144, 165, 167
Black 12, 21, 22, 25, 38, 47, 51, 61, 65, 72, 80, 83, 85, 87, 88, 91, 96, 108, 109, 128, 155, 165, 184, 189, 190, 192, 193, 195, 198, 207, 210, 215, 230, 242, 303, 304
Black Lives Matter 25, 197, 198, 230
Borderline Grill 33
Braddock, Kurt 229
Brady 260, 263, 269, 270, 277
Brady bill 263
Brady Campaign to Prevent Gun Violence 277
Brady Comprehensive Plan 270
brain 3, 9, 11, 27, 29, 40, 43, 88, 91, 99, 100, 102, 104, 105, 107, 109, 113, 119, 129, 132, 135, 140, 158, 162, 169, 176, 208, 221, 222, 227, 237, 242, 303, 306
breach and attack 96, 97, 129, 199
Brennan 238, 239, 299
bullying 35, 134, 135, 137, 139, 141, 143, 145, 147, 151, 153, 155, 157, 160, 168, 252, 281, 287
Burger, Warren 275
Bush, George 261, 262, 272

cable news 28, 241, 242, 300
Camden 26
Canadian Security Intelligence Service 214
Cattell, Raymond 137
CDC (Centers for Disease Control) 4, 23, 163, 174, 271
Center for Mental Health Services 121
Charleston, 96, 97, 108, 109, 165, 185, 200, 201
Charlottesville 179, 185, 187
Christchurch 21, 32, 179, 199
church 1, 12, 37, 97, 108, 109, 185, 186, 200, 209, 212, 214, 215, 250
Clinton, Bill 260, 261
college 12, 17, 21, 33, 35, 36, 39, 47, 48, 53, 73, 75, 109, 130, 131, 183, 186, 207, 212, 245, 294, 295, 301, 304
Columbine 8, 19, 30, 31, 60, 74, 76, 87, 90, 93, 94, 96, 106, 149, 150, 156, 198, 242, 243, 245, 249, 252, 292, 293, 307, 310
Columbiners 30, 243
commonalities 30, 39, 143, 156
conspiracism 4, 219, 220, 288
conspiracy mindset , 4, 219, 221, 223, 225, 227, 229, 231
conspiracy theories 183, 196, 197, 219, 220, 222, 224, 226, 228, 231, 238, 240, 268, 298, 300
contagion 4, 8, 23, 201, 244, 253, 298, 300
content moderation 4, 238, 239, 298, 299
copycat 4, 30, 244, 245, 252, 253, 298
Coronavirus 12, 230
Covid-19 12, 25, 198, 256, 300
crisis 4, 5, 42, 100, 128, 223, 231, 271, 275, 278, 286, 287, 296, 297
Cullen, Dave 31, 92, 150
culture 3, 12, 25, 56, 68, 74, 76, 78, 112, 119, 125, 135, 136, 140, 142, 162, 178, 182, 183, 188,

201, 216, 218, 233, 235, 237, 239, 243, 245, 247, 249, 251, 253, 254, 256, 274, 279, 298, 304, 305, 309

Dark Tetrad 147, 148, 201, 231
Dark Triad 147, 148, 209, 220, 224, 231, 269
Dayton 19, 21, 22, 215, 239
dehumanization 96, 106, 107, 214
Densley, James A. 15, 36
Department of Homeland Security 184, 268
depression 111, 113, 115, 117, 119, 120, 122, 124, 126, 140, 141, 149, 167, 175, 193, 285, 286
Diagnostic and Statistical Manual of Mental Disorders (*DSM*) 35, 125, 127, 138, 140, 143, 163
District of Columbia v. Heller 262
domestic terrorism 3, 16, 18, 178, 180, 184, 191, 192, 226, 231, 298
Domestic Terrorism Act 192
domestic violence 15, 214, 256, 264, 308
Don't Name Them 251, 300

8chan 21, 188, 238, 239, 298, 299
El Paso 19, 22, 32, 97, 179, 191, 201, 239, 258, 298
elementary school 2, 7, 8, 12, 61, 62, 65, 66, 78, 152, 154, 198, 232, 245, 283, 291, 292
empathy 3, 96, 109, 146, 148, 157, 167, 173, 180, 203, 206, 214, 217, 247, 268, 281
epigenetics 118, 174, 280
Everytown for Gun Safety 277
explosives 13, 18, 24, 26, 30, 31, 79, 82, 83, 92, 93, 192, 198, 199, 227, 230, 267, 288
extreme risk laws 270

Facebook 2, 84, 109, 191, 193, 198, 199, 206, 211, 227, 230, 232, 238, 298, 300
FBI 4, 12, 14, 16, 45, 86, 87, 110, 111, 133, 184, 185, 198, 199, 210, 226, 230, 245, 251, 261, 264, 267, 297
Federal Gun Control Act 259
Finland 32
firearms 13, 15, 16, 19, 24, 27, 29, 32, 36, 37, 39, 66, 68, 74, 83, 86, 91, 93, 131, 192, 193, 200, 216, 254, 256, 258, 261, 265, 266, 269, 270, 272, 274, 275, 282, 287
Five-Factor Model 138
forensic psychology 23
foreshadowing 33, 59, 61, 65, 70, 77, 86, 187, 228
4chan 188, 225, 238
fringe fluidity 224

Gage, Phineas 170, 172
gamification 250
gender 56, 106, 107, 157, 168, 178, 183, 194, 202, 204, 212, 216, 217, 222, 234, 235, 279, 288
ghost guns 270
Giffords, Gabriele 129, 130, 132, 277, 295

Giffords Law Center 277
Gilroy 19, 20, 22, 32, 33, 97, 179, 239, 263
Glendale 213
Gordon, Mary 103, 137
grievances 3, 18, 26, 29, 34, 39, 41, 45, 47, 50, 53, 54, 57, 59, 77, 106, 109, 130, 152, 168, 184, 203, 208, 217, 244, 279, 280, 298, 305, 308, 309
Grossman, Dave 98, 99
gun buyback 272, 273
gun death rate 256
gun safety legislation 4, 254, 255, 269, 275, 276
Gun Violence Archive 14
guns 4, 14, 15, 19, 22, 24, 28, 36, 38, 47, 61, 65, 68, 72, 80, 85, 88, 92, 93, 131, 191, 199, 213, 226, 227, 231, 254, 263, 265, 277, 282, 288, 295, 297, 301
Guns and America 14, 15

Harris, Tristan 198, 236
Harvest Music Festival 7, 33, 266
high school 19, 21, 22, 30, 35, 53, 73, 84, 87, 89, 90, 92, 130, 149, 150, 155, 206, 207, 209, 213, 245, 249, 251, 252, 291, 292, 303, 307, 309
hospital 12, 63, 67, 116, 128, 172, 198, 295
Humphrey, Michael 229

ideation and foreshadowing 59
Imageboards 238, 250, 308
imminent threats 293, 294, 297
incel 202, 207, 209, 210, 214, 230
Injustice collector 3, 44, 46, 50, 53, 57, 145, 152, 201, 268
insanity 112, 113
Instagram 20, 33, 83, 85, 213, 236, 238, 240
insurrection 185, 226, 228, 239, 300, 301
internet 4, 23, 29, 51, 60, 72, 74, 85, 109, 136, 142, 144, 157, 168, 179, 188, 197, 201, 203, 209, 210, 231, 233, 235, 237, 239, 241, 243, 244, 253, 264, 282, 283, 287, 298, 301, 306
Interpersonal Neurobiology 302
involuntary celibates 3, 202
involuntary commitment 295, 296
Isla Vista 47, 53, 57, 60, 107, 152, 153, 165, 202, 204, 205, 213, 248, 295

Jewish 37, 195, 201, 225, 304
Johnson, Daryl 259
Johnson, Lyndon 268
Jones, Alex 14, 15, 166, 232, 244, 245

Kelly, Mark 132
Kennedy, John 259
Killeen 212
King, Stephen 251, 259, 263, 301
Knight Templar 54, 60, 153, 200

Langman, Peter 34, 36, 38, 77, 150
Las Vegas 7, 32, 33, 36, 266, 269

leakage 59, 77, 86, 93, 94, 109, 131, 187, 208, 214, 226, 249, 288, 289, 291, 292, 295, 297
Littleton 19, 30, 88
lockdown drills 1, 7, 9, 11, 279

Machiavellianism 143, 147, 148, 151, 224
major depressive disorder 124, 125
manifesto 5, 21, 22, 24, 26, 37, 49, 52, 54, 55, 57, 60, 75, 76, 143, 152, 153, 167, 181, 189, 191, 200, 201, 212, 231, 239, 241, 251, 253, 267, 288, 289, 295, 298
media 2, 4, 13, 15, 20, 22, 24, 25, 28, 30, 33, 39, 66, 76, 79, 84, 85, 108, 110, 125, 133, 136, 140, 143, 150, 152, 155, 157, 158, 165, 184, 187, 188, 199, 200, 210, 213, 219, 224, 227, 230, 232, 234, 236, 238, 240, 242, 244, 247, 250, 253, 274, 275, 277, 279, 282, 284, 287, 288, 295, 297, 302, 304
Melcroft 215
mental health concerns: in adults 285; in children/teens 284
mental illness 3, 20, 35, 37, 77, 110, 118, 121, 122, 128, 132, 134, 140, 144, 154, 155, 158, 166, 174, 177, 201, 209, 258, 260, 263, 264, 286, 295, 296
military 7, 10, 19, 20, 22, 27, 32, 37, 40, 61, 65, 73, 82, 87, 92, 97, 99, 186, 188, 191, 193, 197, 199, 206, 210, 215, 226, 231, 248, 249, 258, 261, 263, 270, 274
militias 178, 184, 191, 193, 222, 226
mirror neurons 104, 105
misogyny 3, 12, 19, 29, 39, 49, 202, 211, 214, 218, 238, 302
Montreal 212
Moore, Michael 30, 243, 301
mosque 12, 21, 198, 200, 298
Mother Jones Magazine 14
movie theater 12, 72, 82, 83, 245, 253
Munich 179, 189
Muslim 21, 54, 56, 153, 184, 189, 200

NAMI 287
narcissism 48, 143, 145, 148, 151, 153, 201, 224, 230, 240, 242, 252, 269
National Crime Victimization Survey 257, 258, 273
National Education Association 11
National Instant Criminal Background Check System 263, 264
National Institute of Mental Health 122
National Rifle Association (NRA) 65, 258, 259, 260, 263, 276
National Suicide Prevention Lifeline 287
National Threat Assessment Center 16, 34
New Zealand 17, 21, 32, 179, 199, 201, 298
Newtown 59, 61, 63, 70, 73, 78, 97, 154, 165, 245, 248, 277, 291
Newtown Action Alliance 277
NICS 261, 263
nightclub 1, 18, 36, 37, 215

Norway 17, 32, 47, 53, 54, 55, 57, 60, 73, 75, 76, 78, 107, 153, 154, 179, 189, 200, 201, 248

Oakland 12, 198
Obama, Barack 65, 189, 190, 193
obsessive-compulsive disorder 68, 71
Oklahoma City bomber 90, 152, 154, 180, 197, 231
Orlando 32, 36, 215
OToole, Mary Ann 45

paranoia 27, 46, 143, 144, 151, 182, 197, 201, 203, 214, 224, 228, 230, 232, 268, 269, 276, 277, 298, 306
Parkland 8, 32, 79, 83, 87, 94, 155, 165, 179, 248, 277, 290, 291, 294
Parkland Cares 277
pathway to violence 3, 4, 14, 16, 45, 47, 49, 51, 53, 55, 57, 61, 63, 65, 67, 69, 71, 73, 75, 77, 79, 81, 83, 85, 87, 89, 91, 93, 95, 97, 99, 101, 103, 105, 107, 109, 111, 133, 150, 157, 169, 182, 210, 214, 278, 279, 305, 306
pattern recognition 23
personality 3, 27, 31, 35, 46, 57, 68, 102, 104, 107, 114, 131, 133, 145, 147, 149, 151, 153, 155, 157, 158, 166, 167, 170, 172, 174, 177, 203, 204, 224, 230, 243, 246
Peterson, Jillian K. 9, 15, 36
Piccolino, Christian 304, 305
Pittsburgh 179, 212
play therapy 10
politicians 2, 141, 142, 149, 189, 191, 224, 225, 229, 232, 265, 279, 289
predatory violence 40, 43, 94, 95
prefrontal cortex 41, 43, 100, 104, 107, 135, 170
prevention 2, 4, 5, 10, 14, 111, 157, 260, 271, 275, 279, 287, 289, 290, 292, 297, 305, 306
Printz v United States 262
psychopathy 141, 143, 146, 148, 151, 167, 269
psychosis 35, 110, 115, 122, 124
psychotherapy 125, 128, 140, 141, 303
psychotic 35, 37, 57, 68, 77, 110, 115, 116, 122, 124, 125, 133, 140, 189, 204, 206, 295, 308
psychotropic medication 71, 77, 122, 128, 132
public mass killer 3, 12, 16, 18, 29, 35, 36, 40, 41, 58, 60

QAnon 225, 226, 228, 239

racism 12, 19, 21, 39, 54, 108, 179, 181, 182, 187, 188, 198, 265, 281, 298, 303, 304
rape 22, 56, 90, 203, 238, 250
Reagan, Ronald 260
Reddit 188, 238, 243
research and planning 3, 79, 81, 90
Richlands 213
right-wing 54, 56, 178, 184, 185, 193, 199, 226, 231
Roseburg 12, 212, 213, 237

sadism 143, 148, 151, 181, 201
Safe Schools Initiative 34
San Bernardino 32
Sandy Hook Elementary School 61, 65, 66, 154, 232, 245, 291, 292
Sandy Hook Promise 277, 291
Sapolsky, Robert 118, 119
Saslow, Eli 303
Scalia, Antonin 262
schizophrenia 27, 37, 68, 104, 115, 117, 122, 124, 126, 128, 132, 133, 140, 141, 144, 165, 167
Schleicher 193
Second Amendment 254, 258, 259, 262, 265, 275, 276
Secret Service 4, 13, 16, 34, 149, 245, 280, 289, 290, 292
See Something, Say Something 291, 293, 297
self-defense gun use 257
semiautomatic 8, 19, 22, 28, 29, 31, 32, 37, 47, 51, 80, 82, 84, 88, 93, 199, 212, 213, 227, 258, 261, 263, 266, 270, 273, 275
serial killer 17, 59, 288
Siegel, Dan 302
sorority 47, 49, 51, 209
Southern Poverty Law Center 183, 197, 214
spree killer 17
Stevens, Jon Paul 262
stress 9, 11, 12, 42, 43, 98, 100, 113, 114, 119, 121, 149, 161, 175, 177, 217, 236, 247, 286, 292, 298, 303
suicide 24, 27, 39, 87, 124, 175, 205, 227, 244, 252, 256, 257, 271, 273, 282, 284, 285, 287, 310
Supreme Court 259, 262, 275, 304
Sutherland Springs 32, 214, 215
synagogue 12, 37, 198, 201

Tallahassee 207, 211
Tasmania 273
teachers 1, 2, 9, 11, 12, 28, 60, 61, 63, 65, 69, 70, 92, 106, 131, 235, 248, 274, 281, 292, 309, 310
Thailand 17, 32, 243
theory of mind 96, 101, 102, 104, 105, 164, 167, 169, 170, 173, 203
Thompson, A.C. 187
Thousand Oaks 32, 33
threat assessment 16, 34, 79, 149, 289, 295, 297, 308
Tiahrt Amendment 261
Toronto 205, 206
toxic masculinity 216, 217

trauma 3, 9, 10, 35, 36, 90, 101, 115, 120, 149, 150, 158, 160, 166, 168, 173, 177, 187, 279, 284, 305, 310
traumatic brain injury 3, 129, 158, 169
travel warnings 2
treatment 25, 53, 69, 71, 73, 78, 83, 87, 112, 114, 116, 117, 122, 124, 125, 127, 128, 130, 131, 140, 142, 143, 145, 146, 151, 154, 157, 171, 174, 209, 213, 217, 264, 286, 287, 293, 294, 296, 309
trends 14, 16, 19, 29, 31, 33, 35, 37, 39, 41, 43
Trump, Donald 187, 189, 191, 193, 197, 200, 225, 226, 228, 230, 300
Tucson 128, 133, 233, 295, 296
Turkle, Sherry 234

Unibomber 231
Unite the Right 185, 186, 192
university 12, 15, 17, 27, 36, 39, 47, 81, 90, 105, 118, 171, 172, 186, 189, 190, 209, 229, 236, 294

victim signaling 151, 214
video 4, 24, 31, 37, 48, 50, 52, 62, 72, 76, 84, 86, 88, 91, 93, 95, 130, 131, 143, 152, 153, 155, 157, 167, 187, 189, 193, 194, 200, 208, 212, 213, 221, 224, 233, 235, 237, 239, 243, 245, 252, 267, 282, 289, 295, 308, 310
video games 4, 72, 233, 240, 245, 248, 250, 282, 308, 310
Violence Project 14, 16, 31, 36, 38, 110, 166, 297
Violent Crime Control and Law Enforcement Act 261
Virginia Beach 32
Virginia Tech 12
virtue signaling 151, 181, 214, 230

Watkins, Jim 239
weapons effect 274
white nationalism 194, 201, 304
white supremacy 3, 12, 20, 21, 25, 37, 109, 178, 179, 181, 183, 187, 192, 193, 194, 195, 196, 197, 198, 201, 202, 203, 209, 230, 268, 303, 305
Winfield 26
workplace rampage killer 18

Yale Child Study Center 71, 74
yoga studio 12, 207, 209, 211
YouTube 48, 84, 86, 87, 130, 131, 153, 188, 208, 221, 224, 232, 238, 240, 243, 245, 283, 289, 295

Zuckerberg, Mark 299

Printed in the USA
CPSIA information can be obtained
at www.ICGtesting.com
LVHW092006181223
766777LV00003B/294